QAnon and On

QAnon and On

A short and shocking history of internet conspiracy cults

Van Badham

Hardie Grant

BOOKS

Published in 2021 by Hardie Grant Books,
an imprint of Hardie Grant Publishing

Hardie Grant Books (Melbourne)
Wurundjeri Country
Building 1, 658 Church Street
Richmond, Victoria 3121

Hardie Grant Books (London)
5th & 6th Floors
52–54 Southwark Street
London SE1 1UN

hardiegrantbooks.com

A catalogue record for this
book is available from the
National Library of Australia

QAnon and On
ISBN 978 1 74379 787 7

10 9 8 7 6 5 4 3

Cover design by Ella Egidy
Text design by Kirby Jones
Typeset in 12.5/18 pt Baskerville Regular by Kirby Jones

Printed in Australia by Griffin Press, part of Ovato, an Accredited ISO
AS/NZS 14001 Environmental Management System printer.

The paper this book is printed on is certified against the Forest
Stewardship Council® Standards. Griffin Press holds FSC® chain
of custody certification SGSHK-COC-005088. FSC® promotes
environmentally responsible, socially beneficial and economically viable
management of the world's forests.

Hardie Grant acknowledges the Traditional Owners of the country on which we
work, the Wurundjeri people of the Kulin nation and the Gadigal people of the
Eora nation, and recognises their continuing connection to the land, waters and
culture. We pay our respects to their Elders past, present and emerging.

To the mother who made me,
and to Ben, Sonia, Emma, Sally and Jessamy
– especially Jessamy –
who make me possible.

CONTENTS

... however much we might
benefit from these devices,
and programmable things
in general, we also have to
be aware that they might not
work exactly the way they were
intended to work or the way
that we expect them to.

'Father of the internet' Vint Cerf in a speech at
Elon University, 9 September 2016[1]

THIS IS THE BEGINNING ...

This is a book about two things: the internet and belief.

In the beginning, the belief was that the internet would be a new frontier of democracy, a platform for limitless, unrestrained expression, a public square where anyone with an internet connection could gather, publish and collaborate. Websites had only existed for four years – browsers for but two – when American writer Steven Levy distilled the optimism of the internet's pioneers in a 1995 column for *Newsweek*. 'After the sound-bite smog of broadcast media,' he wrote, 'this passionate embrace of ideas and creativity is clean, fresh air.' Levy saw in the internet's uncensored realms a place to export the glories of America's First Amendment. Here, citizens of all nations could experience free speech without fear.[2]

There were some grounds for optimism. Back in 1974, five years on from the first computer-to-computer conversation, the international community of researchers working on computer-based communication accepted a proposal with profound consequences. An exchange of ideas between

French and American researchers had inspired the latter to develop a universal technical protocol for communication that enabled everyone's networks of computers to engage with other networks more easily, linking them all together in an 'inter-network'. The 'internet' created was global, neutral and – by design – had no central control.[3]

Throughout history, hard data has been the hoarded, precious treasure of powerful aristocrats, secretive guilds or priestly castes, but the developing architecture of the internet democratised information. Now anyone could read or post without having to seek permission, and the new borderless digital wonderlands of what was dubbed 'cyberspace' inspired great idealism in those with lofty, liberal goals. Here was a place where collaborations could be forged among a community of equals, as Harvard's David Weinberger reflected in 2015.[4] Belief prevailed in those formative decades, he wrote, that engaging with the internet's democratic structure would 'transform us and our institutions in ways that reflect those values'.

This was the spirit with which many welcomed the arrival of social media. The doors of old media gatekeeping were wrenched open. Self-selected hordes of 'citizen journalists' and 'content creators' poured onto the new platforms. Mobile internet technology allowed anyone to seize the means of media production wherever they were, and whenever they liked, with only a phone in their hand.

It all seemed like such a good idea at the time.

There were early auguries that the loudly insisted liberatory potential of the internet may follow a meandering path. It's worth noting that Steven Levy's 1995 column appeared amid a thorny political debate about how to safeguard children from an internet that was already heaving with porn. Perhaps the first portent occurred as early as 29 October 1969, the day the very first computer-networked message was sent. A research team at UCLA was attempting to transmit the word 'LOGIN' to a team awaiting it 500 kilometres away at Stanford University. UCLA managed only to send a holy-sounding 'LO' before the computer crashed.[5]

The Canadian media theorist Marshall McLuhan had predicted the internet years before the Californian computer-lab shenanigans. His 1964 book, *Understanding Media: The extensions of man*, is perhaps most famous for his oft-quoted observation 'the medium is the message', but in the same book McLuhan also reasoned that technology would inevitably create media that was globally networked and participatory.[6] In our thoroughly internet-addled present, those less inclined to believe divine signs than to read screamingly obvious metaphors may indeed stare back at the internet's inauspicious UCLA debut, consider McLuhan's observations and conclude 'the medium appears unstable, and the message is a problem'.

We are now five decades into humanity's use of the internet. I am of the last Western generation that retains any memory of what life without its daily use was like. It's almost three decades since I opened my first email account, chose my first online alias and joined my first IRC (internet relay chat). In that time, the internet has certainly delivered its promised new frontiers. Unfortunately, a lot of them are just fresh digital territories to experience ancient analogue problems.

Trolling. Dogpiling. Doxxing. Swatting. Swarming. Cyberstalking. We've created new words to describe the evolving manifestations of old human viciousness that the internet's lawlessness has facilitated. As a feminist journalist who maintains an active presence on social media, I'm of an internet demographic that has had the historically unprecedented experience of a mass harassment that is not merely public and international but searchable and shareable.

Instead of 'granting citizens of all nations the experience of speaking without fear', the internet has digitised new sources of individual and collective terror. Its much-vaunted capacity to platform content whenever and wherever has provided raw freedom to bully and harass, slander and defame, threaten, berate, humiliate, stalk, violate and abuse.

It's also meant the proliferation of disinformation and conspiracy theories on a global scale, relentless propaganda campaigns, the promotion of hateful ideologies, the celebration of violence and even active recruitment to terrorist and extremist causes, with lethal results.

Tech writer Nick Carr reminded readers of *The Guardian* over a decade ago that the prophetic McLuhan warned us about the dangers of the internet before it even existed. 'McLuhan understood that as media become more interactive, they also become more potent tools for manipulation and control,' Carr explained.[7] In *Understanding Media*, McLuhan described the vulnerability of 'our senses and nervous systems to the private manipulation of those who would try to benefit by taking a lease on our eyes and ears and nerves'.

This image of sensory possession has echoed against my

skull through the conception, research and writing of this book. Those who 'surrendered' to interactive media, feared McLuhan, would find themselves 'with no rights left'.[8]

My interest in the internet's extremist underworld resulted from my experience of its attacks. Within only a few months of commencing work at *The Guardian* in 2013, I found myself on the very public online radar of misogynists, racists, homophobes and outright fascists. I was the subject of attack videos and hateful memes and subjected to constant trolling. In the wake of the online attacks came ones offline too. Parcels of anonymous material began to appear at my doorstep; my Twitter account was hacked; I was stalked, harassed and assaulted in the street. International Neo-Nazi website *The Daily Stormer* published a hit piece with my photograph and a written incitement to run me over in a car.[9]

I was desperate to understand how and where I'd gained a reputation so villainous that it could inspire such treatment. Certainly I was keen to identify those who stirred the harassment and to work out what their possible benefit may be. I began the practice of creating online personae that allowed me to lurk in the communities that drove my abuse so I could pre-empt their attacks. As I did, I found myself becoming fascinated by the individuals who allowed themselves to *be* stirred – those who, as per the McLuhan quote, wilfully 'lease' out their eyes and ears to conspiratorial thinking. The internet has, at least, realised its potential as a storehouse of global information, so what would motivate a user to so forcefully avoid the facts at their literal fingertips and surrender instead to made-up stories designed to manipulate and control?

It's a question that's remained with me over years now spent lurking and watching as internet manipulation and disinformation campaigns have grown to a geopolitical scale. In 2014, a self-recruited online army of misogynist video gamers organised a hate campaign that became known as 'Gamergate'. Insisting there was a feminist plot to ruin game entertainment, they targeted gaming identities Anita Sarkeesian, Zoë Quinn and others with oceanic levels of fact-free harassment. By 2016, an adherent of the online 'Pizzagate' conspiracy theory shot up a Washington restaurant. The shooter had been convinced by internet propaganda that Hillary Clinton was killing and eating children in the restaurant cellar. In 2021, after the 'pandemic year' of coronavirus lockdowns trapped humanity indoors with the dangerous combination of internet connections and fear, adherents of the entirely groundless QAnon conspiracy theory committed acts of terrorism and murder under the influence of their beliefs. On 6 January 2021, many QAnon believers joined the physical mobilisation that marched on the US Capitol Building. They shared chants to hang Vice President Mike Pence, they fought police, they breached the building … and some died.

This book charts the history and events of specifically the Gamergate, Pizzagate and QAnon internet conspiracy cults. The aim is to identify how bad-faith political actors aligned to a mixture of opportunistic greed and far-right causes have weaponised the internet in the service of 'private manipulations'. This book also examines how they're able to 'lease' the minds of those who follow them. It began as an article I wrote for *The Guardian* in 2020, responding to pleas for advice from some of my regular readers who had loved ones drifting towards conspiracy thinking and couldn't seem to argue them out of it.

My piece was titled 'If your friends or family have fallen for an internet conspiracy cult, here's what you should do'. It argued my sad discovery that there's no persuading people out of conspiratorial thinking with reason and evidence. Rather, what appears to be an intellectual or psychological problem is actually one of socialisation. What this book posits is that the cure for unreason is not reason. It's to keep contact alive with humans who you don't want to become lost to this.

I was overwhelmed by the response to that piece. In the first place, I was contacted by hundreds of people sharing their own encounters with internet cults, including some old, dear friends who'd been otherwise embarrassed to talk about loved ones who'd 'fallen down the rabbit hole'. In the second place, I found myself incorporated into the conspiratorial mythos of QAnon believers. More than one tweet I found myself tagged into insisted I was merely serving the interests of the cult's legendary child-killing 'cabal'. 'The conspiracy cult is *The Guardian!*' was one comment among a collection that reached me on Facebook. '#PatheticJournalism by people who support the sexualisation of children and the normalisation of paedophilia,' read another. 'Both *The Guardian* and Van Badham disgust me!'[10]

This book does not subscribe to the gloomy 'technodeterminist' thesis that lays blame on the internet as a tool of inherent evil, corrupting humanity with inevitable, unstoppable force.[11] The argument here isn't that human beings are powerless against what internet technology does to us, because the internet does not have universal effects on the billions of people who use it daily. Rather, this book is about how various political and cultural movements have weaponised the internet's capacity to spread lies, and also those individuals at their keyboards who've made an active choice to believe those lies – whatever harm to others or themselves may result from doing so.

There is a powerful antidote to the nightmarish fantasies of internet conspiracy cults: the truth. In telling this story, I owe a debt to the legion of journalists who have doggedly investigated the individuals and events of the conspiracy movements, as well as to the academic researchers exploring these subjects. To further enhance my understanding, I've also interviewed psychologists, disinformation scholars, extremism monitors, politicians and those ordinary people who bear the damage of the internet cults and have sought out space to talk about it.

Most crucially, I've spent the past year researching this book undercover in the conspiracy community. Enmeshed among believers, I've gained insight into individuals who avow these beliefs as well as the language, symbols and values of most meaning to them. Hundreds of conversations with these people inform not only the detail of this book but also an empathy that has developed in me even for those who wilfully believe things that are hatefully – dangerously – false. Behind claims that Tom Hanks bathes in children's blood, or that there are 300,000 captives hidden under the streets of Melbourne, or that murderous alien lizard people walk among us, there are human beings who must be engaged with as human beings if the rest of us are to stand any chance of defusing these beliefs.

'What if I don't want to help them anymore?' wrote a Reddit user, u/the_cnara, responding to my 2020 *Guardian* article on the question of engagement with believers. 'I'm just angry now, the relationships are destroyed,' they said. 'I don't want them in my life after this even if they let it go.'

This book makes an emphatic point that the cost of not helping is too high. A recent report for American radio network NPR analysed the social impact of conspiracy communities and warned of how disinformation has been leaking from the internet's dark, extremist corners and into mainstream politics.[12] What results from these 'disinformation superspreaders' is defective decision-making that poses a threat to public health and safety, strains families and undermines the very fabric of democracy. It is no coincidence that, as per McLuhan, those attempting to take lease on the eyes and ears and nerves of communities in the orchestration of online conspiracy theories are drawn from the ranks of political actors who vigorously oppose democracy.

Writing for *The Conversation* in 2018 about her research into modern conspiracy thinking, social psychologist Professor Karen Douglas from the University of Kent was careful to point out that the popularity of conspiracy theories is not a phenomenon unique to the internet. Douglas instead reminded readers that 'conspiracy theories have always been with us'.[13] The difference now is that 'the internet fuels them in new ways and enables the deepening of conspiracy theorising in some online communities'. Social scientist Joan Donovan offered to NPR's journalists a compelling theory as to why the fabulist tales of the conspiracy cults had such an emphatic purchase online. She suggested it was because the truth was often pretty boring and didn't play that well on social media.[14]

My experience learning the truth about internet conspiracy cults for this book was many things, but boring was not one of them. 'Disturbing' is a more accurate word; so is 'distressing'.

This is a tale of murder and attempted murder, political dark arts and manipulation, hate, extremism, violence and near-inconceivable cruelty. It's a study of the power of fantasy and an attempt to map the structure of a chosen delusion that's currently inspiring ordinary people into extraordinary behaviour with the political potential to endanger us all. It is McLuhan's old warning borne out in real-world detail.

The power of participatory media to delude people into terrorist acts used to be the stuff of nightmare fiction. Fellow Canadian and horror filmmaker David Cronenberg explored McLuhan's theories of 'senses and nervous systems' surrendered to media manipulation in his 1983 movie *Videodrome*.[15] In the film, the undead, videotaped villain Dr Brian O'Blivion, a media theorist and fictionalised version of McLuhan, seeks to hybridise humanity and technology into a malleable 'new flesh'. To do so, he employs cable television and analogue video technology to broadcast a signal called Videodrome, which has the power to mutate the brain.

It's impossible to ignore the film's parallels with the lure of today's internet conspiracy thinking. *Videodrome*'s anti-hero Max Renn (played by James Woods) allows himself to be seduced – quite literally – by a desire to participate in the fantasies O'Blivion's new media offers him. O'Blivion's hope, he tells Max from a videotape, is for the broadcast of Videodrome's corrupting signal to provoke the individual brains of its audience into a mass mutation. Thus, the power of Videodrome to produce and control hallucination within the mind is the power to change reality. By the film's end, Max has been manipulated into murder, conceiving himself as indivisible from a gun that's grown into his hand.

When Cronenberg made *Videodrome* in 1983, it was just a horror movie. Now, as this story I'm about to tell you explains, the hallucination is here.

I am worried about how widespread these crazy ideas are. Was walking down a street in the neighborhood late last year and a tradie shouted out to *@TurnbullMalcolm* and me 'Hi paedophiles'. It was truly bizarre. It really shook me. The guy was very snarky and weird.

@LucyTurnbull_AO on Twitter, 15 June 2021

1. A SMALL ROLE IN A REALITY TV SHOW

QAnon first arrived in Australia's mainstream political consciousness via a disturbing article published in *The Guardian* on 2 October 2019.[1]

In it, journalists Christopher Knaus and Josh Taylor broke a story exposing the relationship between Australia's conservative prime minister, Scott Morrison, and a man that the article referred to exclusively by his Twitter handle, @BurnedSpy34.

@BurnedSpy34, they asserted, was married to a close friend of the prime minister's wife, Jenny. The journalists had seen photographs of the women together, and also of the prime minister's wife with @BurnedSpy34, and @BurnedSpy34 with Morrison. The relationship between the families was longstanding. The women had been friends since their schooldays, the couples had attended each other's weddings, and public Facebook messages were open about the connection between them.

The Guardian had established that this woman, the wife of @BurnedSpy34, had even been recently employed on the prime minister's staff, in a taxpayer-funded position. Her job had no actual policy or advisory responsibilities, although its proximity to the PM obliged a security clearance. It seemed that a personal largesse may have been indulged by the prime minister through providing her a job, but potential largesse was not the most disturbing element of the article.

What disturbed most was that the journalists had identified @BurnedSpy34 as the author of numerous tweets citing the QAnon conspiracy theory. For a year, this man with a close personal relationship to Australia's prime minister had publicly shared content claiming the world was secretly run by a shadowy cabal of paedophiles comprised of the world's elite. The leader of the battle against the cabal, ran the theory, was no less than Donald Trump, then the serving forty-fifth president of the United States. @BurnedSpy34 had publicly suggested at least two of these elite paedophiles were Morrison's own factional rivals.

@BurnedSpy34's opinions amassed him more than 21,000 followers on Twitter – not an inconsiderable number, particularly in Australia. His work promoting these theories had been praised as 'world-class' by fellow QAnon adherents who gathered on the unmoderated imageboard website 8kun.

The ranks of Australia's 'extremely online' community of daily Twitter and Facebook users needed no introduction to what was signified in the coded, loaded language of @BurnedSpy34's posts. Since QAnon's internet arrival two years earlier, advocates of it like @BurnedSpy34 had made their presence loud and visible within the small-swamp, shared-hashtag ecology of Australia's online political conversation.

The echoes in @BurnedSpy34's tales of secret Satanists gobbling children were familiar to anyone who had followed the strange events of the 'Pizzagate' conspiracy theory in the United States three years earlier. Knaus and Taylor helpfully provided not only a summary of QAnon's shared belief in Luciferian villainy but repeated a warning issued by the FBI that the QAnon movement was potentially inspiring 'domestic extremists'.

By October 2019, the impact of extremist internet discourses and the shadowy, anonymous online communities growing around them was a potential domestic threat Australia could no longer ignore.

From where did you receive/research/develop your beliefs?

The Internet, of course. You will not find the truth anywhere else.

The Christchurch gunman via Twitter and 8kun, 15 March 2019

Back in March of 2019, in Australia's close Pacific neighbour New Zealand, a gunman had brutally assaulted two mosques in the sleepy southern city of Christchurch. He murdered fifty-one people and injured another forty in an ideologically motivated, Islamophobic domestic terror attack. Once arrested and arraigned for trial, Australians learned, with horror, that not only was the gunman an Australian himself, but his ideological violence resulted from a radicalisation process that had begun at home.

Only twenty-eight at the time of the murders, the gunman was just fourteen years old and at high school in the regional New South Wales town of Grafton when he'd started to engage online with the extreme right-wing discussions hosted on imageboard website 4chan, and, later, 8kun. A manifesto purportedly written by the gunman and uploaded to the internet in the hours before his crimes was saturated with memes and popular in-jokes that circulated in these places. 'Subscribe to PewDiePie!' he cried out before he started shooting, invoking the name of a popular YouTube personality whose name was regularly bandied about the internet as a bit of a joke. Explaining his murderous worldview, the gunman said he'd found YouTube a 'significant source of information and inspiration'.[2]

Not everyone who engages in discussion about extremism is an extremist. Not all the discussions hosted on 4chan or 8kun promoted violence. Not everyone who engages with a website becomes a murderer, and yet, not every website provokes democratic governments into requesting that telecommunication companies block their content for domestic security reasons.

But 8kun was that website. The recommendation to block had been at the behest of Scott Morrison's own government. The Christchurch gunman had live streamed his murders to the internet as he committed them, using a camera strapped to his helmet – 'making a snuff film for the social media era' as

Foreign Policy magazine described it.[3] 8kun was one of the sites that had allowed the footage to be published and circulated by users on its platform, even when other platforms such as Facebook activated a site-wide deletion. Communication companies complied with the Australian government's directive, and websites including 8kun, 4chan, LiveLeak, Voat and ZeroHedge were blocked in both Australia and New Zealand until the footage of the violence was removed.

This was the current affairs context in which *The Guardian* informed Australians of the relationship between its prime minister, Scott Morrison, and his 8kun-aligned friend, @BurnedSpy34.

Australians didn't need to remember 8kun by name or know of QAnon yet to be reminded that there were strange, dark corners of the internet where political extremists were aggressively sharing ever more marginal political ideas. Shutting down websites and FBI extremism warnings are serious and unusual events, and the tweets published by the prime minister's friend were extreme.

Q Post 128 asks some incredible questions.
Q isolates the war into the very essence of this fight.
It is for our mind!

@BurnedSpy34 on Twitter, 9 July 2019

@BurnedSpy34 – who on Twitter also liked to call himself 'Burn Notice' – was otherwise known as Tim Stewart. After

The Guardian's original story broke, Australian news site *Crikey* profiled him as a fifty-something 'family man' and that at one point he'd run an online health food enterprise named Fruit Loop.[4] He was, like Scott Morrison, an avid supporter of Australian rugby league team the Cronulla Sharks.

Interviews with his sister, Karen Stewart, confirmed that as a quartet, Tim and his wife, Lynelle, had been friends with Scott and Jenny Morrison since their early twenties.[5] All devout Christians, they had attended Maroubra Baptist Church together. Tim and his son Jesse went to Sharks games with Morrison. A photograph of Tim circulated online: smiling, balding and trim in a charcoal V-neck t-shirt, the prime minister in a black polo next to him, and both drinking bottles of Big Wave, a tropical-flavoured, light-ale craft beer.

Crikey further revealed that Tim Stewart was a former bankrupt. Originally a town planner, according to his sister, Tim had moved into property development, with disastrous results. The business failed. Investors lost a lot of money.

After the bankruptcy, his sister – an accountant – was placed in control of his financial affairs. Tim blamed the bank for his misfortunes. 'He didn't take responsibility, but I'm sure he felt responsible,' says Karen. Tim's parents had lost money in the failed business as well.

He came out of insolvency in 2015, and Karen says other family members believe the loss of the business was a 'trigger' for what happened next. Tim had flirted with various conspiracy theories over the years, including believing the 'birther' theory, pushed by Donald Trump, that claimed Barack Obama was secretly born in Kenya. Tim had discussed ideas gained from the far-right 'sovereign citizen' movement; it claimed laws were a legal fiction that those who declared themselves sovereign could choose to ignore. 'It was when he was a born-again Christian that I thought he was probably most normal,' Karen says. After his bankruptcy, he started talking about the existence of a 'secret banking system'. He also started seeking out new friends on Twitter, chatting online.

One of the friends he made was Peter 'Eliahi' Priest. Priest was a jeweller from Australia's Gold Coast who had a known association with local Neo-Fascist group the True Blue Crew. He was a conspiracy theorist who variously claimed to be a designate consul of the Democratic Republic of the Congo, a CIA infiltrator and personally in possession of three kilograms of uranium. Online, Tim also met Isaac Kappy, a Hollywood bit-player who had a walk-on part in the movie *Thor* and a small role in reality TV show *Vanderpump Rules*. Kappy was known for looking a bit like Disco Stu from *The Simpsons*, for allegedly trying to choke Paris Jackson and for accusing actor Seth Green of paedophilia.[6]

Calling himself a 'Hollywood whistleblower', Kappy had aired his claims about Green and other celebrities on the live stream of far-right radio show host Alex Jones's conspiracy theory website, *Infowars*, as well as in wild, self-shot Twitter 'Periscope' videos he released directly to the internet. Kappy's 'evidence' for crimes amounted to little more than his own insistence that words like 'chicken' and references to cars he'd heard in Hollywood conversations were codewords used by paedophiles to communicate their dark desires.

It was thin, but it was enough to draw the interest of Tim Stewart, as well as Tim's young adult son Jesse. They joined an ongoing conversation with the men and others online who shared their conspiratorial worldview. Karen Stewart thinks Tim may have first been brought into contact with Isaac Kappy by another Australian conspiracy theorist, Fiona Barnett. Barnett had achieved brief mainstream media notoriety in 2015 for airing sensational allegations in the wake of Australia's Royal Commission into Institutional Responses to Child Sexual Abuse; she claimed she had been abused by politicians and the crimes had been covered up by police. That media interest dissipated when it was revealed that Barnett also alleged it was satanic ritual abuse by no less than three Australian prime ministers as well as US President Richard Nixon, and organised by the CIA. She told stories about watching children fed to Dobermans, cult leaders using tractors to execute people and personally meeting with Jesus.[7]

The Stewarts' contact with Kappy was in 2018, and a mysterious poster online known only as 'Q' had been feeding stories about secret paedophile cabals through 4chan since November the previous year. Karen Stewart recalls that the conversations Tim Stewart was already having online brought him and Jesse into contact with the Q posts very early. 'I think most of what they were doing was on Twitter,' says Karen, 'because I don't think they'd have the ability to even be on the 4chan or 8kun message boards.'[8]

The online conversations had made fast friends of the Stewarts with Kappy and Priest. Kappy even flew from the US to Australia and stayed with the Stewart family at their home in the Sydney suburb of Botany, and Priest flew down from Queensland to join them. They spent days together, 'just talking for hours about paedophilia', according to Karen Stewart. Karen saw footage of them that they'd recorded with Fiona Barnett, 'doing an interview with these people in America'. As Karen's concern for her brother's new interests grew, Tim Stewart had started sharing calendars supposedly from 'Luciferian' devil worshippers online.[9] These contained detailed annual schedules for when to sacrifice children, rape children at orgies or drink animal blood.

On the lighter side, Alexander Downer seems to have influence with all sorts of famous families who have a paedophilia shadow over them.

@BurnedSpy34 on Twitter, 25 October 2018

On Twitter, Tim Stewart shared scans of a photocopied, decades-old, fifty-page document titled 'Satanic cult awareness' dating back to the 'satanic panic' of the 1980s.[10] This was a conspiracy-theory-fuelled moral panic that insisted organised, satanic sexual predators were corrupting children through degrading rituals of sexual abuse, and infamously provoked 12,000 accusations in the United States alone – not a single one of which could be substantiated.

Stewart also spread bizarre theories about Scott Morrison's Liberal Party colleague Alexander Downer.

Australia's former foreign minister, Downer had found himself involved in a strange international intrigue dating to 6 May 2016. Long retired from the parliament, he was by then Australia's high commissioner to London when a mutual friend had organised for him to meet American Trumpist operative George Papadopoulos for drinks in a London bar. Over the course of their subsequent inebriation, they discussed Trump's chances in the upcoming US election. Papadopoulos had expressed confidence in his candidate's victory on the basis that the 'Russians might release some information which could be damaging to Hillary Clinton', Trump's opponent from the Democratic Party.[11]

Downer, struck by the security implications of this statement, duly sent a cable back to Canberra, informing Australian intelligence of what Papadopoulos had said. Two months later, on 22 July, the WikiLeaks website published a trove of 19,252 private emails and 8034 attachments that had been illegally obtained through a hack of the computers belonging to the Democratic National Committee, the governing body of Clinton's party. Specifically, the hackers had targeted John Podesta, the chair of Hillary Clinton's presidential campaign.

Alarmed, Australian intelligence shared with their American counterparts the content of Downer's conversation. A suspected connection between Papadopoulos's remarks and the published leaks spurred the FBI to pursue their 'Crossfire Hurricane' investigation into Russian electoral interference, which began on 31 July.

In the wake of Trump's election to the presidency on 3 November 2016, loyal Trump supporters online had made something of a bête noire of Downer due to his role in the investigation. The Trump-aligned community that gathered on the 4chan website described Downer as a 'tremendous faggot' and a 'partisan cunt'.

As the months passed, and more became known about Downer's role, Tim Stewart's own coalescing internet community – the QAnon community – busied themselves poring over records of Downer's history, searching out evidence to prove Downer was compromised, and nefarious, and that his report merely pursued a predetermined path as a dedicated Trump antagonist.

Using his @BurnedSpy34 account, what Tim Stewart did on Twitter was to repeat these spurious accusations about Downer with the claim that Downer's role in the Papadopoulos story was somehow linked to a 1996 child abuse inquiry that had taken place when Downer was foreign minister. While that inquiry had certainly uncovered historic stories of sex abuse perpetrated overseas by some Australian diplomatic staff, there was never any suggestion these incidents involved Downer. For a start, he'd only been the foreign minister for less than three months when the inquiry took place.

Facts did not dissuade Tim Stewart from his insinuations. There were several threads impugning Downer. 'It's no coincidence that Downer did NOT want Trump elected,' he tweeted on 25 October 2018.[12] His son Jesse went even further. On 14 November 2018, a long thread on the subject of the child abuse inquiry was tweeted from Jesse's @Jesse_onya_m8 Twitter account. One tweet in the thread read:

Downer had great reason to panic when @realDonaldTrump became president. He knows that Trump and US military are going after elite pedophiles. Trump's war against the illuminati is very real. Their pedo empire is crashing down. Justice is coming.

The final tweet in the thread was signed off with QAnon hashtags: #Qanon, #WWG1WGA and #TheStorm.

Downer was not the only local target of @BurnedSpy34's accusations. Julie Bishop had been a conservative cabinet colleague of Scott Morrison's for six years of government, most of which she'd also spent in the position of foreign minister. A factional ally of Alexander Downer's, in August 2018 Bishop lost an internal party ballot for the leadership to Scott Morrison when their parliamentary Liberal Party moved to replace then prime minister Malcolm Turnbull. Morrison supplanted Turnbull, Julie Bishop retired to the backbench, and in April 2019, a week before she announced her retirement from politics completely, the @BurnedSpy34 Twitter account suggested that she may have signified her involvement within the supposed global paedophile cabal by allowing herself to be photographed wearing red shoes: 'The media references almost sound as if a message is being sent … "Red shoes". "Special occasion".'

Once more, the son doubled down on the father's remarks. On 2 February 2019, @jesse_onya_m8 tweeted:

Why does Julie Bishop love showing off her red shoes? Why Does Alexander Downer love wearing fishnet stockings? Same sick cult as their friends, the Clinton's, Podesta's and the Deep State in The US?

This tweet, like others, was hashtagged #QAnon #GreatAwakening #WWG1WGA.

Again, while there were numerous photographs of Bishop's shoes, there was no evidence anywhere to suggest she had any connection to organised child abuse. The *Guardian* journalists Knaus and Taylor raised this point directly when they interviewed Tim Stewart in 2019. 'If you want to do your research into the US context, the red shoes are purported to be very much a paedophilia shout out,' Stewart told them, 'and there are some extremely odd photos of large groups of men in suits wearing red shoes, many of whom are promoting paedophilia.' Karen Stewart told ABC TV's *Four Corners* program how this QAnon belief had been explained to her: 'If people wear red shoes … they're wearing red so that when babies are slaughtered and the blood falls on the ground, that no one will see the blood spatter.'[13]

The claims about Bishop and Downer weren't even the most outlandish on Tim Stewart's Twitter timeline. Esoteric references to 'battle' and a violent war between forces of 'Ci-vil vs E-vil', dark and light, were riddled through oblique accusations about weaponised 'mind control' and secret societies. He used quasi-religious, esoteric language as well as code terms without obvious translation. On 22 August 2019, he described living in a 'realm of control & evil', while a couple of weeks later on 11 September he declared, 'Animal sacrifices are returning.' There were many links to unsourced stories about vanishing children. The names of notorious sex offenders – like Jeffrey Epstein – were mentioned often, and certainly among Stewart's rambling interpretations of supposedly prophetic statements made by the still-unidentified 'Q'.

On 18 March 2019, Tim Stewart received both a massive boost to his following as well as the ultimate vindication for writing this kind of material when one of his Twitter threads was shared directly by Q in a post on 8kun. In the thread, Stewart had attacked John Podesta, the man whose hacked emails were at the centre of the WikiLeaks dump. He'd described Podesta as 'a treasonous spirit' and warned 'Darkness will be exposed by its disregard for authority and due process'.

Public association with an account that broadcast somewhat unmoored content like this raised questions about Scott Morrison's personal judgment, both in the media and in parliament. In the wake of the *Guardian* story, on 21 October 2019, Senator Penny Wong used the Senate Estimates Committee process to quiz representatives from both the government and the Department of the Prime Minister and Cabinet about Scott Morrison's connection to Tim Stewart and what she called Stewart's 'extraordinary and bizarre views'. She was trying to establish whether 'information from this person has been passed directly to the Prime Minister'. She asked then finance minister Mathias Cormann directly: 'Is the partner of that person on the Prime Minister's staff? Has a QAnon conspiracist been invited to either Kirribilli House or the Lodge?' Cormann, and the departmental staff, took Wong's questions on notice.[14]

Those questions remained unanswered in the Australian parliament a year later. On 20 October 2020, a full twelve months after *The Guardian* had originally broken the @BurnedSpy34 story, Penny Wong again raised questions in Senate Estimates about the proximity of Tim Stewart to the prime minister. She formally requested details of the vetting process for Lynelle Stewart's security clearance. Throughout this time, Stewart's wife, Lynelle, had continued to work in her publicly funded, undefined role on the prime minister's staff at his Sydney residence, Kirribilli House.

This time, the immediate provocation for Opposition questioning was the revelation that Twitter had suspended Tim Stewart's accounts from its platform. Towards the end of 2020, Twitter had begun a broader international crackdown on QAnon content due to 'clear and well-documented informational, physical, societal and psychological offline harm on our service'.[15] A Twitter spokesperson told *The Guardian* that the @BurnedSpy34 account had been 'permanently suspended for engaging in coordinated harmful activity'.

It was a matter of public interest, said Wong, to establish there was no 'vector of influence' being exerted over the Australian prime minister by a conspiracy movement. By 2020, it had been public knowledge for a year that the QAnon movement had been identified by America's FBI as an extremist threat. In Estimates, Deputy Secretary of Prime Minister and Cabinet Stephanie Foster told the gathering that Lynelle Stewart had passed police checks. She was 'not aware' that Tim Stewart had been banned from Twitter, even though the banning had received broad media coverage. 'I do find that surprising,' Wong said. 'You do a fair bit of media monitoring.'[16]

Objections were raised to Wong's questioning in Estimates by Mathias Cormann, who was still the finance minister at that time and a powerful member of Morrison's cabinet. *The Guardian* reported Cormann complaining to Wong that it was inappropriate to scrutinise Lynelle Stewart's employment 'because of what may or may not be the views of her husband'.

Cormann claimed at Estimates that his knowledge of the prime minister's friendship group and residential staffing arrangements was not deep. Only two weeks earlier, Scott Morrison had announced that Cormann would be nominating for the role of secretary-general of the Organisation for Economic Co-operation and Development (OECD), so monitoring Lynelle Stewart's Instagram feed to determine her level of adherence to conspiracy cult beliefs was perhaps not chief among his preoccupations at the time. It might explain how he could have missed posts from @lynniestew5 that were spattered with QAnon propaganda. Amid family snaps and many photos of sunsets, Lynelle Stewart posted pictures of herself with the prime minister's wife and children, views from Kirribilli House, and QAnon-style memes. Two of the latter appeared on 7 and 18 April 2018, both with the QAnon slogan #thegreatawakening and links to her husband's QAnon-themed website, *Sideways Step*.

Did this make Lynelle Stewart a QAnon believer? Karen Stewart claims it would be impossible to live with her brother and not become one, citing the example of Jesse, the couple's QAnon-militant son. 'You couldn't do it,' Karen says. '[Tim] would absolutely brainwash you. You'd hear it all day, every day.' She also tells a story to illustrate the degree of marital loyalty she says is characteristic of the pair. At a family gathering, drinks were flowing freely when Tim announced, with some conviction, he had the ability to talk to cockroaches. The table fell silent, but before Tim could be challenged, Lynelle quickly backed him up, nodding that yes, she'd seen it, she'd absolutely seen him talking to cockroaches.

Karen also suggests QAnon's talk of 'spiritual warfare' and a world run by Satanists speaks to those – like Lynelle and Tim Stewart and the community around them – who already have an evangelical Christian framework to their beliefs. 'If she didn't believe it herself, she was certainly willing to endorse it,' says Karen of her sister-in-law, pointing out, 'she let Isaac Kappy and Eliahi Priest stay in her house.'

You know #theGreatAwakening is in full swing when the Australian Prime Minister @ScottMorrisonMP mentions #RitualAbuse.

@Jesse_onya_m8 on Twitter, 22 October 2018

Tim Stewart claimed his political beliefs were not something he shared or discussed with his friend, the prime minister of Australia. He told *The Guardian* in their first article about him that he had never sought out any discussion with Morrison about QAnon. 'I have never spoken to Scott about anything of a political nature,' he said. 'The idea of me talking to him about this … it's just not true.'[17]

Despite the Stewarts' closeness to the Morrisons, Lynelle's job and the frequent, documented visits of the Stewart family to Kirribilli House, it was, of course, entirely possible that this was the case. It was Morrison's government, after all, that had shut down Australia's access to Q's home of 8kun in the wake of the massacre in Christchurch. On 4 June 2021, when the prime minister was asked at a press conference about his relationship with Tim Stewart, he readily disavowed QAnon. 'I find it deeply offensive that there would be any suggestion that I would have any involvement or support for such a dangerous organisation; I clearly do not,' Morrison said. The questions were being asked of the prime minister in advance of the *Four Corners* investigation into the relationship going to air. On 6 June 2021, the prime minister's office sent the *Four Corners* producers a terse note. It described the investigation as 'a personally motivated slur against the Prime Minister and his family' and criticised the program for 'raising the profile of what the Prime Minister clearly deems a discredited and dangerous fringe group'.[18]

Discredited and dangerous as that group may have been, there were sources suggesting that they were perhaps not entirely without influence upon the Australian prime minister.

In 2017, the Australian government had concluded a special inquiry into historic allegations of child abuse within various Australian organisations. The Royal Commission into Institutional Responses to Child Sexual Abuse was an initiative of the Labor government that preceded the conservative election victory in 2013. The commission heard testimonies of abuse suffered within organisations from the Scout movement to schools, yeshivas, yoga ashrams and a swathe of religious institutions. The emotional four-year inquiry culminated in a national apology to abuse victims, delivered by Prime Minister Scott Morrison on 22 October 2018.[19]

It was a British blogger, Richard Bartholomew, who remarked on a strange inclusion within Morrison's apology speech, an inclusion that in 2018 did not attract any mainstream comment in Australia. Bartholomew's blog was dedicated to 'religion, media, culture and conspiracy theories', with a particular interest in tracking the influence of conspiracist movements in news reports on current affairs. His blog post on 26 October 2018 was concerned with a particular sentence in Morrison's speech: 'The crimes of ritual sexual abuse happened in schools, churches, youth groups, scout troops, orphanages, foster homes, sporting clubs, group homes, charities, and in family homes as well.'

Bartholomew acknowledged that the use of the word 'ritual' in the context of Morrison's speech was perhaps synonymous with 'systematic' or 'methodical'. Yet in the conspiracist world Bartholomew wrote about, he said, 'the phrase "ritual sexual abuse" (or "ritual abuse") obviously more readily evokes the familiar idea of secret Satanic cults committing depravities with impunity.'[20]

Bartholomew had become aware of Morrison's speech because it was hailed on social media by one Mark Watts. Watts was a UK-based online journalist who had been one of the chief public spruikers of what became the disastrous 'Operation Midland' in 2014 to 2016. This was a police investigation into historical child-sex offences based on allegations of supposed victim Carl Beech, whose story of abuse by a '#VIPaedophile' ring Watts had championed. Beech had named prominent public figures and told lurid tales. 'He said that the head of the British Army had abused him on Remembrance Sunday and that soldiers had pinned poppies into his skin,' to mock the war dead, Bartholomew says. 'The abuse he alleged was not just sexual but also gratuitously sadistic, bizarrely so.'[21]

It was also a lie. After two years, the destruction of several public reputations, inconsistencies in the allegations and an overwhelming lack of evidence, the police turned their investigation back on to Beech himself. On 2 November 2016, a police search found him in possession of hundreds of images of child sexual abuse across various devices, dozens of which depicted acts of extreme sexual violence.[22] He'd accumulated these at the very time he himself had claimed to police to be a victim of abuse. Ultimately, none of his stories could be corroborated, and Beech himself was charged with six counts relating to the abusive images in his possession, one of voyeurism, one count of fraud and twelve counts of perverting the course of justice, and he was sentenced to eighteen years in prison. Some of the targets of his false accusations did not live to see their names cleared.

Even with Beech so comprehensively discredited, his champion, Mark Watts, according to Bartholomew, remained 'generally credulous about this sort of thing'. When Watts shared a *Guardian* article on Twitter about what he described as Morrison's 'fulsome apology' to ritual sexual abuse survivors, Bartholomew investigated. He traced scraps of conversation about the speech flowing around the accounts of Watts and others on Twitter. What Bartholomew read suggested to him that whatever Morrison may have meant by 'ritual sexual abuse', the speech saw Morrison embraced by accounts Bartholomew knew to be aligned with the relatively new QAnon conspiracy. Bartholomew quoted a tweet on his blog from one @StormIsUponUs: 'The new Prime Minister of Australia Scott Morrison must be a rider in #TheStorm. Here he is making an unprecedented statement on the cabal-engineered epidemic of child ritual abuse.'

Significantly, Bartholomew observed conversations on Twitter that insisted that this phrasing from Morrison vindicated Fiona Barnett, the Australian woman who'd achieved some niche internet infamy with sensational 'VIP Satanic ritual abuse' claims. Bartholomew recognised Barnett's name from a story he'd seen her share with other conspiracy theorists. In it, she'd claimed her abuse was coordinated by Nazi mind-control experts who'd been imported into various countries by the CIA after the Second World War with a secret mission to create super spies.[23]

Bartholomew's views may have stayed confined to the blogosphere if not for *The Guardian* breaking its first @BurnedSpy34 story, and then another Australian journalist, David Hardaker of *Crikey*, picking up Tim Stewart's trail.

Prayer request. The Australian Luciferian cult just threatened my life. They told me to be silent or else.

@FionaBa47662575 on Twitter, 6 November 2018

On 31 October 2019, Hardaker published an article entitled 'Scott Morrison's conspiracy-theorist friend claims he has the PM's ear – and can influence what he says'. The article named Tim Stewart as @BurnedSpy34, which *The Guardian* had not. It also observed that Stewart had begun his Twitter account on the very day Scott Morrison assumed the office of prime minister, 24 August 2018. The account's bio was 'Totally burned. Dropped in a new city'. Stewart's first tweet declared, 'A fresh start. Rebuilding a new identity.'

That identity, wrote Hardaker, had been quick to praise Scott Morrison online when, only a few weeks into the job, the new prime minister moved to introduce harsh mandatory sentencing laws for convicted sex offenders. The move was opposed by the Law Council of Australia but supported, with passion, by Tim Stewart. 'Australia has had notoriously short sentences for pedo's,' wrote Stewart at the top of a Twitter thread, explaining the changes with a ready set of well-informed tweets, as Hardaker observed.

The *Crikey* journalist had also found a collection of tweets published by Tim Stewart and Jesse Stewart on the day of the National Apology to Victims and Survivors of Institutional Child Sexual Abuse. It wasn't only that these were arguably self-congratulatory in tone, or that they praised Scott Morrison in an explicitly QAnon context. It was also that they claimed the direct influence of Fiona Barnett on Morrison's use of the words 'ritual sexual abuse' in his speech, with all their satanic, conspiratorial associations. 'A new conversation began today in Australia,' @BurnedSpy34 had tweeted. 'It was a stepping stone to be sure, but we took the step. @ScottMorrisonMP took control of the narrative powerfully and commenced phase 1 of our restoration.' And he added, 'Well played: @FionaBa47662575.'

@Jesse_onya_m8 also acknowledged Barnett's influence, and with even more directness. 'Scott Morrison mentioned #RitualAbuse in his speech today,' he wrote, 'as requested by Fiona ... Big step in a good direction for Australia. Scott is a patriot.'

In isolation, these tweets weren't credible evidence of Tim Stewart exerting influence over Scott Morrison, whatever his tone. People spuriously big-noting themselves on the internet is, perhaps, half the internet. Hardaker, however, had something more. His article linked to a Facebook video uploaded by Eliahi Priest. Since the time when Priest had flown down to Sydney from the Gold Coast to talk about paedophilia, hang out with Isaac Kappy and – so he claimed in a Facebook video – smoke spliffs with Tim Stewart in the Stewarts' backyard, the relationship between the two friends had broken down, and with some acrimony. Priest was not only verbally railing against Stewart on Facebook but he was sharing screenshots of their personal conversations across social media complete with detailed explanations.

Writing in *The Australian* newspaper in 2021, Stephanie Rice pieced together events that she suggested were the source of the Priest–Stewart split.[24] Among Eliahi Priest's somewhat boutique collection of interests was an obsession with Australia's infamous Nugan Hand Bank, a merchant bank that had collapsed in 1980 after the apparent suicide of one of its founders. Formal investigations found that the bank had engaged in questionable financial practices and tax-evasion schemes, but rumours that it had been involved in drug smuggling or was a CIA front could not be substantiated. Its shadowy reputation was not assisted by its surviving co-founder shredding documents and fleeing Australia via Fiji in a fake beard rather than facing authorities, nor by the same man turning up in Idaho thirty-five years later running a tactical weapons company that supplied US Special Forces. The whole wild story had supplied rich fodder for conspiracy theorising for decades. As Stephanie Rice discovered, it was Eliahi Priest's insistent belief that, as prime minister, Scott Morrison should be investigating Priest's personal claims that Nugan Hand had hidden a $15 trillion fortune that could reshape the world economy. Where Tim Stewart had fallen foul of Priest was in Stewart's reluctance or inability to leverage his relationship with Scott Morrison to ensure Priest's Nugan Hand claims were investigated by the government.

Priest did, in fact, have reason to believe that such leverage could be brought to bear. On 27 July 2019, months before *The Guardian* broke its @BurnedSpy34 story, Priest published his communications from Stewart on Facebook. In these, Tim Stewart conferred with Priest about how he was going to get the words 'ritual sexual abuse' into Morrison's national apology speech. 'I am organizing an intimate strategy for the PM, re the ritual phrase,' wrote Stewart. 'I'm just preparing a message to Scott now re Monday. Once he's awake mate, he will kick arse.' He'd also shared with Priest a message he'd sent to his wife, Lynelle. 'An army of victims and therapists would specifically love it if Scott's apology referenced ritual abuse victims,' it said. 'This exact wording is a key phrase for victims. Think of this like a code that sends a direct and clear message that they have been heard by Scott specifically.'[25]

On the day of the national apology, Stewart was bullish about their prospects. 'I think Scott is going to do it,' he wrote to Priest. 'Pretty sure speeches at 11. I hope he says it. Scott is very aware of the enormity of today.'

Priest showed his Facebook audience that Stewart had mentioned 'Scott' to him no less than fifty-four times. Priest also had images: photos of Stewart with Morrison; a group photo of Priest, Tim Stewart and Jesse with Isaac Kappy; and an image of a Zoom meeting he said he'd been asked by Stewart to set up. This featured the four with Fiona Barnett, purportedly to strategise the inclusion of 'ritual sexual abuse' into Morrison's speech.[26] It was understandable, perhaps, how frustrated Priest became at Tim Stewart's reluctance to push his conspiracy theory on Scott Morrison, given Stewart's success at getting the prime minister to so publicly commit to pushing his own.

I am not a violent person.

Yes, I advocate harsh justice for traitors who commit heinous crimes so long as due process has played it's course.
Yes, I swear a fucking shitload.
Get the fuck over it, have a teaspoon of cement and harden the fuck up.
Fucking sick of weak pieces of shit.

@NeganHQ on Gab, 22 June 2021

In 2021, the story of Tim Stewart, Jesse Stewart and questions about QAnon's 'vector of influence' over Scott Morrison resurfaced. This time, it was the national broadcaster's flagship investigative journalism show, *Four Corners*, that was sifting through Eliahi Priest's message records and interviewing Tim Stewart's family members, trying to gauge the level of purchase an internet conspiracy theory had over an Australian prime minister.

In the intervening years from 2018 to 2021, the established facts of the Stewart family and their intervention into the national apology hadn't changed, but the world around them certainly had.

In 2018 and 2019, the disturbing presence of QAnon was something that hovered on the edges of the Australian consciousness, mostly among the extremely online. In 2020, with entire Australian cities trapped indoors with their computers waiting out the containment of coronavirus, *everyone* was extremely online. The boundaries between online and offline worlds were the haziest they'd been in internet history. Tripping over those boundaries came QAnon, inspiring a nebulous army of keyboard acolytes pushing claims of 'deep states' and 'paedophile elites' into every possible corner of social media conversation.

'QAnonners' seemed to materialise everywhere, from Facebook yoga groups to trending topics on Twitter to online family get-togethers. If the encounters with its imagery of battle and 'dark to light' apocalyptic language weren't disturbing enough, footage coming out of far-right anti-lockdown protests around the world and specifically Trump 2020 re-election campaign events in America brought the slogans, themes and costumes of Q#characters into confronting visual view. Testimonies were growing of families, households and intimate relationships riven; those who'd 'gone full QAnon' were aggressively polarised against those who hadn't. On 6 January 2021, a mob of Trumpist protesters attempted to violently compel American lawmakers to overthrow the 2020 presidential victory of Democrat Joe Biden by breaching Washington's Capitol Building, intending to hunt down the congressional representatives and senators who opposed them. As images of the violence travelled around the world, the amount of QAnon merchandise visible among the violent crowd was unsurprising.

By the time *Four Corners* went to air, the explanations by Tim Stewart's sister and both of his parents about the behaviour change QAnon beliefs had effected in their loved ones were chilling enough. But when they talked about Tim travelling to a place to which they couldn't follow or reach him, there was something that was now very recognisable to the broader community about their fear.

David Hardaker from *Crikey* had followed up with Tim and Jesse Stewart a couple of weeks after the 6 January riots. While Tim Stewart adamantly denied any suggestion he supported violence of the kind that had just erupted on Capitol Hill, Hardaker noted the online rhetoric of both father and son embraced the key tenets of the Capitol rioters, blending the language of esoteric religion with that of patriotism and revolutionary fervour. Both were insistent the election Trump lost to Joe Biden had been unfairly stolen from him. Kicked off Twitter in its post–6 January QAnon purges, Jesse had relocated to his father's new platform on the unmoderated hard-right platform Gab. Here, Jesse's language had grown more extreme. He accused Joe Biden of being a member of the Illuminati, an alleged secret society of all-powerful, world-event-manipulating masterminds who have been a mainstay of conspiracist belief for years. He showed that he was a fervent anti-vaxxer. He aggressively denounced perceived enemies as 'commie, pedo enabling fucks'. He called Alexander Downer a 'little spy bitch boy and traitor to Australia'. He threatened to hang Scott Morrison's party rival Malcolm Turnbull.[27]

Four Corners revealed that the broader Stewart family had become so concerned by the extremist beliefs espoused by the pair, they reported Tim and Jesse Stewart to the national security hotline, several times. They'd heard the angry rhetoric in person. When Jesse realised that Karen had been speaking to journalists, he flooded her mother's phone with abusive messages and berated Karen on Twitter. Comparing Jesse Stewart's @jesse_onya_m8's tone on Twitter to that of his new incarnation as @NeganHQ on Gab, the word Karen kept repeating in her head as she read them was 'radicalisation'. A friend insisted she report them to the Australian Security Intelligence Organisation (ASIO). Karen now believes that neither of them will ever speak to her again.[28] Karen also told *Four Corners* that she didn't understand 'why the prime minister would want to be seen to be with someone who has such radical beliefs'.

It was a question that Labor Senator Penny Wong attempted to put to the government – for the third time –

in a Senate Estimates hearing on 25 May 2021. It was a couple of weeks ahead of the *Four Corners* broadcast, and the senator was aware the prime minister's office was not answering incoming questions from journalists regarding Tim Stewart. The senator wanted to know if Scott Morrison had yet been briefed on the security threat posed by QAnon. In the year since the last question she had posed about this, the threat had elevated. The conspiracy theory had been weaponised by hostile international actors as a vehicle for disinformation. The New York Police Department had identified the theory as anti-Semitic. She noted allegations that Tim Stewart had described 6 January as 'one of the greatest days on earth'. She asked Morrison's cabinet member Simon Birmingham, 'What measures, if any, were in place to prevent Mr Stewart having access to confidential information about the Prime Minister?'[29]

The government, again, took her questions on notice.

The political implications of the relationship between Scott Morrison and zealous advocates of deeply fringe positions deserved such scrutiny. Over the years there had been repeated warnings about QAnon from the FBI. Australia's own national security services had expressed dire concern about extremism arising in communities like 8kun. In the weeks after the Capitol riots in Washington, adherents of the QAnon theory featured heavily in the number of criminal indictments that were served, some for the most egregious of crimes.[30] 'It's a national security concern, for sure,' says Miles Taylor, a US security expert who'd served the George W. Bush administration and, for a shorter period, Donald Trump's, 'and one that the government must be more forthright and transparent about, especially when people hold those views who are close to a country's leaders.'[31] There were serious implications regarding the proximity of local QAnon acolytes to the prime minister and their direct familiarity with government security processes around facilities like Kirribilli House.

What would this knowledge mean when Australia's government changed? What would it mean when QAnon's priorities did? As the coronavirus pandemic wore on, QAnon adherents online adopted more extreme anti-vaccination positions. On 22 February 2021, @NeganHQ responded to images of Scott Morrison being vaccinated while wearing an Australian-flag face mask with two posts on Gab. 'What a pathetic loser,' said one. 'In a single moment, the Australian Prime Minister has disgraced our flag,' said another. By 30 June, @NeganHQ was calling Scott Morrison 'Scommie' and accusing him of 'forcing vaccines on certain industries'. These appeared in the context of Gab posts like one on 28 April 2021:

'I'd pay two grand to see [certain people] hanged,' @NeganHQ said.

The *Four Corners* exposé of the Stewarts had included an interview with Miles Taylor, the US national security expert, about the American experience of QAnon's security risk. He told the program: 'These conspiracy-theory trends like QAnon are a danger to the country. The vitriolic rhetoric on some of these message boards could jump the tracks into violence very, very easily. We were worried about that, and it wasn't just a law enforcement concern. We started to view it as a real national security threat.'[32]

Security was only one concern stirred by the saga of Scott Morrison and the QAnon family. Questions had to be asked about the prime minister's political judgment. Back on 18 November 2019, David Hardaker at *Crikey* had run a new story about the 'ritual sexual abuse' comment in the prime minister's apology speech. The prime minister's office had told *Crikey* in advance of Hardaker's article that Morrison's use of the term came from a bipartisan reference group of survivor advocates and members of parliament (MPs). This group had spent four months consulting with affected communities to advise on the apology ceremony and the apology itself, but documents and interviews revealed to Hardaker that 'ritual sexual abuse' had not been in their recommendations. It was not mentioned once in a twenty-page briefing paper they prepared. One panel member told *Crikey* she'd only ever heard the term used by conspiracy theorists. Another member, survivor advocate Chrissie Foster, told the journalist that if the term had been mentioned, the group would have recommended, explicitly, against its use.[33]

Instead, Morrison had seemingly allowed his language, through his friend Tim Stewart, to be influenced by Fiona Barnett. At the time, she had even tagged him into a tweet about it on 17 October 2018: '@ScottMorrisonMP When you issue your "National Apology to Victims and Survivors of Institutional Child Sexual Abuse" this Mon 22 Oct, please acknowledge victims of "Ritual Abuse" by using these very words. This will gain you credibility with the many RA victims and the therapists.'

It was one thing for a head of government to consult with a diverse range of views. It was entirely another for those views to be from someone who made videos of herself claiming to have been fed a baby's dismembered face in a child-raping satanic blood orgy once staged at the Bathurst City Hall for cricket legend Richie Benaud's birthday.

So what was to be gained? Why do it?

Maybe it wasn't merely bad judgment. One could suggest that the powerful might maintain proximity with conspiracy theorists out of some genuine shared belief, or in a subdued expression of values that are culturally or ideologically simpatico. That's possible.

Alternatively, one could consider that the recent relationship of organised politics to the internet conspiracy cults has been informed by far more cynical calculations. As the evolving story of this book details, there are numerous political actors who have manipulated online conspiracy theorists into becoming their unpaid digital propagandists. Blogging in the wake of Morrison's apology speech, Richard Bartholomew suggested the casual mention of a loaded term like 'ritual sexual abuse' was perhaps deliberately ambiguous. 'It may be that he wanted to signal his belief in the phenomenon without having to invest political capital in it,' he wrote at the time.[34] Democratic electoral victories are made from accumulating small electorates, and maybe conspiracy cults are just cheap chunks to win.

Less discussed in the analysis of Scott Morrison's political relationship with Tim Stewart were the unsettling questions provoked in its opposite direction.

Tim Stewart was a politically interested person. He was engaged enough about current events to be tweeting about political identities like Alexander Downer and Julie Bishop. He was immersed in daily conversations online about exposing cover-ups, he harangued his extended family about his beliefs, and he did political stuff with his son. Yet Tim Stewart had said that he'd 'never spoken to Scott about anything of a political nature'. It was worth asking: if so, why not? If you wanted laws changed and criminals arrested and a 'great awakening' that would transform the shape of all society, why wouldn't you be broaching it with the actual politician that you knew?

By 2 October 2019, the day Tim Stewart told *The Guardian* that he never talked to Scott Morrison about politics, his old friend had established himself as the dominant actor in Australian politics. Morrison's triumph over Julie Bishop and other rivals in the Liberal Party leadership contest was something he won through astute backroom dealing and his own political ruthlessness. In May 2019 he also fought and won a federal election. He ran a political party, a government and a cabinet – he was expert in political power and had himself made powerful with that expertise.

So how could Tim Stewart persist in QAnon beliefs about a 'cabal of elites', a 'Deep State' and 'shadow government' when the real state – the real government – was the same guy who drank light ales with him? How does an anonymous internet prophet come to exert more influence over someone's political reality than a prime minister hanging out with you at a Sharks game?

Addressing these questions obliges a journey in several directions. One of these is into the conspiracist mindset, to understand how it spawns and what encourages it to continue. Another explores the ancient myths that fuel the fantasies of modern paranoia, another still the agendas of those opportunists and grifters who feed voraciously on conspiracist belief.

Then there's a path to be followed deep into the rough, dark territories of the internet's subcultures, such as the imageboard websites 4chan and 8kun. These were the spaces that were creating Q, forming Q, for many years before Q first appeared.

Van Badham is a noxious feminist whore whose cunt smells like dingo shit.

Anonymous on 4chan, 9 November 2016

2. GATEWAY DRUGS

To understand the self-sealing, reality-excluding phenomenon that is QAnon – its origins, characters, implications and the near totalising belief of its adherents – the place to begin is in the abstract, esoteric worlds of the internet's 'imageboard' websites. QAnon emerged as a mysterious conspiracy theory posted on the imageboard 4chan in late 2017 and not long after moved to another imageboard, 8kun, where it made a permanent home.

Imageboards are a form of website in which users engage an unfolding public discussion with contributions made by posting text, images or both. The individual 'boards' within the site are different discussions, arranged around a diversity of topics, and typically the users are anonymous. Comments accumulate in a free-flowing conversation where anyone can say what they like because no one has to know who they are. Imageboards are a platform to say the unsayable. They are immersive and exclusive, with their own language and powerful rituals of participation.

4chan and 8kun are the most infamous of the modern internet's forums, and the communities that they've spawned have evolved into active, visible subcultures offline. It was within these cliquey, self-referential spaces that the conspiracy cults of Gamergate, Pizzagate and QAnon all first formed. Some might claim the structure of the imageboards made such movements inevitable. The imageboards were also the places that birthed the alt-right.

Head to the 4chan homepage today and its front page offers an index. Anyone who visits the site can join conversations about fashion, sports and literature, as well as politics and a range of pornographic genres, including Japanese *ecchi* and *hentai* erotic material, subgenres of manga/anime (*ecchi* a kind of playful, softcore sexual content and *hentai* a kink or fetish animated hardcore pornography that revels in the abnormal or perverse).

Japanese influence runs through 4chan. 4chan's founder, New Yorker Christopher Poole, known online as 'moot', had become interested in Japanese imageboards via his participation in a subforum that ran on the comedy website *Something Awful*. It was called 'Anime Death Tentacle Rape Whorehouse'. As a conversation dedicated, simultaneously, to the Japanese anime genre, provocation and smut, many ADTRW users had familiarity with Japanese-language imageboards that embraced and showcased the same kind of content. A favourite of the group was Futaba Channel, also known as 2chan.net.

Wishing to re-create the Futaba experience for an English-language user base, in 2003 Christopher Poole sat down with the source code for the Futaba website to use as a model and laboriously translated its Japanese text with the help of Alta

Vista's Babel Fish online translation software. He built his own imageboard site, dubbed it 4chan and launched it on 1 October of that year. From the beginning, he advertised his new site towards the anime fans of ADTRW. It attracted those who had chafed at the moderation of comments that *Something Awful* had imposed on their conversation.

The way 4chan worked was to eschew the registration process required by other sites. Instead, posting could be completely anonymous, and discussions were refreshed and maintained only for as long as participants kept engaging with their content. What kept a discussion at the most-viewed top of the page was not what an editor or an admin determined should go there but whether people were still discussing it. When a discussion became unpopular, the site deleted it.

An online anime forum run by mob democracy – with no names, no rules and no accountability – perhaps sounds adolescent in concept. This is unsurprising. On the day he launched 4chan, Christopher 'moot' Poole was only fifteen years old.

wtf is happening to my computer
is this the work of the evil hacker christopher poole?
Anonymous on 4chan, 24 October 2018

While Poole kept his age and identity a secret, the anonymous, lawless platform the teenager had created found an energetic following. More boards were added, expanding the site's purview far beyond its anime origins, gathering people into boundary-less conversations about weapons, cars, history, philosophy. 4chan's combination of text-and-image-based discussion rapidly spawned a new, infinitely regenerating language of online slang, shared jokes and visual memes, from the funny-cat-photo humour of LOLcats to the surprise insertion of clips from Rick Astley's 1980s pop hit 'Never Gonna Give You Up' into otherwise unrelated videos, a prank known as 'rickrolling'.

4chan's structure for promoting content incentivised the creation of sensational material that generated reactions. Whatever was the most inventive, controversial or plain outrageous discussion attracted attention that in turn brought it before more users (and by 2014, the site had an estimated 22 million users every month). Anything less interesting vanished. The baiting, response-provoking mockery of internet trolling became an art form here. 4chan's screens constantly refreshed with creative ways the channers had found to humiliate and abuse one another. A reputation for gross content was also well earned. One notorious 4chan conversational genre was 'poop stories', where some users uploaded pictures of their bowel movements.

Not all users were embracing 4chan's lack of restrictions merely to indulge in its lack of taste. Before the end of 2003, 4chan boards were already being flooded with child sexual abuse images.

Legal action saw to the removal of these images, but the question of whether a teenage boy was really the best person to platform free-speech absolutism on the internet was left unasked. The free speech of others in fact laid a burdensome regulatory responsibility onto Christopher Poole. The teenager found himself having to source a loose team of volunteers to monitor the threads and remove snuff content and child sexual abuse images, while he dutifully referred bomb threats and other criminal activity to the FBI.

He also became preoccupied with trying to work out how to monetise the site. For all its growing infamy, 4chan demanded hosting space that made it more costly than profitable to run. Advertisers were reticent to be associated with a site that hosted unpredictable content like tentacle porn, 'cock shots' and photographs of self-harm and defecation. That was 2009. Five years and millions of monthly site visitors later, 'moot' had started and then dropped out of college and was still living out of a two-bedroom apartment with his mother.

Meanwhile, the 4chan community's structural politics of shock, mockery and irony were manifesting influence beyond the site, in unforeseen ways.

A string of separate news reports over the years chronicled how 4chan had platformed images of animal cruelty, illegal hacking, more child sexual abuse images, cyberbullying campaigns and even the harassment and stalking of a vulnerable and abused eleven-year-old who went by the internet name of 'Jessi Slaughter'.

In 2010, and courtesy of a webcam owned by a friend, Florida-based Jessi was making YouTube videos about the 'emo' music and fashion that was popular at the time. One day, the tone of the videos took a sharp turn. Schoolyard rumours claimed Jessi had bragged about a sexual relationship with Dahvie Vanity, the lead singer of emo band Blood on the Dance Floor, and these rumours made their way to social media. Jessi responded with a furious denial on YouTube, hitting back at 'cyberbullies' in an invective-laden rant that contained the memorable threat 'gonna pop a Glock in your mouth and make a brain slushie'. The emotional video went viral.

The discovery of the video was met with delight by 4chan users. Jessi was denounced as a 'whore', images and words from the video were repackaged into endless jokes and memes, and a flood of mockery swelled into a river of harassment. Jessi's father, Gene, joined in Jessi's next YouTube video to harangue the harassers, roaring lines like 'You done goofed!', which made him a sensation on 4chan in the worst possible way. In addition to relentless internet harassment, Jessi – and Jessi's family – were 'doxxed', meaning their phone numbers, addresses and other details were published online. They were subjected to abusive phone calls, bomb threats were phoned into Jessi's school and thousands of dollars of unwanted deliveries turned up at the family home.

The family came apart; Gene was arrested for punching Jessi. The year Jessi turned twelve, Gene was dead of a heart attack. Socially isolated, harassed and humiliated, Jessi spent some time in foster care. Meanwhile, Dahvie Vanity responded to his notoriety by releasing a song that quoted Gene's rant on camera. Other lyrics complained about damage to his reputation caused by an unnamed, malicious slut.

In 2018 – years after the story of the tearful, bullied child and the enraged father had been absorbed into impersonal internet folklore – Jessi Slaughter alleged on a Tumblr blog that Dahvie Vanity had groomed and raped them from the age of ten. By 2019, there were no less than twenty-one women alleging Vanity had also sexually assaulted them, most when they were only minors. Journalists discovered Vanity had two previous arrests for raping children.[1]

Even when these events became known, 4chan commenters remembered Jessi Slaughter not as a person but as a shared tribal experience. Being able to claim you were around 4chan 'for Jessi Slaughter' was a badge of veteranship, with a sort of heritage status. 'Should've bullied that whore more holy fuck,' someone wrote in 2021.

Improbably, 4chan could be darker. Channers enthusiastically shared stolen intimate images of people. Doxxing was sport. Users even shared images of animal cruelty and human murder. In 2014, when a 33-year-old man from the US state of Oregon brutally murdered his partner, he uploaded photographs of his victim's body to 4chan from the crime scene. It was captioned: 'Turns out it's way harder to strangle someone to death than it looks on the movies.'

What happened on 4chan resurrected old debates about internet censorship. In 2010, Australia's News.com.au ran critical comment from Professor Matt Warren, from Deakin University's School of Information Systems. Warren was adamant that an unfettered internet presented obvious dangers, and there shouldn't be free access to it. He wanted it controlled and censored, and people to be held accountable for their actions on it.[2] Similar calls were reported in French media. In 2014, the website www.emmayouarenext.com

appeared; it had a countdown clock, promising to drop nude photos of actor Emma Watson at a certain time. When the time came, the site transformed to that of a marketing company – supposedly retained by celebrities – promoting the hashtag #ShutDown4chan with an open letter to Barack Obama. 'The recent 4chan celebrity nude leaks in the past 2 months have been an invasion of privacy,' read the letter, 'and is also clear indication that the internet NEEDS to be censored.' It was when a journalist from *Business Insider* noticed the letter was signed 'Brad Cockingham' that people realised this, too, was a prank.[3] The internet was a slippery place. 4chan would not be censored.

In 2011, joint research from MIT and the University of Southampton deemed that the disinhibition of 4chan users was due to their online anonymity; there were no reputational consequences on the platform, no matter how extreme the speech or how radical the content.[4] This birthed a culture of intense competition among users to make ever more shocking contributions. 4chan, wrote *Wired*, had developed its own rules of the internet, and Rule 36 was: 'There is always more fucked up shit than what you just saw.'[5]

Whatever combination it came in, the murders, tortures, bullying, poop stories and porn on 4chan established that its currency was outrageousness. It was an outrageousness that drew the attention of radical political actors, and it was about to have profound political implications.

What can we do individually to stop the spread of globalism and defeat the globalist message at home and abroad?

<u/skankhunt92> Does regular garlic repel psychic vampires?

<u/SirSeizureSalad> No, but the 2nd amendment does.

Reddit, 23 February 2017

Over the course of 4chan's years, channers had not only competed to outrage one another within the site's internal strands, they formed and mobilised groups to wage disruption on the external world. They did things like raid other people's internet activities, called in bomb threats to an NFL stadium, and made a swastika a trending topic on Google. They organised with other online communities to overwhelm an online Greenpeace poll to name a humpback whale 'Mr Splashy Pants'.

More darkly, they'd mocked pop star Justin Bieber by starting a #CutForBieber hashtag. Channers used fake images of self-harm to encourage Bieber's real fans to demonstrate their opposition to reports of the pop star smoking marijuana by hurting themselves in 'protest'. In 2014, channers mocked up an online campaign that tried to convince girls to post online nudes under a #LeakforJLaw hashtag, supposedly in solidarity with the actor Jennifer Lawrence, whose own nudes had recently been hacked and circulated – by 4chan. Another time, anti-feminists in the

4chan community started an #EndFathersDay hashtag, trying to smear the feminist movement by pretending they were an authentic women's campaign. Both stories were picked up and promoted by international news organisations who hadn't tumbled to the hoax.

The political potential of internet-based collective mobilisations was realised early by a left-libertarian hacker presence on 4chan. A loose collection of users who had originally been involved in 4chan's miscellaneous imageboard (known as /b/), the group started channelling small 4chan-style pranks against various targets in 2006, like taking down the website of a far-right radio host. They called themselves 'Anonymous', after the automatic identity that every new user was provided on 4chan.

In January 2008, Anonymous released a menacing computer-narrated YouTube video of storm clouds, declaring war against the Church of Scientology. 'For the good of your followers, for the good of mankind – for our enjoyment – we shall proceed to expel you from the internet,' promised the video, and 'systematically dismantle the Church of Scientology in its present form.'[6] Not only did Anonymous then attack the Church of Scientology's computers, the group encouraged people out on the streets around the world to physically protest against the church. Emboldened, Anonymous's computer attacks over the next few years shut down websites and leaked data from banks, governments, political parties, jihadist groups, security companies and major corporations. Anonymous backed the Arab Spring uprisings, and in 2011 claimed credit for taking down forty websites that featured paedophilia content, publishing the names and identifying information of 1500 users of the sites. They were described as 'the first internet-based superconsciousness'.[7]

Anonymous fought oppression and for justice, but a hard-right-wing presence centred around 4chan's 'Politically Incorrect' discussion board – known as /pol/ – was also emerging. Long-marginalised proponents of fascist and Neo-Nazi ideologies were gaining the confidence to express their ideas in the sly, are-they-or-aren't-they-serious imageboard language of trolling, pranks and memes.

In April 2017, Jacob Siegel of *The Daily Beast* updated an article he'd first published in June 2015.[8] That was the year that Christopher Poole – who had already stepped down as 4chan's administrator – sold 4chan to Hiroyuki Nishimura, the creator of Japan's 2chan, the site that had originally inspired Poole.

In his article, Siegel chronicled the channers' growing indulgence of the iconography and language of ancient hatreds over the length of the previous decade. Nazism, woman-hating and anti-Black racism had become dominant themes in online conversation. Their use of extremist imagery soundly mocked the piety of inclusive 'politically correct' modern manners as well as the earnestness of the individual social justice activists that channers encountered online. An example was 4chan's 'Ebola-chan' meme in 2014. Styled like an anime character, Ebola-chan was created in response to the lethal contemporaneous Ebola disease outbreak in Africa. She had wide eyes and pink pigtails that curled into Ebola cells. Calling her 'the viral goddess of love and Afrocide', channers offered her jokey online prayers and venerations in the expressed hope she would kill millions of Black people. In service to the meme, channers managed to publish material on a Nigerian website that claimed Ebola was a demon unleashed on Africa by white racists. They instructed readers not to trust the Western doctors treating Ebola, insisting they were worshippers of the demon. Fortunately, the prank was quickly identified as a troll.

Amid this kind of plausibly ironic racist tastelessness, explained Siegel, the authentic far right realised that a place where 'bad words and old slanders [were] being bandied around as a kind of satire' was a place where they could hitch their fascism. They could 'make ancient blood hatreds feel like something new again', and all under the cover of humour and irony.

4chan's absurdist, bombastic and highly visual rhetorical style was arresting and impactful. Unsurprisingly, as its content spread into social media beyond 4chan, its language and its style were aped – and adopted – on these other platforms too.

The most notable transmission was to Reddit. Started in 2005, Reddit is a bulletin board style of website where discussions (called 'subreddits') are also formed around topic areas, with a community of users 'upvoting' or 'downvoting' content into more prominent view. Founded by a pair of college roommates from the University of Virginia, from its inception Reddit also promised a free-speech experience. Its distinction from 4chan was that self-started community discussions were frequently framed around breaking news stories.

For this latter reason, Reddit calls itself 'the front page of the internet'. It's had some mainstream legitimacy to do so. In 2006, Condé Nast, the publishers of global magazine titles *Vogue, GQ, Wired, Vanity Fair* and *The New Yorker,* had bought the site for US$20 million.

By 2015, though, that 'front page' had been denounced by the Southern Poverty Law Center as 'a black hole of violent racism'.[9] The same year, Reddit's CEO tried to take action against subreddits that were facilitating harassment. This occurred in a context of sustained user revolts against her attempt to manage the site, and she soon was forced to resign. *Gawker* reported that Reddit communities with names like 'CoonTown' collected thousands of subscribers who came to see videos of brutal violence against Black men, content that featured in the top 2 per cent of the site's traffic. Jacob Seigel denounced it in *The Daily Beast* as the internet's single largest gathering place for racists.[10]

That this kind of hard-right, radical publishing had all begun as edgy, ironic satire on 4chan was irrelevant. Eventually, wrote Siegel, 4chan's /pol/ board and the racist forums on Reddit attracted people who either did not know or never cared if the intent of the hate was ironic; they just came for the racism. They built on that enterprise, too, he said, quoting the American Neo-Nazi Andrew Anglin on the influence 4chan had on *The Daily Stormer*, an explicitly Neo-Nazi website that Anglin had founded in 2013. Anglin told Siegel that the *Stormer* had readily looted images and emulated the rhetorical styles of 4chan. It was a successful move, said Anglin. Their website had really taken off.

For the decade leading up to the time that Siegel's article was published, advocates of far-right politics on 4chan's /pol/ board gradually began to refer to themselves as 'the alt-right'. It was a term that had been popularised by another explicit Neo-Nazi American, Richard Spencer, who started using it around 2008. Spencer headed a white nationalist think tank called the National Policy Institute. It pushed old far-right ideas with repackaged terminology, advocating for things like 'scientific racism', 'white identity' and the supposed supremacy of Western civilisation. Spencer's aim in popularising the term alt-right was to provide a unifying identity to a loose collection of unaligned Neo-Fascists and white nationalists wherever he found them and organise them into a 'big tent' movement. In 2010 he began publishing a webzine called *The Alternative Right* to express these ideas.

The alt-right Spencer had identified manifested on 4chan and other social media. It was extremist but it was also politically chaotic, a mishmash of established hard-right movements with differing positions, maverick ideologues and random internet bandwagoners whose beliefs were still in flux. One thing its proponents agreed upon was that racial white identity was under lethal attack, and there was growing agreement about who was responsible: 'political correctness' was the problem and 'social justice warriors' (SJWs) were to blame.

The white man needs to take back the indie game
scene. Cunts have proven corrupt and incompetent,
possibly Jew-influenced.

Anonymous on 4chan, 19 August 2014

The fringe influencers of the online alt-right tested many
channels to exert disruption in the real world. In 2013, the
release of a small, text-based independent computer game
sparked a 4chan mobilisation that would prove history-
making, and the alt-right seized an opportunity to participate.

The computer game was called *Depression Quest*. Its
developer was Zoë Quinn, a then 25-year-old American
who had built the game in collaboration with a writer
and musician. Quinn's personal experience of living with
depression and ADHD had inspired its creation. Within
40,000 words of interactive text, the player's task in *Depression
Quest* is to navigate the day-to-day challenges of living with
depressive illness. Quinn released it to the gaming platform
Steam in August 2014 for free, because when she was first
diagnosed with depression at fourteen, Quinn's parents had
not been able to afford any professional help. 'I can't in good
conscience hold back offering someone something that could
help them start making real changes in their life,' Quinn
explained.

It was a benevolent gesture, and the game became
incredibly popular. Within eighteen months, *Depression Quest*
was downloaded more than one million times. There was,
however, almost immediate criticism from gamers whose
preferences were, perhaps, for more visual, less cerebral

gaming entertainment. That criticism wasn't limited to 'It's just boring and is entirely all reading', like one early review on the game's Steam listing page.[11] It included rape threats. It included death threats. Curiously, these were not levelled at either of Quinn's male collaborators.

Depression Quest was an example of quirky, indie-style gaming entering the spaces of the mainstream, and there were established online gamer communities who did not like it. Games exploring intimate themes – like this one about managing mental illness, or other contemporary titles about cancer treatment, menstruation or relationship breakdown – were drawing the interest of games media. The public attention sat uncomfortably with audiences who preferred the splashing-blood, shoot-'em-up aesthetics of game franchises like *Call of Duty* or *Grand Theft Auto*.

It wasn't just a question of aesthetics. It's easy enough to not play a game that doesn't appeal to you, or to skip an article about a product you're unlikely to buy. The issue was a culture that had developed around gaming, in places like in-game chat, 4chan, Reddit and in specialised game forums, that fiercely defended itself as a preserve of a narrow social identity – one to which, from its conception to its creator, *Depression Quest* did not conform.

Rape threats and death threats weren't the climax of what the internet did to Zoë Quinn. They were barely the beginning.

Australian sociologist Michael Salter and his American counterpart Lori Kendall are theorists who study the intersection of gender with online identity. Both have made the blunt point in their work that from the 1980s on, the 'early adopters' of computer technology, gaming and the internet in the West were young, white, heterosexual men.[12] In an influential essay he wrote about online abuse, Salter noted that an identifiable '"geek" variant of masculinity' had even emerged within computing and gaming communities as the use of digital technology had spread. Older ideals of masculinity may have lionised physical strength or warrior prowess or virility; now, wrote Salter, 'technical mastery came to serve as an alternative foundation for masculine identity'. Within gamer spaces, the worth of a man was not about how many bricks he could lift or fights he could win or girls he could bed. It was about how smoothly he could illegally download a new Metallica album or solve all the puzzles in *The Legend of Zelda*.

As games developed multiplayer platforms, so too did players affect aggressive personas in their competitive gameplay. A subcultural vernacular developed in these spaces that was heavy with insults and wilfully brutal. Obscene, abuse-laden lingo spread from the in-game chat to the places where gamers congregated on social media. Unmoderated discussions like 4chan were described by tech writer David Auerbach as a 'nonstop barrage of obscenity, abuse, hostility, and epithets related to race, gender, and sexuality'. This had the effect of concentrating the slender demographics of gaming communities even further: anyone who complained about abuse was subject to more, and worse.

The broader social reality, by the 2010s, was that participation in gaming and internet culture was diversifying rapidly. Rather than remaining the preserve of young, white heterosexual men, by 2014 British studies were showing that women were more than half of the games market, and by 2015 the Pew Research Center established that white, Black and Hispanic Americans were equally likely to be gamers too.[13] Australian research determined that the average age of gamers had shifted from twenty-four in 2005 to thirty-four by 2015; 78 per cent of gamers were aged eighteen or over.[14]

At the same time as mainstream games companies were adapting their content to meet their new markets, feminists and other cultural theorists started challenging attitudes that represented game culture as an overwhelmingly male domain.

This increasing visibility of women particularly in what had been male-dominated space was interpreted by 'geek variant' masculinists as an affront. To the self-cloistering communities within spaces like 4chan that heaved with such people, feminist criticism was a wilful incursion to be resisted, lest the very notion of masculinity itself be overrun.

In 2012, the experiences that a young Canadian gender studies academic, Anita Sarkeesian, had with this 'resistance' presaged much of the strange madness that was also about to visit itself on Zoë Quinn.

MOOT IS A HAIRY MAN WHORE WHO SUCKS ANITA SARKEESIAN'S AND ZOE QUINN'S HAIRY SMEGMA COVERED J E W DICKS

Anonymous on 4chan, 8 December 2014

Anita Sarkeesian was a graduate student at York University in Canada. Her research critiqued the representation of women in genre tropes across popular culture, and she maintained a website with a YouTube channel, *Feminist Frequency*, that documented her work. In June 2012 she launched an online Kickstarter fundraiser to make a series of videos that extended her analysis to video games. 'I love playing video games but I'm regularly disappointed in the limited and limiting ways women are represented,' Sarkeesian wrote in her pitch asking for contributions.[15] To make *Tropes vs. Women in Video Games*, she needed six thousand dollars to cover production costs.

'[T]its or back to the kitchen, bitch,' came one comment.

'LESBIANS: THE GAME is all this bitch wants,' came another.

They continued: 'You are a hypocrite fucking slut'; 'I'll donate $50 if you make me a sandwich'; 'She needs a good dicking, good luck finding it though'; 'I hope you get cancer :)'; 'Back to the kitchen, cunt.'

And more. Thousands and thousands more, across all platforms where Sarkeesian had a presence – two thousand within a week on her YouTube channel alone. A post on *Feminist Frequency* reported that a 'coordinated attack' had mobilised, trying to get Sarkeesian's accounts banned, sending her torrents of abuse – including rape and death threats – even editing her Wikipedia page to describe her as a 'cunt' and transforming her profile picture to porn. On her Tumblr, Sarkeesian identified that 'a dozen or more different people were working together to vandalize' the Wikipedia entry alone.[16]

The abuse of Anita Sarkeesian was so intense, it became an international news story. French website *Madmoizelle* pegged the blame for the attack squarely on 'a bunch of 4channers doing everything on the Internet to destroy her'.[17] It seemed that someone had brought Sarkeesian's Kickstarter to 4chan's attention, as they had abuse victim Jessi Slaughter and so many other targets before.

The joke at the time was that 4chan did more to resource a feminist critique of gaming than Sarkeesian could have ever managed on her own. In the wake of publicity about the abuse, donations made in solidarity with Sarkeesian flowed into the *Tropes vs. Women in Video Games* fundraiser. She had asked for $6000. She received $158,922.

The videos got made but laughs for the woman herself were thin on the ground. Anita Sarkeesian's life was transformed: the engaged and eager 28-year-old academic became a woman made famous for her public abuse, because that abuse didn't stop when she surpassed her fundraising goals, or even when she made her videos. The attention from 4chan had made her into a new kind of internet celebrity: the online feminist folk villain.

Over the next few years the abuse and death threats continued, and there were ongoing attempts to hack her accounts, shut down her sites and dox her. The attention had made her videos hugely popular, but while she was provided with international platforms in the media and at conferences to discuss her work, she was subjected to bomb and mass-shooting threats at public appearances. She was falsely reported to the FBI and IRS for investigation. She was sent images that depicted video-game characters raping her and had a video game made about her. It was called *Beat Up Anita Sarkeesian,* and in it the player punches an image of her face until it is misshapen, cut and bloody.

She was also the subject of conspiratorial, crowd-funded amateur documentaries. Two men behind these films, Jordan Owen and Davis Aurini, worked sometimes together, sometimes apart, but shared a mission to prove Sarkeesian was a fraud and manipulator. Their most infamous project was a crowd-funded documentary called *The Sarkeesian Effect.*

Aurini self-identified as an 'intellectual' and shared prop-heavy white nationalist opinions on a YouTube channel and on Reddit. He was rumoured to hang out on 4chan's /pol/ board. Owen was also a YouTuber, as well as a gamer, and a composer of 'modern orchestral dance music'. Both men were enraged that Anita Sarkeesian had been recognised for her feminist advocacy at events like the Game Developers Choice Awards and denounced her in *The Sarkeesian Effect* as 'a bully like [the video game industry] had never encountered before, a bully that used guilt and political correctness to have her way'.[18]

Their films and public comments repeated the online myth that her stories of harassment were a lie – a pity-eliciting grift to propel her to fame and riches – even as their own projects actively harassed her.

For all the exuberance of their attempts to have Anita 'cornered', the only major revelation of Aurini and Owen's film was that she got her correspondence delivered to a post-office box rather than a street address. An insistence of

Aurini's that she had lied about reporting her harassment to the police turned out to be incorrect. When the police located her harassment reports, Aurini retorted online that this news merely 'compounded' his questions rather than answering them. His reasoning for this was without explanation.

Writer David Futrelle from the anti-misogynist website *We Hunted the Mammoth* followed the story of the Sarkeesian films and blogged about it. He saw a genuine desperation within these projects for 'the terrible things people say about Sarkeesian to all be proved true'. For a start, there was the issue that they were sourcing money from people on a promise to validate the energy 'half the internet' had put into hounding her.[19]

There was also, Futrelle observed, a monstrous, sometimes admitted, envy of Sarkeesian among these people. She was able to raise more money from her projects than they could for theirs. She was invited to game industry parties when they were not. Her work was influencing a mainstream conversation. Futrelle described a pressing, psychological need he saw in Jordan Owen to delegitimise her. Any suggestion that Anita Sarkeesian may not be the creature Owen wanted her to be, wrote Futrelle, 'actually seemed to plunge him into something close to an existential crisis'.

Around these men, their projects, the online movement against Anita Sarkeesian and forums like 4chan, a new ecology was growing. The internet is the technology that offers the vastest storehouse of humanity's learned truths in all our history, yet the accessibility of internet communities, their global reach and the rapidity of their communications were creating spaces where participants could affirm and reaffirm wilful myths to any audience that was eager to believe them. Years later, this phenomenon would be called 'post-truth'.

When it came to the likes of Anita Sarkeesian, the scheming 'SJW' villain her antagonists wanted her to be was a far more compelling story than the video-game-playing feminist academic she really was. The same keyboards and screens used to demonise her as an agent of a 'politically correct' conspiracy were ones on which a mere few clicks could establish she was not a demon at all. The very proximity to empirical evidence made the deliberate choice to ignore it more conspicuous – and disturbing.

'CONSPIRACY THEORIST' – A PERSON THAT RESEARCHES A SUBJECT AND THEN USES LOGIC AND CRITICAL THINKING SKILLS TO FORM AN EDUCATED OPINION INSTEAD OF JUST BLINDLY BELIEVING WHATEVER THEY SAW ON TV.

Flat Earth Research on Facebook, 15 October 2019

Researchers of conspiracy thinking have identified three reasons why such thinking appeals to people.

The first is what they call an *epistemic* provocation, when people are seeking to furnish their knowledge of something about which they are curious and wanting to feel accurate and certain in that knowledge.

The second reason for conspiracy thinking has an *existential* motive. The political theorist Philip Tetlock has identified that conspiracy theories come from people's need to exert control over their environment, to feel more safe and secure within it.[20] When people feel a lack of control over the sociopolitical instruments that govern them – like, perhaps, the government, the economy, corporate power or the media – the result can be psychologically disempowering. Conspiracy theories offer a 'compensatory satisfaction', which means that believers use the illusion of a superior, 'insider' knowledge to regain a sense of control over events that distress them.[21]

Thirdly, conspiracy thinking can derive from a *social* motivation. Ascribing nefarious behaviours and the blame for negative events to an 'other' can be a way of boosting a positive image of the self, or attributing valour, cleverness or moral superiority for an in-group. 'Conspiracy theories [seem] particularly appealing to people who find the positive image of their self or in-group to be threatened,' observed a group of researchers from the University of Kent. 'Research suggests that conspiracy belief is stronger when people experience distress as a result of feeling uncertain.'[22]

In 2014, the year Zoë Quinn launched *Depression Quest* on the games platform Steam, what was happening politically on 4chan began a fateful intersection with conspiracy-minded fellow travellers.

The white, male, heterosexual in-group on 4chan was suffused with far-right provocateurs, and also heaved with users paranoid about feminist entryism to a world of gaming that they'd embraced as an interchangeable metaphor for their own masculinity. It was this same year that *The Guardian* reported that women players now made up 52 per cent of gamers.[23]

It was August that year when Zoë Quinn's ex-boyfriend hit 'publish' on a 10,000-word blog treatise that discussed the end of their relationship. Titling it *thezoepost*, he shared it to gamer community forums on the sites *Something Awful* and *Penny Arcade*.

In it he denounced Quinn as a liar, a cheater, a manipulator and a hypocrite. He published intimate details and wild allegations about Quinn's sex life, a trove of their private messages and personal photos. He told people not to work with Quinn, not to trust Quinn and implied Quinn was sleeping with people for prospects of career advancement. He named one of these people as a writer at *Kotaku*, the games review website.

He'd only known Quinn for a few months. Quinn described their relationship as 'intermittent', short-term and 'toxic'.[24] They broke up in a hotel room in April 2014. There was sex and there was violence. Bill Zoeker, a friend of Quinn's, arrived there when the ex had gone and 'could clearly see bruises' on Quinn's arm. Quinn had been expressing concerns to friends about the relationship for months, and '[s]uddenly the whole situation became very real to me,' Zoeker said of that night.[25]

Sometime later came another complication: Quinn was pregnant. There were emotional texts exchanged with the ex about the pregnancy, but Quinn was alone, and had an abortion.

Now that same ex had written 10,000 words of obsessive abuse about a relationship that had lasted a total of five months. Later he bragged to journalists about how he'd spent the weeks after the break-up researching and filing all the information he could obtain on Quinn, workshopping proposed content for a revenge post among his friends, coming up with ideas for how he might maximise what he wrote to go viral. He didn't mention the pregnancy, the abortion or Quinn's allegations of violence, but he was especially proud of linking Quinn's supposed infidelity with 'five guys' to the Five Guys Burger and Fries burger joint chain. He knew the association would make meme-rich material.

Then, he published. It was removed from *Something Awful* and *Penny Arcade* within hours, but he'd also published it as a WordPress blog. Someone shared it to 4chan. Zoë Quinn's ex says it wasn't him.

Quinn was at a restaurant in San Francisco with friends and her new boyfriend, Alex Lifschitz, when word came from another friend that *thezoepost* existed. The restaurant event was a farewell party: Lifschitz was leaving the US to take up a job offer in France; Quinn would be joining him. The evening soured as more friends got in contact to tell Quinn the post was spreading, and that 4chan had seized on it. As Quinn's friends and community mobilised to try to get it taken down, the pace of sharing was exponential. Through mobile internet technology, it was possible to watch Quinn's life transform in real time.

'4chan is all up in arms over it,' reported the enormously influential British gaming blogger and YouTuber @Totalbiscuit in a blog post on 19 August, trying to tease out just what so many were then watching unfold.[26] What

4chan had seized upon in *thezoepost* was the claim about Quinn's sexual relationship with the *Kotaku* writer. In the impulsive, instantaneous and unaccountable world of 4chan, some community members decided that *Kotaku* had reviewed *Depression Quest* favourably because Quinn had what @Totalbiscuit described as 'intimate relations with some of the writers'.

Kotaku hadn't actually reviewed *Depression Quest*. Not at all. Quinn had been mentioned by that particular writer only once, and before their romantic relationship began and in a feature – not a review – about a number of other developers.[27] This fact was easily discoverable and, also, irrelevant to the burgeoning discourse about who 4chan wanted Zoë Quinn to be. @Totalbiscuit made the point about 4chan at the time: 'It's difficult to tell what is true and what is not … there's always going to be ridiculous stories and trolling attempts.'

The truth was that similar communities to those that had feasted on Anita Sarkeesian had found themselves a pretext to now devour Zoë Quinn. The ex-boyfriend's post served as something like a scarlet letter, pinning on Quinn's alleged promiscuity an avatar for the corruption of modern gaming. Jesse Singal from NYMag.com saw the 'deliberate and malicious' craft that had gone into *thezoepost*, and its precise dog whistles to 'these sad, specific ideas that a segment of the gaming community has about women being duplicitous and breaking men's hearts'.[28] Arthur Chu from *Slate* saw it too. 'The "crazy bitch" story [is] a very potent trope to use,' he told *Boston* magazine. 'It's a very nasty, very calculating train of thought, and it worked.'[29]

Zoe quinn is wrong and also a whore.
Anonymous on 4chan, 23 September 2014

In the wake of *thezoepost*, what the online activists of 4chan, Reddit and communities across this niche of the internet decided was that the feminists and other 'SJWs' were not only exerting unnatural ideological influence upon game culture with Sarkeesianist 'bullying' and 'guilt' but were using sex to lure journalists, games studios, conference organisers and the whole infrastructure of the games industry into bed with their cause. It was nepotism, favouritism, transactional, unethical! And *thezoepost* offered proof that the social justice concerns expressed about gaming were illegitimate, that 'feminism is cancer', and that – to quote a popular 4chan refrain – 'all women are whores'. That, by default, made the furious channers fearless defenders of 'ethics in games journalism'.

Years later, Quinn wrote a book, *Crash Override*, that described subsequent events. Every one of her personal internet channels – every social channel, every professional channel – was suddenly choked with targeted abuse. Images of horrific violence were posted with threats to inflict the same. Someone found Quinn's phone number and home address and released them online, so there were threatening phone calls from strangers in the middle of the night. Old nudes taken when Quinn was much younger were found and distributed. They printed them out, they masturbated on them, and they mailed them. To Quinn's friends. To work colleagues. To family members.[30]

Kotaku went so far as to put out an explicit statement decrying the accusations. The mob did not care. They unleashed what they assured themselves was a righteous misogyny, and hate material targeting Zoë Quinn spread from 4chan to Reddit, where Zoë Quinn's ex turned up to do an 'ask me anything' public interview. It jumped to forums run by online publications like *The Escapist*, YouTube videos were rapidly made, and there were discussions stirred across Twitter and on secret chat channels where a certain kind of gamer liked to cluster. 4chan forums that in the past had infamously platformed real-life mass murderers were now hosting calls for the death of Zoë Quinn.

The creator of *Depression Quest* had seen internet attacks when the game had launched, but no one had seen anything like this. The abuse lasted for days. Then weeks. Then months. This wasn't a mere attack – it was a campaign. Originally, the accounts participating in the abuse on Twitter had hashtagged their material under the somewhat revealing moniker #Quinnspiracy. A subreddit was also set up under this name.

As the days passed, the attacks spread to anyone who defended Quinn, anyone perceived as Quinn's ally, or anyone deemed a 'social justice warrior'. *Boston* magazine reported that within a week of *thezoepost*, 'strangers threatened to kill other women in the industry' and the campaigns against men who publicly supported women were unsparing.

Zoë Quinn's father was harassed. Alex Lifschitz's new employer in France was besieged with online attacks until his job offer was retracted. Phil Fish, a game developer who'd stood up for Quinn, was hacked. His social security information, passwords, websites, PayPal details and the financial data of his company, Polytron, were all compromised. In despair, he sold his company. 'To every aspiring game developer out there: Don't,' he tweeted. 'Give up. It's not worth it. This is your audience. This is videogames.'

Unsurprisingly, Anita Sarkeesian was also swept up in more abuse. On 25 August 2014, when Sarkeesian released her most recent *Tropes vs. Women in Video Games* video, someone tweeted her residential address at her. She was forced to flee her home.

On 27 August, the movement got a bigger name and clearer public identity due to tweets from Adam Baldwin. Baldwin was a 52-year-old actor who'd sustained himself for decades with mostly small parts in genre films and made-for-TV movies. He'd enjoyed something of a midlife career renaissance when he was cast in *Firefly*, the short-lived space-fi TV series by *Buffy* creator Joss Whedon. *Firefly* developed a cult following with a strong Venn overlap with the 'geek' community, and Baldwin was soon on the pop-culture convention circuit that a lot of gamers attended. By 2014 he'd acquired a Twitter following of 190,000 people as well as a conversion from previously liberal political beliefs to hard-right views.

That day in August, Baldwin tweeted a link to some conspiratorial YouTube videos that attacked and maligned Zoë Quinn. He added a hashtag: #GamerGate. The attempt, wrote the Australian sociologist Michael Salter, was to signify 'the allegations against Quinn were indicative of a broader political scandal or conspiracy, a la Watergate'.[31]

The hashtag was readily embraced because it had numerous uses. Firstly, it liberated the campaign focus beyond Zoë Quinn and towards any target that might be identified as a challenge to the 'gamer' identity. Secondly, it positioned the self-identified gamer advocates as victims of a considered scandal. The very concept of a '#GamerGate' was polarising: you either believed that gamers were, indeed, rising up against scandalous injustice and were recruited by the #GamerGate believers, or you were among those waging injustice against them.

It also provided a tribal identity to the campaign participants who started calling themselves 'Gators'. They created new spaces on the internet to engage with one another on #GamerGate subjects, like the infamous dedicated subreddit r/KotakuInAction. All over the world, Gators even organised offline 'meet up' events to hang out in person and socialise. 'My voice is still a bit rumbly after last night – not used to talking that much,' one participant in Melbourne enthused after an event on 6 June 2015. 'I may have talked people's ears off.'

That this stuff had been pushed by Adam Baldwin gave #GamerGate the veneer of celebrity. His specialised, cultural Twitter reach pushed the discourse into the consciousness of the pop and entertainment media even as it reached corners of online 'geek masculinity' that weren't necessarily inhabited by devotees of 4chan. It also demonstrated early the use of Twitter in #GamerGate's campaign mobilisations, as if something toxic brewed in the subcultural cauldron of 4chan and its communities could be tipped into a river and poison a whole town.

The poison was certainly spreading. Among the movement's growing list of victims was outspoken #GamerGate critic and indie game developer Brianna Wu, who received forty-eight death threats in six months. She and her husband had to hire a security detail and begin living under assumed names. On 28 August, games writer Leigh Alexander decried game culture on website *Gamasutra*. She described a community of people so estranged from regular social interaction and professional life that they could make fantasy creatures of SJWs and games journalists and indulge in online wars against them; human consequences were felt by other people.[32] She was tagged into 13,296 tweets in the next six weeks. Actor and gamer Felicia Day wrote a blog post admitting that witnessing the way #GamerGate spread had intimidated her from speaking out about it – and within a single hour of publishing, she was doxxed. Her home address was supplied in an anonymous comment under her own post.

Of the online weapons for harassment in the Gamergate arsenal, Twitter had a specific effectiveness. It was a forum where almost every conceivable target – from game developers to journalists to feminists – had a public presence and an audience watching on.

Twitter's capacity to host secret 'direct message' conversations among groups, its hashtag feature and its lists of trends meant that teams of Gamergaters could work together to amplify attacks through a hashtag like #GamerGate until the topic started to trend. When it did, the substance of the attack became visible to every Twitter user, and easily flowed to other social media sites from there. It was a means to give global reach to false rumours and lies. On Twitter, you could bully, threaten and humiliate someone in front of the entire online world.

As Twitter lacked a capacity for a mass blocking of accounts, someone trying to personally inoculate themselves from a deployed mob had to manually go through every account that was abusing them and block each one, which meant they had to experience and re-experience every attack. Randi Harper, a DevOps (development operations) engineer, was herself subject to these kinds of Gamergate attacks. She grew so frustrated at their volume and imposition on her time that one night she just stayed up and created 'ggautoblocker'. It was a computer script that pre-emptively filtered out Gamergaters and #GamerGate content before it could reach her. She shared the script online. Unsurprisingly, it was popular.

Then, '[t]hings kind of blew up overnight,' as Harper told Opensource.com. After she released ggautoblocker, she 'became even more of a target' and 'started having to deal with the ways that harassment could cross over to real life'.[33] Harper was stalked and inundated with physical hate mail at her home. There were email campaigns directed at her employer to have her fired, others that threatened her family. Pizzas were turning up at her home address, and there were even false reports filed with law enforcement to draw armed raids by police. This last practice was nicknamed 'swatting'.

It was extraordinary harassment, and yet a compounding frustration for Gamergate victims was that anonymity made its perpetrators very slippery.

unite we have our chance to destroy feminism.

Both reddit and tumblr is hopping on the zoe quinn hate bandwagon. go to tumblr, twitter and reddit to educate them. feminists are finally open for debate.

use hashtags and link the behavior #zoe #anita #dina use the imgur pics show them how they all lie about everything.

THIS IS #OPERATION-BRING-FEMINISM-DOWN

Anonymous on 4chan, 20 August 2014

In a 2016 paper for the journal *Games and Culture* titled 'The long event of #GamerGate', Danish IT academic Torill Elvira Mortensen analysed what gave Gamergate its vicious energy as a movement.[34] It replicated the leaderless and anonymous structure of 4chan and defied attempts to hold anyone to account for what it did. When any Gator was challenged about the attacks, wrote Mortensen, their defence resorted to a 'no true Scotsman' fallacy. The repeated claim was that no true Gator would 'harass, threaten, hack, or dox other people,' Mortensen explained, 'and if it happened, either in the name of GG or not, it was supposedly the work of somebody unaffiliated with the movement.'

What gave Gamergate the appearance of an organic movement was, in fact, its inconsistencies. Though he'd been ambivalent about *thezoepost* when it appeared, @Totalbiscuit had been blogging about the questionable closeness of games media to the games industry for years. He embraced Gamergate as an opportunity for critical reckoning. His posts on this subject to his 400,000 Twitter followers and two million YouTube subscribers were a conceptual world away from what was being done by people like one seventeen-year-old boy who weaponised Gamergate infrastructure to terrorise every girl who had ever turned him down. The problem was that an organised campaign was taking place that perhaps neither the boy nor @Totalbiscuit fully realised they were in.

In her article subtitled 'The long event of #GamerGate', Torill Elvira Mortensen compared the effect of this apparently leaderless structure to a swarm. The participants, she explained, weren't formally organised – or even entirely aware of what was happening around them – but they took behavioural cues from those they were in closest proximity to online.

Like a swarm, their behaviour was not determined by a clear plan. Instead, there were core groups of individuals using demands for 'ethics in games journalism' as a cover to run a campaign against feminism. They'd worked out where and how to kick an internet beehive in such a way that angry bees could be relied upon to do the rest.

Mortensen said Gators believed themselves to be self-organised and that their movement was one of 'equality'. While some personalities drew more attention than others, leadership was something that participants understood with a certain 'I am Spartacus!' air. On 4chan, they openly fought about tactics. 'DO NOT MAKE THIS A GENDER ISSUE NO MATTER WHAT,' one channer admonished his comrades on 21 August 2014. 'Our goal is to change minds, and nobody EVER changes their mind in stupid gender wars.' The point of the movement, reminded another channer the same day, was 'about nepotism and corruption in the gaming industry'.

'[B]ut really its about pol hating women,' responded another.

'No, we love women,' someone replied. 'We hate manipulative whores.'

Tactical bickering and dissimilarities in belief springing up within Gamergate discussions helped to affirm the Gators' self-image of rugged online individualists, each empowered to make the choice – or not – of whether to attack the movement's targets in tandem.

It was romantic and idealistic self-recruitment to a grand heroic narrative. 'The perpetrators do not see themselves as perpetrators at all,' Anita Sarkeesian explained in a public speech on the subject, a month after #GamerGate had kicked off in earnest. 'They see themselves as noble warriors.' The shared denial that women were being threatened was crucial to maintaining belief in a heroic, crusading identity. 'We are blamed for the abuse we receive and regularly told that we are either asking for it or inventing it entirely,' she said.

In response to her ongoing comments on this theme, #GamerGate accounts addressed her directly: 'Go fuck yourself stupid cunt. Learn your shit before you try to make something out of nothing, GamerGate is not hating on women,' someone calling themselves @GBaMBuscH tweeted at her on 16 October 2014. @Totalbiscuit was more polite when he accused her of 'insert[ing] herself into the conversation' in one of his YouTube vlogs. On 3 October 2014, on Twitter, Adam Baldwin demanded Brianna Wu publicly apologise for ever claiming any of her harassment came from Gamergaters because she 'couldn't prove' who was behind the attacks.

What became conspicuous about a movement so avowedly committed to the cause of ethics in games journalism was that while condemnation of the media abounded, analysis and critique of the actual journalism was sparse. Critiques of feminism, women and the details of women's bodies were plentiful. On 31 August 2014, a channer appraised one of Gamergate's favourite targets with typical discernment: 'No tits, too much cellulite in the ass, sagging labia lips,' they offered, 'and that was before she got fat.'

Newsweek commissioned social media analysts Brandwatch to audit the two million #GamerGate-related tweets posted between 1 September and 23 October 2014. Using a representative sample (25 per cent of them), Brandwatch found that the 10,000 tweets levelled at Zoë Quinn were fourteen times the number of posts tagging Nathan Grayson, the male journalist whose 'ethics' were supposedly compromised by the sexual relationship they were having. Between them, Gamergate targets Anita Sarkeesian and Brianna Wu – neither of whom were journalists – were tagged in #GamerGate tweets more than 70,000 times. It was 'more than all the games journalists *Newsweek* looked at, combined'.[35]

'Neither of them has committed any supposed "ethics" violations,' *Newsweek* observed. 'They're just women who disagree with #GamerGate.'

<rd0952> i want someone to do some serious damage to feminist social media

<rd0952> like actually inhibit their spread

<Silver|2> whats the plan?

<rd0952> not just annoy them or bring up controversy

<naga_Samir> You would have to oust someone as taking advantage of other feminists by use of social media and propeganda

<Silver|2> Like Anita?

#burgersandfries IRC chat log, 21 August 2014

Christopher Grant, editor of the gaming website *Polygon*, was succinct about the impact of the Gamergate campaign. 'They failed to root out, uh, the "corruption in game journalism" that they insist is there, which after two months of a loud and noisy campaign they haven't found,' he told a radio interviewer. 'Doesn't exist, but what they have done is chase women out of their homes.'[36]

Zoë Quinn and Alex Lifschitz may have been driven into hiding by the Gamergate attacks, but they weren't frozen there. As they migrated from one friend's home to another to maintain their safety – at one point even living in a disused elevator shaft – they monitored what was happening and thought through their response. Quinn had tried to pursue action through official channels, but the tech platforms were unresponsive and, beyond the advice to 'just stay off the internet' – somewhat impracticable for two people working in it – the law did not know what to do. When the harassment didn't die down, Quinn and Lifschitz devised a different strategy.

The monstrous caricature created by *thezoepost* and the abuse that followed depicted Quinn as self-seeking neophyte, another feminist grifter who had appeared within the games community just to ride its opportunities to unearned praise, income and tickets to cool things. In reality, Quinn was a creature of the same internet culture as the channers and the Gamergaters and had been since adolescence. Quinn had learned to code and hack in the same secret online crannies where the most hardcore channers hung out and the whole concept of 'geek masculinity' had spawned. Quinn had made friends there, had tested out adolescent personas there, had – admittedly, as a younger person – participated in pranks and bullying from there. 'If #GamerGate had happened ten years earlier and to someone who wasn't me,' Quinn wrote in *Crash Override*, 'I might have been on the other side.'[37]

Now themselves besieged, Quinn and Lifschitz went to visit Quinn's former online neighbourhoods. It didn't take them long to find some Gators. On the old IRC network, for example, a group of channers were having strategic discussions about how to ruin Quinn's life on a channel they'd called #burgersandfries. The couple learned that Quinn's ex-boyfriend himself was appearing in these conversations, providing pep talks maligning Quinn's character to cheer on the participants.

On 5 September 2014, Zoë Quinn started to publicly release some highlights from these discussions. In response, someone from #burgersandfries dumped a full transcript of their channel logs to the internet. They insisted inspection would reveal that Quinn was a liar who had 'cherry-picked' information.

David Futrelle of *We Hunted the Mammoth* described this response as a tactic in itself. Called 'doc dumping', the idea is to overwhelm potential readers with a single piece of data that is chaotic, complicated and a chore to sift through. Futrelle said they were counting on people not to read '3756 pages, in 10-point type' of overlapping, heavily self-referencing conversations – but Futrelle did.[38] So did a team of researchers from Robert Gordon University and Dundee and Angus College in Scotland.

The evidence they found supported Futrelle. 'The words "ethics" and "ethical" appear, collectively, only 146 times,' he observed, within a log that also contained 4778 mentions of Zoë Quinn, and ongoing, lengthy, repeated speculations about the texture of Quinn's vagina. The Scottish researchers cited 69 mentions of the word 'slut' in the discussion, with 71 of 'whore', 173 of 'bitch', 114 of 'cunt' and 265 of 'rape'.[39]

There were more discoveries. What the Scottish researchers also found was a range of tactics that a surprisingly small group of internet-adroit Gamergaters was using to create what Futrelle described as 'the illusion of a vast grassroots uprising'.

On 21 August 2014, the #burgersandfries group was assigning which 4chan forums should activate the different elements of the Gamergate campaign; user @Rd0951 helpfully suggested: '/v should be in charge of the gaming journalism aspect of it. /pol should be in charge of the feminism aspect, and /b should be in charge of harassing her into killing herself.'

They advised one another on how to overcome bans and other restrictions on the accounts they were using. They affected false online personas to thicken out their ranks and padded them with fake bios and credentials. They created reams of 'sockpuppets' – false accounts – and a mass of them were deployed especially on Twitter and Reddit to make it look as if their numbers were larger.

'I need to make some throwaways to post this on Reddit with,' wrote user @JCtheDenthog in such a conversation on 21 August.

'I'll make a fake account just to retweet it,' @Trigger responded.

'I'm thinking of making a few sleeper cell twitter accounts,' offered @Roberts[OPEC].

The group organised events like 'threadbombing', where actions were coordinated to simultaneously spam discussions with their material while overwhelming the capacity of human site admins to moderate them. They adapted strategies to get around spam filters. On 18 August, user @hresvelgr advised adding various image content to the posts that would both avoid filters and spark interest:

USE A PIC THAT DRAWS ATTENTION.
ASSES.
TITS.
ETC.
BANE.
SHREK.
MAKE IT A BIG POST FOR YOU.

All of this was used to 'amplify the signal, and the noise', the Scottish researchers explained. On imageboards, it forced all other discussions off the site, with anonymity fanning a false perception that these subjects were all people in the group wanted to talk about.

The political technique being used here was known beyond the internet as 'astroturfing', the pretence of being a grassroots movement and faking both organic and popular support. While the participants exchanged methodologies for hacking and doxxing and other manipulations of computer technology, the Scottish researchers discovered the group was also channelling many old political tactics through the new online media.

The researchers traced discussions among these secret organisers about how they wanted to align with influential people, what human and technical resources were at their disposal and how they could make most efficient use of these in their campaign. The anti-feminists identified high-profile allies who might amplify their messages and add legitimacy to them, like other indie game developers, or feminists who might have an ideological difference with Quinn, or even just more girl gamers to deflect accusations of misogyny. There were schemes to provide 'public relations cover', like a plan to send a card to Anita Sarkeesian that condemned her harassment, even at the same time they were actively organising more of it. 'Start following companies and personalities that support gamergate, and express support towards those who need it,' a chat participant advised as they identified places to recruit new activists in the campaign. They devised and delivered recruitment copy.

Lists of enemies were drawn up and shared. The Scottish researchers reported that academics who spoke out about Gamergate were to be 'considered fair-game'. The researchers spoke from direct experience: the paper's lead author had tweeted about the 'deeply unhealthy stream of attitudes' they had observed in #GamerGate discussions online and was assailed with replies containing YouTube clips denouncing Zoë Quinn for infidelity. One tweet he received linked to an image archive. It contained naked selfies stolen from Zoë Quinn.

Torill Elvira Mortensen was right to compare Gamergate's operations to a swarm. The chat logs revealed that behind the swarm, a small cabal of queen bees was running a war room that the other bees didn't know about. 'This then is the modus operandi of the cyber-mob,' concluded the Scottish researchers.

<le_nodman> I just hate this whole political agenda
shit in my video games

#burgersandfries IRC chat log, 25 August 2014

Was it political? Yes. An organised campaign to harass and terrify women out of a cultural space was inherently political, but Gamergate was not merely motivated by political forces and using political tactics. It was drawing the attention of some ambitious political actors.

By 2014, 4chan was saturated with jokey, ironic meme-making Neo-Nazis and other hard-right activists who readily embraced Gamergate as an activist opportunity. What journalists and anthropologists were coming to understand was that there were direct links between the burgeoning alt-right white supremacist movement and an established community of online misogyny. Exploring the rise of the alt-right in Quebec, the *Montreal Gazette* observed that the movement's most prominent members 'didn't stumble into extremism by leafing through a dog-eared copy of *Mein Kampf*'.[40] Their identification with alt-right ideas 'began with a slow-burning hatred of women'.

It was a process that Canadian journalist Nora Loreto had seen up close. She'd once made a glib joke on Twitter about wanting to smash up the camera equipment of a right-wing 'news' website that had misreported a sensitive story. The tweet went viral, and Loreto was subjected to a brutal online sexist and sexualised abuse campaign from the far right that lasted for months. She made a blunt point: 'misogyny,' she told the *Gazette*, 'is a gateway drug.'[41]

Activists of the alt-right were using the misogyny whipped up by Gamergate as a recruitment channel. As the Gamergate campaign rolled on, it was showing those activists where their channels reached. The slut-shaming of Zoë Quinn found ready amplification in the 'men's rights' (MRA) movement and the 'pick-up artist' (PUA) online groups who were already susceptible to traditionalist, hard-right beliefs. Canadian anthropologist Amy Hale explained the link to the *Montreal Gazette*: inflexible attitudes about status and personal entitlement were challenged by movements like feminism. 'Fascist ideas,' said Hale, 'provide them with a clear hierarchy that places them at or near the top.'[42] There were many such articles on this subject published in Canada in 2018. In April of that year, a hard-right misogynist murdered ten people and injured sixteen others when he drove a rental vehicle into a busy pedestrian area of Toronto.

Writing five months after Gamergate had started, *Guardian* columnist Jason Wilson argued that what alt-right activists offered online misogynists was an idea that married white supremacy and Gamergate misogyny. This idea was 'cultural Marxism', an all-purpose reds-under-the-beds conspiracy theory that had been pushed by the Western hard right at various strengths for decades. Wilson explained the key insistence of the cultural Marxist theory was that elites within 'the most important cultural institutions, from universities to Hollywood studios', were sleeper agents of a Marxist plot. From sites of powerful cultural influence, went the theory, these Marxists 'promoted and even enforced ideas which were intended to destroy traditional Christian values and overthrow free enterprise'. The fronts for this cultural Marxism were the 'social justice' movements for 'feminism, multiculturalism, gay rights and atheism'.[43]

The hatreds nurtured by this theory were ancient as well as paranoid. The hard right held the Frankfurt School of twentieth-century Marxist philosophers responsible for cultural Marxism, given how much the school's theory explored the relationship of culture to ideology. It was hardly unknown among them that the school's most prominent members were researchers with Jewish backgrounds. The phrase 'cultural Marxism' itself was a dog whistle to old anti-Semitic myths about secret power, corruption and an enemy within. Torill Elvira Mortensen's research observed a theme in online pro-Gamergate discussions that 'claimed Jews and western academics have joined forces to pacify White men and planned to hand the power of the "western world" to the Jews or Islam by encouraging politically correct digital games'.[44]

It was through the cultural Marxist conspiracy framework that Adam Baldwin took to Twitter in November 2014 in a now-deleted series of tweets that claimed '"leftists" with a "totalitarian impulse" were trying to impose their "political crap" on "gamers" as part of a "culture war"'.[45] It made sense if you considered that within the conspiracist framework Baldwin shared, feminists and their SJW allies were attempting to ruin or steal video games for cultural Marxism. Gators could therefore justify to themselves that harassing feminists, Jews, Black Americans or anyone from the internet was in truth the work of cultural patriots fighting a nefarious foreign incursion. That the inclusive values on which the modern liberal democratic state is based were being shredded for them in the process was not Adam Baldwin's concern.

PUT BANNON ON THE MAP YOU SON OF A BITCH

Anonymous on 4chan, 15 December 2016

The hard-right American political operative Steve Bannon was very interested in Gamergate. He had come into contact with the burgeoning online gamer community in 2005, two years after the creation of 4chan. Bannon was running his own boutique investment firm at the time he was introduced to the work of a Hong Kong–based company called Internet Gaming Entertainment (IGE) as a potential investor. At the time, the online role-playing game *World of Warcraft* had exploded in popularity and had ten million subscribers. The game mechanics obliged the earning of virtual 'gold' to purchase desirable in-game goods, and IGE's business model was 'gold farming'. They employed low-paid Chinese workers to play the game and earn 'gold', which the company then sold on for real money to lazier or less adept players. Bannon organised his former employer, the merchant bank Goldman Sachs, to assist by injecting $60 million into IGE and he went on the company's board.

Bannon had reasons to be interested in IGE's world beyond a financial opportunity. Born into a family of Catholic,

Kennedy-voting trade union members, Bannon had earned a degree in urban planning, become a naval officer, worked at the Pentagon, collected a master's in national security studies and then an MBA at Harvard, switched careers to merchant banking and made a fortune. He became a vice-president at Goldman Sachs and even a film and television producer. He backed Sean Penn's movie *The Indian Runner* and Julie Taymor's *Titus*. Thanks to an early investment in the company that produced it, Steve Bannon also received returns every time the globally syndicated *Seinfeld* TV show went to air.

Along the way, Bannon's politics had radicalised sharply to the right. In 2017, *Salon* published an extraordinary story about his conversion. Bannon was a young naval officer on a destroyer deployed to the Persian Gulf during the Iran hostage crisis in 1980. A complex hostage rescue plan was executed by the Democratic Carter administration – and failed. A helicopter crash amid the withdrawal killed eight troops. It was a catalysing political moment for Bannon, said *Salon*: not only was his national pride wounded by these disastrous events but, apparently, his masculinity was too. Bannon was more than aware President Jimmy Carter had been considered an exemplary naval officer in his day, earning an outstanding reputation and prestigious posts. Bannon, on the other hand, was barely rated by his superiors as better than average. *Salon* claimed that the young officer took Carter's failure in Iran as a personal slight. He switched his allegiance to the Republicans, backed Ronald Reagan against Carter and, before he switched careers to finance, worked in the Reagan White House.[46]

As the years passed, Bannon's resentment towards Carter swelled into disillusionment with the entire American establishment as he travelled from the military to politics to the commanding heights of market capitalism. By 2014, the year that Gamergate began, Bannon was dropping fascist references into public speeches. He quoted Julius Evola, a long-dead and long-discredited anti-modern Italian philosopher who'd collaborated with the Nazis at the height of the Third Reich and whose work argued that 'equality is an illusion' and published papers with titles like 'Woman as thing'. Bannon was also an admitted intellectual companion of Russian Neo-Fascist philosopher Aleksandr Dugin, with whom he shared opposition to secularism, multiculturalism and egalitarianism. Bannon was avowedly opposed to immigration of any kind and preached American isolationism. He was denounced as a white nationalist, but he called himself an 'economic nationalist'.[47] His was a hard-right agenda from the political fringe, but as the years passed, Bannon was increasingly determined to realise it in the mainstream.

Bannon's investment in IGE returned valuable political insight into the gamer community, although the business itself was a failure. Enraged *World of Warcraft* gamers who denounced 'gold farming' as a form of cheating organised protest campaigns through their online communities. They flooded game companies allowing gold farming with complaints until their pressure caused the game makers to effectively ban the practice. It destroyed IGE.

Bannon was left in awe of the brutal effectiveness of what he'd seen. He'd discovered an online demographic clique of people with the time to spend all day on computers, and who had the knowledge and ferocity to wreak hell at perceived incursions on their territory. 'These guys, these rootless white males, had monster power,' Bannon said.[48]

In the years following the collapse of IGE, Bannon's residual payments from *Seinfeld*'s syndication flowed in, and his commitment to his hard-right political project deepened. After the Democrats won the 2008 US election, the losing Republican vice-presidential candidate, Sarah Palin, had emerged as a favourite with the nascent, right-populist 'Tea Party' movement. Bannon was recruited to do some work for her, producing propaganda films ahead of a potential 2012 tilt at the presidency. By this time, he'd fallen in with the maverick right-wing 'gonzo' journalist Andrew Breitbart. Breitbart admired an earlier documentary Bannon had made about Ronald Reagan and started calling him 'the Leni Riefenstahl of the Tea Party'.[49] Bannon revelled in the comparison with Adolf Hitler's greatest film propagandist.

Palin's candidacy for the Republican presidential nomination fizzled out in 2011, but it was Bannon's relationship with Breitbart that was to prove of more political value. Breitbart had put his name to an anti-establishment, populist new site that he'd started in the mid-2000s as the right-wing answer to *The Huffington Post*, and Bannon was a founding member of the board. From his friend, Bannon had come to appreciate the wisdom of 'the Breitbart doctrine'. This was the belief that 'politics flows downstream from culture', and that it was culture-makers who shaped the political values among the people that politicians would be then obliged to follow.[50]

To make politics change, Breitbart advocated, you had to drive cultural change. Through their efforts making news sites and propaganda movies, Breitbart and Bannon were organising to do precisely what their ideological comrades had insisted a 'cultural Marxist' conspiracy had been doing for decades: they were taking over influential cultural institutions to recruit their power to their side.

This further proves that there's no significant difference between Cultural-Marxist shitlibs and limp-wristed cuckservatives. Both accept and abide by the Cultural-Marxist agenda that has inundated and is destroying our society and nation.

Philo-Identitas √Identitarian, comment on Breitbart.com,
22 October 2017

On 29 February 2012, 43-year-old Andrew Breitbart was walking around his Los Angeles neighbourhood when he suffered a sudden, massive heart attack and died. His death left Steve Bannon with an even more important inheritance than his doctrine. Bannon had himself appointed executive chairman of *Breitbart News* and took control of the operation with the assistance of a capital injection of US$10 million from the hard-right tech-billionaire Mercer family.

What Bannon understood as a political activist as he took the reins at *Breitbart* was that the internet had opened a new and little understood battlefield for an ideological information war.

Between the day Christopher 'moot' Poole launched 4chan and the day ten years later that *thezoepost* went viral, Facebook alone had grown from a million users to 890 million. Channers had an intimate and advanced understanding of the digital terrain that more recently arrived netizens did not. The harassment of Anita Sarkeesian had drawn mainstream news attention to the events within internet subculture, but the gullibility with which that press had fallen for the #EndFathersDay and #CutForBieber hoaxes revealed the poor handle that mainstream culture had on what was happening there. Few appreciated just how much 'monster power' the 'rootless white males' on the internet could unleash.

But, as someone whose $60 million investment in IGE had been destroyed by *World of Warcraft* message boards, Steve Bannon certainly did.

With Sarah Palin a bust for the 2012 US election cycle, Bannon's attentions had turned towards finding an appropriate Republican candidate to support in the 2016 elections. In 2013 he met with the infamously anti-immigration Alabama senator Jeff Sessions to encourage him to run. Even when Sessions said no, Bannon continued building an internet-based war machine in the knowledge a candidate would eventually materialise, almost as an afterthought. In the meantime, Bannon invested in three cultural properties to politically weaponise 'information operations' on intersecting fronts.[51]

The first addressed the 'legacy media' of mastheads and broadcasters, and their developing presence online. At the same time the new digital media front was gobbling the capacity of old media newsrooms to sustain themselves with advertising, Bannon launched a non-profit think tank called the Government Accountability Institute (GAI). It resourced the impoverished newsrooms with detailed research, seeding stories about Bannon's opponents and ideological enemies, which a news-hungry mainstream press could then more easily pursue. Bannon understood that stories targeting individuals on the left did more reputational damage when published in left-leaning mastheads than right-wing ones, and he prioritised driving stories towards them. The GAI-published books – like one called *Clinton Cash* – were effectively compendiums of this kind of material, using the established media apparatus of book promotion and discussion in the mainstream media to disperse this 'information' about their chosen targets.

More quietly, Bannon and the Mercers had also taken control of the American subsidiary operation of a company called SCL Group. Formally, SCL specialised in behavioural research and strategic communications, but those who knew more about its precise services described their work as 'cyberwarfare for elections'. The subsidiary was called Cambridge Analytica. In receipt of 230 million illegally obtained tranches of personal data scraped from Facebook accounts, the company was building a data model using AI to channel targeted political-persuasion material to unsuspecting Facebook users.

The third front was *Breitbart News* itself. Bannon relaunched the site after Breitbart died, hiring the same web designers who had built sites for liberal-associated brands like NPR, PBS and Discovery. 'Andrew wanted this aesthetically to look as good as anything on the left,' said Bannon after the launch.[52] The *Breitbart News* mission, announced the site's new editor-in-chief, Joel Pollak, was to 'transition from a blog site that occasionally broke news to a comprehensive site that led the news cycle'. To closer associates, Bannon himself described *Breitbart* as his 'killing machine'.[53]

As Bannon accumulated his assets, he kept an eye on the online gaming community. According to his biographer, Joshua Green, 'he thought they could be radicalized in a kind of populist, nationalist way'.[54] As Bannon continued to build *Breitbart News* into what by 2016 he would openly call 'the platform for the alt-right', Gamergate appeared, like a gift.[55]

Not only had its hate campaign against Zoë Quinn demonstrated the 'monster power' Bannon wanted to harness to his own movement, but its rubric demand for 'ethics in games journalism' carried with it an implicit mistrust of establishment media, which Bannon was keen to amplify and enhance. If 'the real opposition' to Bannon's project – as he told a journalist in 2018 – was 'the media', kids stirred up into an online crusade for 'ethics in games journalism' were Bannon's to win.[56]

Where does /pol/ stand on Milo Yiannopoulos?
Would gay libertarians who bash liberals be allowed
into the Fourth Reich?

Anonymous on 4chan, 29 December 2015

Milo Yiannopoulos was a British university dropout who'd had a short tenure as a clickbaiting tech blogger for the UK's *Daily Telegraph*. After leaving the *Telegraph* following a rumoured expenses scandal, he was most notable for starting an online tech journal, *The Kernel*, with himself as owner and editor, which had been forced to close amid claims of unpaid wages.

Yiannopoulos's style of journalism was to call women at technology conferences 'dickless wonders' and pick visible, public fights with celebrities like Stephen Fry. Steve Bannon approached him to write Gamergate stories for him at *Breitbart*.

Although he'd previously described gamers as 'unemployed saddos living in their parents' basements', Yiannopoulos eagerly took up *Breitbart*'s offer to champion their cause in its pages.[57] Aggressively branding himself as a fearless provocateur, the platform gave Yiannopoulos the opportunity to 'say the unsayable' in front of an audience that was baying for it, and to cultivate a notoriety-based celebrity.[58] His politics were on the far right but hardly had the commitment or explicitness of Bannon's. Yiannopoulos's identity as a gay man with a Black partner and a hazy, self-styled persona that alternated between Catholic and Jewish – depending on his audience – was useful for shielding *Breitbart* from accusations of being homophobic, racist or anti-Semitic.

In the streams of targeted Gamergate material *Breitbart* published throughout 2015, Yiannopoulos denounced Zoë Quinn as merely profiteering from 'professional victimhood', claimed in a series of articles that Randi Harper was 'a deeply troubled, hateful, and damaged human being', published even more about how Anita Sarkeesian was 'stupid' and uneducated, and declared Brianna Wu was 'unstable' and 'mentally disturbed'.[59] While attacking them, he claimed they'd invented stories of being attacked. He repeated the old lines from *The Sarkeesian Effect* that these women were the real bullies and Gators but the scapegoats of their scorn.

As Gamergate continued through 2015, and then 2016, readers of Yiannopoulos's *Breitbart* column were encouraged to follow him on Twitter, where under his swelling @Nero handle he invoked mobs into the mass abuse of chosen targets. The most infamous was the persecution of Leslie Jones, a Black female actor punished for having the temerity to star in a female-led remake of *Ghostbusters*. The cruelty that Yiannopoulos instigated against Jones was so extreme, Twitter took the then highly unusual step of blocking him from the entire platform.

Yiannopoulos's reputational assassination of Gamergate's favourite female villains extended to attempts to savage their professional lives. He alleged they were 'incompetent in their chosen fields', lacked talent, were corrupt, lied and had unearned favour.[60] While the now mononymic 'Milo' snapped up speaking gigs and TV appearances, signed book deals and sold t-shirts that declared 'feminism is cancer', a team of forty-four largely unpaid interns who he had sourced from 4chan collaborated to research and write his articles and speeches for him. *Breitbart* retained a 22-year-old recent university graduate, Allum Bokhari, who was rumoured to − ahem − heavily contribute to Yiannopoulos's writing duties there.[61] *The Guardian* declared Yiannopoulos 'a shallow, amoral actor who plays the bad guy for money'.[62]

In reality, he was worse. Attempts to denounce Yiannopoulos as a racist white nationalist or member of the alt-right were responded to by the free-speech champion with aggressive legal action levelled at the *Los Angeles Times*, *The Forward*, *Business Insider*, *Glamour*, *Fusion*, *USA Today*, the *Chicago Tribune*, *The Washington Post* and CNN.

Meanwhile, Bannon had him promoted to tech editor of *Breitbart* and his profile was building. It was part of a 'grand plan', wrote *Buzzfeed*, for Bannon to transform him into 'a conservative media star capable of magnetising a new generation of reactionary anger'.[63]

Listen to Trump's campaign speech. It's actually good, all of his ideas are dead on and he is completely transparent.
Trump would seriously make a great president. He knows how to run the show, he's ruthless, and he can't be bought off.
Anonymous on 4chan, 17 June 2015

When Donald J. Trump descended a golden escalator at Trump Tower, New York City, on 15 June 2015 and announced he'd be running for president, Gamergate was still running. On 19 June, Yiannopoulos published 'Donald Trump, king of trolling his critics, should be the internet's choice for president' in his *Breitbart* column.[64] Within four days, he was abusing *Gamasutra*'s Leigh Alexander.[65] Within another week, his campaign began against Randi Harper. By November 2015, Yiannopoulos was summoning the 'rootless white males' of channer culture to his banner at *Breitbart* with exhortations to their grievance and their sense of victimhood. Concepts like 'the patriarchy' were bullshit, he told them – the real victims in society were the white cishet men online who'd ever been called losers or shitlords or manbabies. If you were one of these men – if you'd ever felt bullied or harassed, victimised or marginalised – you now had a champion. Milo Yiannopoulos was the man for you.[66]

Buzzfeed's Joseph Bernstein reacted with incredulity to Yiannopoulos's appeal. Here he was, said Bernstein, encouraging 'young English-speaking white men, perhaps the least victimized group of people in the world', to think of themselves as victims, their in-group under direst threat.[67] He was grooming them for conspiracy thinking.

Bernstein was right to identify that Yiannopoulos's words had the whiff of 'the campaign trail'. The flattery and the nurtured victimhood were tactical attempts by Bannon, through Yiannopoulos, to 'activate [an] army' with the same grievance narrative that defined the Republican candidate he was now backing for president. 'They come in through #Gamergate or whatever,' Bannon told his biographer, Joshua Green, 'and then get turned onto politics and Trump.'[68]

Two years later in 2017, it was Joseph Bernstein, again, who revealed in *Buzzfeed* just how dark those politics were. He'd received a leaked cache of Yiannopoulos's emails and exposed that Yiannopoulos had been sourcing advice on his tech stories and political ideas from outright white supremacists.

These included the ex-con, Neo-Nazi hacker Andrew 'weev' Auernheimer, who ran systems administration for *The Daily Stormer*; the authoritarian neo-feudalist Curtis Yarvin; and Devin Saucier, a prominent white nationalist and member of a neo-pagan, far-right 'white power wolf cult'.[69] Yiannopoulos described Saucier as his best friend.

A pipeline had been created.

Yiannopoulos was crowdsourcing ideas from the extremist right that were passed to and developed by his 4chan offsiders, whom he called his 'Trufflehounds'. The stories were laundered of their origins through the editorial processes at *Breitbart News* and channelled to *Breitbart*'s audience via Yiannopoulos's tech brand. The organic communication networks of channers who recognised their own preoccupations in what was produced drove and distributed online conversations. They made their own propaganda informed by the messaging – memes – and as their cultural products flowed 'downstream', they carried political influence into the wider world.

The observation that 'what begins on /pol/ and leaks out into Twitter has a way of colouring media coverage' actually appeared as a quote in a Yiannopoulos article he'd been encouraged to write by the white nationalist wolf-worshipper Devin Saucier.[70] As Yiannopoulos's profile grew, so came the entreaties from those who – in public, at least – had claimed to be politically moderate. They wanted his help – his reach – in settling old scores, gaining protective favour perhaps, or stretching their own distribution. Tech writer David Auerbach, who had once decried 4chan as a 'nonstop barrage of obscenity', categorically denied to *Buzzfeed* he had ever sent an email to Yiannopoulos – which was by then in *Buzzfeed*'s possession – containing 'background information about the love life of Anita Sarkeesian'.[71] He did admit to *The New Republic* that he had contacted Yiannopoulos, though, about a 'Wikipedia related scandal'.[72]

What Bannon had seen the potential for in Gamergate – what it had become – was a ruthlessly efficient model for propaganda and influence operations on the internet.

Australian researchers Michael Jensen and Tom Sear study influence operations. The term traditionally describes campaigns run by hostile foreign governments to affect social attitudes or disrupt the decision-making processes of a target population. It can also apply to the actions of political parties, or activism or even corporate interests. Influence operations involve an intersection of highly calibrated propaganda techniques and community organising. In a 2018 article, the Australian researchers explained there are two dominant models of persuasion in the public sphere. The first is a *rational* model, where people accept claims when they're backed by evidence. The second is a *narrative* model, where people believe as fact the stories that resonate most with them.[73]

In 2018, the Australian researchers were writing about how Russian influence operatives employed the narrative model of information to push political messages through online channels. For the Russians, it was valuable to know what lies people wanted to believe so strongly that they didn't demand evidence for them. It made their targets far easier to manipulate.

Jensen and Sear demonstrated in their paper how Russian influence operations had used Twitter to target the Australian public sphere. They showed how seemingly innocent online activities like a #MakeTVShowsAustralian Twitter hashtag campaign was about identifying communities with which they might then nurture relationships. It's relationships, according to Jensen and Sear, that have a powerful influence on where political opinions are formed and how voting decisions are made.

The gamers that gathered around the anonymous imageboards like 4chan formed a community where masculine identities were fragile because participants felt they no longer had control over the games industry that they'd embraced to define them. Their furious reaction to a perceived incursion by Anita Sarkeesian had exposed their obsessions and paranoias – that 'pressing psychological need' David Futrelle had seen in Anita Sarkeesian's antagonists to be supplied with claims the world was other than it was.

Zoë Quinn's ex-boyfriend was a digital native who calculated where to drop the right narrative into the right place for this desperate, conspiratorial energy to ensure its distribution and perpetuation. When a narrative was powerful enough, those captured by its romance, perhaps, and the tribal identity it gave them, volunteered their own time to staff the secret chat channels, operate the sockpuppets, dox the accounts and send the mutilated photographs to Zoë Quinn's dad.

Gamergate showed it didn't matter how easily disprovable the narratives were. If enough people just wanted to believe in these fictions, an entire apparatus spawned around them all to keep it going.

In internet realms built by white, Western teenage boys, there were no regulations on speech, and gatekeeping was weak and discretionary. The barriers that had kept Nazis, fascists and all variations of white power wolf cultists out of cultural institutions since the Second World War did not exist here. These people seized on any space and every narrative vehicle that might offer them opportunities to weave their dark mythologies.

There were grifters at the ready, too, just as willing to invest in popular made-up stories as the fascists were – people like Yiannopoulos, who liked the money and infamy that Gamergate brought him and adored the attention. There were also people like Mike Cernovich, an opportunistic lawyer wanting to build his brand on the internet as a writer, maybe, or political commentator, or internet-misogynist swami. He threw himself in front of the Gamergate audience with blogs claiming 'young men have it rough' and offered legal advice to Zoë Quinn's ex when the young man was finally – finally – served a restraining order.

Then there were people like Steve Bannon and the billionaire Mercers, who had secret plans and ambitious agendas and were out to 'activate an army'. They were people who knew – because they had think tanks and stolen data and money and they made it their business to know – tactics to summon the swarm that Torill Elvira Mortensen talked about.

Once you knew which stories to tell, villains to curse and suggestions to drop, Gamergate and what came after it showed that once a swarm of people voluntarily chose a narrative model over empirical reason, their situation could be manipulated by one person as motivated as a vengeful ex-boyfriend in a direction to do anything. To hound a woman from her home, or falsely call a lethal SWAT team to her house. To join a racist mob against an actress, to march into a family pizza parlour with a gun. To vote for Donald Trump. To riot for him. To murder someone.

In September 2014, Gamergate had been running for a month. Christopher 'moot' Poole, the creator of 4chan, had now turned twenty-six. He'd spent some time in Europe, got some perspective on his life, and he was done. He unilaterally banned all Gamergate content from 4chan. There was a new controversy week after week, he explained to *Rolling Stone*. The stress, he confessed, had worn him down. He was abused by Gamergate-supporting channers for it. They flocked, instead, to 8kun.[74]

Anonymous you are so dumb

Anonymous And you're not white and never will be

Anonymous on8kun, 1 December 2019

8kun had been launched by a guy called Fredrick Brennan in 2014. A nineteen-year-old American, Brennan had grown up in rural poverty and with osteogenesis imperfecta, a mobility-limiting and very painful condition also known as brittle bone disease. When his father couldn't manage his care anymore, Brennan was shuffled through the foster care system.

Computers had become his escape from isolation. Known online as 'Hotwheels', he'd been on 4chan since he was twelve, delighted by its irreverence, its limitlessness, and the community of pranksters and edgelords it attracted. Brennan believed in free-speech absolutism. He later told an interviewer from *Wired* that as a channer purist, he'd grown to resent the power Christopher Poole wielded over the content on 4chan.

One night, high on magic mushrooms and nursing an obsessive loathing of Poole, he started to build an imageboard that would push the limits of acceptable discourse online even further than 4chan did. Brennan's creation, 8kun, was a free-speech wonderland – and a safe and anonymous harbour for the expression of violent woman-hating, explicit racism and raw anti-Semitism to shock the most seasoned of channers.

When Poole shut 4chan's doors on Gamergate, Brennan opened 8kun's wide. Traffic on his site went from a hundred posts a day to five thousand every hour. Offensive content got 8kun kicked off hosting platforms. There was plenty of it. 8kun allowed anything that wasn't illegal in the United States of America. 'Anything' included paedophile forums, softcore photos of children, rape porn, photographs of self-harm and Nazis. Lots and lots of Nazis.

Brennan was in such a dark place at this time in his life that he published an op-ed in no less than Nazi site *The Daily Stormer* arguing that his own tortured body was an argument for eugenics.

How bleak to consider the optimism of the internet's pioneers back in 1995 compared to this. Back then, *Newsweek*'s Steven Levy had envisioned the internet as a passionate embrace of ideas like 'clean, fresh air'.[75] That liberal dream had led to a place where paedophiles rubbed shoulders with Neo-Nazis, and a volunteer army of online misogynists – desensitised by a decade of channing, whipped into a frenzy by Gamergate, carefully manipulated by ambitious political actors like Steve Bannon – was coming to join them.

What would happen? Answers were provided too soon.

In 2013, tech magazine *Wired* interviewed Peter Kirstein, a computer scientist who'd built and run the UK's first internet connection in the 1970s. What did he think of the modern internet? 'None of us had any idea what the internet would become,' he told them. 'We thought it was only going to be of interest for us academics.'[76]

Instead, as the 2010s ticked on, unfettered hate and conspiracy were raging wild across a site built by a physically hurting, parentally abandoned teenage boy. By 2019, counterterrorism analyst Clint Watts had warned *The Washington Post* that 8kun was a place where lone wolves could find a pack.[77] And also by 2019, the three racist killers of the respective Christchurch, Poway and El Paso attacks chose 8kun to drop their manifestos and announce their intentions to murder. In the wake of their attacks, 8kunners cheered the deaths of the innocent victims.[78]

Fredrick Brennan was now a young adult in 2019. He'd sold 8kun to a guy called Jim Watkins in 2015 and quit an ongoing role as site administrator three years later. In the wake of the murders in El Paso, Brennan joined calls for the site to be shut down. It was a safe space for domestic terrorists, he said – and he wanted the nightmare to end.

It was 8kun – this place of nightmares, and terror, and unrestrained id – that would offer a home to the emerging QAnon movement late in 2017.

But before that happened, the far extreme of the new internet culture went to visit a pizza place.

I never bought into that pizzagate crap. I'm not saying there isn't a possibility that it might be true, but there's nowhere near enough evidence to convince anybody with decent critical thinking skills. That being said, I though it was pretty funny when some guy showed up to Comet Ping Pong armed and ready to take out pedophiles.

Anonymous on 4chan, 27 December 2016

3. CHEESE PIZZA

Sunday morning, 4 December 2016, was rainy in Salisbury, North Carolina. Edgar Maddison Welch woke up early with at least three guns in his house and too much on his mind.

Maddison, as he preferred to be called, had not been his usual self for months.

In October, 28-year-old Maddison had been driving to his night shift at Salisbury's Food Lion warehouse when his car struck a thirteen-year-old boy named Kenyatta Belton, who'd been walking along the street outside Food Lion with some friends.

Maddison – who had plans to become an emergency medical technician – got out of his car and stayed with the injured boy until police arrived. Kenyatta was bleeding badly from a wound to his chest. A man among those who ran to help him created a tourniquet to stem the flow of blood. When the police arrived, they applied a second tourniquet.

Witnesses said Maddison hadn't been driving well, but police determined that he wasn't speeding, and no charges were laid. Kenyatta had to be airlifted to hospital. He'd sustained broken bones, injuries to his torso and legs, and had a head injury. It would be a long stay.

The Welches were a well-known family in rural Salisbury. 'Smallsbury' was a town of only 30,000, and Maddison's grandfather had once owned the local radio station and been a county commissioner. Maddison's dad, Harry, had also served in local government. His mother, Terri, was a nurse and a volunteer firefighter. Community-minded people, they took in foster children and sheltered abandoned dogs. They were 'a family of rescuers', his mother said.[1]

In the weeks that followed the car accident, it became clear to the family that Maddison was racked with guilt. He was concerned about the potential long-term impact of the accident on Kenyatta Belton's life. Maddison started to have nightmares. Terri noticed his personality shift. He'd always been an energetic and outgoing person, but he grew melancholy and quiet. His family suggested he might get some help. Maddison declined.

His friends usually described Maddison as a thrillseeker, but after the accident, the young man who'd liked hiking and shooting and being outdoors withdrew into his home. His parents got the feeling he was watching more TV than usual, maybe playing a lot of video games.

He was actually spending a lot of time on the internet, again. A few years earlier, he'd been quoted in the local newspaper, the *Salisbury Post*, saying that long-distance hiking had helped him to overcome an internet addiction.[2] Now he was back online, and in the weeks leading up to 4 December, Edgar Maddison Welch was reading a lot of internet reports and watching online videos. The content he consumed was troubling him.

The Thursday just gone, for example – 1 December, the day before Kenyatta Belton had told Facebook he would finally be discharged from hospital – Maddison had been on a YouTube binge. He'd become fascinated by conspiracy theories, and the internet rabbit hole he'd gone down that night was, typically of late, a dark one. The videos talked about child rape and molestation and how networks of predators appeared to be everywhere. Sensational reports suggested these abusers were hiding in plain sight, sometimes in positions of authority. Sometimes, the videos said, even in the highest levels of government.

Although Maddison was only twenty-eight, he'd already been married, left his marriage and become the primary carer to his two daughters. He lived with them. He loved them. He was a beloved uncle to his sister's kids too, the fun uncle who took them fishing and surfing and skateboarding. Children were important to him. The idea of organised paedophiles out in the community abusing children was terrifying and enraging. It preyed on his mind. That Thursday night, he texted friends and his girlfriend, insisting that action had to be taken, trying to recruit them to do … something.

He didn't say anything to his parents, but he told his friends that he'd started to plan. The internet had offered him 'intel' on where the most powerful paedophiles were meeting and gathering. He'd learned that an innocuous suburban frontage in another city was hiding the trapped child victims of a trafficking operation. Maddison wanted to go there, he said, and take a stand 'against a corrupt system that kidnaps, tortures and rapes babies and children in our own backyard'.[3] He mooted taking extreme measures. It'd be worth 'sacrificing the lives of a few for the lives of the many', he told his friends.

His girlfriend warned him against doing 'something stupid'. Maybe, suggested a friend, he should conduct some 'recon' on this place before just going in somewhere 'guns blazing'.[4]

Maddison continued his planning. Then Sunday came.

The morning was cold as well as wet. It was early winter, but only six degrees. Edgar Maddison Welch got out of bed early. He dressed himself in jeans and a navy hooded sweatshirt and pulled a dark woollen beanie over his head, past his eyebrows. He'd told his family he had some things to do. He loaded his Toyota Prius with a Colt .38-calibre six-shot handgun, a twelve-gauge shotgun, a folding knife, a 9-millimetre AR-15 long assault-style rifle, at least twenty-nine rounds of ammunition, a box of shells and a change of clothes. Then he got into the car. Soon he was on a 550-kilometre drive to Washington, DC.

I have been talking to people around me and here in my little town absolutely no one has even heard of the scandal. So you can imagine how difficult it is to begin to explain it to someone who is completely out of the loop.

Olcore on Voat, 13 December 2016

What was Maddison Welch thinking about on his long, grey drive north? When he started the car, he told himself it was with the intention of having a 'closer look' at a restaurant basement in a north Washington neighbourhood.[5] Despite all the guns in the car, he'd decided his journey would be just to 'shine some light' on the rumoured goings-on. Then, he'd turn around and come home.[6]

Washington was at least a five-and-a-half-hour drive from Salisbury, and that's a long time to be alone with your thoughts on a cold, wet day. Maddison's turned to the nature of evil, and where his own responsibility might lay in stopping it.

In recent years, Maddison Welch had become a religious man. His parents didn't like to remember it, but as a teenager Maddison had been chaotic. He'd racked up a record that contained a couple of drug charges and drink-driving offences. His name appeared on a forged prescription and he was convicted for underage drinking. He'd been in a substance-abuse treatment program. As recently as April 2013, Welch had pleaded guilty to a charge of impaired driving, recording a blood alcohol content of .09.

In recent years, he'd grown aggressively devout. Friends told stories of a time they'd taken acid in front of him and he responded by chanting Jesus's name to cast 'demons' out of them.[7]

Now he was an adult, and lately he'd committed himself to helping people – from a neighbour who needed a porch fixed, to travelling to Haiti with a group from his local Baptist men's association to rebuild houses after an earthquake. Although in his time he'd dropped out of community college and had a history of beginning new careers – as an actor, a writer, a firefighter – only to end them, there was no question he'd embraced his obligations to his little girls. He worked twelve-hour night shifts at Food Lion so he could parent them during the day.

Maddison regularly posted Facebook content of the girls captioned with Bible quotations. He had Bible verses tattooed on his back that spoke to his new sense of adult conviction: 'Even the youths shall faint and be weary, and the young men shall utterly fall. But they that wait upon the Lord shall renew their strength; they shall mount up with wings as eagles; they shall run, and not be weary; and they shall walk, and not faint' (Isaiah 40: 30-31).[8]

In the car, his mind sought divine guidance as he remained preoccupied with thoughts of barbarity and suffering. There is certainly enough historical resonance along the highways between Salisbury and Washington to provoke anyone to introspection on this theme. The route runs through Richmond, the capital of the short-lived Southern Confederacy, and Maddison's car hurtled through the landscape of some of the most vicious fighting of America's civil war. Manassas, Fredericksburg, Petersburg: these are places more notable for who once died there – and for what – than for whoever's living there now.

Maddison's home town, Salisbury, itself rests on a monument to suffering. The Salisbury National Cemetery that now houses America's war dead was built upon a site of infamous Civil War cruelty, Salisbury Prison.

Here the Confederates had originally interned conscientious

objectors and family men who refused to enlist for the South, but by 1864 a facility built to house 2500 was packed with an extra 10,000 Union Army prisoners of war. Not even roofs were provided to accommodate the excess, let alone sewerage. Lice-ridden men starved and died in their own filth by the thousands. An uprising of the unarmed prisoners was put down by Confederate guards who fired shrapnel balls at them from cannons. Hundreds were mutilated, hundreds were killed.

As Maddison Welch drove 500 kilometres to confront evil elsewhere, a bronze statue in the centre of his home town – built to honour the 'Southern cause' of Salisbury Prison's mass-murdering jailers – remained unmolested. Seven metres tall, *Gloria Victis* was inscribed with the words *'Deo Vindice'*, 'vindicated by God'.

Maddison sped over grey roads and past colourless trees further away from Salisbury. He was not thinking of how poisonous, false ideas and propaganda had spurred hundreds and thousands of Americans into the death and ruination of civil war. He was thinking of what the internet had told him about a sex ring raping children in the basement of a Washington family restaurant, and his mission to 'protect the defenceless' grew more desperate in his mind.[9]

As his car approached the city, Maddison felt like his 'heart was breaking'. He sent his girlfriend a Bible quotation via SMS, claiming some kind of anointment by God.[10] He mounted his smartphone on the car's dashboard and recorded a message to his daughters as his ringed fingers gripped the steering wheel.

'To my girls,' he began, and his speech broke with a long, sad pause. 'I love y'all more than anything in this world. I can't let you grow up in a world that's so corrupted by evil without at least standing up for you ... and for other children just like you. Like I've always told you; we have a duty to protect people who can't protect themselves. I hope you understand that one day. I love all of y'all.'[11]

Maddison Welch wanted to 'do some good' in the world.[12] Just before 3 pm, he parked his car just off Connecticut Avenue in northwest Washington, DC. He left his shotgun and shells in the car but fastened the loaded six-shot revolver to his hip and hung twenty-nine rounds of ammunition across his chest. Holding the 9-millimetre long assault rifle, he walked through the front door of a pizza joint called Comet Ping Pong.

am i missing something? its a restaurant that has
ping pong, what else is there to see?

Anonymous on 4chan, 3 November 2016

The established facts of Comet Ping Pong were that it was a hipsterish place that marketed itself to families, situated in the friendly, affluent Chevy Chase neighbourhood of Washington, DC. The city is divided into four quadrants, and Comet's home in the upper north-west quadrant is sometimes derisively referred to as 'Upper Caucasia'. It was a warehouse conversion with high ceilings and a leafy outdoor area, with a games room full of playable ping-pong tables.

The owner was James Alefantis, a chef and restaurateur with a background as an art curator. The restaurant was decorated not only with industrial surfaces but a rotating selection of new work from local artists. The ping-pong tables would regularly get cleared out for concerts. Many punk bands played Comet – including legendary local act Fugazi – and bands playing other music too, as well as drag acts and performance art. The venue hosted benefits, fundraisers, all-female punk showcases and community events.

It had a reliably urbane clientele. Alefantis was an out gay man; his ex was the infamous David Brock, a former conservative operative who'd turned progressive and become the founder of the watchdog group Media Matters for America. Comet was a place where punks, political progressives, the LGBTQIA+ community and their friends could share hot wings, dipping plates and meatball pizzas. There were squash blossom salads and cheesy broccoli for vegetarians. Everyone recommended the cocktails.

This was information you could glean from an online Yelp review, or an article in *The Washington Post* or a magazine like *Slate*. But Maddison Welch hadn't been intrigued into loading his car with guns and driving all the way to DC by broadsheet reviews of Comet's 'Ca-lamb-ity J's' pizza.

He'd been learning about Alefantis's restaurant for the last three days on Facebook. Alex Jones – the host of *Infowars*, a conspiracy theory website with a live stream that Maddison liked to watch – had talked about the place and tweeted about it too. So had many less-identifiable people generating content on social media sites like Reddit and 4chan, Twitter and Facebook.

They weren't discussing the food. What eventually found its way to Maddison Welch via Jones and others was online speculation about a relationship between the restaurant and the Democratic Party's 2016 presidential nominee, Hillary Clinton.

On 2 July 2016, Clinton had been the Democrats' presumptive nominee for a month when an unidentified person who claimed to be a 'high-level' analyst with America's Federal Bureau of Investigation participated in an 'ask me anything' question-and-answer forum on 4chan. They called themselves 'FBIAnon' and said they had information to leak about the charitable foundation run by Clinton and her husband, Bill Clinton, a former US president. The Clintons got paid 'in children as well as money', FBIAnon said.

'Does Hillary have sex with kidnapped girls?' asked someone in the chat.

'Yes,' responded FBIAnon – and, once started, this rumour quietly circulated around untraceable corners of the internet for months.

The rumour grew a little louder when, on 22 September 2016, international tabloid *The Daily Mail* broke a disturbing story. They had photographs and 'sexting' messages exchanged between disgraced Democratic congressman Anthony Weiner and a fifteen-year-old girl. Responding to the story, the FBI raided Weiner's home. On a seized laptop, they discovered emails from a woman named Huma Abedin. Abedin was not merely Anthony Weiner's unhappy wife – she was also Hillary Clinton's former deputy chief of staff and now vice-chair of Hillary Clinton's presidential campaign.

This Weiner scandal was opportune timing for Clinton's opponents and the Republican presidential nominee, Donald Trump. Republican activists fomented suspicions around questions that the laptop's cache of emails provoked.

Republican efforts were assisted on 7 October when Julian Assange's WikiLeaks website began daily releases of 20,000 pages of emails hacked from the accounts of another prominent Democratic Party identity, John Podesta. He was Abedin's superior, the chair of the Clinton campaign.

Podesta's emails were internal campaign communications from what was supposed to be a private, personal account. They discussed strategic decisions and office tensions, even restaurant bookings. When they were leaked to the internet, the anonymous rumour about Hillary Clinton and the 'kidnapped girls' began to re-emerge.

Long before any of the Weiner/Abedin/Podesta email events took place, Hillary Clinton had herself been investigated by the FBI for her use of a private email server when she was the US secretary of state. The FBI had raised concerns that by using the private server, she'd improperly conducted official communications of classified material. Eventually, their investigation discovered no serious impropriety. Clinton was cautioned and publicly chastised by the then head of the FBI, James Comey, and the case was closed. In the wake of the discoveries on Weiner's laptop, on 28 October 2016, James Comey informed US Congress that he was reopening that prior investigation to determine if the Weiner emails may be relevant to it.

It was eleven days before the US election, and these stories about emails saturated all media.

On 29 October, the day after Comey reopened his email investigation, a user with the handle 'Fatoldman' appeared on Thee RANT, an anonymised, unofficial internet chat site that was popular with New York City police officers. They posted a claim that 'the feds were forced to reopen the hillary email case [because] apparently the NYPD sex crimes unit was involved in the weiner case'. The message was screencapped and shared to Twitter by another anonymous user, 'Eagle Wings', whose handle was @NIVIsa4031.

Eagle Wings had a very bare personal bio and a generic profile image on their Twitter account and yet had a follower count the size of a celebrity's, over the hundreds of thousands. In August 2017, *Politico* identified them as a power-user within secret Twitter 'war rooms', where Trump-supporting activists met to share and distribute pro-Trump content that was often also then amplified by automated accounts, known as 'bots'.[13]

Ten hours after Eagle Wings shared the rumour, someone calling themselves 'Carmen Katz' – ostensibly from the town of Joplin, Missouri – published a Facebook post on her personal page about the Comey investigation. 'My NYPD source said its much more vile and serious than classified material on Weiner's device ...' wrote Katz. 'Hillary has a well documented predilection for underage girls ... We're talking an international child enslavement and sex ring.' Katz furnished her allegations with a reference made to the high-profile convicted sex offender Jeffrey Epstein.

Before the extent of his abuse of young girls was revealed to the public in 2008 criminal proceedings, Epstein was a wealthy financier, and known to have palled around with Hillary Clinton's husband. It was a matter of record that Epstein had even offered Bill Clinton the use of his private jet. By the time of Epstein's trial, the aircraft itself had become infamous. It was reported that this plane had been nicknamed 'the Lolita Express' by locals who lived around an airport that Epstein frequented with his conspicuously younger companions.[14]

The Carmen Katz Facebook post was screencapped and shared to Twitter by an account named @DavidGoldbergNY, with a caption claiming the Weiner emails 'point to a pedophilia ring and @HillaryClinton ... at the center'. It received 6369 retweets.

Within hours, a website called *Godlike Productions* posted the news that 'at least 6 members of Congress, several top leadership from federal agencies, and others all implicated in a massive child trafficking and pedophile sex ring' – and that this ring was operated 'directly' by the Clinton Foundation.[15] On 1 November, the *Conservative Daily Post* site ran the headline 'FBI confirms evidence of huge underground Clinton sex network' above an article that claimed: 'A source from the FBI has indicated ... a massive child trafficking and paedophile sex ring operates in Washington, D.C.'[16] There were no sources named, and the only document to which it linked was a *New York Post* story about Anthony Weiner's laptop that made no mention of either trafficking or a sex ring.

Many of the links between these sources were drawn together in an extraordinary piece of investigation by *Rolling Stone* journalist Amanda Robb. She followed them towards a man named Douglas Hagmann, a self-claimed private investigator from Erie, Pennsylvania.[17]

On 2 November, Hagmann brought the story off chat sites to the attention of internet broadcaster Alex Jones. As a guest on Jones's *Infowars* broadcast, Hagmann claimed to an audience of potentially as many as 7.7 million people that a 'source' in the New York Police Department had briefed him on the 'sexual angle' of the emails in the trove on Weiner's laptops. 'I don't want to be graphic or gross here,' said Hagmann, '… [but] Hillary did in fact participate on some of the junkets on the Lolita Express.'

With the Carmen Katz post circulating, and the platform provided to Hagmann's claims by Alex Jones, it didn't take long for passionate Donald Trump fans who gathered on the Reddit discussion board r/The_Donald and various forums on 4chan to start looking for links between the rumours about Clinton and the contents of the hacked Podesta emails.

They pored over months of Podesta's correspondence. It documented everything from resolving policy contradictions to managing infighting among the campaign staff. Along the way, the self-appointed investigators also learned the details of Podesta's family relationships, the events that he went to and the circles he moved in … and that he liked to eat pizza. A lot.

When will the Establishment Media hammer Hillary Clinton on the explosive WikiLeaks email revelations from her campaign chairman John Podesta?

Breitbart on Facebook, 16 October 2016

John Podesta was from an Italian-American family. He enjoyed a particularly close relationship with his brother, Tony, who was a Democratic Party fundraiser and Washington lobbyist. John often gave interviews about how much he loved to cook, and in 2015 the Podesta brothers worked together on a food-themed fundraiser for Clinton's incipient campaign. James Alefantis – who ran the Comet Ping Pong pizza restaurant – was a good friend of Tony Podesta's. He was one of the featured guests at the Clinton fundraiser. It was reported in *Politico*.[18]

When pro-Trump channers and 'redditors' went through the hacked Podesta emails and saw the number of references to pizza, pasta and walnut sauces, they didn't see someone from a family with a love of food. They saw a powerful member of the Washington political elite and codewords for covert activity.

An email to Podesta spoke of a handkerchief he'd left behind at a meeting decorated with 'a map that seems pizza-related'.[19] This item provoked intense speculation as to the hidden meaning of its symbols. Someone remembered that 'CP' had once been 4chan slang for 'child pornography' and concluded that 'cheese pizza' meant the same.[20] Then, in November, a channer helpfully suggested how other food terms mentioned in John Podesta's emails might be decoded:

'Hotdog' = boy
'Pizza' = girl
'Cheese' = little girl
'Pasta' = little boy
'Ice cream' = male prostitute
'Walnut' = person of colour
'Map' = semen
'Sauce' = orgy

Podesta's emails made 149 references to pizza and 41 references to sauce alone. Reading these as codewords for acts of paedophilia was to establish a narrative of gluttonous, relentless, unforgivable sexual cruelty. The assumptions drawn from these readings melded with the rumours about Hillary Clinton as a sexual predator that FBIAnon, Fatoldman, @DavidGoldbergNY, the poster on the *Godlike Productions* website and Carmen Katz had all published, and that Doug Hagmann had spoken about on *Infowars*.

A horrified and disgusted community of amateur internet sleuths worked backwards from the codewords to flesh out a shared understanding of how Clinton, Podesta and their associates may be operating. A 2008 email to John Podesta from James Alefantis offered Comet Ping Pong as the venue for an Obama campaign fundraiser. Interest coalesced around the restaurant as a venue for nefariousness at the highest political level. Soon enough, an Instagram post from James Alefantis was found that furnished their worst suspicions – it depicted Barack Obama himself playing ping-pong with a child.

Someone scrutinised the signage at Comet Ping Pong, producing a meme that circled the crescent moons and five-pointed stars in its logo, attesting that this was the unholy iconography of Baphomet, the goat-headed occult deity of the Crusades era. Someone else retrieved a WikiLeaks file that purported to be an FBI briefing on 'Symbols and logos used by pedophiles to identify sexual preferences' and saw traces and shapes of paedophile codes in graphic symbols used in the Comet Ping Pong letterhead and on its menu.

Within the unmoderated realms of anonymous internet discourse, the power of relentless insistence was transforming speculation to conviction.

An image ripped from James Alefantis's Instagram account of a windowless cement space was deduced to be a 'kill room' for disposing of spent and surplus children. Another photograph sourced from his account featured a man in a black shirt that read 'I [heart] L'Enfant' flanked by two other men, who were shirtless and in boxer shorts. It was presumed the t-shirted man was Alefantis, brazenly promoting a paedophilic lifestyle; *enfant* is, of course, French for 'child'. It's also the name of a Washington bar, as well as its nearby metro station. Both are named after the city planner of Washington, Pierre Charles L'Enfant.

On a website called *Victurus Libertas* ('Freedom to Live'), run by a Texan couple called 'Jim' and 'Angie', an account purporting to be FBIAnon published police illustrations of suspects in the UK's infamous Madeleine McCann child-kidnapping case and claimed the hazy portraits were the Podesta brothers.[21]

As a flood of posts and online photographs burbled with allegations of child torture and abuse going on beneath his restaurant, James Alefantis became aware of engagement spiking across his social media accounts. There was a sudden bump in his number of Instagram followers, as well as those subscribed to the Comet Ping Pong accounts on Instagram and Facebook. The new engagements were rarely positive. 'We're onto you,' said one comment. 'I will kill you personally,' said another.[22]

The presidential election campaign was in its final days, and the tension between Clinton supporters and those backing Donald Trump was running hot. Yes, Alefantis was cheering for Clinton, although they'd never actually met. Yes, his political loyalties were a matter of record. Yes, combative partisanship on the internet had come to define the 2016 campaign. But by 4 November, Alefantis realised that what was happening to him and his business went far beyond mere electoral scrapping.

Death threats and accusations of paedophilia were not only coming via Instagram, Facebook, Twitter and as text messages and phone calls. They even appeared on the restaurant review website Yelp. Relentless, unremitting accusations of participation in child abuse and murder bombarded not only Alefantis but those in Comet Ping Pong's forty staff, like bartender Josh Vogelsong. Vogelsong had been working at

Comet since 2011. He also performed as a drag queen called 'Donna Slash' and helped book acts for the venue. He'd taken photos of himself and various shows at the restaurant and posted them on Instagram. 'PAEDOPHILE CHILD MOLESTING ASS PIECE OF GARBAGE,' commented a user called @debbieoconell_ on a post of his. 'Dumb bitch, or whatever the fuck you are,' said user @rb.sad. 'We're gonna slit your throat and bathe in your blood,' said someone else.[23]

Alefantis had never seen anything like it. Alarmed, his young employees gathered to help him search out online what may have been provoking the onslaught of hate.

That day, 4 November, Alex Jones from *Infowars* had released a YouTube video. In it he lamented 'all the children Hillary Clinton has personally murdered and chopped up and raped'.[24] It racked up 427,000 views.[25] Jones was echoing remarks made that day by Erik Prince, a national security adviser to the Trump campaign and the brother of billionaire conservative activist Betsy DeVos. Prince had gone on Breitbart radio some hours earlier, claiming that '[b]ecause of Weinergate and the sexting scandal, the NYPD started investigating' Hillary Clinton's secret activities. He insisted that 'they found a lot of other really damning criminal information ... Hillary went to this sex island with convicted pedophile Jeffrey Epstein'.[26]

The Comet Ping Pong staff discovered a trove of blogs, chats, videos, memes and internet broadcasts across Reddit, 4chan, Instagram and elsewhere that proclaimed a connection between Clinton and other murderous Democratic Party paedophiles and their family pizza restaurant. Photographs customers had posted of their children enjoying meals at Comet Ping Pong had been ripped from their social media accounts and shared as 'evidence' of abuse.

By 4 November, the accusations weren't limited to child molestation and murder, either. They now extended to claims of black magic and Satanism, with some ferocity. The proof cited wasn't just the crescent moons of Comet Ping Pong's outdoor signage. Within the WikiLeaks emails, accusers had found a mysterious message from a woman called Marina Abramović to Tony Podesta, dated 28 June 2015. It read:

> *Dear Tony,*
> *I'm so looking forward to the Spirit Cooking dinner at my place. Do you think you would be able to let me know if your brother's joining?*
> *All my love, Marina*

This email had also been mentioned by Alex Jones on 4 November. He called it 'one of the most disturbing WikiLeaks revelations to date'.

Having seen for myself in Videos on the Internet that was posted with Marina Abramovic's Spirit Cooking by herself who is closely associate with Pondesta and is mention in Wiki Leaks email. She is doing a Satanists ceremonial. My eyes do not deceive me and I don't need anyone to tell me that I didn't see it.

DWagner12, comment on *Breitbart*, 6 December 2016

For people willing to see paedophile symbols on restaurant menus, a link between Marina Abramović and the Podesta brothers was rich treasure. The black-haired woman was seventy years old but looked far younger. She was Eastern European, and apparently born in a country – Yugoslavia – that could no longer be found on a map. She called herself a 'performance artist'. Images of Marina Abramović on the internet depicted her almost universally wearing blood-red, black or white robe-like dresses, and engaged in surreal rituals. She draped scorpions across her face. She caressed skulls. If you googled her name and 'Spirit Cooking' – as mentioned in the email to Tony Podesta – you could find a 1997 video of her painting nonsense, poetic instructions on a cement wall with pig's blood encouraging observers to eat their pain.

Alex Jones was speaking about Abramović when he said 'reports that FBI agents see Hillary Clinton as "the antichrist personified" now make a lot more sense'.[27] The same day that James Alefantis and his staff were trying to make sense of their sudden internet notoriety, #SpiritCooking was the top trend on American Twitter. A tweet with that hashtag was shared over a thousand times comparing the artist to Jeffrey Dahmer, the prolific American serial killer. One of Gamergate's opportunistic bandwagoners, lawyer Mike Cernovich, referenced the 1997 video to explain that what Abramović and the art world claimed were performances were actually 'sex-cult rituals' that existed as a demonstration of the elite power held by people like the Clintons.[28] 'It's done openly to taunt the public. It's a form of power and control,' blogged Cernovich. Someone else online found a picture posted by James Alefantis of Marina Abramović 'holding a bundle of sticks'.[29]

Abramović – who in reality was a performance artist, and one of significant international renown – was quick to issue a condemnation of the rumours. 'This is taken completely out of my context,' she explained, outraged. 'It was just a normal dinner.'[30] Only ten people had even attended that night – it was a reward for Tony Podesta donating to one of Abramović's Kickstarter fundraising campaigns. The 'Spirit Cooking' in the email was just a joke, she said, a reference to the name of her 1997 performance which used the pig's blood and awkward poetry to satirise the notion of artist-as-guru, and the very genre of 'self-help'. As it was, John Podesta couldn't even make it to the dinner at the artist's house, and – Abramović stressed – '[t]here was no blood, no anything else. We just call things funny names, that's all.'

But the audience of *Infowars*, 4chan, Reddit, Twitter and the other sites amplifying the #SpiritCooking hashtag weren't reading the exclusive interview Abramović gave to *ARTnews*. They weren't following up expanded reportage in *New York* magazine, or in the US imprint of *The Guardian*.

The world of the Podesta brothers and Marina Abramović was one where those who wielded political power met those wielding cultural power in the columns of cosmopolitan masthead magazines, long before they met in person.

It was a world that did not touch Maddison Welch, who jammed in parenting, abortive career attempts and the internet between his long shifts at the Food Lion. The communities that surrounded James Alefantis and his staff were casually entertained by irony: drag queens dancing around in fake blood or punk bands in hooded robes pretending to summon rockstars from the dead. The online people suddenly joining their audience at the invitation of Alex Jones and Reddit threads were not in on the joke. The queer, punk and high-art scenes that produced these spectacles were unknown to them, and their attempts to link the out-of-context images to a narrative featuring Hillary Clinton, the Podestas, performance art and a pizza restaurant followed the desperate logic of a nightmare.

That same 4 November, a Reddit user called u/DumbScribblyUnctious published a thread that compiled the dominant accusations of the developing story. That thread, 'Comet Ping Pong – Pizzagate Summary', appeared within r/The_Donald, soon gaining its own dedicated subreddit, r/Pizzagate. Twenty thousand people subscribed. 'Pizzagate' entered the language – a new word to describe the internet's wild story about the satanic Clinton campaign.

The same day, noted Amanda Robb in *Rolling Stone*, a reporter named Cassandra Fairbanks – at the time working for a Russian state-owned news agency, *Sputnik News* – was furiously pushing out the rumours to her not-inconsiderable Twitter following. When she tweeted 'I've literally spent the last hour wondering if podesta ingested sperm mixed with breast milk with his brother', a user called @GodlessNZ responded to her: 'Tweets assembling under #JohnMolesta and maybe #PizzaGate.' As a hashtag, #PizzaGate became an international concern within hours.[31]

It had been a mere two days since 'private investigator' Doug Hagmann had spruiked these still unsubstantiated rumours about Clinton on Alex Jones's *Infowars*. With only four days to go until the election, it was unsurprising to see prominent advocates of the Trump campaign seize upon this viral story about his opponent. *The Daily Beast* reported that not only had the story of Clinton's satanic association run on right-wing news site *Drudge Report*, but the Fox News personality Sean Hannity tweeted a story from his own website entitled 'LEAKED EMAIL appears to link Clinton Campaign Chairman to bizarre occult ritual'. Actor James Woods – once upon a time the star of *Videodrome* – was one of the high-profile Twitter accounts that kept the story trending.[32]

As a hashtag, #PizzaGate was gaining speed as well as reach on Twitter, in no small part due to the participation of some highly active accounts retweeting #PizzaGate content. At least three thousand accounts shared the hashtag at least five times; a klatch of these were accounts that shared as many as nine hundred tweets a day. Amanda Robb noticed that there were sixty-six known Trump campaign operatives engaging with one or more of the most prolific #PizzaGate tweeters. Trump strategist Michael Caputo followed 146 of them. Trump's 'spiritual adviser', the pastor Paula White, followed seventy-one. The son of retired Lieutenant General Michael Flynn – who was himself advising Trump on national security – followed fifty-eight.

This is a great place for Washington elitist to RAPE
CHILDREN and hide their SEX CRIMES!!! The pizza's
a little doughy though:(

(three stars)

Craig C on Yelp, 11 November 2016

Perhaps there are people who can tweet nine hundred times
in a day, but activity on Twitter at that level of concentration is
usually attributed to bots. The automated algorithms behind
bots are programmed to respond to things like keywords
and hashtags with an action – like a retweet, a 'like', or a
line of generated text. Someone – or someones – had set up
bots to respond to tweets about #PizzaGate, and by doing
so promoted the hashtag as a trending topic, which drew the
attention of more live users. Greater engagement – especially
from high-profile accounts, like the Trump supporters – made
the topic more visible, which in turn drew greater engagement
and provoked more visibility.

For James Alefantis, the visibility meant that by 5
November, journalists from mainstream media outlets had
become aware of the story now swirling around him. Will
Sommer, a reporter from the *Washington City Paper* at the
time, rang sometime after 9.30 pm that night. Sommer left
Alefantis a voicemail asking, 'Do you know about this online
conspiracy theory that you're running a child-slavery ring out
of Comet with Hillary Clinton?'[33] When Alefantis spoke to
him, Sommer asked Alefantis if he'd like to respond to the
allegations about kill rooms and child-sex dungeons under his

restaurant that were going viral on Reddit. Alefantis didn't even know what Reddit was.

Will Sommer's piece about what was happening to Comet Ping Pong appeared in the *Washington City Paper* on 6 November. In it, an adherent of the #PizzaGate stories – a Twitter-using Trump supporter quoted by Sommer who called himself 'Pizza Party Ben' – insisted 'strange coincidences' surrounded the restaurant, and suggested people investigate it for themselves. The article also quoted a Reddit conversation that asked, 'Does anyone want to run surveillance on Comet Ping Pong?'[34]

Someone already had. Posing as a customer, someone had posted a photograph taken of Comet's interior to Twitter, claiming to have found a 'spooky' locked door.

Alefantis had told Sommer he blamed the 'bizarre theories' about Comet on the presidential campaign. Between that interview and 8 November, the day of the election, the #PizzaGate hashtag was still a live topic. Bizarre theories were running wild across blogs, Facebook pages and unattributed websites.

Online activists were trying to keep the #PizzaGate story going even on election day itself. On 8 November, @BrittPettibone – a writer who had tens of thousands of followers – tweeted a drawing of children with the words 'sexualised children, child abuse, pools, and bondage ... a look inside Hillary Clinton's friend Tony Podesta's house' as a caption. She also reposted the #PizzaGate hashtag, and another tweet: 'We should expose this.' Dozens of responses agreed.

'Dozens' on Twitter seemed an unremarkable political event when more than 133 million Americans were physically out casting votes. Will Sommer himself had concluded in his piece for the *Washington City Paper* that Pizzagate appeared little more than 'just a desperate attempt to slime Clinton's campaign a few days before the election', given it was an election Clinton was heavily favoured to win.[35]

Trump had consistently lagged Clinton in voter-intention polls. A gaffe-heavy campaign and his repeated unpreparedness for policy questions had given mainstream media pundits little reason to doubt those polls were true. Yet as the votes rolled in, it became apparent that although Trump had lost the popular vote by some margin, a targeted electoral strategy aimed at winning over slices of voters in populous swing districts had delivered him a majority of states in the US electoral college.

Trump won the election. Rowan County, which contained Maddison Welch's hometown of Salisbury, North Carolina, gave Trump a thumping 66.54 per cent of their vote.

In solidly Democratic Washington, DC, a disappointed James Alefantis had the comfort, at least, of believing that the attacks on his restaurant would disappear with Trump's victory. In the last week of the election, the phone calls and harassing emails had not stopped at his restaurant's doorstep. Other shopkeepers in the neighbourhood were being harassed as well.

The rumour persisted that tunnels connected torture rooms under Comet to dungeons and basements elsewhere. A Google review of the French bistro across the road contained allegations of child abuse. Emails and phone calls demanded other local businesses explain why the shops had chosen certain symbols to decorate their logos and other graphic properties of their businesses. Another local pizza shop owner – this one a Trump voter – was told his shop logo was a symbol for child pornography. The logo depicted ... a slice of pizza.

There were one or two days of post-election relative peace. Then Alefantis learned that Pizzagate had not ended with Hillary Clinton's political career. The community of believers in the Pizzagate story grew even more energetic. On 20 November 2016, @BrittPettibone rallied the Twitter troops. '#Pizzagate is a world-wide citizen investigation now,' she wrote. 'It cannot be stopped. At this point, the truth being brought to light is inevitable.'

'Pizzagate is not going away, this story will be huge!' Mike Cernovich tweeted two days later.

Nearly two weeks after the election, online Pizzagate posters were still encouraging one another not to 'let up'. Amanda Robb at *Rolling Stone* found articles that proliferated on obscure websites and in Facebook groups under headlines like 'FBI: Rumors about Clinton pedophile ring are true'.[36] These repeated internet chatter and ignored disproving evidence that had been accumulating from mainstream media sources as far back as 1 November. That date was when fact-check site *Politifact* had suggested an article's claims of an 'underground Clinton sex network' – that relied solely on the hearsay of someone called WartHog76 – were, perhaps, a little thin.[37]

Weeks after this, the stories continued to appear on fringe websites with names like *YourNewsWire*, *AmericaTalks*, *The Vigilant Citizen*, *Planet Free Will*, *Living Resistance*, *The New Nationalist* and *Before It's News*.[38] The accusations grew. A site with the legitimate-sounding name *The European Union Times* ran an article that claimed Clinton was a known witch who the FBI itself had outed as the biblical Antichrist. It was illustrated with photos of Marina Abramović holding a ram's head.[39]

James Alefantis had locked down his own social media accounts, but he started getting calls from customers, his family members and his friends that the online harassment was now targeting them. His general manager's wife had asked her husband to quit his job to escape the terrifying messages deluging their social media. Other Comet staff were counting how many #PizzaGate posts were appearing on Twitter every minute – sometimes, there were as many as five. A friend of Alefantis's at MIT's Media Lab was watching the #PizzaGate mentions and the stories told in them bloom online and called Alefantis with a warning: 'this thing is out of control'.

Comet's general manager, Bryce Reh, described the experience to *The New York Times* as '[l]ike trying to shoot a swarm of bees with one gun'.[40]

In desperation, Alefantis contacted the FBI, the police, Facebook, Twitter, YouTube and Reddit for help stemming the online swarm, and to try to get the articles taken down. The online platforms were mostly unresponsive. Yelp, at least, published a warning on its website that reviews of Comet couldn't be trusted due to an ongoing controversy. Online commenters had been claiming that there were pieces of dismembered children in the food.

While authorities tried to work out the line between a constitutional right to free speech and the rights of innocent people subjected to an out-of-control harassment campaign, there were, at least, police stationed outside Comet Ping Pong when an unfamiliar customer turned up during a busy shift the night of 16 November.

Did you guys know that the entire nation of Turkey is obsessed with #pizzagate? It's talked about on the streets and in coffee shops.
You can't stop kek. It's coming, he's real. Pizza gate is real.

Anonymous on 4chan, 21 December 2016

Wednesday, 16 November 2016 had been another big day on the internet for Comet Ping Pong's victimised staff. Earlier that day, the #PizzaGate hashtag had been shared by a popular Turkish television anchor with close to 200,000 Twitter followers.

At the time, Mehmet Ali Önel was employed by a pro-government TV network. The Turkish government was under some scrutiny from the Obama State Department for proposing some laws offending human rights. The suggestion from the hardline government of Turkish President

Recep Tayyip Erdogan was to decriminalise child rape and molestation if offenders married their victims. The international community was in uproar. Önel was one of numerous Erdogan supporters who took to Twitter and reused the #PizzaGate hashtag to accuse America of hypocrisy. 'USA #PizzaGate shaken by paedophilia scandals,' Önel tweeted.

A comprehensive report in the *Daily Dot* revealed that the Turkish pro-government papers – including mainstream mastheads *Sabah*, *A Haber*, *Yeni Şafak*, *Akşam* and *Star* – were suddenly reporting Pizzagate as a serious breaking news story, using the images and claims that were running unverified and unchecked on Reddit.[41] The participation of mainstream Turkish media in the hashtag ratcheted up the popularity of Pizzagate as a Twitter trending topic again.

Only the day before this happened, James Alefantis had given an interview to the *Washington City Paper*, speaking of his exasperation at the internet hate campaigns but pledging the restaurant remained 'completely safe' inside. 'None of these people are going there,' he told journalist Laura Hayes, 'they're cowards.'[42]

Less than a day after Önel's tweeting, the night of 16 November in America, the trending #PizzaGate hashtag stirred a sometime naval reservist and enthusiastic grassroots Trump campaigner into making a visit. In his Twitter bio, Jack Posobiec claimed that he was 'fmr CBS news', although he had never worked for them. Mostly known – if at all – for being a *Game of Thrones* blogger, Posobiec had made an online name for himself through pranks and provocateur-style trolling.

Although he later claimed that he went to Comet Ping Pong merely to 'show it was a regular pizza place', that Wednesday he arrived with a friend, ordered some garlic knots, let his friend order beer, and then began a live broadcast with his phone of himself 'investigating' the restaurant.

'I don't know what's going to happen to me,' he told the camera, explaining he was there for an 'IPOE', a military acronym that means 'intelligence preparation of the operational environment'. Posobiec also claimed in his video that, depending on what did happen there, his friend had a phone at the ready to call emergency services.

When Posobiec took it upon himself to walk into Comet's back room and film a child's birthday party that was taking place there, the Comet staff intervened. The manager asked the police officers stationed outside for some assistance, Posobiec was refused service and asked to leave. Posobiec was given the food and drinks on the house and did leave the premises at police suggestion.

As a result of Posobiec's broadcast, the #PizzaGate hashtag received its largest reach yet. @BrittPettibone tweeted in response: 'You're my hero for doing this, Jack. Never let go.'

Asked later about the incident, Posobiec repeated his line that he was merely seeking evidence to disprove the online claims about Comet. By that time, of course, he'd already recommended that 'sub-sources' – that is, other people who believed in Pizzagate – go in there, with hidden cameras, and seek out evidence of their own.

On 21 November, *The New York Times* reported on what was happening to James Alefantis and Comet as a national news story. Alefantis, his staff and his friends had been turned into human bullseyes, said the *Times,* by those who pushed false articles, and by those who believed them.[43] *Snopes,* the respected internet fact-checking site, published a point-by-point debunking of the Pizzagate story on the same day.[44]

It didn't seem to matter. Two protesters turned up outside Comet that night. Alefantis happened to be there – he exhorted the men to search the premises and disabuse themselves of any idea that sex tunnels or kill rooms were present. The men came inside, found nothing, and left, although not before telling him the place was a dump.

Among others, *The New York Times* article quoted a musician called Amanda Kleinman about her experience of the ongoing abuse by the Pizzagater community. Kleinman had a band called Heavy Breathing, which had performed at the restaurant numerous times. Her music clips on YouTube had been inundated with hateful comments. The comments directed at her on Twitter were so awful that she deleted her account.

The abuse was 'endless', said James Alefantis. It was scary. The restaurant was receiving up to 150 abusive phone calls a day. Alefantis unplugged the phone.

The online stalking of Comet Ping Pong staff, friends and customers had grown so extreme by 22 November that the site administrators of Reddit took the uncommon step of shutting down the r/Pizzagate subreddit. They were enforcing their moderation policy. 'We don't want witch-hunts on our site,' they explained in a statement.[45] Posts from redditors sharing photos and private information about those connected to the restaurant had been agglomerating rapidly. It wasn't just that the Comet staff had their personal phone numbers and home addresses circulated online, or that people were turning up to film James Alefantis's house and interrogate his neighbours. Property tax records were published. Someone had even shared the details of John Podesta's Netflix subscription.

Dozens of other websites had also been sharing photographs of children with a connection to Comet – kids who'd appeared in the restaurant's social media pages, perhaps, or whose parents had merely 'liked' the restaurant online. These kids were as young as five years old. Alefantis was horrified. 'Someone should be prosecuting these people,' he told the *Washington City Paper*.[46] Their families were already hiring lawyers, trying to get the photos taken down.

Rather than impede the spread of the rumours, Reddit's act of closing its dedicated subreddit was seized upon by the Pizzagater community as evidence of exposed elites engaging in a desperate cover-up. Pizzagaters claimed censorship and announced they were relocating their community to Voat, a 'free speech' discussion site with very limited moderation. It had experienced its most significant recent growth after Reddit adopted an anti-harassment policy.

One of the former r/Pizzagate moderators announced the impending relocation to Voat on the r/The_Donald subreddit, and in martial terms. The 'entire mod team and everyone else is tightening up our opsec and putting on our battle-armor', they said, using the military abbreviation for 'operational security'. The subsequent discussion aped the language of a holy crusade. The closure of the r/Pizzagate subreddit was described as an 'unspeakable act'. 'We have all made life insurance videos,' someone else said. 'We have all vowed to continue this fight. You have only increased our number. This morning we were numerous, tonight we are legion.' Almost 150,000 tweets on the subject flowed in the wake of these announcements.

Despite the Reddit ban, the exposé in *The New York Times*, the takedown in *Snopes*, the police encounter with Jack Posobiec and everything else, Alex Jones at *Infowars* published a new video the very next day, entitled 'Pizzagate is real'.[47]

In the segment, he recapped the supposedly incriminating contents of the Podesta emails. He gave the impression he was quoting John Podesta from the emails when he said, 'We're going to have the six-year-old, the seven-year-old and eight-year-old in the hot tub for your entertainment down at the ranch house. They can be a little persnickety, but they are also willing and enjoy it.'[48]

None of these words were Podesta's. Jones was exaggerating the contents of an exchange between Podesta and some friends about how they were going to carpool their children to a pool party. 'Bonnie will be Uber service to transport Ruby, Emerson, and Maeve' didn't make it onto *Infowars*.[49]

Jones instead told his audience, 'Something's going on. Something's being covered up. It needs to be investigated.' He told them this in a video on 27 November that went for half an hour, in which he claimed he would soon be 'getting on a plane' and turning up at Comet Ping Pong himself. 'I couldn't sleep last night,' he said, for thinking about Comet, the child sex trafficking that was said to be going on there, the 'satanic art' on its walls. 'I may take off a week,' said Jones, 'and just only research this and actually go to where these places are and stuff.' He urged his audience to 'investigate it for yourself' – he qualified that he personally lacked 'the self-control to be around these type of people'.

Only a few hours later, Jones published another video on the same subject, this one called 'Down the #Pizzagate rabbit hole'.[50] He published another – 'Pizzagate: The bigger picture' on 1 December.[51]

That night, Edgar Maddison Welch was watching him.

Maybe gaslighting really did take over the world and there's a conspiracy to brainwash people by making them doubt their judgement and substitute someone else's.

thicktail1730947 on Voat, 8 December 2016

It had been more than a month since Maddison Welch had been behind the wheel of the car that hit Kenyatta Belton and put him in the hospital. On 1 December, Kenyatta was still in that hospital. Kenyatta's public Facebook posts from that time don't mention pizza, John Podesta, 'kill rooms' or even the US election. They contain Facebook Live videos shot by a bored child from his hospital bed – images of an unadorned hospital room, the tired smiles of visiting family members and the exhausted face of his father.

The kid doesn't quote the Bible, wave an American flag or denounce a European performance artist for suspected witchery. His public updates read: 'I have to use the bathroom and I can't' on 7 November, and 'Wtf I been in the hospital a month and I'm good I'm ready to go home' on 23 November. On 25 November he asks, 'Some one call me', and, later, 'They will not release me out this hospital'. A day later came an update: 'Getting released next Friday.' That made the date he would finally go home Friday, 2 December.

Kenyatta Belton's Facebook updates were set to public, and they were easy to find. Maybe Maddison Welch checked in on the suffering of the hospitalised kid that he'd hit with his car, maybe he didn't. There's no public record of him doing so. There is, however, a record of what Maddison Welch was watching on the night of 1 December. His interest in the fantasy child victims of 'Pizzagate' was retained in the memory of his mobile phone.

That night, Thursday, Maddison had been watching YouTube videos on his mobile. He sent a text message about it to his girlfriend. He told her that he'd been watching 'Pizzagate' videos, and that the content made him 'sick'. Maddison didn't stop watching the videos. He watched more, and for the next few hours. He also visited the website of Comet Ping Pong pizzeria.

A little after 8 pm that night, he sent a text message to another friend, known as 'B'. It said '*Watch PIZZAGATE: The Bigger Picture on YouTube*', which was the name of the video Alex Jones had just uploaded. It included a link to YouTube.

Not long after he contacted B, Maddison got a call from another friend, known as 'C'. They may have spoken, they may have not, but afterward they had an SMS conversation. C wrote at 8.28 pm *Tell me we r going to save the Indians from the pipeline*, which most likely referred to a political stand-off that was then taking place between the Standing Rock Sioux Tribe and the US federal government over the construction of a gas pipeline through Sioux land.

Maddison was unconcerned about the Sioux. *Way more important, much higher stakes,* he responded, *Pizzagate.*

Sounds like we r freeing some oppressed pizza from the hands of an evil pizza joint, replied C.

Youtube tonight, talk in AM, said Maddison.

I'm in, said C, at 8.35 pm.

Now, Maddison contacted B again, asking him to get in touch so they could all go together to C's place in the morning. He repeated his request for B to check out the YouTube links. B said he'd get back to him in the morning.

Did they meet the next morning? At 2.58 pm the next day, 2 December, Maddison Welch texted C again. He really wanted to meet. He wanted to know whether C had any 'army buddies' in the area.

C did. Maddison asked, *[he] down for the cause?*

C suggested it would depend on the cause.

Raiding a pedo ring, said Maddison, *possibly sacraficing the lives of a few for the lives of many. Standing up against a corrupt system that kidnaps, tortures and rapes babies and children in our own backyard.* Maddison said the *cause was defending the next generation of kids, our kids, from ever having to experience this kind of evil themselves.*

I'm sorry bro, Maddison continued, *but I'm tired of turning the channel and hoping someone does something and being thankful it's not my family. One day it will be our families. The world is too afraid to act and I'm too stubborn not to.*

A few minutes later, C and Maddison spoke on the phone. When that call ended, Maddison texted his girlfriend and said he was going round to C's. B also sent Maddison a text message, saying that he'd be there too.

This was Friday. On Sunday, at 6.42 am, B texted Maddison again, suggesting they should meet. Maddison responded that he was on the way. *Hell moths Fucking yeq,* replied B at 6.52 am, likely attempting to type *Hell motherfucking yes* and losing to his phone's autocorrect.

By 8.42 am, Maddison appeared to be by himself in his car. This was when an exchange of text messages took place between him and his girlfriend. She had woken up at Maddison's house to find that he wasn't there, and that she'd been left alone with his two children. She was concerned. Her messages to him increased in concern over the course of the day.

Edgar Maddison Welch had a history of substance abuse and was experiencing symptoms of trauma after an accident in which he'd hospitalised a child. He had discussed plans with friends to engage in a guerrilla raid likely to result in a loss of human life. He was a legal gun owner in North Carolina, and he had three guns and ammo in his car.

At 11.06 am, from his car, he made a video for his family. He loved them, he said. He hoped he 'showed it'. He hoped he'd be able to tell them again, in person. 'If not,' he said, 'don't ever forget it.'

Is it really that hard to believe that maybe, just
maybe there are lunatics who take everything they
read on /pol/ seriously and then sperg out? Every
social platform is bound to have a few crazies.

Anonymous on 4chan, 5 December 2016

The fantasy universes of the internet may be limitless, but
the world itself is small. As Maddison Welch continued his
rainy drive into Washington, journalist Christine Grimaldi –
a Washington local, and my friend – was lunching at Comet
Ping Pong with two friends.

The three of them had been meaning to leave much
earlier, but one of her friends had brought her kids, and the
kids were having so much fun playing ping-pong that the
women kept ordering drinks. They talked and laughed.
Comet was a neighbourhood fixture, and popularity kept
it busy. Despite everything it had endured on the internet,
Comet's vintage sign with its stars and moons was still lit
up on its green facade, the tables still had red-and-white
chequered tablecloths. The paintings and murals chosen by
James Alefantis – the work of his artist friends – were still on
the walls.[52]

Just shy of 3 pm, Christine and her friends settled their bill
at Comet and parted ways. Christine's husband was still on
his way to pick her up, so she slipped into Politics and Prose,
a bookstore a couple of doors down, to collect a novel that
she'd ordered. As she did, Edgar Maddison Welch parked his

Prius near Comet, not far from the corner of Connecticut and Nebraska avenues.

He approached the front door of the restaurant through which Christine had not long left. His AR-15 assault rifle was displayed across his chest. His loaded .38 revolver was holstered at his hip, and he carried a folding knife. The man who'd told his family he wanted to 'stand up' for children then marched with deadly weapons into a family restaurant where children played ping-pong while their parents had drinks and ate pizza. There were still kids playing ping-pong when Maddison Welch arrived.

The customers, the staff and the children at Comet Ping Pong were terrified. Welch walked through the restaurant, heading towards the back, where the ping-pong tables – and children playing at them – were.

As he did, Comet staff crept along the restaurant aisles from table to table and in low voices urged the customers to get out of the building and find safety in the street. Two middle-aged men, Gareth Wade and Doug Clarke, had only just ordered pizza and beer when a trembling waiter told them there was a gunman in the building – and then Welch himself approached their table. He told them to get out, and they ran, joining the adults and children fleeing from the restaurant, some still with pizza in their mouths.

Welch turned towards the kitchen.

James Alefantis was at a church fair while this was happening. He found out what was going on when the shift manager called. She was crying. 'A guy came in with an assault rifle,' she said, explaining that police were already on the scene. The response had been swift. The manager told Alefantis police were stopping traffic, securing the area and directing fleeing staff and customers into a firehouse down the block, across the street.

Police were in the process of locking the block down, establishing a perimeter, evacuating the surrounding businesses and moving everyone to safety. A police helicopter was on its way. So was James Alefantis, who – even after everything that had happened – could not comprehend why a man with an assault rifle was roaming his pizza restaurant.

Inside, that man was proceeding slowly. Around him was a moment frozen in time. People had vanished, but the tables were still laden with chequered tablecloths and napkins, half-drunk drinks, half-eaten food. The smell of fresh pizza still hung in the air.

Maddison Welch didn't allow himself to be distracted by the scene. He was here to bust the infrastructure of a satanic global paedophile ring that involved at least James Alefantis, the Podesta brothers, Hillary Clinton and an Eastern European woman who posed with goat skulls. The internet had told him Comet Ping Pong was where these criminals met, where their deeds were done. He'd been told there were raped and tortured children hidden in the basement of this restaurant, next to kill rooms where used-up child victims were extinguished.

He was searching for that basement now, with his assault rifle slung across his chest. He was looking for a staircase, a false wall, a locked, 'spooky' door ... Maybe he was straining to hear the sounds of trapped children calling out to a yearned-for rescuer who had finally arrived. There had been hundreds of thousands of tweets about this restaurant, spread by people who called themselves journalists – spread by Alex Jones, spread by senior Republican party identities. There were blogs, message boards and an ocean of Facebook comments all insisting the allegations were established facts. Mike Cernovich, the lawyer, had put his own name to such on his blog: 'Clinton's inner circle includes child traffickers, pedophiles, and now members of a "sex cult",' Cernovich had said.[53]

Where were the abused children being held? As he moved through the restaurant, Welch had explored the back room and found nothing. Now he was searching the kitchen and – finally – found a locked door. Could this be it? The door to the basement stairs?

Did Maddison Welch's heart suddenly thrum faster with this discovery? Did he float and tremble with a wave of adrenalin as he handled the lock? Maybe his hands shook. Maybe they were slippery with perspiration. He picked up a nearby butterknife and jammed it into the lock, trying to pry it open. Did he imagine he could hear the screams of children beyond the door?

The knife wouldn't open the lock. Maddison became frustrated. He had told his family he had a duty to protect people who couldn't protect themselves. He dropped the knife. He stood back from the door and pointed the assault rifle at the lock. He shot at the lock. Again. And again.

Still, the lock didn't break, the door didn't open. Maddison dragged some furniture towards the door and climbed on top of it, peering around the weakened door's edges into what lay behind.

Maddison Welch had come to rescue children from a basement. He was staring into a storage closet that contained some cooking supplies and the remains of a computer he'd just shot with an assault rifle.

It confounded him.

In the alley behind the restaurant, one of Comet's kitchen staff heard the three loud bangs and didn't know what they were. He'd been fetching fresh pizza dough from a freezer that Comet shared with another restaurant nearby when Maddison Welch had marched in the front door a few minutes earlier. He'd missed the panic, the terrified evacuation. He was walking back into the kitchen carrying the dough, and he saw the man with the rifle.

Maddison and the kitchen hand made eye contact, and Maddison swung to face him with the rifle in his hands. With the AR-15 pointing at him, Comet's employee forgot about dough, pizzas and everything else and bolted in fear of his life, running onto the street through the now empty restaurant's front door.

As the kitchen hand found a police officer and breathlessly described what was happening inside, Maddison Welch searched the restaurant again.

There were no hidden rooms here. There were no tunnels. There were no trapped children, or sex criminals, or evidence of sex trafficking or abuse of any kind. There were no stairs to a basement. There was no basement at all. Outside the restaurant, the gathered police were broadcasting calls for him to drop his weapons, come out onto the street and surrender.

Maddison Welch put his rifle down on a beer keg, and his revolver on a table. Twenty-three minutes after he'd walked into Comet Ping Pong, he walked out again. There were masses of police in the streets; they were pointing guns at him. A helicopter flew overhead.

Maddison raised his hands over his head. Police directed him to expose his waistband, to establish he was now unarmed. They told him to walk backwards away from the restaurant, which he did, towards a zebra crossing. They told him to lay on the ground. As Maddison was put into handcuffs, two people who'd fled Comet when he'd arrived confirmed to police that the man on the road was the man they'd seen enter the restaurant with an assault rifle.

What was he thinking, Maddison Welch of Salisbury, North Carolina, when he was lying with his face pressed against the tarmac, a pale, solitary man in blue t-shirt and jeans? Did he think that his 'raid' had been worth it, while the metal cuffs cut into his wrists?

Did he think about Alex Jones, who had urged his viewers to 'investigate' Comet for themselves? Did he start to review the blogs, the quotes, the 'word of mouth' that had insisted to an audience of millions of Maddisons that Pizzagate was real?

Arresting officer Sergeant Benjamin Firehock asked Maddison why he had come there. The arrest affidavit reports he replied that he'd heard reports on the internet, from other people and the radio that Comet Ping Pong was hiding trafficked children in secret rooms and that he had come armed to help rescue them.

Maddison Welch had come to Washington prepared to sacrifice 'the lives of a few for the lives of the many'. The sacrifice he actually made was of his role as a father in the lives of his children. He faced an inevitable jail sentence that would likely last significant years of their childhoods. All for the sake of saving other children who didn't exist, who were never in a basement, who were invented, fantasy creatures of internet smear campaigns and political convenience.

The arrest proceeded without incident. Maddison Welch complied with all police instructions and was taken into custody.

@washingtonpost Comet Ping Pong Congrats to Edgar Maddison Welch – the fastest crisis actor ever busted

@devilchasnme on Twitter, 6 December 2016

Christine Grimaldi left the bookshop. She and her husband heard more and more sirens on the drive home but only learned precisely what she'd managed to escape when they checked the internet back at home.

James Alefantis and his staff were allowed back into Comet Ping Pong later that night. Back to the drinks that were still on the tables, the chequered tablecloths, the cold, uneaten slices of pizza, the frozen moment in time.

Alefantis had no desire to remain in that moment. He and his staff cleaned up and repaired. By the weekend, Comet Ping Pong was back in business. The smell of fresh pizza thickened the air as loyal local crowds – shocked by the recent events, and the man with the gun – flocked to its tables to demonstrate solidarity and community, to eat and to drink.

Elsewhere, in the same city, Edgar Maddison Welch had been issued a white plastic jumpsuit by correctional officers and spent his first nights of many in jail.

In the aftermath of the incident, a swarm of journalists descended on the story of Pizzagate. A factual record of its events was set down. Mainstream media outlets, academic journals, authors and analysts dissected the lies that made up Pizzagate. They studied the means by which its myths were disseminated within the unique ecology of the internet through bad-faith actors, and opportunists, and more hapless participants.

Any thought that Pizzagate was a phenomenon that would now resolve into concluded history through a neat intersection of facts with the machinations of the law was, however, mistaken.

What Pizzagate established was that skilful manipulation of social media could manufacture political narratives so compelling they could overwhelm reality. This wasn't a new insight for researchers of propaganda and disinformation, but the image of a man in jeans shooting up a computer cupboard because he'd been convinced Hillary Clinton was raping babies inside it alerted many, many others to a pressing and volatile modern danger.

The Obama administration – by December 2016 in its dying days – warned of a problem everyone could suddenly see. 'There's no denying the corrosive effect that some of these false reports have had on our political debate,' said Obama's press secretary, Josh Earnest, the day after Welch's arrest. 'It's deeply troubling some of those false reports could lead to violence.'[54]

The power of those false reports was such that the arrest of Maddison Welch did not end them. Pizzagate was a story with symbolic furniture so ancient to Western myths and fairytales it awoke genuine familiarity and connection in those who consumed its pieces. Old stories of nefarious 'elites' stealing children to practise satanic abominations on their bodies have been used to demonise heretics, witches, other marginalised groups, political enemies and Jews for centuries.

Historian Michael Barbezat, now at the University of Western Australia, saw repeated in Pizzagate a phenomenon that fellow historian Norman Cohn had described in the 1990s as the 'nocturnal ritual fantasy'. The subterranean labyrinths, secret symbols and tortured innocents of Pizzagate, wrote Barbezat, have been lurking in the Western cultural subconscious since the Romans. The eternal theme of these stories is a heroic struggle against the forces of this darkness by those who are righteous enough to stand up to it.

Pizzagate offered anyone with the means to speculate on a message board, cheer on Alex Jones from home or march into a pizza joint with a gun an opportunity to demonstrate heroism. In a world where day-to-day life consists of more mundane – and morally complex – struggles with work, parenting, family, relationships, drugs, alcohol or money, the appeal of moral simplicity is understandable. Facts are poor competition against an epic narrative of easily achievable personal glory.

This was the framework set by Pizzagate that ensured the persistence, resurrection and reinvention of its central claims. The internet forums that created Pizzagate now explained the inconvenient truth of Maddison Welch's arrest away. *The Washington Post* reported on 6 December that it only took hours for Pizzagaters to decide that Welch was not one of them. 'Some suggested he was a "false flag",' said the *Post*, a decoy planted by the elites 'who had been used in an elaborate plot to conceal the truth'.[55]

At his trial in June 2017, Maddison Welch pled guilty to interstate transportation of a firearm and assault with a dangerous weapon. He began a four-and-a-half-year sentence in prison.

The made-up story of child sexual exploitation by Hillary Clinton and Democratic Party child-murderers that had landed him there knew no such confinement. Its symbols and events were already being repurposed into the founding mythology of an evolving new community known as QAnon.

Adrenochrome doesn't exist endogenously you fucking mongoloid larper. Take your fake patrolman gun and blow your brains out.

Anonymous on 4chan, 31 October 2017

4. 'ARE YOU ALL LARPING AS LARPERS?'

HRC extradition already in motion effective yesterday with several countries in case of cross border run. Passport approved to be flagged effective 10/30 @ 12:01am. Expect massive riots organized in defiance and others fleeing the US to occur. US M's will conduct the operation while NG activated. Proof check: Locate a NG member and ask if activated for duty 10/30 across most major cities.

This was the first post since attributed – although not without some disagreement – to the online identity who would become known as 'Q'. (The 'M' in the post presumably stood for US 'Marines' or maybe US 'Marshals', 'NG' for the US National Guard.) It appeared on 4chan's /pol/ board at 16:54:29 on 28 October 2017.

It was one of several anonymous postings on /pol/ that day repeating a rumour that the arrest of Hillary Clinton was imminent. Such rumours had been around for a while. Clinton had lost the presidential election to Trump a year earlier, but the fantasy of her incarceration was yet a mainstay of Trump supporters, who'd been chanting 'lock her up' at his rallies since July 2016. 'Lock her up' had been chanted at the 2016 Republican convention as Trump became the party nominee, at Trump rallies across the country, at every conceivable public opportunity by Trump hangers-on.[1]

What Clinton's crime was supposed to have been was never entirely clear, but you could always find unprovable insistence in the internet's most unaccountable corners that she was selling uranium to the Russians or raping and eating children under Washington pizza joints. Or maybe she had something to do with slave colonies on Mars? Trump never spoke directly about Pizzagate, but its conspiracy myths persisted on the internet and helped to furnish an online reputation for Clinton as a deceitful, criminal character.

So posts claiming 'Hillary Clinton will be arrested' or that she and John Podesta would be killed didn't detonate on 4chan like breaking news. They got responses like 'large if verified', 'fake and gay' and 'ok, keep me posted'.

'Larp intensifies' posted others, as well as 'LARPPPPPPPP' and 'Your moma will die you idiotic larper'.

There was a good reason for the tone, the style and even the abbreviations of such posts. They were entirely consistent with the practice of a 4chan LARP.

LARPing has always seemed like a cool idea to me,
but I have never met a LARPer who didn't make my
skin crawl.

Anonymous on 4chan, 5 March 2010

LARP is an acronym for 'live action role-playing' games.
A sly, ironic playing of such games was a 4chan tradition.
No understanding of the origins of the QAnon movement is
possible without an appreciation of the LARP and the geek
culture that spawned it.

Players in a role-playing game adopt fantasy personas or
characters with which to engage one another. The objective of
any role-playing game is to generate and maintain a dynamic,
real-time narrative while staying in character. The gameplay
consists of players responding to improvised and spontaneous
challenges from other players.

Children's games such as 'doctors and nurses' and
'mothers and fathers' are role-playing games at the most basic
level. Children create personas that mimic the social roles
performed by the adults around them. There are no rules,
and the game essentially lasts until the children lose interest
in their characters.

More structured, adult forms of role-playing games have
existed throughout history in different cultural contexts.
Historical re-enactments, theatresports and military exercises
are all arguably variations of the role-playing game. In the
1970s, Dave Arneson and E. Gary Gygax combined their

passion for tabletop strategy games with a role-playing concept and created a game called *Dungeons & Dragons* (*D&D*).

Individual players within a *D&D* game each make up a heroic persona, and the group of players travel as a war party through an imagined realm created by one of their own. This player is known as a 'Dungeon Master' (or DM) and plots the game's events that lie ahead of the others. The game takes place seated around a table, players taking notes with pen and paper. The course of their adventures is determined by character choices and a throw of the dice.

From the beginning, *D&D* was not for everyone. It was complex and technical and took hours just to learn how to play. Highly competitive, it became a cultural site of the emerging 'geek masculinity' long before anyone knew what the internet was.

Even so, the game achieved a cult popularity, with millions of game editions sold. It wasn't long before the gameplay format that it popularised was adapted for playing as an even more immersive 'live action' role-playing experience, beyond the tabletop.

In a live#action role-playing game, players dress up as characters in costume and physically interact with one another in that character, with play taking place in a real environment reinterpreted as a fantasy setting. LARP organisations like Amtgard run online promotions for live#action sword-and-sorcery-themed medieval battle events governed by a set of standard rules. Although the LARP equivalent of a *D&D* Dungeon Master (known as a 'Game Master' or GM) still creates a basic story and scenario and establishes the rules, the players control their character's individual decisions. A group of Australian researchers who study LARPs have explained that to make this dynamic functional, players have to accept certain boundaries and a social contract of behaviour before the game begins so that conflicts can be avoided later on.[2]

What results for LARP players is a personalised yet deeply immersive fantasy experience – a near total escapism. Conspicuously, some LARPers over-attach to the game scenarios, as well as within the practice of LARPing itself, allowing the emotions affecting their game personas to affect their personalities outside of the game. Role-players call this phenomenon 'emotional bleed'.

Psychologists have identified that escapist activities attract people seeking relief from distressing preoccupations.[3] Something like LARPing gets them away from discomfort and personal awkwardness, perceived marginalisation or social pressure. Escapist activities are about a concentration of a person's focus, which in turn creates distance from the self, lowering someone's self-awareness and decreasing their self-evaluation. While these are pleasurable experiences for the individual, they can compound that person's social dysfunction, especially within a broader peer group. The stereotype of the LARPer as a costumed, obsessive fantasist is an object of mockery.

The ghosts of geek masculinities past haunt the cultural framework of geek masculinities present. Their pop cultural artefacts, frames of reference and language are shared from generation to generation. Channers who've never been away from a computer long enough to even play a game of *D&D* still know what LARPing is.

The word is used as an insult, with a specific political meaning. In 2017, a Reddit user named u/renolcc gave an eloquent translation of a LARPer. 'It just means someone is pretending, particularly in the sense of pretending to be some kind of hero for their political position,' u/renolcc wrote, 'or like talking big online about some kind of political action you're going to take, or that should be taken, without any real intention of leaving your computer and doing anything for real.'

But LARPer had another, more complex meaning on 4chan than just a subcultural sledge. In the ever-renewing, anonymous waterfall of ephemeral discussion on its imageboards, LARPing was being revived by the ever-competitive channers as an online game of conversation.

4chan researchers use various techniques to tease out the dominant subjects and chains of discussion from the chaotic, constantly refreshing content found there. One of these is to excise from a board's archive all posts that don't contain the word 'the'. All short, non-substantive comments disappear. Researchers from the Q Origins Project using this technique saw a 4chan stripped of chatter.[4] Trawling through months of posts that preceded the arrival of the post attributed by some to Q on 28 October 2017 – and across a variety of 4chan's boards – they noticed that hundreds of variously self-identified 'insiders' kept appearing with fanciful stories about secret knowledge and hidden insight. Each individual made attempts to goad other channers into engaging with their claims.

The posters called themselves names like CIAnon,

WhiteHouseInsider, HLI (short for 'high-level insider'), FBIAnon. Like any committed LARPer, they turned up to play already in character. They'd make mysterious posts and drop hints about possessing insider information that related to a subject at hand, they'd take questions and respond with oblique replies. The social contract of the 4chan LARP was negotiated without explicit acknowledgement. The actual gameplay was convincing those who happened to be present that the particular conspiratorial pitch being offered was worth investing in as a shared, ironic reality.

Channers called the practice LARPing, outright. While hundreds of attempts crashed and burned to dismissive interest or none at all, successful LARPs were rewarded with group recognition of their chosen identity and the collective willingness to keep playing along.

The 4chan LARP wasn't some kind of method-acting exercise about saying believable things in a believable way until the audience caught you out in a contradiction or you revealed an impostor's mistake. Rather, it celebrated the temerity to expand into an imaginative spiral of ever grander, weirder claims. HLI began their LARP with vague insistence of political knowledge and some mysterious suggestions about contemporary political events. Over the progression of the LARP, though, their revelations began to include such things as the 'hidden truth' about the birth of historical Jesus. As a researcher from the Q Origins Project remarked, 'A very high-level insider, indeed.'[5]

FBIAnon of Pizzagate appeared within the same forum, with their wild insistence about the secret crimes of Hillary

Clinton. While the pipeline of Pizzagate influencers took the account at its word, amplifying the claims far beyond 4chan and into a social media maelstrom, those who stuck around on 4chan got to see the same FBIAnon account expound entirely unrelated, fabulist suggestions about a Jewish plot to take over America.

There was no believable logic to it, but logic and believability were never the point. The art of the 4chan LARP was about flattering illusions that everyone already knew were illusions. What followed was a theatrical improv game of 'Yes, and?' by the /pol/ crowd to furnish the details of a false, expanding mythos. Someone claiming to be in the FBI and outing Hillary Clinton as a child molester didn't have to provide a true story for the idea of it to be comforting to people who hated her. The fantasy of being selected as part of a special audience to receive this information had its own gratification.

So entrenched was LARPing culture within 4chan that six weeks before Q first appeared, users were floating the notion of LARPing as LARPers. A post made on 19 September 2017 distilled the tenor of 4chan's internal cultural moment:

> *This board is fucking taking a toll on my head.*
> *I've become pretty racist since joining here, but all these posts saying that you all larp and are for real, its fucking confusing.*
> *Is it a mix of parking fags and alpha males? Or are you all larping as larpers? Or are you genuinely larpers? Or genuinely racist? Or larping as all of these?*
> *For all you know I could be larping right now, this place is beautiful.*

I'm convinced at this point that Steve Bannon
checks /pol/ regularly

Anonymous on 4chan, 20 May 2016

On 28 October 2017, when an unexceptional, anonymous post appeared on 4chan's /pol/ board claiming 'Hillary Clinton will be arrested between 7:45 AM – 8:30 AM EST on Monday', it looked like another wilful statement, and typical of a genre.

It might even have been read as a solidarity gesture. A year into his presidency, Trump was embattled. Just that week, the US Special Counsel Robert Mueller filed the first set of charges from his investigation into pro-Trump Russian meddling in the 2016 US election. The White House had also been forced to respond to the testimony of twelve women who'd accused Trump of sexual harassment, and a story broke in *The New York Times* that placed the president's son and senior members of his campaign team at a pre-election meeting in Trump Tower that seemed to have been set up by the Kremlin.

Back in 2016, the Trumpist vibe on 4chan had been far more optimistic. At the same time that Don Jr was meeting with mysterious Russians in Trump Tower, aggressive loyalty to Trump was flourishing in communities on Reddit and 4chan. 'Lock her up' sentiment always had a receptive audience there. On the night of the 2016 election, reported *The Washington Post*, people on 4chan celebrated Trump's victory with statements like: 'WE WON THAT. HOW DO YOU FEEL GUYS. BITCH IS GOING TO JAIL.'[6]

Trump was inaugurated as president on 21 January 2017. By 28 October, nine months had passed and Hillary Clinton had not been arrested. She faced no charges. She was not 'going to jail'.

In the weeks after Trump's surprise election, channers had claimed his victory as their own. 'I'm fucking trembling out of excitement brahs,' ran one breathless 4chan post of 9 November 2016. 'We actually elected a meme as president.'[7] That meme had expert help: Steve Bannon had become chief executive of Trump's then-struggling campaign a mere eighty-eight days before the election and was widely credited with turning Trump's fortunes around. Bannon was rewarded for the election victory with appointment as chief strategist and senior counsellor to the new president. He also received a seat on the US National Security Council.

Bannon saw himself as Thomas Cromwell in the court of the Tudors, and his influence was felt quickly. 'His is an ethno-nationalist vision in which America leads a clash of civilizations,' reported Paul Waldman in *The Washington Post*.[8] Attempts to ban entry of people from Muslim countries to the US, restrictions on immigration, usurping the authority of the National Security Council and a commitment to build a border wall to keep out Mexicans were controversial and divisive Bannon-led policies. He was ambitious to do far more.

The new administration, however, did not operate with the discipline to which Bannon may have been accustomed.

Bannon thought Don Jr's meeting with the Russians was 'treasonous', for a start.[9]

A meme may have been fun to elect, but in office it was chaotic. Less than a week in, Trump had the FBI director, James Comey, brought to the White House for dinner. The new president clumsily suggested to the long-term public servant, 'I need loyalty, I expect loyalty.'[10] Comey later testified to a US Senate Intelligence Committee that he responded that he was 'not on anybody's side politically and could not be counted on in the traditional political sense'.[11] The mood at that dinner then shifted markedly.

By Valentine's Day, Trump's national security advisor, Lieutenant General Michael Flynn, had been forced to resign when it surfaced he'd lied to the vice-president about the nature of his communications with a Russian ambassador.[12] Trump had called in Comey to the Oval Office, suggesting that Comey might find a way of letting Flynn off from the growing trouble he was in. Comey refused and, within a couple of months, was fired. He found out at a Los Angeles FBI field office when the words 'Comey resigns' flashed across a television set on the wall.

Dysfunction dogged the Trump administration. There were multiple scandals every week. The frequency of these scandals did not lessen their capacity to shock.

Between 11 and 12 August 2017, a mass mobilisation in Charlottesville, Virginia, brought the alt-right together with Neo-Nazis and the Ku Klux Klan in an event called 'Unite the Right'. Images of a torchlit parade of demonstrators chanting 'Jews will not replace us' alarmed the world.[13] Violence broke out with counter-protestors, and a demonstrating white nationalist drove his car into a crowd of them, killing a woman named Heather Heyer, and injuring nineteen other people.

Republicans as well as Democrats condemned the participating far-right groups, and the violence. Trump, however, infamously declared there were 'very fine people' on 'both sides' of the protest. According to *The New York Times*, this line came from Bannon. He'd 'cautioned the president not to criticize far-right activists too severely for fear of antagonizing a small but energetic part of his base'.[14]

Trump's statement was denounced as a dangerous and irresponsible false equivalence. The public outcry was enormous.

Trump was still a year out from the US congressional midterm elections at this point in 2017, but the violence in Charlottesville galvanised a broad coalition of opponents. A series of bad polls across August had the NBC news network dub Donald Trump 'Mr 30%'.[15]

On the campaign trail, wrote *Vox*, Trump had been in strategic lockstep with Bannon as he stoked resentment of immigration, Muslims and the Black Lives Matter movement among white voters. Their tactics had chafed against what the Republican Party establishment had considered acceptable.[16] Now, Trump and Bannon had made it to the seat of government, where rather a lot of the old Republican Party establishment was still hanging around.

The party elites did not like Bannon. There were ongoing leaks from the White House of internal clashes. There were also reports of fights between Bannon and the president's daughter Ivanka and her husband, who Trump had also appointed as advisors – Michael Wolff reported that Bannon had called Ivanka 'dumb as a brick'.[17]

Trump's lack of interest in the 'granular detail' of his own policies led the press to dub Bannon 'Trump's brain'.[18] Anti-Trump poster campaigns across US cities made the demand to 'Impeach President Bannon'. Bannon's sizeable profile did not win him greater affection from the president. He was increasingly marginalised from Trump's favour. By 18 August, less than a week after the violence in Charlottesville, Bannon was out. Accounts differ as to whether he was fired or chose to leave, but whatever the case, he was on his way back to *Breitbart*. Leaving with him was his talent for detail in policy implementation. Several key Trump projects – like extreme and aggressive deportation policies and travel bans – were either watered down or stalled.[19]

It wasn't the only derailment that the ambition of the pro-Trump far right had suffered.

I'm surprised no one is talking about the fact that this collapse and others like it show that the 'popularity' of someone on twitter (or even reddit) clearly includes bots, paid posters (i.e Russian, etc) as well as people who are just following to hate on these personalities.

ReadMoreWriteLess on Reddit, 29 December 2017

In 2016, Milo Yiannopoulos had finally been banned from Twitter. He threw a party to celebrate, news that was covered by *Vanity Fair*.[20] In November 2016, even as they called him 'Donald Trump's alt-right poster boy', Yiannopoulos was the subject of a flattering profile in London's *Evening Standard*.[21] By February 2017, his trajectory was heading dangerously mainstream. He was scheduled for a slate of campus speaking appearances, had a book deal with Simon & Schuster, had been invited to speak at the Conservative Political Action Conference (CPAC), was still holding down his column for *Breitbart* and had just been a featured guest of the influential HBO show *Real Time with Bill Maher*.

Over a period of four days, it all fell apart. A sixteen-year-old Canadian girl had found obscure podcast recordings of Yiannopoulos defending the idea of thirteen-year-olds enjoying sexual relationships with older men.[22] She campaigned to bring these comments to the attention of the CPAC organisers.

A line had finally been crossed. Somewhat karmically, this new Yiannopoulos scandal blew up on Twitter. He lost his book deal, had his speaking engagements cancelled, was booted from a horrified CPAC and even had to quit *Breitbart*. *Vox* reported that the Canadian teen took the action she did because Yiannopoulos had come to represent a place she did not believe 'the conservative movement should go'.[23]

Later, at the start of October 2017, footage also emerged that had been shot over a year earlier, in April 2016. It was of Yiannopoulos singing 'America the Beautiful' to Neo-Nazi Richard Spencer and a crowd of his sieg-heiling comrades in a

Dallas bar. At that point, even Bannon was obliged to disown his former protégé.[24] The pair's billionaire backer, Robert Mercer, also started to quietly re-evaluate his patronage.[25]

The gloomy context perhaps explains 4chan's online hunger for some happy, if fanciful, stories about Clinton going to jail. Perhaps a little anti-Clinton LARPing was like listening to a greatest hits album from a broken-up band. It wasn't surprising that even a poorly written LARP attempt, like claiming her arrest, attracted interest. Into this conversation, Q made what is popularly accepted as their first, still anonymous, post.

Ninety minutes later, a second post appeared on /pol/, and their familiarity with the 4chan form was obvious.

Mockingbird

HRC detained, not arrested (yet).

Where is Huma? Follow Huma.

This has nothing to do w/ Russia (yet).

Why does Potus surround himself w/ generals?

What is military intelligence?

Why go around the 3 letter agencies?

What Supreme Court case allows for the use of MI v Congressional assembled and approved agencies?

Who has ultimate authority over our branches of military w\o approval conditions unless 90+ in wartime conditions?

What is the military code?

Where is AW being held? Why?

POTUS will not go on tv to address nation.

POTUS must isolate himself to prevent negative optics.

> *POTUS knew removing criminal rogue elements as a first step was*
> *essential to free and pass legislation.*
> *Who has access to everything classified?*
> *Do you believe HRC, Soros, Obama etc have more power than Trump?*
> *Fantasy.*
> *Whoever controls the office of the Presidecy controls this great land.*
> *They never believed for a moment they (Democrats and Republicans)*
> *would lose control.*
> *This is not a R v D battle.*
> *Why did Soros donate all his money recently?*
> *Why would he place all his funds in a RC?*
> *Mockingbird 10.30.17*
> *God bless fellow Patriots.*[26]

A cascade of rhetorical questions was consistent with the style of a 4chan LARP, and this second post was dripping with references to terms that had been bandied about 4chan and the conspiracist internet for years.

'Mockingbird', for example, suggested the theory of 'Operation Mockingbird'. Back in the 1970s, journalist Carl Bernstein reported America's CIA had an established practice of working with media agencies to provide 'journalistic cover' to its operatives abroad.[27] They also made use of contacts, local knowledge and information from reporters who worked as foreign correspondents. The Mockingbird conspiracy theory wildly extrapolated this specific history to insist masthead journalists were domestic spies, and the mass media was but a front for the CIA's manipulative domestic operations.

'Huma' referenced Huma Abedin, Hillary Clinton's long-term aide and deputy campaign manager, whose disastrous marriage to disgraced congressional representative Anthony Weiner had been the subject of much conspiratorial speculation during Pizzagate. When these posts appeared, Abedin was in the process of divorcing Weiner; he was by then in jail for his sexting of a minor. The 'AW' likely was referring to him.

'Soros' was George Soros, a Hungarian-born Jewish financier. During the Nazi occupation of Hungary, Soros's father hid his young son and risked his life to save other Hungarian Jewish families from extermination. After surviving the Second World War's brutal fifty-day siege of Budapest in which 38,000 civilians were killed, as an adult, Soros became a billionaire and channelled a mind-boggling 64 per cent of his personal fortune to progressive causes. *Forbes* magazine identified him as the most generous giver in America, and his conspicuous generosity had long made him a conspiracist favourite.[28]

Those familiar with the ideological flavour and LARP culture of /pol/ could perhaps sniff a well-known code buried in the post. 'Do you believe HRC, Soros, Obama etc have more power than Trump?' this poster asked. Positioned against the iconic and powerful Trump were Clinton, the feminist, Soros, a Jew, and Obama, a Black man. Huma Abedin was a practising Muslim and Anthony Weiner was also Jewish. They were identities emblematic of the 'cultural Marxist' conspiracy that the racist hard right on /pol/ had been pushing for years.

Over the course of the next twenty-four hours, what appeared to be the same account posted a further ten times. The first post appearing on the morning of 29 October 2017 shot for a 'birth of historical Jesus'–level gambit. It made the Pizzagate-esque claim that 'Many in our govt worship Satan'.

Language that would later become liturgical to future QAnon adherents appeared in these early posts on 4chan. Much of it was long-established LARPer parlance. 'Some of us come here to drop crumbs, just crumbs,' opened the second post of 29 October. 'Crumbs' meant clues and suggestions. The MegaAnon account was promising to drop 'HUGE BREADCRUMBS' about the hidden meaning of a Trump speech back on 5 October.

The poster-that-would-become-known-as-Q, concluded the post with 'Sit back and enjoy the show', suggested that 'Patriots [were] in control' of the oblique military activities – like arrests – to which their posts referred. 'The show' referred to the oncoming spectacle of predicted events. Again, 'enjoy the show' was something MegaAnon had said back on 12 October. This was when MegaAnon had been advancing a conspiracy theory that '((((they))))' – using in this case the anti-Semitic (((echo))) symbol to mean a supposed Jewish elite that ran Hollywood – 'negotiated their plans of throwing [now convicted sex offender Harvey] Weinstein under the bus with Weinstein himself'.[29]

A first reference to 'the great awakening' was also deployed in a post attributed to Q from 29 October, within a rant about Black voters backing Democratic candidates. 'At some point the great awakening will occur,' promised the post, 'whereby these false local/national black leaders are corrupt and paid off to help keep the black pop poor and in need.'

These 29 October posts consisted mostly of rhetorical questions again. The suggestions they made were indistinct and the writing inexplicit. Perhaps that was the point? A hazy narrative formed over the course of that day that was essentially a retread of Pizzagate; the repeated insistence was that Democrats were corrupt and that Hillary Clinton and the Clinton Foundation and others had something to do both with missing children and millions of dollars of hush money paid to others.

The posts further suggested that not all Republicans could be trusted, the military knew something about it, a host of evil characters were complicit in it, and the press was covering it up. There were more mentions of Obama, Soros, the transnational Islamist organisation the Muslim Brotherhood and Hispanic gang MS-13. References to conspiracy favourites the KKK, uranium sales, the Rothschild family and JFK were also sprinkled among the texts.

Unlike the villain-dominated legends of Pizzagate, this emerging story posed not just a depiction of a powerful and hidden evil but proposed the existence of a hero too.

Donald Trump.

Donald Trump is a fucking hero HANG THESE BASTARDS IN A PUBLIC GALLERY.

@Jamie30476465 on Twitter, 10 July 2021

Yes, the story as it developed was that no less than Donald Trump was fighting to rescue the missing children from the clutches of Hillary Clinton and her satanic myrmidons. According to the early posts widely attributed to Q, Trump had apparently 'installed his people' to fight the corruption and was 'in control' of a process to bring the evildoers to justice.

Within a few days of Q's first post, other users on 4chan were creating threads about them with titles such as 'Calm before the storm'. This referenced a glib quote Trump had made to journalists while posing for press photos with a group of American military leaders on 5 October 2017. Back then, cameras were flashing when Trump asked the gathered press, 'Do you know what this represents?'

The press didn't know and asked him.

'I don't know,' replied Trump. 'Maybe it's the calm before the storm. Could be the calm. The calm before the storm.'[30]

At the time, the new president's forays into foreign policy had inflamed tensions between the US and nuclear power North Korea, as well as strained affairs with hostile Iran. Military action had been discussed. Trump was being photographed with military leaders. The journalists present pressed the American president to explain what 'the storm' was.

'You'll find out,' was all he said.

Donald Trump had come to the presidency with no political experience, and his handling of the office since his election had become characterised by gaffes, untruths and profoundly dangerous strategic mistakes. There were internal ructions due to domestic decisions like the 'Muslim ban' and questionable White House personnel choices. In addition to the problems with Iran and North Korea, he'd also started a trade war with China and embraced the authoritarian leaders of Saudi Arabia, Turkey and Egypt. *Foreign Policy* magazine described the twenty-day tenure of Michael Flynn as national security advisor as 'more like a stint in rehab than a period of government service'.[31]

Back in 2015, Scott Adams – the cartoonist behind *Dilbert*, and a Trump admirer – had started to publish blogs wistfully claiming that Trump's rivals for the Republican nomination were a case of mere two-dimensional chess players taking on a '3-D Chess Master'.[32] Adams proposed that Trump had triumphed over more experienced political operators – like Jeb Bush – in the Republican primaries because of an almost preternatural strategic ability.[33]

Two years later, while Trump's real-world actions wreaked real-world chaos, Adams's chess-master notion was revived in the imagination of Trump's supporter communities on 4chan and Reddit. 'HOLY FUCK HE'S PLAYING 4D CHESS ON A 3D CHESSBOARD AGAINST PEOPLE PLAYING 2D CHESS,' an anonymous channer screamed in early October 2017 in a /pol/ discussion speculating whether Democratic Party attempts to impeach the president were a strategy to start a civil war. Chess mastery echoed as a meme through the information pipeline that was now built around these kinds of ardent pro-Trump discussions. In the r/The_ Donald subreddit, things like comic strips and panel memes were appearing of Hillary Clinton trying to play tic-tac-toe against Trump, who was featured as a floating giant brain.

On 18 February 2017, Trump claimed at a rally in Florida that there had been a major terrorist incident the previous evening in Sweden, which he appeared to blame on immigration. The Swedish embassy was swiftly in touch with the US State Department; no such incident had occurred. Trump was mocked mercilessly online. Even former Swedish prime minister Carl Bildt tweeted: 'Sweden? Terror attack? What has he been smoking? Questions abound.'[34]

This meme that insisted on Trump's grand mastery was fiercely deployed in his defence. '4-D chess once again from Trump,' tweeted right-wing internet personality Paul Joseph Watson, who was also a presenter for the Alex Jones show *Infowars*. 'Create controversy over #SwedenIncident – force media to talk about Sweden's multicultural hell.' Established here was an aggressive explanatory frame for excusing Trump's errors and unpredictability. It was seized upon by the president's political allies, particularly Fox News.

The frame was then repeated through the right-wing media to the point of cliché, provoking condemnation from former world chess champion Garry Kasparov as well as an analysis in *The New York Times*.[35] The danger of this, warned writer John Herrman, was in how effectively the meme acted to cement for Trump's supporters 'an explanatory bridge' between two 'observable tendencies' that should otherwise alarm them: 'that Trump keeps doing unexpected or abnormal things; and that his political opponents, and the media, can't seem to stop him.' Creating a myth of Trump's strategic genius posed great danger to those backing-in a political leadership that was, in reality, careless, haphazard and impulsive.

This myth of Trump the unmatched strategic mastermind was the established frame in which the Q posts appeared. An in-control, righteous hero who was wrestling a chaos beyond sight offered a far happier scenario than Pizzagate's doom-laden universe of unchecked spirit-cooking and child abuse.

God Emperor Trump will MAGA!
u/TheKingOfNeptune on Reddit, 12 February 2019

On the morning of 29 October 2017, a new (as yet still anonymous) Q post appeared, urging channers to remember 'There are a lot more good people than bad, so have faith'. Even so, the poster was at pains to remind 4chan readers that the stakes remained high. 'These people worship Satan,' the poster insisted about an hour later, in a tone more conversational than the military affect of the first few posts. Lest this conversationalism soften the author's image, a post appeared less than half an hour later reaffirming their seriousness and legitimacy as a source. 'Military Intelligence ref above is the absolute biggest inside drop this board will ever receive,' they wrote.

An observation made by later commentators was that whistleblowers didn't typically drip out – let alone foreshadow and promote – their leaks. Reflecting on the posts in an influential *Medium* essay, Reed Berkowitz made the point that real leakers tend to deliver all the information they have in one go, and with as much speed as possible, in order to minimise their risk of being identified and caught.[36]

Why a supposedly high-level military or intelligence official would similarly decide the best place to divulge state secrets was a forum best known for Neo-Nazis, Gamergate and internet hoaxes wasn't even the question. The question was why something written with such apparent po-faced seriousness wasn't being torn apart by a 4chan crowd that habitually denounced arriviste posters as 'newfags' and harassed them into eventual silence.

The content of these posts wasn't so shocking or revealing that the /pol/ audience was stunned into sudden reverence towards them. They came in the wake of FBIAnon, HLI, MegaAnon and many others.

The researchers from the Q Origins Project are confident that the poster who became known as Q chose to start posting on 4chan because Q was a long-term 4chan user.[37] The voice used was an effortless fit into the written tradition of 4chan LARPing. This was why there were no brutal callouts of this 'newfag' as there would have been if a newcomer without the specialised, subtle appreciation of the established tone had appeared. Revealing for researchers is how the posts are without the frank racism or open anti-Semitism that characterises 4chan's habitually barbaric language, yet all 4chan users present for the conversation recognise their author as one of their own. 'The poster was deeply, deeply familiar with 4chan culture,' one researcher said. 'They understood not merely how to speak the language but how to dog whistle in it.'

A further tip-off to Q as a 4chan native, according to these researchers, was a reference made to conservative Republican Party identity Trey Gowdy in Q's third-ever post. In context, a quote from Gowdy seemed to be illustrating the argument that Special Counsel Robert Mueller, at the time investigating Trump for possible collusion with Russia, was actually working with Trump, in secret, to expose the Satan worshippers within the US government's midst. The passage ran:

Why did POTUS meet Bob under the cover of FBI Dir interview?
Bob is unable to serve as Dir per the law.
Gowdy comments on Comey (history will ...)
POTUS has everything.

The quote from Gowdy struck the 4chan researchers as an odd detail, because it was so obscure. It was something Gowdy – then a congressional representative from South Carolina – had said in a little-heeded interview on Fox News six months earlier on 16 May 2017.[38]

Gowdy's remark referenced a press conference James Comey had given in 2016, when he was still FBI director, in which Comey publicly chastised Hillary Clinton for her use of a private email server. 'History will be much kinder to Jim Comey in that July press conference than the Democrats were,' Gowdy had said. 'I think he had access to information that, because he is a stand-up guy he's not gonna disseminate classified information.' As it turned out, the 'classified information' that had provoked Comey to give that press conference was an intelligence document the FBI was fairly sure had been faked and supplied by Russian agents.

Gowdy's quote was not particularly newsworthy at the time and was even less so nine days later on 24 May 2017, when *The Washington Post* broke the story of the Russian fake.[39] Apart from a write-up in hard-right news website *Daily Caller* the day after it was said, Gowdy's quote was long out of the public conversation and had disappeared from view ... unless, it seemed, you were on 4chan. Here it had been an item of anonymous discussion in 4chan's /pol/ threads in the days before Q began posting.

The Q posts from 28 and 29 October 2017 are archived today as if they were independent utterances, but their original context was within a dynamic 4chan conversation. Q's earliest posts – which did so much to foreground the later mythos and language of the QAnon movement – spoke to posts made by other anons on the /pol/ threads that day.

If indeed these earliest posts were all composed by the same author, that's a high level of engagement with the forum; it indicates the author is familiar and comfortable with the form. 'This person has spent many hundreds and most likely many thousands of hours on 4chan in general and on /pol/ in particular,' concludes one of the Q Origins Project researchers, 'reading this material that is already circulating there, and now basking in it. So why is Q on 4chan? Because Q lived on 4chan. Q grew up on 4chan.'[40]

There was another reason that the posts may not have met with fiery dismissal on the /pol/ board. By October 2017, 4chan had become known in the mainstream consciousness as an engine of Trump promotion. It was attracting an audience of Trump supporters more inclined to wilful belief than wild iconoclasm.

There were people watching /pol/ now who were inclined to look past 4chan's habit of irony, its history of pranks, and its tradition of LARPs. QAnon adherents who claim to have been active on 4chan when Q's prophecies began insist that 4chan users claiming to be whistleblowers or insiders proved themselves to be credible by an ability to rapidly answer questions within the discussion. These people say that the relentless intrusions by LARPers improved their own ability to scrutinise what was real from what was a troll. They believed other anonymous users who said they could verify the claims of the original anonymous source. 4chan was credible, one of these people tells me, because it had platformed the 'staff of companies sharing how to get freebies, people finding a place to confess anonymously [and] hacking activism'.[41]

There were people deeply invested in the belief that 4chan's anonymity created a community of equals. Despite Q's targeted references and specific finger-pointing, they refused to suspect the account of an agenda.

A captivating comedy of Executive-branch adventure as a hapless basement-level White-House writer gets wrapped up in the world of secrets, sex and spies.

Mike Nunn, review of Peter Benchley's *Q Clearance* on *Goodreads*, 15 May 2013[42]

In one of the first posts of 28 October, the author-who-would-soon-become-known-as-Q had foretold that 'massive riots' would result from Hillary Clinton's impending arrest. Then there'd be others – Clinton's co-conspirators – who'd also be arrested trying to flee the US. This was expected, said more posts, so the National Guard had been activated. This was all supposed to take place on 30 October 2017.

It didn't. On 30 October, a Monday, Hillary Clinton was not arrested. She did not face any 'extradition'. There were no riots. There was no National Guard mobilisation.

Q returned a day later – and when Q did, on 31 October, not a word was said about those events promised to happen the day before, events that had failed to come to pass. Instead, a fresh post appeared headlined with an image. It was of Emanuel Leutze's propagandistic 1851 painting *Washington Crossing the Delaware*.

This famous patriotic painting depicts the American revolutionary leader George Washington on one of the humble cargo boats his forces used to launch a surprise attack on the British during the War of Independence on Christmas night, 1776. Washington's crossing of the Delaware River enabled a much-needed victory for the rebels at Trenton, New Jersey, and is believed to have turned the tide of the revolutionary war.

The text of the post was another list of rhetorical questions about Hillary Clinton, George Soros and the Muslim Brotherhood, and suggested spurious connections between them. This list included, conspicuously, one question that read: 'Has POTUS *ever* made a statement that did not become proven as true/fact?'

It was a curious claim to make of President Trump – he'd been caught out in twenty-eight public lies in that month of October alone – but it certainly spoke to the frame of Trump as a 'chess grandmaster' of dissembling and cunning that had been built up by his mainstream allies for months.[43]

The poster spoke with confidence about yet-to-take-place events, even as more rhetorical questions were asked. A mere thirty-two seconds after the *Washington Crossing the Delaware* post appeared on /pol/, a subsequent post insisted '11.3 – Podesta indicted and 11.6 – Huma indicted'.

This new post continued, 'Wizards and warlocks (inside term)' would ensure 'Satanic evil' would not be allowed to endure. 'PS, Soros is targeted,' it promised. Later that night, the poster's confidence extended to 'Get the popcorn, Friday & Saturday will deliver on the MAGA promise'.

More promises about John Podesta's impending arrest were made the next day, claiming his arrest would happen '11.4'. Furthermore, 'Confirmation (to the public) of what is occurring will then be revealed,' read the post, 'and will not be openly accepted. Public riots are being organized in serious numbers in an effort to prevent the arrest and capture of more senior public officials. On POTUS' order, a state of temporary military control will be actioned and special ops carried out.'

This post, of 1 November 2017, was the one where the poster referred to themselves as a 'Q Clearance Patriot' for the first time. It was an interesting identity for the poster to claim.

A 'Q clearance' is a legitimate US government security clearance, but one that pertains to Department of Energy workers obliged to access restricted data concerning nuclear weapons and related materials. Why a government worker in the atomic energy space would be privy to information about impending judicial processes – and sharing it on 4chan – remains a fascinating question.

Coincidentally, *Q Clearance* was also the name of a satirical Cold War spy novel about atomic energy workers by Peter Benchley. Benchley was a former speechwriter to Lyndon Johnson. He also wrote *Jaws*.

There were plenty of other fascinating questions raised by the flurry of posts from the 'Q Clearance Patriot'. One was the variation in tone between the posts. There were no rhetorical questions in the first post on 1 November. It began grandly, in the manner of political speech, with an appeal to 'my fellow Americans' and a pledge to take back 'our great country (the land of the free) from the evil tyrants that wish to do us harm and destroy the last remaining refuge of shining light'.

The next post, made only twenty-two seconds later, was more religious in nature, even as it asked readers to 'Follow the questions from the previous thread(s) and remain calm, the primary targets are within DC'. Whilst warning readers – in the direct language of conspiracy theory – of 'false flags', or deceptive, covert operations that would sow confusion as the predicted events took place, Q implored 'above all, please pray'. Before concluding the post with 'God bless my fellow Americans', Q misquoted the Bible. 'For God so loved the world that he gave his one and only Son, that whoever believes in him shall not perish but have eternal life. Love is patient, love is kind' was a mishmash. The first half is John 3:16, briefly the most googled search term in the US when, in 2012, an NFL footballer who'd once painted the verse number onto his eye black coincidentally threw 316 yards to win an upset game. The second half is from 1 Corinthians 13:4–8 and is frequently recited at weddings.

The post ended with '4,10,20'. In context, one could be forgiven for thinking this referred to Mark 4:10–20, a section of the Bible in which Jesus proclaims 'The secret of the kingdom of God has been given to you. But to those on the outside everything is said in parables'. This may be overestimating Q's biblical scholarship; researchers from the Q Origins Project instead point to subsequent Q posts that reveal '4, 10, 20' are the positions of the 'DJT' letters in the alphabet.

Was Q more than one person? The posts appearing an improbable few seconds apart from one another suggested either the material was being drafted before it was sent or that it had more than one author. The latter could explain the wild variation in tone.

After an analysis of the posts for *Business Insider*, investigative data reporters Angela Wang and Sawyer Click made the point that 'any number of people could have posted messages as Q'.[44] 4chan's board only provided 'a thread-level identification number to each poster'. Q in one thread could've been someone else in another. Fredrick Brennan, the creator of 8kun, told Wang and Click, 'There is no way to say how many Q's there were' in the 4chan posts. 'People were just playing a character,' he said. 'It's impossible to figure out who started Q just because the people who started Q didn't do anything to identify themselves.'

this roleplay bullshit is getting out of hand. mods need to start banning you retards.

Anonymous on 4chan, 31 October 2017

In recent years, the term 'meme' has come to describe one of the specifically visual jokes that get transacted through the internet, but meme more broadly means any cultural text or system of behaviour that's copied, adapted and passed on from one person to another. Publishing Q-like exhortations on 4chan to 'have faith', 'trust in your president' and 'enjoy the show' in a swirl of conspiracy-rich language could have been a role-playing game attracting more than one Dungeon Master. Established LARPers were definitely engaged in the developing Q story. MegaAnon, one such established LARPer, was explicitly addressing the Q posts as early as 4 November 2017.

The Q Origins Project researchers consider MegaAnon 'phenomenally successful' among the /pol/ LARPers for their ability to sustain a conspiracy narrative.[45] They date MegaAnon's first post to 23 May 2017. From that point, MegaAnon's story flowed with references to old conspiracy favourites like the murder of Democratic staffer Seth Rich, the Clintons, Huma Abedin and Weiner, JFK, George Soros, uranium sales, the Rothschilds and the Saudis. There were also many, many cloaked anti-Semitic claims about Jews in the alt-right's (((echo))) notation.

Trump was a hero in MegaAnon's tales too, although with far less pomp and infallibility than Q would later afford him. 'I voted for him (duh),' MegaAnon said on 7 June 2017, 'but only republican I'll ever excitedly run to the polls to vote for as President, is [Trey] Gowdy.' A mere twenty minutes earlier, MegaAnon had posted: 'Trump doesn't say or do ANYTHING that's not intentionally executed.' The same day, they also said, 'What we are witness, starting with Comey's testimony, is the "4-D chess", that everyone elludes to, when describing this administration.'

'How do you know that Q really had the right language for 4chan?' say the Q Origins Project researchers. 'Because MegaAnon ... explicitly praises Q.'

Indeed, MegaAnon offers the Q Clearance Patriot the ultimate praise, writing on 5 November 2017: 'Brah is on point ... he's doing a fantastic job.'

The admission here, say the Q Origins Project researchers, is that Q's 'pro-style' is better for /pol/ than MegaAnon's, and 'You cannot get a better endorsement than the most prominent name in your field saying you are better at what she does than she herself is'.[46]

On 1 November, Q's pro-style lay not only in a rainbow of different tonalities but in promising 'Proof to begin 11.3'. There were seventeen Q posts over the course of that same day. Self-aggrandising claims made on 31 October about how these supposed revelations were the 'Biggest drop on Pol' and 'Biggest drop to ever be provided on Pol' were repeated: this was, said Q, again, the 'Biggest advanced drop on Pol' – just in case the noise of MegaAnon or HLI or any of the other LARPs was still competitive. By 2 November, the boast had ballooned to 'the biggest "inside" "approved" dump in American history'.

In these posts, Q resurrected the old, familiar frames of Pizzagate with some exuberance. 'The pedo networks are being dismantled,' Q assured. 'The child abductions for satanic rituals (ie Haiti and other 3rd world countries) are paused (not terminated until players in custody).' All followers had to do was wait until the plot-twisting arrests of 3 November.

Those who remained engaged with the threads in the meantime were told over the next two days of mysterious 'devices' planted in the White House that could 'actually cause harm to anyone in the room'. Other posts carried more rhetorical questions about oblique foreign relations. 'Follow Huma,' Q repeated, and suggested something politically labyrinthine was going on in North Korea. There were references to 'Donna running for cover'. These pertained to former Democratic National Committee chair Donna Brazile.

Brazile had been chair of the DNC for Al Gore's presidential campaign in 2000, the first African American woman to run a presidential campaign for a major party. In late July of 2016, she returned as an interim appointment to her old post after Debbie Wasserman Schultz had been made to step aside. A set of hacked WikiLeaks emails – like those that would later draw Pizzagate down on John Podesta

– indicated that Wasserman Schultz had shown favouritism towards Hillary Clinton over Clinton's internal rival for the Democratic nomination, Bernie Sanders, in the Democratic nomination process.

Since Gore's defeat, Donna Brazile had spent fifteen years as a commentator for news network CNN, but in October 2016, yet more hacked DNC emails released by WikiLeaks revealed that she'd shared CNN debate questions with the party to assist the Clinton campaign. This revelation came at the height of 2016's presidential contest. Brazile resigned from her CNN job.

A year later, Brazile was in the news again because she was releasing a tell-all book about the Clinton campaign. She'd been the subject of a *Breitbart* article just a few hours before Q was making posts about her – and the subject of twenty more *Breitbart* pieces within the course of the week.[47]

While Q's claims about impending arrests, 'pedo networks' and 'wizards' and 'warlocks' were fanciful, posts about Brazile and others showed Q was attuned to wider conversations being held within the right-wing discursive pipeline that Gamergate had strung together and Pizzagate had literally weaponised. There were also four stories in *Breitbart* that mentioned Huma Abedin in the month before Q appeared. One of these was published the day before Q's first 'Follow Huma' post.[48]

Even so, Q's was still a fringe conversation – arguably, just a LARP by one player, maybe more. It may have stayed mere conspiracy-flavoured infotainment for the exclusive enjoyment of 4chan's /pol/ community were it not for two rumoured 4chan moderators. Online, they were known by the names PamphletAnon and BaruchTheScribe. While Q's predictions for 3 November 2017 did not come to pass, their combined efforts ensured it would always remain one of the most powerful dates in Q's historical calendar.

... let us find truth – wherever it may lie. Whether it is convenient, or inconvenient. Whether it disappoints you, or fills you with hope. No matter which, it is the truth after all which will set us free.

@TracyBeanz on Twitter, 20 December 2017

When 3 November came, its hours passed without much delivery on Q's promise of excitement. Just as had happened with the non-arrest and non-indictment of Hillary Clinton four days earlier, no arrests or indictments against John Podesta took place. There were no riots, the military had not mobilised, the 'Emergency Broadcast System (EMS)' did not provide 'a direct message (avoiding the fake news) to all citizens', as Q had insisted it would, back on 1 November. On 3 November, Q's first post of the day led with 'Where is John Podesta?', asked some rhetorical questions about airport security and then declared 'Podesta's plane has military escort (i.e. tag) and is being diverted (forced down)'. Q had, however, added a get-out. Apparently, there was a 'Short delay'.

Podesta was nowhere near a 'forced down' plane on 3 or 4 November, but he'd still managed to make news. Trump had dog-whistled that very day to the right-wing trashing of Podesta's reputation in front of a gathered press pack as he prepared to leave on a tour of Asia. It was 'disappointing', Trump said, that his own Department of Justice was investigating his relationship with Russian influence. 'They should be looking at the Democrats,' Trump said. 'They should be looking at [John Podesta] and all of that dishonesty.'[49] On the preceding Monday of that week, the DOJ had recommended charges be brought against Trump's own former campaign manager, Paul Manafort.

In Australia, 3 November was already 4 November, and Podesta was being mentioned in local reports from the Australian Broadcasting Corporation detailing how Russian actors had managed to hack those DNC emails more than a year earlier and visit disaster on Hillary Clinton's campaign.[50] The hacking had been so complete, the report revealed, that Clinton's own personal telephone number had been publicly disclosed. The ABC reported that on 7 October 2016 – the day the Podesta hack was released by WikiLeaks – Clinton's phone was 'buzzing with crank messages' to the point where Huma Abedin had to 'call staffers one at a time with Mrs Clinton's new contact information because no one dared put it in an email'.

Q had existed for less than a week, spoke like a LARP and already none of its heavily amped, self-promoted predictions had come true. Then, sometime on 3 November, a woman who called herself @TracyBeanz released a video to YouTube with the title '/POL/- Q Clearance Anon – Is it #happening???'. 'I do not typically do videos like this,' she began. She explained that she was drawing attention to the

Q posts on 4chan 'just in case this stuff turns out to be legit because honestly, it kind of seems legit'.

@TracyBeanz was a small-time YouTuber who ran a channel with ten thousand subscribers. Her real name was Tracy Diaz. She'd campaigned for Republican Ron Paul's short-lived presidential run in 2012, and then for Trump in 2016. Her writings 'questioned' the established facts of the Sandy Hook massacre and 9/11, she was a Pizzagate advocate and she believed Amazon was owned by the CIA.

She was involved in a network of conspiracy theorists that included George Webb, the guy who on 14 June 2017 managed to shut down part of a seaport in Charleston, South Carolina by spreading an unfounded online rumour that a ship sailing into it was bearing a 'dirty bomb'.[51] The claim was investigated and found to be false by the US Coast Guard, and authorities sought out the source of the threat. Ohio-based Webb was questioned by the FBI the next day. Local police had found him drunk in his car.

Diaz had blogged that earlier in 2017 she had agreed to participate in an interview with two people who claimed to be documentary filmmakers.[52] It turned out they wanted to discuss Webb. Diaz did not take note of their names, she couldn't tell them where Webb got the information he peddled or who his contacts were. The interview concluded, and Diaz says her 'intuition told [her] there was a pretty good chance these people weren't documentary filmmakers'. In her bio, Tracy Diaz describes herself as an 'investigative journalist'.[53]

In 2018, NBC journalists Brandy Zadrozny and Ben Collins pieced together a trail of Diaz's blogs and videos and reported that the so-called 4chan moderators PamphletAnon and BaruchTheScribe had used her to bring Q to popular attention.[54]

BaruchTheScribe was a South African web programmer whose real name was Paul Furber. PamphletAnon's real name was James Coleman Rogers. The two NBC journalists found Rogers in Facebook posts. He self-identified as a Trump supporter and participant in the 'meme war' that the 4channers believed had led Trump to victory. On Facebook, Rogers recirculated memes that made Pizzagate claims – namely, that Democrats raped and murdered children. When the Q Clearance Patriot appeared on 4chan, Furber and Rogers saw a potential vehicle for promoting a particular world view.

'A bunch of us decided that the message needed to go wider,' Furber told NBC, so he and Rogers started identifying appropriate YouTubers to be their broadcasters.

It's unsurprising that Diaz was receptive. The pitch was that building a following for the Q Clearance Patriot's posts would bring bigger audiences to all of them. At the time, Diaz was recovering from a bankruptcy in 2009, juggling family and a job. She was relying on Patreon and PayPal donations promoted on her channels to fund the content she was making on them.

The 3 November video she made not only shared the contents of the Q posts but featured Diaz trying to decipher their references and explain their meanings. This was an approach she'd taken in earlier videos, where she'd dissect and discuss 'drops' from WikiLeaks. The 'Q drops' offered a combination of conspiracy thinking with a puzzle challenge for her audience of interpreting what the cryptic posts might mean. It proved more popular than anything else she'd ever done. This first video clocked up 250,000 views.

Diaz repeated the formula and her online following grew in all directions. She made dozens of Q-themed videos, all of them soliciting donations. NBC quoted her in one of them acknowledging that '[b]ecause I cover Q, I got an audience'.

Diaz's growing YouTube popularity wasn't the only value that she brought to the project of PamphletAnon and BaruchTheScribe to amplify Q. The 4chan moderators had originally wanted to direct the Diaz video-viewers back to 4chan to harvest their attention there. Diaz disagreed – directing her viewers to 4chan would involve having to teach them the complex protocols of imageboard communication and channer culture and might demobilise them. 'Instead,' she wrote on her blog, 'I recommended we start the CBTS Reddit board.'[55]

'CBTS' stood for the Trump quote 'calm before the storm' and it had already appeared in Q's posts. Diaz knew that Reddit's more user-friendly interfaces would be easily grasped by anyone who came to investigate more of the Q story. By January 2018, the subreddit r/CBTS_stream was created by Diaz, Furber and Rogers, who were also its original posters and moderators. In their article for NBC, Zadrozny and Collins recognised that the move to Reddit was a watershed moment for the incipient QAnon movement. There was already a conspiracist community established on the platform, and the r/CBTS_stream tapped into it, growing their audience as they drove discussion about each new Q post.

Subreddits and other forums incubate mini-ideologies. When the ideology has attracted a sufficient mass of pissed-off young people, it moves to Twitter and begins attacking journalists and politicians. *I'd like to read a research paper about this life cycle.*

@Noahpinion on Twitter, 6 March 2021

The pipeline that Diaz helped build for Q between 4chan and Reddit was an example of what a group of researchers from the University of Alabama, University College London, Cyprus University of Technology and Telefonica (a Spanish multinational communications company) described as a kind of 'web centipede' – a chain of influence – in an academic study back in 2017.[56] Their team had tracked millions of posts made by social media users to determine where the URLs (web addresses) of heavily shared 'news' links were first popularised.

What surprised the researchers was just how much 'fringe communities on Reddit and 4chan serve as an incubation chamber for a lot of information'. According to the paper's co-author, Jeremy Blackburn from the University of Alabama, 'Many online hoaxes, false or misleading stories have been traced back to users on these platforms ... The content and talking points are refined until they finally break free and make it to larger, more mainstream communities.'[57]

The researchers cited Pizzagate as an example of this happening. A pipeline could be traced from the hoax 'flourishing' on 4chan and Reddit to its spread into broader consciousness via Twitter. From there it could be spread to Facebook, Tumblr, Instagram or anywhere else.

They'd crunched enough data to prove what once had only been anecdotal: 4chan exerted a 'surprising level of influence' on the spread of information beyond its imageboards. 4chan's 'lax moderation' and zero barriers-to-entry gave disinformation stories enough of a platform to find an audience. If that audience saw an opportunity in a story to harm a preferred target, to influence political behaviour, to pursue a profit or to deliver enough 'lulz', they'd promote and share it, whether it was true or not.

On Reddit, wrote the researchers, subreddits functioned as 'tightly-knit' communities. If 4chan's disinformation penetrated these groups, it incubated. From here, it gained a collective weight of internal agreement before gaining a velocity that powered its spread to other subreddit communities and elsewhere.

If the disinformation then reached Twitter, it could propagate rapidly – not least because automated 'bot' accounts could be activated by vested interests to amplify it and give it the illusion of popular validation. Posting behaviour from bots, wrote the researchers, could influence the posting behaviour of the real users who existed beside them.

The 'web centipede' didn't just form an information pipeline. It operated as a conscious or unconscious influence operation. Everyone who engaged with its content was recruited into the dissemination of propaganda. Jeremy Blackburn summarised the research on Twitter in the language of memes. He illustrated an information transmission chain from 4chan through Facebook to Fox News using an image from the body-horror movie *Human Centipede*.[58]

Tracy Diaz made videos on YouTube about the 'Q' she'd seen on 4chan, and she spread that content to Reddit. As it turned out, she didn't just bring a Reddit audience to the Q story. She also brought four thousand Russian-operated Twitter accounts.

> Russia, Russia, Russia! That's all you heard at
> the beginning of this Witch Hunt Hoax ... And now
> Russia has disappeared because I had nothing to do
> with Russia helping me to get elected.
>
> @realDonaldTrump on Twitter, 30 May 2019

According to *The Washington Post*, the word 'disinformation' came into popular English use in the 1980s and derived from a Russian word, *dezinformatsiya*.[59] The 1952 edition of *The Great Soviet Encyclopedia* described this as 'dissemination (in the press, on the radio, etc.) of false reports intended to mislead public opinion'. Apocryphal stories claim that the word describing the practice was invented by Joseph Stalin himself.

By the time Tracy Diaz had started bringing Q to the broader public in 2017, knowledge of recent Russian disinformation activities in the United States was finally widespread. Media sources had reported since 14 June 2016 that Russian hackers had been behind the attack on the computers at the DNC.[60] On 22 September 2016, Democratic congressional representatives Adam Schiff and Nancy Pelosi had issued a joint statement revealing that briefings to Congress by intelligence services confirmed a Russian plan to interfere with the 2016 elections was well underway.[61]

Russia publicly denied the accusations, but American security agencies confirmed on 7 October 2016 that the hacks that had thrown the Democratic campaign into such chaos had been directed by the Russian government. After Trump's victory, *The Washington Post* reported on 9 December 2016 that the CIA had concluded the point of Russia's disinformation activities was to 'boost Trump and hurt Clinton'.[62]

On the day of the first Tracy Diaz Q video, Special Counsel Robert Mueller was still leading a public Department of Justice investigation into Russian influence operations in America. The attempt was to establish the level of Russia's direct involvement with the Trump campaign. When Mueller's investigations concluded in April 2019, he'd identified that to 'provoke and amplify political and social discord in the United States', Russian operatives had run a complex propaganda campaign through a social media 'troll farm'.[63]

The so-called troll farm was Russia's Internet Research Agency (IRA), an organisation based in St Petersburg and funded by 'an oligarch with ties to Russian President Vladimir Putin'. Reports about Mueller's findings in *The Washington Post* explained that IRA operatives set up fake accounts and established front groups across a diversity of internet platforms. Tasked with attracting followers to polarising and divisive positions to build political mistrust and sow chaos, the troll farmers 'churned out' online disinformation that seized upon existing political fractures within American society.[64]

Mueller would not make his detailed, itemised pronouncement that 'the Russian government interfered in the 2016 presidential election in sweeping and systematic fashion' until 2019.[65] The presence of Russian influence operations in the 2016 US presidential elections had become established fact by 2017, but details of its continuing activities were not completely known. It took researchers from Reuters until 2020 to analyse enough granular data to discover that since-banned Russian-backed accounts on Twitter had been pushing @TracyBeanz's Q promotion from the start.[66]

These researchers found that #QAnon was 'the single most frequent hashtag tweeted by accounts that Twitter has since identified as Russian-backed', and this began in November 2017. There were four thousand of these accounts and they repeated the word QAnon itself 17,000 times. Reuters noted that the first mention of QAnon on Twitter was from an account called @CrusadersPost, and it was made as early as 2 November.

@CrusadersPost was an account that shared content from 'obscure Russian officials'. The Reuters researchers discovered it had first contacted Tracy Diaz in April 2017, months before Q had appeared. Back then, Reuters said, the account subsequently encouraged Diaz to promote content from MegaAnon, the LARP account that had preceded Q on 4chan. The same month, @CrusadersPost had tweeted birthday greetings to Tracy Diaz, and offered to help her out on 'a new project'.

'YOU ROCK,' Diaz replied.

Russian information operations of 2016 were certainly a coordinated campaign to swing the election to Trump. Trump won, yet the disinformation campaigns continued. Why? Because what Trump represented to the Russians was not an end point to their political interference but a symbol of its reach. The ongoing goal was to discredit and undermine Western democracy. Trump was but one of many Russian vehicles to do just that.

QAnon was another. Disinformation scholar Nina Jankowicz from America's Wilson Center says, 'Just as in 2016, when the Kremlin seized on narratives that furthered American political polarisation – such as the Black Lives Matter movement or gun rights – QAnon was a perfect movement through which Russia could continue to divide America, and all the other countries where Q spread.'[67]

The campaign objectives are broader than just to spread chaos. 'Division keeps Russia's adversaries distracted, and concerned with their own domestic affairs,' says Jankowicz. 'Meanwhile, Russia continues its foreign adventurism – supporting Assad, for instance, or building up troops and fomenting war in occupied Ukraine.

'It also serves Putin's whataboutist narratives at home,' she says. 'When Western democracy is failing, Putin can point to this and say to Russian protestors and activists, "Is this what you want?"'

Less than a week before Q's first post appeared on 4chan, @TracyBeanz published a blog post. In it she described a 'longing for truth' in the face of corrupt, malfeasant government. She spoke of a determination to 'weed out' lies told by a power structure that was inauthentic and obscure. Any reluctance to confront this authoritarianism was something she described as a 'hood' that people 'had worn over their eyes' and was blinding them.[68]

There certainly was a corrupt and malfeasant authoritarian government that was blinding people to its aims, but it was Vladimir Putin's Russian Federation. Tracy Diaz believed she was 'changing history' with the work she was doing. She was, but she was doing it as an unwitting agent of a malicious foreign power that sent her birthday greetings even as it recruited her into a disinformation pipeline.

Or did Tracy Diaz know better? 'After her first Q video on Nov. 3,' Reuters reported, 'the number of Russian tweets pushing Diaz' handle surged to 40 monthly through the following spring.' The more Q content she uploaded to YouTube, the more the Russian operatives online promoted her. By the time of the Reuters report in 2020, @TracyBeanz had gone from ten thousand YouTube views to ten million. Along the way, Reuters said, she was 'amassing undisclosed donors' on her sites. Tracy Diaz had built enough of an income stream through her YouTube channel that it became her full-time job.

You will see her begging for money on Patreon as she says it is for 'research', but it's just her browsing 4chan and taking gullible idiots money over a LARP that she knows is a straight up troll. Sorry sad bastards, real anons will kill this shit now.

Anonymous on 4chan, 21 November 2017

The amplification provided to the Q posts thanks to Tracy Diaz, BaruchTheScribe, PamphletAnon and four thousand Russian-backed Twitter accounts enabled their creep far beyond the self-referential and ironic 4chan LARPer space where they'd originated. Mediated through YouTube, then Reddit, then Twitter, the legs of the 'web centipede' of Q content then extended into Facebook. There was a collection of statistics that made this extension a significant concern.

Firstly, as 2017 became 2018, the user demographics of Facebook were in the process of shifting from a young person's platform to one hosting older users.[69] That year, users over fifty-five became the second-largest demographic group on the platform. Later-life Facebook adoptees were restocking a user base that the youthful twelve to twenty-four age groups were leaving. Research had established that social media use had many appeals for older people, not least of which were improved social connectivity and overcoming loneliness and isolation.[70] A 2015 study had already suggested that people born between 1946 and 1964 were spending more time online than even the digital natives of the millennial generation.[71]

Of concern were statistics borne out in later research from a study by NYU and Princeton in 2019.[72] Analysing the sharing patterns of Facebook users in the 2016 election, these researchers discovered that users over sixty-five 'shared nearly seven times as many articles from fake news domains as those aged between 18 and 29'.

What made the Q posts even more dangerous in this context was that they'd existed online for months before receiving due scrutiny from either the mainstream press or other institutional overseers. Michael Golebiewski and danah boyd, researchers for Microsoft, coined the term 'data void' to describe this phenomenon and consider its dark online implications in a 2018 paper for *Data & Society*.[73] Golebiewski and boyd explained that if a Google search was unable to deliver credible sources on a certain subject, the algorithm would simply deliver whatever it could find. This mechanism was ripe for manipulation by internet-based operatives who could push otherwise little-mentioned terms in niche corners of the internet and build search-engine heft behind them. In this way, fake news content or propaganda could gain 'hidden virality' before the platforms, media or other institutional authorities even knew it was there to do something about. Journalist Matt Binder applied the point in a 2018 article for *Mashable* that in those months when Q was posting in a data void, even people attempting some basic verifications of Q's claims were led by Google searches towards conspiracy websites, blogs and other unreliable or bad-faith sources.[74]

A bleak warning came from technology academic Brian Friedberg in a piece about this for *Wired* in 2020: the longer infectiously bad ideas go undebunked, the greater their spread and the greater their purchase.[75] Meanwhile, the NYU/ Princeton researchers had found that the expanding cohort of internet users in their sixties lacked 'the level of digital media literacy necessary to reliably determine the trustworthiness of news encountered online'. The simple effect of ageing on memory was a compounding factor. 'Memory deteriorates with age in a way that particularly undermines resistance to "illusions of truth",' the researchers said.

The risk of manipulation was clear. Even without the effects of age or inexperience, 'social endorsements' of content made by people who Facebook users personally trust serve as powerful 'credibility cues' to reinforce false information. This phenomenon of familiarity leads people to believe what they are told by known contacts over information supplied by experts at a distance to them. The devilishness of Facebook is that it allows strangers to take on the guise of familiarity with a minimal exchange of verifiable information. Online relationships form without the care and scrutiny to which they're subjected offline. Older people with low digital literacy were uniquely vulnerable to the corrupting form of influence from new, unmet Facebook 'friends'.

The third relevant phenomenon was how Facebook's algorithms started recommending QAnon content to people who weren't even searching for it. Researching pro-Trump, anti-vaccine and anti-lockdown groups on Facebook was all it took for a *Guardian* reporter to have QAnon content suggested by the platform's algorithms. A few simple keyword searches from that point guided the reporter to hundreds of QAnon Facebook groups and accounts.

This experience was related in a major investigative feature about QAnon's digital footprint by *The Guardian*'s Julia Carrie Wong, who found the other reporter's experience was not unusual. Brian Friedberg confirmed to *The Guardian* that after liking and joining a couple of these groups, Facebook fed him more and more suggestions of the same. 'I really do not think that QAnon as we know it today would have been able to happen without the affordances of Facebook,' he said. Wong's investigation had discovered 'documented pages, groups and accounts' on Facebook associated with QAnon numbered 'more than 3m aggregate followers and members'.[76]

Even allowing for the likelihood of overlap among groups and accounts, the figures bore out the predictions that Brandy Zadrozny and Ben Collins – the NBC journalists who charted the rise of Tracy Diaz – had made back in 2018. They noted that QAnon content was migrating from 4chan to Reddit and YouTube, and then to Facebook, where dozens of public and private groups provided it with a new, receptive audience. Again, the information incubated within these forums was refined and repackaged and shared. 'Meanwhile,' they wrote, 'Diaz kept making videos, racking up hundreds of thousands of views.'[77]

Back on 4chan, Q kept posting, dropping biblical quotes, conspiracy tropes, pop culture references, rhetorical questions and appeals to the familiar symbols of American patriotism amid the 'crumbs'. They were now signing off messages as 'Q', rather than 'Q Clearance Patriot' or the more oblique 'Alice & Wonderland' as they had before. This last was a phrase repeated at least twenty times, sometimes around veiled hints that referred to Hillary Clinton and a mysterious connection to Saudi Arabia, although others believed that former president Barack Obama was Alice because he'd once thrown an *Alice in Wonderland* themed party. On 4 November, Q also posted a visual meme, reading 'The strongest weapon in the United States is a patriotic American' in front of a US flag.

The posts were also nodding to the known bugbears of the online right. A post on 6 November had the tone of the right-wing Gamergaters who complained about the women-led *Ghostbusters* reboot:

> *Why are most forms of media left-wing?*
> *Why is H-wood left-wing?*
> *Why is the narrative so important?*
> *Why do liberals defer to racism w/o proof?*
> *No proof.*

Some posts were barely more than lists of words, arranged as if in urgency, reading like a minimalist poem. On 5 November, a post included:

> *Old.*
> *Connection.*
> *News.*
> *Bad actor.*
> *London Mayor.*
> *Background?*
> *Affiliation?*
> *Connection to Queen?*
> *British MI6 agents dead.*
> *When?*
> *How?*

It was gobbledegook but written in the style of coded messages shared by undercover agents in spy movies. A river of posts saturated with acronyms for American intelligence agencies gave it all the air of insider knowledge, writing for people who were already *au fait* with the terms. Between August and September 2018, the Q posts even used the term 'Red October' to refer to hopes of a Republican landslide in the upcoming US midterm elections. *The Hunt for Red October* is, of course, another spy novel, a bestselling one, written by Tom Clancy.

Following the posts was fun in the way an old action movie like *Jaws* was fun. You could be thrilled by the story as long as you didn't look at the monster too closely.

If you did, however, fact-check Q's claim that, for example, the Reserve Bank of Australia was one of a list of 'ROTHSCHILD OWNED & CONTROLLED BANKS' (11 November 2017), you'd discover that the bank was under 100 per cent state ownership and always had been. There was no actual monster, just a prop department and a mechanical shark.

is this just someother wanna be cicada 3301 fags or is it legit

Anonymous on 4chan, 11 July 2021

With exhortations to readers to 'follow', 'paint the picture', 'keep digging' and 'get organized', Q was inviting readers to participate in a fantasy adventure of downed planes and mass arrests, secret wars and pursuit of the seemingly indefatigable supervillain, Hillary Clinton. 'Crumbs will make bread,' Q promised on 6 November, and that 'bread' was a coherent plot that readers had to piece together from the posts with their own personal leaps of imagination.

Q had already framed the solve-it-yourself puzzles with appeals to in-group elitism back on 4 November. 'Remember,' Q said, 'information is everything, the flow of information is no longer controlled by the MSM [mainstream media] but by you/others.' It was an irresistible proposition to those whose mistrust of mainstream media had led them into the audience of self-appointed YouTube 'journalists' like Tracy Diaz.

Even in those earliest days, the Q posts could be described as a game of clues and interpretation. Such games had been infamously played through 4chan before. In 2012, a mysterious decryption puzzle had been posted to the platform posing a friendly challenge. 'Hello,' ran a message that offered the image of a cicada to decode. 'We are looking for highly intelligent individuals. To find them, we have devised a test.' It was signed '3301'. The puzzle architects of what became known as 'Cicada 3301' buried clues within clues in a challenge that led players through the pages of obscure William Gibson novels to translating Welsh poetry to QR codes attached to lampposts across five different nations, from Poland to Australia. The identity of the puzzle makers was never revealed, and the clues evaporated at a certain point. It captivated the imagination of those who encountered it, with suggestions that it may have been a recruitment tool for a specialist spy agency, or a secret society of cryptographers, as opposed to, perhaps, an international friendship group of widely read CompSci PhD students amusing themselves online with some digital *D&D*.

Cicada 3301 was too specialised and difficult for just anyone to play. Alternatively, as QAnon developed, it enticed and tantalised players with references that were familiar, flattering to their powers of deduction and politically affirming. With its rhetorical questions and codewords, its similarity to a clue-based game was noticed by professional game makers such as Reed Berkowitz.

Berkowitz's 2020 *Medium* essay, 'A game designer's analysis of QAnon', is one of the best structural analyses of QAnon's appeal there is. Berkowitz specialised as a maker and researcher in the niche fields of experience fiction, interactive theatre, alternative reality games (ARGs) and live games for educational purposes, building 'games designed to be played in reality'. Yes, he built LARPs.[78]

What Berkowitz identified in Q was something of a 'dark mirror' that inverted how a game is supposed to work. Games like Cicada 3301 are designed to follow a preordained plot, and players traverse an emotional journey through it as they engage and solve accumulating puzzles. The bane of the game designer, Berkowitz explains, is the psychological phenomenon of 'apophenia', which describes a tendency to read connections or meaningful patterns into things that in reality are unconnected and random.

In a traditional game, when players start to insist that patterns exist between unrelated things, they wander away from the game plot, the action doesn't progress and the real puzzle remains unsolved. In the video game *Ghost of Tsushima*, for example, the wandering samurai player-character is at one point tasked to find their way up to a mountain shrine by swinging from tree branches across a gorge. If the player fails to notice the tree branches, apophenia may encourage them to believe that a ridge of rocks are the path because they follow a path-like line. The game isn't designed for the rocks to be scaled, and in any attempt to do this, the samurai will fall and die. Although the game resurrects the player, if they persist in their belief the rocks are the path they will never reach the shrine. The plot will never move forward. The samurai will just keep falling into the gorge.

Berkowitz suggests in his essay that Q's endlessly unanswered rhetorical questions, unexplained clues and open-ended propositions functioned within its 'dark mirror' to keep the samurai forever stuck in the gorge.

Instead of answers or solutions, Berkowitz described Q's posts as a process of 'guided apophenia'. He used as an example a suggestion from Q in an early post on 21 November 2017: 'Their need for symbolism will be their downfall. Follow the Owl & Y head around the world'. The recommendation was rooted in an unquestioned insistence that the supposed child-murdering elites compulsively signified to one another their membership of this cabal. Those following the Q posts rapidly supplied a composite image of celebrities making what could be argued was an 'owl' symbol, creating masks for their eyes with their fingers.

In this way, a series of unrelated images of people making an almost mindlessly common hand gesture became a type of 'proof' for those enmeshed in Q's stories of symbolism and satanic association that the legendary cabal existed. The same went for the red shoes that provoked conspiracists to denounce Australia's former foreign minister Julie Bishop as a murderous paedophile.[79] 'Find the match. "Red shoes",' Q had exhorted on 15 August 2018, bringing Bishop under this unfounded scrutiny.

Red shoes, of course, are hardly unusual. There has been a 'red shoe trend' reported in the fashion press every year for at least the past decade.

Berkowitz observed that the community of self-described 'anons' growing around the Q posts as the months passed were repeatedly encouraged into wildly misinterpreting the random data presented to them. Q's believers may not have seen an agenda operating in the posts, but Berkowitz did; Q pointed at random events, and those playing along imposed connections between them through sheer force of ideological will. The point, Berkowitz said, was that whatever interpretative conclusion was reached by these people, it would always end up reinforcing the propaganda message Q was pushing.

Whether Q was actually an ideological mastermind – or group of them – directing a complex disinformation campaign, or the sophisticated influence operation of a hostile foreign government, or just a channer whose LARP had spun wildly out of control didn't matter. The intent of Russian influence operations in these online spaces was always to encourage political and social discord in targeted countries and communities; the Russian operations had amplified Q because Q was doing that work for them. Q's posts encouraged followers to mistrust some of the most powerful sources of truth and icons of freedom in Western society. Q drops created villains of democratic government, a free media and individual Western cultural leaders, from pop stars to the pope.

And Q made villainising fun. In April 2020, Adrian Hon, another designer of alternate reality games, was quoted by both *Los Angeles Magazine* and *Wired* explaining Q's entertainment appeal. 'QAnon is popular partly because the act of "researching" through obscure forums and videos and blog posts, though more time-consuming than watching TV, is actually more enjoyable because it's an active process,' Hon said.[80] *Wired* made the connection that the game that QAnon got people to play worked so well online because it was 'the quintessence' of internet culture. 'The web has always been about making willy-nilly connections,' wrote *Wired*'s Clive Thompson. 'This links to that which links to this.'[81]

QAnon also worked as sophisticated persuasion because it recruited the player/reader/'anon' into actively persuading themselves. Within the 'anon' community that was forming around the 'Q drops' and their interpretations, the shared illusion of solving Q's unsolvable riddles delivered self-satisfaction, camaraderie and peer group approval, even as it entrenched demonisations of people and institutions that were based entirely on lies. Those connecting unconnected dots, wrote Reed Berkowitz, convinced themselves their conclusions had been reasoned out through pure logic. There's a hit of dopamine – the brain's reward chemical – that comes whenever people solve puzzles or gain knowledge through their own efforts, he explained. Feeling this sense of reward motivates people to seek out more puzzles to solve.[82]

It's what made the 'Q drops' as dangerous as they were addictive.

Don't take this as an attack, but how did you grow
your audience Tracy? Mostly thru Qanon right?
When exactly did you know it was a LARP? Why
didn't you tell your followers the truth? You were
contacted by the same people that contacted
Defango, so you knew.

four20, comment on Steemit, 2018

According to NBC, within weeks of starting the r/CBTS_ stream Reddit board, Tracy Diaz and her comrades were soon spending 'all their waking hours in chat rooms on the gaming-focused forum Discord analyzing and decoding Q messages'.[83] She and the two former 4chan moderators had collected tens of thousands more followers on their various platform channels. By March 2018, the Reddit board had 20,000 subscribers.

Then it was banned by Reddit. Q's urgent, life-and-death, end-times rhetoric had been absorbed with some intensity by the growing online community of people who called themselves 'anons'. Reddit administrators identified that the QAnon community in the subreddit r/CBTS_stream were inciting violence as well as harassing and doxxing perceived enemies.

Yet such was the growing popularity of Q that the traffic just relocated to a new subreddit called r/TheGreatAwakening.

By September 2018, numbers had swelled; there were 70,000 people congregating there, sharing stories of satanic child snatching, government conspiracy and Hillary Clinton's endless misdeeds. This subreddit was also soon banned for encouraging violence. *The Atlantic* reported there had been death threats against Hillary Clinton.[84] The community had also doxxed a man from Minnesota they had misidentified as a mass shooter.[85] Despite a #DiscreditReddit campaign run on Twitter to protest the bans, by September 2020 Reddit proceeded to ban a further seventeen QAnon subreddit communities.

Paul Furber, the 4chan moderator and South African web programmer, had been kicked from r/CBTS_stream before the banning even happened, deemed as threatening to another user. When Diaz, Rogers and the other moderators were also booted from the Reddit site, they sought other platforms through which to promote their profit-making Q material.

Through the r/CBTS_stream board they'd made contact with Jerome Corsi, an established conspiracy theorist who'd become an editor for Alex Jones's *Infowars* website. Corsi was the author of a bestselling book called *Where's the Birth Certificate?* It promoted the conspiracy theory that Barack Obama was not born in the United States and therefore was not eligible to be president. It was published, unedited, three weeks after Obama had released his birth certificate and proved beyond doubt his place of birth was the USA.

The NBC journalists had closely charted the Corsi connection to the new-generation conspiracists. Although he later walked back his involvement in Q's growing online community, Corsi joined efforts at message-decoding within the r/CBTS_stream subreddit very early. As soon as December 2017, Rogers and Furber were guests on *Infowars*. After the originating group was purged from Reddit, Rogers and his wife, Christina Urso, leveraged Rogers' budding conspiracist profile to begin a YouTube presence named *Patriots' Soapbox*.

NBC described it as a 'broadcast of a Discord chatroom with constant audio commentary from a rotating cast of volunteers and moderators', and it was a 24-hour live stream of these people posing Q's riddles and trying to work through clues from the posts. With 46,000 subscribers, Rogers and Urso advertised their preparedness to take donations through PayPal, cryptocurrencies or mail.

Emerging here was a phenomenon concurrent to that of Q, something that commentator and tech consultant Benjamin T. Decker called the 'conspiracy entrepreneur'.[86] Although Diaz and Rogers had started to attract criticism within their original forums for profiteering from their projects, Q's following still grew and attracted others to join the cottage industry they had started. New Q-themed podcasts, vlogs, chatrooms and other products appeared across platforms, aggressively harvesting donations.

Journalist Adrienne LaFrance was interviewed by NPR radio in 2020 and described an entire economy of people trying to make money from QAnon whom she'd encountered while writing an investigative feature titled 'The prophecies of Q' for *The Atlantic*. She wrote of Etsy stores where people hawked Q-themed jewellery, bumper stickers, t-shirts – indeed, anything at all with the letter Q on it.[87] Writing for *The Daily Beast* in 2018, reporter Kelly Weill had also seen this commercial opportunism on the Pinterest website. More popularly known for hosting fan art, recipes and inspiration boards for home renovations, the Pinterest page of a San Francisco jeweller Weill had found retailed Q-themed earrings next to 'best dad in the galaxy' money clips.[88]

LaFrance observed that a whole community of Q influencers had an investment in the QAnon theory that wasn't merely about spreading its ideas: the economy around the conspiracy was as important to these people as the conspiracy itself. Their motivation to promote Q was obvious.

As these Q industries matured rapidly around the platforms, the poster behind Q had also made a new platform decision. On 25 November 2017, the 230th post that was attributed to the internet's new prophet appeared not on 4chan but on Fredrick Brennan's old imageboard, 8kun.

It appeared with a 'tripcode', a kind of internet ID generated to preserve anonymity while still identifying posts as being from the same author. It read:

Test

Test

4Chan infiltrated.

Future posts will be relayed here.

Q

Hotwheels doesn't own it anymore. some ex Marine
or something owns it now.

Anonymous on 4chan, 30 December 2018

Despite the influx of users that had come to his site during Gamergate, Fredrick Brennan's capacity to maintain 8kun had been limited for some time. The site had struggled with bandwidth limits, it kept getting kicked off hosts for its offensive content and it failed to make money. Then, one day, Brennan received an email from a stranger who offered both his site a new host and himself a curious business opportunity.

The email had come from Jim Watkins. He and his son, Ron, were an American expat father-and-son team based in the Philippines, and they approached Brennan with a scheme to ensure 8kun's future.

Jim was ex-army. He had begun his internet career running a porn website called Asian Bikini Bar. He had what *Wired* described as a 'web' of business interests, including in tech and property development.[89] He also owned an organic food company and apparently a pig farm on the outskirts of Manila. In 2014, Jim proposed to rescue 8kun if Brennan moved to Manila to work for him and live in a condominium that he owned. Brennan took the job. Soon enough, he sold 8kun to Jim Watkins, but Brennan continued as the site's administrator.

Watkins tried to monetise 8kun's reputation for notoriety. His schemes included selling an 8kun cryptocurrency that users could buy to send their threads to the top of the site. He launched a shambolic news service called *Goldwater* under the tagline 'Banned, biased, honest' that Watkins himself hosted, and he began a company that recorded audiobooks.[90] Watkins had also bought the old 2channel website, the Japanese one that had spawned 2chan/Futaba and inspired Christopher 'moot' Poole to build 4chan.

While Watkins pursued these projects, Fredrick Brennan watched bemused from late 2017 onwards as the growing audiences for the Q posts started to seek them out at their new home on 8kun. Diaz, Rogers and Furber organised a presence here too. The redditors and Facebook users were coming to 8kun to read Q's 'drops' at their source. These people were conspicuously unfamiliar with the protocols of imageboard culture, but they were desperate to engage. 'We joked about it for years,' Brennan posted on Twitter, 'but #Qanon is making it a reality: Boomers! On your imageboard!'[91]

But was it even Q who the Facebook boomers had followed into the internet badlands of 8kun? When Q relocated to the new imageboard, rumours circulated that Q's identity had been stolen, and that the posts had been hijacked. The rumours that Q's incarnation on 8kun was Ron or Jim Watkins or both of them began and have endured for years.

Committed 'anons', typically, did not care about the identity of the Q Clearance Patriot. NBC had once quoted a tweet by a devotee around the time that Coleman Rogers was suspected of being the mysterious Q. 'NO ONE cares who Q is,' roared the tweet. 'WE care about the TRUTH.'[92]

Besides, as early as 29 October 2017 – within only a day of Q's first post – suggestions had already begun that Q's original poster had been replaced by an impostor.

To assume that Q's predictions were welcomed on 4chan with the credulity that they later found elsewhere would be a mistake. The /pol/ board was a village of nihilists and cynics who told themselves wild stories for fun, and the stories had to be good to get the crowd's encouragement to continue.

4chan LARPing was an anarchic competition, but it still had losers. In the hour or so after the first two Q posts, within the same conversation, a channer was aggressively posting with the desperation of someone ignored: 'Hillary's arrest is only the beginning … the election anniversary to be wild …' Their frustration at a lack of engagement was palpable: 'I'm telling you guys,' they whined, 'Hillary is getting arrested, and no one believes me just like the media do not.'

Another channer responded in the manner more typical of the forum: 'youre a dumb piece of shit making up nonsense,' they shot back, 'i hate hillary but she is never going to jail.'

Under no circumstances would a god fearing christian would be a part of pedo club. This in fact the jews fault. The jews made them do it. Yeah its tha jews.

Anonymous on 4chan, 3 July 2021

5. THE GREAT AWAKENING

The visibly ballooning influence of Q and the suite of QAnon conspiracy theories posed a series of terrible, real-time questions to Western political modernity. Some of these had been answered in ages past, and in the most terrible of ways.

What happened if you married an adaptable set of paranoid conspiracy theories to an insecure population experiencing a period of tremendous social change? What if the most extreme and violent accusations imaginable were levelled at targets in the language of a holy and patriotic war that promised to make heroes of its warriors? What if these accusations were grounded in thousands of years of cultural messages that promoted dehumanisation and hate? What if it all cloaked itself in pious symbolism, and seized at powerful religious pretexts for its actions?

Technological change had added new, disturbing questions to this dire list. What if those conspiracist ideas could replicate as fast as they were generated through a global information pipeline? What if technology had fractured the very notion of a shared majority truth? What if political actors – foreign adversaries, ambitious ideologues, media grifters, populist demagogues – had an interest in maintaining that fracture? What if their own profit came from chaos? What would happen?

QAnon answered that question.

So is anyone concerned with the public perception of Q followers if normies start saying we're all nazi Jew haters?? I mean there are some serious red pills here, and some newcomers might get scared off. I'm ready for the Zionists to be exposed and this cabal driven from the Earth. I hope the world is!

Unknown commenter on Voat, via u/Owen_Meany on Reddit, 23 September 2018

The attraction of Q's obscurantist prophecies was that the story Q was telling was participatory. The scroll of hints, allusions and rhetorical questions that unrolled post by post invited readers to break codes, make connections and assemble the coherency of Q's narrative for themselves.

A community formed of people who devoted themselves to translating Q's cryptic posts and ascribing a meaning to them. They called themselves 'bakers'.[1] This was a pun on Q's references to 'crumbs, just crumbs', which meant the clues that appeared in the posts. Q even thanked them by this name in posts. 'We thank you for your service, Bakers,' Q said on 21 February 2019.

The bakers gathered in groups on various social media platforms. They 'researched' the meaning of each 'crumb' together, excitedly anticipating the next drop's appearance. Their first task was to determine what each acronym used by Q was meant to spell out, and what the various appearances of numbers or letters or punctuation marks in the posts might signify. Were they coordinates? Dates? Passages of the Bible? Q presented pop cultural references to decode, named characters to identify, quotes to attribute and symbols to locate in a historical context. 'Everything has meaning,' Q insisted as early as 4 November 2017, repeating the suggestion across seventeen subsequent posts. This directive drove the bakers to wild conclusions about what the oblique, endlessly unexplained utterances may mean – they called these assemblages 'dough' or 'bread'. Making connections between unconnected things was not an individual miscalculation here: it was a collectively encouraged apophenia.

In his essay about QAnon as the dark mirror of gaming, game designer Reed Berkowitz called the accumulation of accepted meaning among the baker communities a 'Darwinian fiction lab'.[2] Platforms like Reddit allowed audiences to 'upvote' content to the coveted most-read spot at the top of the page. Facebook's algorithms did something similar, marking the most liked, most engaged-with posts as the most 'relevant' and therefore most attention-grabbing within its own internal communities. When it came to translating

Q's posts, wrote Berkowitz, what happened in these groups was that the 'correct' answer was the one weighted as most popular.

Berkowitz found it ingenious, comparing it to artificial intelligence powered by groupthink: what the group found the most entertaining or gripping explanation of a crumb was the one that got accepted and then amplified. Such explanations were then called a 'proof' by the bakers. It was likely a deliberate pun; in culinary baking, 'proofing' is the term for a fermenting lump of dough's final rise before it goes into an oven and becomes bread.

Fed by Q's posts, the story – fermented among the bakers before being shared outward in its final form – was every bit as dramatic as the urgent tone of Q's spy-style communiqués. This was unsurprising; many of the references Q wove into the posts came from sources of literary fiction, film and TV, as well as from a library of established conspiracy theories that had floated around the internet for years. Q appeared to be something of a Tom Clancy fan. The spy-thriller author's 1991 book title *The Sum of all Fears* was a phrase repeated in eight of Q's drops. The title of Clancy's 1989 novel, *Clear and Present Danger*, appeared as a phrase eight times. *The Hunt for Red October* (1984) had twenty-six mentions. There were six mentions of spy-thriller author Robert Ludlum's most famous character, Jason Bourne. But Q wasn't afraid to engage other genres. References to movies including action thriller *Iron Eagle* (1986), *Godfather III* (1990), *The Matrix* (1999), *Speed* (1994) and *Snow White and the Seven Dwarfs* (1937) nestled alongside the hoary tropes of conspiracy favourites from 'black ops' to JFK and the Vatican Bank.

The conclusions that the bakers reached did, of course, flow back to Q in the dynamic replies that followed each 4chan or 8kun post. Whoever was operating the Q account could engage and develop whichever of the ideas had most use to the Q project. It was targeted market research, in real time.

Q certainly knew how to engage that market. The poster offered congratulations to the 'anons' for the conclusions they supplied. It was a powerful source of encouragement, reward and vindication for these people to find their 'research' cited in a drop by a watching Q. What an honour it must've been for Tim Stewart, occasional houseguest of Australian Prime Minister Scott Morrison, when one of his @BurnedSpy34 Twitter threads attacking John Podesta was dropped online by the great Q, direct.

Q's repeated encouragement to readers was essentially intended to develop and support the creation of a community that wouldn't challenge the veracity of the stories Q was telling them. The mainstream media, Q insisted, could not be trusted; it was in the evil service of Pizzagate's devious, satan-worshipping and deadly cabal of elites: 'THEY USE THE MEDIA,' howled Q on 30 June 2018. 'THEY USE HOLLYWOOD. THEY USE POLITICAL LEADERS. THEY ARE LOUD.' It was significant that Q declared that these elites included political leaders from all parties, and all nations: Q's positioning as somehow bipartisan allowed followers to convince themselves the posts were objective and independent.[3]

The narrative established that the participants of the evil cabal shared a lust for power, wealth and enduring beauty that transcended illusions of partisan difference. In the hands of the bakers, this central premise was moulded around Q's statements to furnish a comprehensive mythos, although the details were subject to variation.

Its central story was that the elites ran a complex international operation of mass child abduction to serve the harvesting of a highly addictive substance called adrenochrome. (Adrenochrome is a real chemical compound; it presents in the human body as a result of the oxidation of the stress hormone adrenaline.) The insistence was that members of the paedophile elite raped and tortured children not only to indulge a depraved carnality, not only to honour their dark lord Satan, but also to provoke the release of adrenochrome from the children's terrified, traumatised, mutilated bodies. 'Children are being kidnapped, tortured, raped, and sacrificed in the name of PURE EVIL,' wrote Q on 28 August 2018. Once the children were milked for adrenochrome, the leaders and celebrities ingested it.

Q never directly mentioned adrenochrome, but the baker community borrowed it from prevailing internet folk-myths to explain how celebrities from the Hollywood Q despised – people like Tom Hanks, Oprah Winfrey and Chrissy Teigen – unnaturally retained their good looks and power. To accuse such well-known, familiar names of venal brutality didn't merely shock. It jarred. It destabilised.

> she flayed the girl face off but the girl still was
> alive, and then she put the girl face on and was like,
> you know, talking to the girl with the girl face, and
> then they say Hillary Clinton cut#... cut her stomach
> open and pull our intestines out while the girl was
> still alive. And then they put a tube up her nose and
> drunk her fucking brain out of her nose.
>
> **Young Pharaoh on Instagram, 24 May 2020**

Not only were the elites accused of killing children but they were also accused of eating them. An amazing offshoot conspiracy theory emerged in April 2018 that proposed the existence of a video named *Frazzledrip* depicting a cannibalistic crime. Rumours spread on Facebook, Twitter and 4chan claiming the video had been found saved under the filename 'Frazzledrip' on Anthony Weiner's seized laptop, tucked in a folder labelled 'life insurance'. Posters claimed that in the video, Hillary Clinton and Huma Abedin had recorded themselves raping and sacrificing a young girl in a satanic ritual that culminated in them filleting the girl's face from her head and wearing her skin as a mask. Various social media accounts claimed they'd seen it – on the dark web, on fringe websites, on YouTube – before it had been taken down. Mostly, people quoted other people who had seen it. A blurry, sepia-toned image said to be a screenshot from the video was widely shared.

It was supposed to be an adrenochrome harvest, *The Daily Beast* reported.[4] Q reminded believers of this rumour on 18 June 2018, two months after the video story took root: 'Weiner HRC/Others – crimes against children.'

These abuses against innocent, kidnapped children by devil-worshipping elites were permitted to continue, went the QAnon theory, due to the complicity of the 'deep state'. The deep state referred to the faceless bureaucrats and organisational elites within government, the media, the military and other institutions – like the CIA – who protected the elites for rewards of wealth and power. For the QAnon faithful, democratic elections were an illusion, as every US government since Reagan was a mere front. An unelected shadow government instead made all decisions – and in secret – to perpetuate the cruel status quo against the interests of the people. 'The "fix" has always been in – no matter which party won the election,' Q said on 14 December 2017. Q claimed both Kennedy and Reagan had resisted the deep state and were shot for their disobedience. Reagan was allowed to survive, and every president since had served its interests loyally.

In the shadow of the deep state, the principled resistance movement of 'white hats' had arisen. White hats referred to brave, virtuous patriots – like Q – hidden within the various branches of government and the military. They were working together on a complex plan to expose their deep state counterparts, the 'black hats'.

It was terminology borrowed from the world of information security, where black hats were malicious hackers and white hats were the security specialists employed to outfox them. In the universe of Q, white hats were campaigning to arrest the depraved elites and rescue the children they had stolen, delivering freedom, justice and liberty for the people as they took down the cabal. White hats in the military were responsible for drafting Donald Trump to run for president. The white hats knew the strategic brilliance that had made Trump a real estate billionaire could win the game of four-dimensional chess needed to outmanoeuvre the elites, the deep state and all the sheep they manipulated.

'Ask yourself an honest question,' posed Q on 14 November 2017. 'Why would a billionaire who has it all, fame, fortune, a warm and loving family, friends, etc. want to endanger himself and his family by becoming POTUS? ... Perhaps he could not stomach the thought of mass murders occurring to satisfy Moloch?'

Moloch is a recurring figure in the Bible, presumed to be a Canaanite deity, and associated with child sacrifice. Depicted in centuries of Western art as a monstrous bull-headed humanoid, arms outstretched over sacrificial flames, Moloch was used as a metaphor for capitalist greed in Karl Marx's *Capital*. In popular culture, he made a cameo appearance devouring people in Fritz Lang's epic 1927 movie, *Metropolis*. More importantly, he got a lot of play on 4chan's /pol/ board. Long before Q appeared, Moloch was a running – and often anti-Semitic – joke among channers, positioned as the incarnation of Jewish evil locked in eternal battle with Kek, the invented ironic god of 4chan. The word 'Kek' substituted on 4chan for a kingdom or community, as well for the concept of laughs or lulz. Trumpist channers frequently depicted Hillary Clinton as a devotee of Moloch. They shared sexual hate fantasies about receiving oral sex from Clinton while calling her a 'moloch worshiping whore'.

Q also made heavy use of the word 'sheep'. This was a term borrowed from decades of conspiracist communications. Sheep or 'sheeple' were ordinary people who maybe even thought they were virtuous patriots going about their lives but were blind or asleep to the reality of the power struggle going on between the white hats and the black hats, good and evil, light and dark. Sometimes it was a wilful blindness that caused sheep to ignore the visible patterns with which the elites arrogantly revealed to one another their membership of the cabal. The mainstream media also deceived and manipulated people with 'fake news' in order to ensure their sheep-like compliance with the deep state agenda. This agenda was totalitarian political control over human life and death itself.

The mission of Q – and the patriots Q recruited – was to wake up the sheep to the truth of the white-hat/black-hat battle being waged around them. There was a need to direct the sheep away from the fake news media – the mainstream media (MSM) – and instead towards the truth told by Q and spread by unimpeachable patriots. 'What is the MSM? Who controls the MSM? Who really controls the MSM? Why are we made to believe the MSM are the only credible news sources?' Q asked on 20 November 2017.

The message within the communities was that patriots did not need to argue the facts to evangelise for Q. Instead, they should suggest that sheep 'do your own research' and refer the curious to the YouTube videos, blogs, Facebook pages and Reddit boards where the bakers were baking bread from Q's crumbs. Shelves of books interpreting Q were being listed for sale on Amazon. If the sheep read the right research, they'd start to 'follow the white rabbit', find themselves offered a metaphorical red pill/'Q pill'– a form of information that would ensure they'd never see the world the same way again.

This terminology was lifted from *The Matrix* movies. In the first of the film series, Neo, played by Keanu Reeves, is a hacker who comes to realise that the world in which he lives is a computer simulation. Accepting an invitation to 'follow the white rabbit' tattooed on a woman's shoulder, he encounters a group of plucky renegades resisting computerised control who offer him a choice. By taking a blue pill, he will erase his realisation, returning him to his former life but keeping him trapped in a lie. By taking a red pill, he will awake from the lie and see beyond the fantasy that's been created to placate humanity.

Neo takes the red pill. The real world is a dystopia, but Neo gains superpowers, becomes a hero and gets the girl.

I can confirm this works best, redpilling by giving hints, thus making it an investigation game, it's the best way to make people curious.

Anonymous on 8kun, 17 December 2017

Anyone who wasn't stirred to 'save the children' enslaved by the depravity of the elites was wilfully resistant to what Q claimed was the truth. This meant that they'd chosen to take the metaphoric 'blue pill' instead of the liberating red one because the truth was too frightening. How frightening? Positively dystopic. On 4 April 2018, Q posts spoke of 'tunnels' under paedophile Jeffrey Epstein's private island, and a dark temple located there. Pizzagate had described tunnels connecting Washington restaurants where stolen children were tortured in basements. Bakers believed children were stashed in tunnels under the streets of New York; discussions on the unmoderated social media app Telegram claimed there were up to 300,000 stolen children imprisoned under the streets of Melbourne, Australia. They were destined for torture and sacrifice. Those who ignored the visible clues of this mass child imprisonment were choosing to remain 'asleep'. 'Reality is hard to swallow,' explained Q on 11 July 2019. 'FAKE NEWS keeps you asleep (sheep) and fixed in a pre_designed false reality (narrative).'

In the meantime, Donald Trump was engaging extraordinary manoeuvres of principled cunning to contain and demobilise the black hats and child-stealing elites. This was why the deep state was using the fake news media to smear Trump with false accusations, mischaracterisation and specifically the allegations that his campaign had actively colluded with Russia. Fortunately, Trump's strategic genius was to use these attacks as a distraction to continue his secret work among the other white hats as they mobilised to bring the elites to justice. Special Counsel Robert Mueller wasn't really investigating Trump for collusion with Russia – this was cunning cover for his covert role working with Trump to flush out the paedophiles. The public theatrics of this were the 'calm before the storm' that Trump had described. 'The storm' to come was the event in which the members of the cabal and deep state would be arrested, tried before military tribunals, convicted and imprisoned in Guantanamo Bay. The storm was a living Judgment Day. 'The President of the United States initiated and confirmed the order when he stated "The Calm Before the Storm",' wrote Q on 4 December 2018.

The mass arrests would no doubt be met with civil disturbance stirred up by the deep state with those groups they'd long manipulated into doing their bidding. For this reason, a military takeover would be enacted. Q had explained as early as 1 November 2017 that the white hats were preparing to shut down communication services and use an 'Emergency Broadcast System' to warn patriots how to stay safe while the military suppressed the riots, and while this had not come to pass on the predicted date, that date was no doubt a cunning misdirection to confuse opposing forces. The likelihood of chaos was why Trump himself had allowed Q to leak the details of this plan on chan imageboards. A core group of patriots pre-enlightened by Q needed to be prepared for the chaos to come, as well as be able to explain the truth to confused sheep as peace was restored.

The storm would deliver 'the great awakening' to all the people. Here light would triumph over dark and all the illusions created and maintained by the deep state could finally be dismissed and 'the truth' revealed. A new golden age would dawn. On 7 December 2019, Q had written:

Knowledge is power.

Think for yourself.

Trust yourself.

Do due diligence.

You awake, and thinking for yourself, is their greatest fear.

Sheep no more.

THE GREAT AWAKENING.

The forces of darkness would fight fiercely, and sometimes everything would appear hopeless. There would be some predictions that might seem to fail to come to pass, but the white hats had many 'false flags' and deceptions of their own with which to surprise and confuse their enemies. Trump always knew what he was doing, so all doubting patriots should remember to 'trust the plan' (Q said this twenty-seven times), remind one another that with Trump in charge, 'nothing can stop what's coming' (eighteen times) and rally together in the knowledge that 'where we go one, we go all' (more than two hundred times).

If chaotic events – like a stuck boat blocking the Suez Canal or a pandemic outbreak or a mass shooting – were to occur, they were probably distraction theatre in the battle being waged to deliver humanity from 'dark to light' (Q used these words around thirty times). The true meaning of events could be explained through consultation of Q's posts, or in discussion with those who translated them. What appeared real was probably a political 'movie' created to hide deep-state nefariousness or to cunningly cover Trump's latest manoeuvre. 'You are watching a "scripted" movie,' Q reminded followers on 11 June 2018. Patriots should sit back, ignore everything that media, government or any other institutional authority told them, trust Q and 'enjoy the show'. There were dozens of suggestions to do this throughout the Q posts.

It was absolutely bonkers, all of it. Everything Q posted and everything the bakers said was a casserole of ignored facts, wild fantasies and desperately wilful misreadings of proven historical events.

Quite beyond the skimpily evidenced challenges these stories posed to what was visibly true, some of their details appeared to derive from something like a half-remembered pop-culture literalism.

A *Los Angeles Magazine* article posed that QAnon's condemnation of Hollywood as some kind of satanic Babylon was 'an exercise in contradiction'.[5] The magazine interviewed political scientist Joseph Uscinski from the University of Miami, an expert on conspiracy theories, who revealed that the disdain for Hollywood that ran through QAnon adherents was so intense it had produced variants of this theory suggesting that those who ran the industry 'turn child actors into shoes'. Even so, he observed, some of QAnon's most engaging storylines were visibly lifted from Hollywood films.

It wasn't limited to references from Lewis Carroll's *Alice in Wonderland*, or the repurposing of Alice's 'white rabbit' and the red-pill/blue-pill tropes from *The Matrix* movies. Q's taste was really very broad.

Adrenochrome, for example, was not actually a fountain-of-youth blood-product drug obtained from the bodies of tortured children. This was fiction. While it certainly is a real-life oxidation of adrenaline, and in some countries substances related to it are used medicinally to treat blood clots, it was not psychoactive nor milked from children's fears, and its fiendish reputation appears to derive from literary sources.

The Daily Beast explained that Aldous Huxley had mentioned it in his 1954 book, *The Doors of Perception*; Anthony Burgess nicknamed it 'drencrom' in *A Clockwork Orange* and Frank Herbert described a character in *Destination: Void* as so high 'he looked like someone who had just eaten a handful of pineal glands and washed them down with a pint of adrenochrome'.[6]

Yet adrenochrome's most famous use was a throwaway joke in the Hunter S. Thompson novel *Fear and Loathing in Las Vegas*, which had also appeared in the Hollywood screen adaptation of the book. In a conversation that claims adrenochrome makes mescaline seem like ginger beer, the drug-addled lawyer character suggests the extent of his own debauchery by insisting that adrenochrome he's ingesting must be harvested from a living human body; he won't get high if it just comes from a corpse.

In reality, whether milked from the living or dead, adrenochrome is ginger beer rather than mescaline. The belief that it had psychoactive properties derived from some experiments conducted by a pair of Canadian psychiatric researchers in the 1950s, one of whom consumed it and claimed to have experienced hallucinations and delusions as a result. These effects have not been replicated in other users. It's worth noting that at the time the Canadians were also conducting experiments with mescaline and LSD.[7]

As for the idea of an energy source derived from the screams of human children, New Zealand magazine *The Spinoff* suggested that it may have seemed familiar because it was also part of the plot in the 2001 Pixar movie *Monsters Inc.*[8] The conspiracy theorists were well ahead of the New Zealanders: a 2020 article in *Wired* reported that claims circulated online that the movie itself was a cryptic reference to what evil Hollywood got up to.[9]

The reputation of Hillary Clinton for starring in snuff films was, similarly, the stuff of wilful fantasy. The sepia-toned image shared online that posters claimed had been taken from *Frazzledrip* showing Huma Abedin's face draped with the flayed skin of a raped girl was in reality far less cinematic. The image used was found to be a blurred photo of an Indian restaurateur named Geeta wearing a paper mask. Her picture had been lifted from an ad that promoted a supper club that Geeta ran in Washington, DC. Internet fact-checkers *Snopes* traced the appropriated use of Geeta in the *Frazzledrip* conspiracy to an obscure YouTube video that had been uploaded on April Fool's Day 2018 and then quickly deleted.[10]

Even the slogan 'where we go one, we go all' – shortened to 'WWG1WGA' – was a clumsily repeated line. In a post on 19 April 2018, Q cited it as a quote from President John F. Kennedy. It wasn't. CBS News discovered it was a line said by the doomed teenage sailors in the underwhelming 1996 boat-disaster movie *White Squall*.[11] Claims by QAnon adherents that the words were inscribed on the bell of JFK's presidential yacht, *Honey Fitz*, have also been debunked. Reddit sleuths from r/Qult_Headquarters and the *QAnon Anonymous* podcast tracked the image of the bell to a tall ship called *Eye of the Wind* – not ever owned or sailed by JFK, but certainly used as a shooting location in *White Squall*.[12] The words 'calm before the storm', incidentally, appear in the *White Squall* trailer too.

Look at the photos of trump rally, yo will find Carolyn in second that smile, look and you will see JFK jr. The son of JFK, he JFK jr. Is alive and is the glue of the earth. I know this to be true, open your eyes, your being you will find.

@DismantlingTheCabal on Telegram, 6 August 2021

As fragile as its grip on the truth may have been, the QAnon story had strength in its adaptability and resilience. The obliqueness of Q's posts lent them an infinitely re-interpretable quality. It allowed them not only to be constantly reread as predictions of future events but also as allusions to conspiracy theories generated elsewhere. Different conspiracist communities could thus be channelled towards Q as some kind of conspiracy omnitheorist.

Reading the Q posts suggests this may have been a deliberate strategy. Q makes numerous references in the posts to President John F. Kennedy, assassinated nearly sixty years ago and the focus of some of the most enduring and widespread conspiracy beliefs in America. As recently as 2013, *The Washington Post* reported that 62 per cent of Americans believed his assassin, single-shooter Lee Harvey Oswald, did not act alone, despite decades of detailed evidence supplied to the contrary.[13]

Q's appeal to conspiracy thinking was targeted to a place where resistance to conspiracy thinking was already soft. On 8 April 2018, Q posted:

> *POTUS & JFK JR.*
> *Relationship.*
> *Plane crash 1999.*
> *HRC Senate 2000.*
> *The 'Start.'*
> *Enjoy the show.*
> *Q*

Unsurprisingly, the bakers in the online Q groups have cooked some Kennedy flavours into the great cake of their Q cosmogony. Having located a photograph of JFK's adult son and Trump together at a New York Knicks game only a few months before JFK Jr's death in a plane crash in 1999, they've invented various links between the murdered president and Q's supposed white hats/black hats war.

Some 'anons' have insisted that Hillary Clinton was behind the plane crash that killed him, claiming that had he lived he may have obstructed her evil ambition to be elected senator from New York. Others claim JFK Jr faked his death, remains alive and is now on a secret mission to avenge his father's death at the hands of the deep state. The Southern Poverty Law Center has reported that 'QAnon supporters believe JFK was about to reveal the existence of a secret government when he was assassinated', and that the younger Kennedy, still alive, 'will soon emerge to either become Q or team up with Trump'.[14]

Rolling Stone went into even more detail. In a piece for the magazine on 3 July 2019, E.J. Dickson reported that hardcore QAnonners didn't merely believe JFK Jr was still alive but also that he planned to emerge from his twenty years spent in hiding to support Donald Trump and become his running mate in the 2020 election. Further, there were claims that a man named Vincent Fusca – recently of Pittsburgh – was actually JFK Jr in disguise, and t-shirts had been made to promote this belief.[15] Although Dickson added that the two men looked nothing alike, the dissimilarity was explained by QAnon believers as a deliberate ruse involving tooth veneers. Trump/JFK Jr campaign t-shirts, *Rolling Stone* pointed out, were already for sale on Amazon.

Was it ironic? It's not always possible to tell. 'Lizard People Matter' t-shirts for sale on Redbubble may seem like a joke, yet polls in the past have indicated that up to 12 million Americans might subscribe to a belief in the existence of vampiric, shape-shifting, alien lizard people.[16] The claim was that stranded extraterrestrial 'saurians' lived among us, disguised, pursuing positions of power to control humanity. They could be recognised, suggested some, by the unexplained scars on their bodies, or by having red hair.

Q makes no direct reference to lizards, reptiles or dragons, but in a post on 29 June 2020, Q quoted a letter addressed to President Trump from the noted Catholic conspiracist Archbishop Vigano, the former Apostolic Nuncio to the United States, alluding to spiritual battle with 'the offspring of the Serpent ... those who serve themselves, who do not hold any moral principles, who want to demolish the family and the nation', among their many other sins. A reference like this was glib, yes – but still enough to widen Q's appeal to the niche community of believers in reptilian humanoids.

In the social media spaces where QAnonners and other conspiracy theorists gather online, no bridge is required between Q's depraved, adrenochrome-drinking elites and, say, blood-drinking, all-powerful 'reptoids'. Whether believers hail from Q's community or that of the saurian-adjacent, all of them understand that the villains they're fighting are one and the same.

Vegas Tenold was an investigative researcher for international Jewish advocacy organisation the Anti-Defamation League (ADL) when he described QAnon's appeal as a 'big tent' conspiracy as the reason for its popularity. 'Part of the genius,' he quipped to *Insider* in a 2020 article, was that 'whatever garbage' you had, 'you could bring it to the party'.[17]

Did adopting such beliefs expose their believers to mainstream ridicule? Sure. An interesting phenomenon that can be observed in conspiracy communities is that, for some, the depth of immersion in the beliefs is proportional to their sensitivity to mockery.

In the posts, Q stoked this sense of marginalisation in the flock. In that letter to the president on 29 June, Q described 'children of light' who were 'the object of a sort of discrimination' while their adversaries – the children of darkness – held 'strategic positions in government, in politics, in the economy and in the media'.

A popular meme still circulates in online QAnon communities that appeals to a deeply felt, shared sense of persecution. Emblazoned with the 'where we go one, we go all' slogan, it features Charlie Brown and Snoopy overlooking a Los Angeles sunset and is captioned: 'Someday, stories will be told about the soldiers of that time … The ordinary people who spent countless hours researching, debating, meditating and praying – and for the truth to continually be revealed to them. Because although they were mocked, dismissed and cast off, they knew their souls had long ago agreed to do the work.'

This quote is attributed to one Dr Russell Everard McGregor, an Australian psychiatrist who was struck off the medical register in February 2020. The NSW Medical Council had been alerted to inappropriate behaviour from McGregor in the wake of a colleague's affair with his wife and discovered he'd made three hundred blog posts to his own clinic website heavily promoting QAnon theories. Investigated by an assessing psychiatrist, McGregor plied him with six hundred pages of QAnon material. A hearing into McGregor's mental state found him paranoid and mentally unfit to continue treating patients, and the chair of the medical council phoned to inform him of his suspension. His response was to call the chair a 'filthy dirty fucking leftwing slut', denounce the council as a 'paedophile protection agency' and claim he'd been struck off due to 'deranged President Trump haters and those who are political sycophants of what the Deep State represents'.[18]

Q's posts position self-identified 'soldiers' – like McGregor – as both bold heroes and plucky underdogs fighting the deep state's all-powerful evil. Again and again, the posts flatter these people as grand rebel-patriots in the historical tradition of George Washington, Thomas Jefferson and Thomas Paine, simultaneously nurturing impressions of their unjust persecution. In a post of 12 March 2019 (repeated on 28 March 2020), Q asked the online audience:

> *Those who attack you.*
> *Those who mock you.*
> *Those who cull you.*
> *Those who control you.*
> *Those who label you.*
> *Do they represent you?*

There's a discernible echo in this of the appeal that Milo Yiannopoulos made three years earlier to his own fan base. 'If you have ever felt bullied,' as he once wrote in *Breitbart*, 'or victimised, or harassed, or marginalised … then Milo Yiannopoulos is for you.'[19]

In both cases, the encouragement is intended to form a simple tribal identity among followers based on their shared experience of victimisation. A Milo/Q-themed champion then rides in against injustice, more than prepared to represent the victims' interests.

These scenarios create easy good-guys/bad-guys binary identities. This binary entrenches the demonisation of the black hats/deep state/elites/intruding gamer-feminists who the hero-champion's rebellion seeks to overthrow. It also neatly slots anyone who mocks or criticises the brave-soldier-patriots into automatic alignment with the enemy.

This was dangerous for Q's followers not only because sowing a persecutory delusion in a group of people is a psychological tactic to ripen their minds for persuasion or coercion, but also because at the heart of the Q project, the loyal 'anons' were being persuaded to believe a sticky, fabulist story that represented ancient, ugly and historically lethal superstitions.

The People will overturn their overlords.

Russell McGregor (@killaudeepstate) on Gab, 7 August 2020

When Joseph Uscinski was interviewed by Adrienne LaFrance for her *Atlantic* feature 'The prophecies of Q', he explained to her that he saw 'conspiracy thinking as independent of party politics'. He instead saw the sticky fabulism of something like Q as a 'form of mind-wiring', organised around acceptance of a universal conspiracist proposition.[20]

Uscinski identified that Q had a religious appeal, especially for American Christians. LaFrance's article subsequently revealed that at the time of their interview, Uscinski's own mother, Shelly, was both a Christian and a QAnon convert. Apparently, Shelly liked that Q quoted the Bible, explained LaFrance. She also liked that Q encouraged people to pray.

In the piece, LaFrance also quoted the historian Norman Cohn, who in 1957 had tracked eruptions of 'apocalyptic thinking' as a reaction to periods of profound economic, social and technological change, occurring 'at periods of time when displays of spectacular wealth were highly visible but unavailable to most people'. Writing in *The Irish Times* sixty-four years later, Richard J. Evans, emeritus professor of history at Cambridge, expanded on Cohn's point about change.[21] He explained that twenty-first-century internet technology had forever transformed how we received information itself: the news is not gradual, it's immediate. Media cycles whirr with a constant churn of events, and information about change floods us; it's overwhelming. The sense of a world in perpetual flux is destabilising. Perhaps this is why conspiracy theories have become 'more popular and widespread' than they'd ever been in history.

Q's conspiracist, Judgment Day–style promise of 'the storm' that would bring about a 'great awakening' and transform all society not only met Cohn's historical conditions for 'apocalyptic thinking', it also used the language of religious revival deeply familiar to American evangelical Protestants.

'Great awakenings' were recorded historical events that had transformed ritual and belief in American churches in cyclical movements since the 1730s and held enduring symbolic and ideological influence over America's political right. In 2006, Republican President George W. Bush sounded like a YouTube Q-influencer when he pondered aloud to a group of conservative journalists the 'confrontation between good and evil' represented by the challenge that terrorism posed to democracy. Among his ideological kin, he suggested a transformational third great awakening dawning in America.[22]

Documentary filmmaker Arthur Jones told Adrienne LaFrance for her *Atlantic* piece that QAnon reminded him of his evangelical-Christian upbringing in the Ozarks.[23] Jones was the director of *Feels Good Man*, a documentary about the doomed attempt by cartoonist Matt Furie to rescue his character Pepe the Frog from its appropriation as a symbol of the alt-right; Pepe has since been adopted by QAnon too. What Q offered Trump-voting evangelicals, Jones suggested, wasn't just a familiar language but also a welcome prospect. By the time of Q's arrival, President Trump had been exposed in the press as an unholy liar, cheat and serial adulterer. The claims Q made allowed those more devout to still believe all of this was yet 'somehow part of God's plan'. Internet magazine *The Outline* also traced in Q's prognostications a Christian tradition of failed, persistent prophecies, including – but not limited to – the return of Jesus Christ, and the coming of Judgment Day.[24]

If Q had purchase on a certain kind of evangelical Christian identity, the Q stories also had a purchase on their fear. Survey data compiled by *The Washington Post* in 2021 explained that a cultural context had been seeded over years of right-wing media 'telling conservative Christians that their religion and their way of life are threatened' and described how Q had operated in that frame.[25]

By 2020, Rupert Murdoch's right-wing Fox News media network was well established as the most trusted by 36 per cent of white evangelical Protestants, according to the independent Public Religion Research Institute. This was 'nearly twice the proportion of all other religious groups'.[26]

Propaganda myths were repeated on Fox, including claims that the Democratic Party openly despised Christians, that they were active haters of traditional Christianity, that Democrats schemed to see Christians destroyed. Fox insisted that Christian values were under daily assault by America's most powerful forces, and that across the country the threats posed to Christians were worse, imminent, everywhere. All of this was said in one single seven-minute monologue from prime-time Fox star Tucker Carlson on Christmas Eve 2019.[27]

There were far more monologues, and panel discussions, and news-like clips from Fox assembled on this theme. Christmas was a ripe time for sources like Fox to spread myths of Christian persecution. Fact-checking website *Snopes* reported that former Fox News identities like Bill O'Reilly had been claiming a leftist 'War on Christmas' and other Christian rituals since at least 2005.[28]

Over the subsequent years, Fox had relentlessly stoked alarmism with stories like a claim on 26 August 2012 that 'Christians victims of rising "hostility" from gov't and secular groups, report says', in which 'hostility' appeared to be campaigns for marriage equality and public healthcare.[29] Fox selectively reported incidents of overseas violence as confirming 'Christians most persecuted group in the world as vicious attacks grow' on 14 August 2017.[30] By 2019, the ongoing refrain had become that Christianity was 'the most persecuted religion on the planet' – at least according to *Fox & Friends* on 30 December 2019.[31]

And this was, of course, only Fox. *Breitbart* published a hundred articles on the theme of 'Christian persecution' in

2020 alone. The impact of the messaging was recorded in data collated by the Public Religion Research Institute.[32] Their studies found that by November 2020, 73 per cent of Americans who identified as 'Fox News Republicans' believed Christians faced active discrimination in America. A further 58 per cent claimed white people were discriminated against. Only 36 per cent believed America's Black population faced discrimination.

Just as *The Washington Post* in 2021 studied the relationship between perceptions of an assailed Christian identity and Q with data, information ethicist Thomas J. Froehlich from Kent State University offered his own academic analysis as to why entities such as Fox News, *Breitbart* and QAnon stoked these resentments so relentlessly. The aim was to accumulate and consolidate political influence, a power base, economic reward and ideological supremacy, even if it was in direct opposition to the interests of their supporters, denigrated democracy or threatened the survival of the country. These media entities imposed a cognitive authority over their audience as they flattered partisan views and encouraged the rejection of competing authorities, Froehlich said. Activating emotional triggers to feed 'anger, resentment, or self-righteousness' among their target market rendered their believers uniquely manipulable as well as volatile.[33]

In the discursive milkshake-maker of pro-Trump QAnonism, the *Post* subsequently found through its analysis that encouraging these attitudes resulted in adherents assigning 'religious significance to the presidency and Trump in particular'.[34]

Ongoing, long-term ideological debates about whether America was a Christian or secular country had effectively been swallowed into a meme that 4chan had started in 2015 – repeated by the likes of Milo Yiannopoulos – wherein Trump was depicted as a giant, armoured 'God Emperor' from the Warhammer tabletop game. The *Post*'s careful polling had drawn out a sentiment that manifested in Christian QAnon believers, in which 'Trump was anointed by God to serve as the great Christian protector from those who would … strip Christians of their rights and liberties'.

Yes, it's called Jews and Corporations you retard.
But they've managed to convince you retards that
it's lizard people and other retarded bullshit.
Anonymous on 4chan, 24 February 2021

It wasn't the only shared value *The Washington Post* had uncovered. The researchers had found considerable shared sentiment between pro-QAnon, Christian nationalist, Trumpist and anti-Semitic positions.

The *Post* researchers had worked alongside the ADL to develop questions that teased out anti-Semitic attitudes among respondents of their poll. They found that the aggrieved Christian nationalists who supported the QAnon theory shared twice as many anti-Semitic beliefs as those who were opposed to QAnon. This was hardly surprising to the researchers, who pointed out that the animating ideas of the Q mythos resided in old anti-Semitic tropes about Jews controlling the banks, the media and the government. It was no great leap for such people to conclude the Jews must also be the puppeteers of the deep state, and the attempts to undermine Trump.

'In other words,' reported the *Post*'s researchers, 'these are not independent forces operating in American politics. Christian nationalism and QAnon support work together to drive up anti-Semitism.'

What always impressed the seasoned 4chan-observing researchers from the Q Origins Project was how Q's understanding of the forum extended beyond not merely how to speak in the language of channing 'but how to dog-whistle in it'.[35] It wasn't that 4chan's toxic swamp of old bigotries and vocabulary of hate rarely uttered in public since the end of the Second World War had left a residue that stuck to Q; rather, Q was a creature of the swamp. When Q whistled, dogs could hear it.

Jason Blazakis, professor at the Middlebury Institute of International Studies and director of its Center on Terrorism, Extremism and Counterterrorism, told the *Los Angeles Times* in 2021 that Q's 'cabals', 'elites' and 'black hats' were 'new words for old terms that have existed for quite a long time'. To the *Times*, Q's story of 'dark forces acting just out of sight' was a recycling of the anti-globalist 'new world order' beliefs that had preoccupied conspiracy communities in the 1990s.[36]

Over the decades of the Cold War, Western conspiracist beliefs had mostly told stories of liberty-thieving, gun-snatching communist agents hiding under every American bed. This narrative lost its villain when the Soviet Union collapsed in 1991. Brian Levin, a director at the Center for the Study of Hate and Extremism at Cal State San Bernardino, told the *Los Angeles Times* that in the absence of an enemy, people were obliged to invent one, so 'they filled that void with an evil global cabal'.

Pizzagate, and then Q, had resurrected this cabal from its 1990s incarnation, although it was made of much older parts – namely, stereotypes of Jews. In his 2021 piece about conspiracist belief for *The Irish Times*, historian Richard J. Evans, one of the most globally pre-eminent scholars of the Third Reich, made the sad point that while conspiracy theories have recruited a vast array of villains in their various iterations, 'it is above all Jews who have been the object of the paranoia they represent'.[37]

The 'Jews will not replace us' chants from the alt-right at the violent 'Unite the Right' rally in Charlottesville in 2017 were a jarring modern return to this old historical paranoia. The event was shocking because it symbolised a return of overt anti-Semitism to the public square. In recent decades, the mediating language and symbols of cabals, 'new world orders' and the (((echo))) symbol represented anti-Semitic hate that – in public, at least – was typically more covert. Unless, of course, you were on 4chan, in which case the anti-Semitism was explicit, outright and omnipresent.

The Charlottesville rally was ostensibly a protest against the removal of a Confederate statue, yet the attendees came in regalia emblazoned with swastikas and Hitler quotes. A banner read 'Jews are Satan's children'.

'They immediately came after the Jews,' wrote Yair Rosenberg in *The Washington Post*.[38] Jews had so long endured as a racist obsession, said Rosenberg, because 'many can often "pass" as white when not wearing traditional Jewish symbols'. He quoted the African American scholar Eric Ward's explanation that in the fantasy racial hierarchy of white supremacy, Jews functioned as dissembling 'demons', using their whitishness as a cover to stir up trouble among the 'subhuman, dangerous beasts' of the other races who supremacists believed were so inferior they were otherwise incapable of revolt.

These supremacist myths about Jewish power-grabbing and deceit had had pushers in corners of Western culture for a long time. Fox News's 'war on Christmas' trope traces directly back to the advocacy of notorious anti-Semite industrialist Henry Ford.[39] In the 1920s, he'd distributed a series of pamphlets accusing American Jews of conspiring to cancel public Christmas celebrations. '[It is] religious attack that they preach and practice,' he wrote in one of a collection of 1921 essays. These were published under the title 'The International Jew'.

Did this cultural history imbue a sly tone within Q's 'Christmas' posts? On 25 December 2017, Q wrote, 'MERRY CHRISTMAS! Celebrate this SPECIAL day in a BIG way. God bless you all.' On 17 December 2019, Q responded to a fan who'd posted a photo of a restaurant called 'Q Mas':

Though, nothing should ever replace 'Christ' in 'Christmas'.
Merry Christmas, Anons/Patriots.
God is on our side.
Q

Worth considering is that Trump himself promised within his 2016 presidential campaign to 'bring back' 'Merry Christmas', insisting that a nebulous liberal conspiracy had managed to obliterate its use as a holiday greeting. 'We're saying "Merry Christmas" again,' he said again at a Value Voters Summit in Washington, DC, in October 2017, in praise of his own presidency.[40] 'Do you remember they were trying to take "Christmas" out of Christmas? Do you remember?' he reminded a crowd of young conservative activists in December 2019.[41] 'They didn't want to let you say "Merry Christmas",' the president said. He returned to the subject at a speech in Georgia in 2020.[42] 'Remember we started five years ago, and I said, "You're going to be saying Christmas again." We say it proudly again. Although they will be trying to take that word again out of the vocabulary. We're not going to let them do that.' He did not elaborate who 'they' may have been.

Q made references that were far less oblique than plausibly deniable Christmas greetings. Q's mentions of the Rothschild banking family and the financier George Soros in the posts employed anti-Semitic stereotypes about vampiric Jewish usury that dated back centuries.

This is some next level historical fantasy revisionism jewry bull shit. It reeks of 'judeo-christian' lies that modern day american and western cucked christians masturbate to.

Anonymous on 8kun, 30 December 2017

Mike Rothschild (no relation of the Rothschilds), tracked more of Q's direct references in a 2021 piece he wrote for the *Daily Dot*, pointing out that Q's 'obsession' extended beyond false claims that the famous Rothschild family owned international government banks (they don't).[43] Mike Rothschild said that Q included them within an 'evil corrupt network of players' alongside Hillary Clinton, Obama and George Soros as well as 'insinuated the family had a hand in creating AIDS; hinted they sold a Black Forest lodge where they hunted humans'. Q also linked them to the NXIVM sex cult. Of Soros in particular, Rothschild said that Q's intimation on 9 September 2020 that the ninety-year-old Hungarian Holocaust survivor had a 'supposed Nazi past' was the cruellest of projections:

Was the Nazi party ever truly destroyed (eradicated)?
Did the belief carry-on [re-deployed]?
... Background of Soros?

Q

Rothschild also summarised Q's assertions: that the nonagenarian used his vast and shadowy wealth to fund domestic terrorism, that he owned voting machines used in an attempt to rig the 2016 election, that he was engaged in devious collusions with the Democratic National Committee and that he funded 'LOSER BOTS' that fought Q's messaging on social media. In addition, Soros apparently took orders from a "sick and evil"' master known only as 'P'.

Q's posts name-checked Soros more than fifty times, often alongside mentions of the Clintons. A separate post about Chelsea Clinton's husband, Marc Mezvinsky, from 13 January 2018, made sure to mention that he'd been raised 'attending a Conservative Jewish synagogue' before the exhortation 'FOLLOW HIM AND FAMILY DOWN THE HOLE TO FIND MORE TRUTH'.

On 4 April 2018, the anti-Semitic dog whistles grew much louder when Q engaged with an explicit image reposted from 8kun. It depicted a stereotypical cartoon of a Jewish man wearing a Star of David around his neck and wading through a tide of blood – labelled as flowing from a gaggle of Eastern European countries – with a knife in hand. It was captioned 'Why do they persecute me so?'. The filename was 'liesofkikes.png'.[44] Q's comment on it was 'The "Chair" serves the Master. Who is the Master? P = C'.

Beyond these stereotypes, suggestions and the cartoon, there was also Q's 'cabal'. Q never directly used the word and yet fed its presence in the narrative by responding to other posters who did. A secret society of rich bloodsuckers who stole innocents and subjected them to the foulest of corruptions is the image of not only the vampire in fiction but the lizard people of conspiracy theory. Both had originated, historically, as metaphors for the shape-shifting, of-us-but-not-us, anti-Semitic stereotypes of Jews.

The cabal narrative's most powerful modern incarnation had come in a notorious Russian text published in 1903 and known as *The Protocols of the Elders of Zion*. What it pretended to be was the secret minutes of an 1897 meeting of powerful

Jews, conspiring in secret to plot no less than the destruction of all civilisation.

The civilisation it described had already been forever transformed by the events of the First World War, and by 1918 its frame of reference was long out of date. In 1920, London's *Times* revealed the text was a mash-up of paragraphs lifted from a mid-nineteenth-century French satire as well as parts of a German Gothic novel, overwritten and embellished by its Russian compiler. Its credibility was the subject of a Swiss trial in 1934–35, and it was publicly declared a fake.[45]

Yet the proven fake was published and republished, translated, copied, shared and recopied, and reached millions of people because there was an audience who was seeking justification for anti-Semitism, and they wanted its claims to be true. It was an immensely powerful document, according to Richard J. Evans, that in the hands of Germany's Nazi party became a 'warrant for a genocide'.[46] The contents were rambling and fanciful, but it had the same function as 'doc dumping' online. The point wasn't to sift through and analyse its details but to publicly claim it as authentic, documentary evidence of Jewish conspiracy. Hitler and Goebbels had both explicitly discussed its use to their shared ideological project. It didn't matter to either of the men whether the text was authentic. Its value was its narrative power to affirm their biases to themselves and to others.

Disturbingly, Evans was writing about *The Protocols of the Elders of Zion* in the context of discussing its similarity as both text and phenomenon to the opus of Q's posts and the discourse those posts had encouraged. The parallels were not limited to similar roles as vehicles of ideological convenience. The 1903 text also repeated the anti-Semitic fiction known as 'the blood libel'.

It may sound familiar. It's a medieval myth with its historical origin in 1144, when a young boy known as William of Norwich was found dead in an English wood. In the years after he died, a lurid story was retrospectively embroidered around his death. It accused a secret conspiracy of Jews of his ritual torture and murder, and of defiling his body to mock the Passion of the Christ. The myth spread throughout Europe. In her book *Culture Warlords*, Talia Lavin describes how the story became one of Jews stealing Christian children 'for the sake of their blood, which Jews bake into matzah, the traditional unleavened bread of Passover'.[47] Then they'd eat them.

That there is an explicit prohibition against consuming blood in Jewish law is irrelevant; the story is not about communicating facts. All Jews were held culturally responsible for the smear made against them. Thus, when on Easter Sunday 1475 the dead body of a two-year-old Christian boy named Simon Unverdorben was found in the cellar of a Jewish home in the Italian city of Trent, local authorities cited the blood libel as the explanation for the death, rounded up eight local Jews to blame for the murder, tortured and killed them. Attempts by a papal investigator to determine the truth of the boy's end were frustrated by the local bishop who had predetermined the Jews were to blame. The myth of the blood libel was fiercely defended again and again throughout the Middle Ages, Lavin explains, because it created an ongoing pretext in which Jews could be scapegoated for anything.

Stories of secret, blood-eating, underground child killers are even older than William of Norwich or Simon of Trent. In an article for *The New Republic* about their reappearance in the myths of Pizzagate and QAnon, Lavin cited Norman Cohn's description of 'nocturnal ritual fantasy' in his studies of European witch trials.[48] Cohn dated it as far back as the Romans. These were a malleable set of accusations, Lavin explained. A social out-group is blamed for ritualistic and perverse behaviours that corrupt and destroy innocents, and that's enough justification for the out-group and anyone who enables it to be destroyed.

The paranoia may not be initiated by political actors, but it self-generates propaganda that those actors are all too ready to manipulate for their own purposes. Cohn's research charted its deployment from Romans against Christians, then by Christians against Jews, then Christians against witches, then by Catholics against perceived heretics.

For her article, Lavin interviewed Dr Michael Barbezat, a medieval historian and research fellow at the Australian Catholic University, and he expanded on Cohn's point. He warned that, historically, when accusations of satanic child abuse are publicly echoed by political leaders, that's when violent persecutions result. For Barbezat, 'Things happen when those with power become interested in the kinds of ideas these marginal thinkers are promoting, or weaponize them.'

As surveys of QAnon believers – like the 2021 one from *The Washington Post* – have shown, recruits to its theories were not drawn exclusively from a pool of anti-Semites.[49] Israeli newspaper *Haaretz* reported that the movement had managed to attract some Jewish acolytes, even if numbers were 'tiny'. Speaking for the ADL, Vegas Tenold told *Insider* magazine he did not consider QAnon 'explicitly' anti-Semitic in its activities.[50] Neither Q nor the 'quniverse' of hangers-on in the baker communities deployed campaigns against targets merely because they'd been identified as Jewish, although there were certainly Q-influencers whose use of the ((((echo)))) revealed sympathy for that position. You also didn't have to spend too much time in the 'research' threads posted on 8kun to discover anti-Semitic speech and chunks of text ripped from books with names like *The Rise of Anti-Christ, Volume 4.*

Felix Klein, the federal commissioner for Jewish Life in Germany and the Fight Against Anti-Semitism, was more specific in his condemnation. He told *Der Spiegel* in September 2020 that QAnon's octopus reach into diverse conspiracy discourses used anti-Semitism 'like an ominous bonding agent' to connect their ideas.[51] The *Daily Dot* reported that a compilation of Q-related posts on 8kun contained 'over 89,000 mentions of "Jews," almost 25,000 of "Rothschild;" and thousands of other, various anti-Semitic slurs'.[52]

Whoever was behind Q was using the historical paths of anti-Semitic extremism to channel overwhelmingly white, Christian followers towards a generic and adaptable Trump-centric extremism. The community used Trump's Jewish son-in-law Jared Kushner, and daughter Ivanka Trump's conversion to Judaism, as a shield against accusations of bigotry or appropriated them as 'good Jews' within a Christian–

Zionist worldview. Alternatively, they used the relationship with Kushner as further demonstration of Trump's political chess mastery, given the anti-Semitic insistence that Jews, in their deviousness, ever played all sides. Notable, perhaps, was that the influential Steve Bannon was reported using the euphemism 'globalist' to describe Kushner in tirades against him at the White House.[53]

There were established ways of scapegoating minorities, explained Michael Brenner from American University's Center for Israel Studies when interviewed about QAnon in 2020, and Q made the minorities 'exchangeable'.[54] What was consistently apparent was an invocation to superstition and stereotype that could soften people towards ideological patterns of bigoted and hateful ideas.

The layers of ancient messaging and the repetition of such old stereotypes gave the theory a cultural familiarity, even to adherents who had never heard of the elders of Zion, or Simon of Trent. It made the context easy to grasp. Recognisability imbued the stories with the grandeur of historical memory and with that came persuasive heft.

Years of absorbing Q's pronouncements and exploring their meaning within online communities transformed Q's audience's conception of itself. In the beginning, Q had identified them as 'patriots' worthy of insider knowledge into some level of domestic spycraft. By 24 June 2020, Q was telling them they had been 'selected to help serve your country' and calling them 'digital soldiers'.

In a 2021 article for *The Conversation*, Timothy Pettipiece, a religion scholar from Canada's Carleton University, saw in

QAnon belief a similar militant energy as within the early Christian sects, dangerously mobilised towards 'overturning their contemporary socio-political order using imagery of demons and holy war'.[55]

'The QAnon story casts Trump as a kind of radical Christian ruler, deputized by God to wage war against the liberal infidels destroying a once great and holy nation,' Pettipiece writes. Q maybe began as a conspiracy theory, but over the years the combination of aggressively paranoid ideas and the tribalistic expression of them had crystallised its nature into that of a cult.

I want the day of the rope now. the globalist cabal must hang.

Anonymous on 8kun, 13 September 2020

The year 2020 set something of a high-water mark for QAnon's online and in-world influence due to an intersection of conditions created by the coronavirus 'COVID-19' pandemic. First diagnosed in China in December 2019, the disease was a previously unknown form of severe acute respiratory syndrome coronavirus and spread both rapidly and lethally. By the end of January 2020, the World Health Organization had declared it a global health emergency. While researchers raced to even grasp the basic nature of the new disease, the rate of infections overwhelmed hospital systems. Within a year, more than 100 million people had caught COVID-19 and nearly three million people had died from it; 500,000 deaths occurred in the United States alone. Many of the medical personnel trying to treat COVID-19 were infected and killed by the virus while doing so.[56]

The spread of the disease was a terrifying event, in no small part because even as its case numbers exploded, the social institutions of medicine, science and government still knew so little about it. In the absence of any available prevention or cure, governments around the world enforced 'shelter in place' and lockdown orders that largely confined populations to their homes and prohibited social gatherings. They further ordered the closing of services, enterprises and events, obliged 'social distancing' regulations to keep people physically separated, shut borders, forcibly quarantined travellers and instituted 'mask mandates' to prevent airborne virus transmission.

These radical government interventions were a shock to civic populations that had no living memory of mass quarantine conditions. Karen Douglas and psychology researchers from the University of Kent had made the point in 2017 that conspiracy belief became stronger when people grew distressed from feelings of uncertainty, and the social conditions created by coronavirus drove distress and uncertainty on a global scale.[57] Prohibited from gathering in person, citizens turned to the internet for socialisation. It was the ripest possible moment for people to experience a vulnerability to conspiracy thinking, and, on social media, an illusion of community masked a web centipede ready to fuel their paranoia and devour them.

Cam Smith, an independent Australian researcher who monitors local far-right and conspiracy communities, witnessed the online radicalisation of vulnerable people in real time. During the uncertainty of the lockdowns, people he'd been observing on Facebook who previously may have expressed doubt around the efficacy of vaccines or been 'a bit worried' about 5G communications technology seemed to get turned towards QAnon fanaticism after even relatively limited exposure to its propaganda.[58]

It didn't matter how far away Australia was from the US or its specific cultural hang-ups. QAnon's omni-conspiratorial adaptations easily absorb regional variations of paranoia; it was attracting followers from all over the world. People would watch maybe a single QAnon documentary that referred to the cabal, said Smith, 'and then all of their posts after that would be just crazy, out there, adrenochrome, eating-children bullshit'.[59]

In *The Conversation*, Timothy Pettipiece explained that QAnon's summation of the 'real cause' of the crisis across the world in 2020 'was an underground religious war being waged by US soldiers against legions of Illuminati demons'.[60] When people who were online, frightened and already susceptible to conspiracy thinking were communicated QAnon messages in the right way, said Cam Smith, it 'could flick a switch in them and they'd just go nuts'.

One such person was Melissa Rein Lively, one of QAnon's Jewish adepts. The Arizona woman had been drawn towards QAnon in May 2020 at the height of pandemic anxiety. She'd been enticed towards its propaganda online through her involvement in the online 'wellness' community.

Originally, she later told an interviewer from *Haaretz*, the social media content she consumed was 'optimistic and uplifting'.[61] It was reassuring to be told that patriots within the government were committed to protecting the public from danger. Then, a QAnon image comparing mask mandates to the dehumanisation process of the Holocaust activated an inherited cultural terror in her. Her switch flicked. Fear drove her towards dark QAnon content that spoke to and reinforced her growing conviction a second Holocaust was coming. Driven deeper into QAnon communities, consuming increasing amounts of propaganda, Rein Lively invested completely in the myth. She allowed herself to be convinced by QAnon that Holocaust survivor George Soros was a secret Nazi.

Addled and terrified, in July 2020 Rein Lively encountered a mask display at a local Target store and lost psychological control. Shouting 'This shit's over!' again and again, she filmed herself violently trashing the display and uploaded the video to the internet. Rein Lively's meltdown – her mid-lockdown unhinging – became iconic and her video was viewed 100 million times. When police came to question her at home about what she'd done at Target, she filmed herself again. This time she screamed at the police that she'd been 'hired to be the QAnon spokesperson' and accused them of arresting her for being Jewish.

The police took her to a psychiatric hospital and she spent a week there. After eight weeks of intensive therapy she was able to gain some perspective on what had happened to her and started to realign with reality. 'The message just hits the right person at the right time,' she explained to *Haaretz* of her experience with QAnon, 'and everything changes.' Relating her 'rabbit hole' journey in another interview, this time with CNN, Rein Lively also described QAnon as a cult.

The cult's activities were not limited to internet propaganda, as effective as that had been on people like Melissa Rein Lively. QAnon adherents were physically mobilising.

What's scarier to you: A virus with a survivability rate of over 99%, or hundreds of thousands – maybe millions – of children being raped?

Will Witt on Facebook, 31 July 2020

In June 2020, a lot of QAnon activity appeared around the Twitter hashtag #SaveTheChildren. It did not refer to the hundred-year-old British humanitarian charity of the same name. It was a discursive hijack by QAnon activists, lending credibility to their children-milked-of-adrenochrome claims. In an example of QAnon's signature conspiracy hybridisation, QAnonners embraced the tenets of pandemic denialism then simultaneously used it to argue the real pandemic was the mass abduction of children sex-trafficked into the evil adrenochrome industry. QAnon discussion groups variously suggested the pandemic lockdowns and mask-wearing were deep-state schemes to snatch more children.

In reality, the pandemic was infecting thousands of Americans every day and the heavily insisted statistics that

QAnon memes and hashtags pushed about child abduction were more QAnon fantasy. A repeated claim that 800,000 children were going missing every year in the US alone was a corruption of figures from media reporting about missing children that had appeared back in 2012.[62] The 800,000 figure referred to the total number of 'missing' reports logged with police over the course of the year. It included children who'd gotten lost, been injured or had run away from home as well as the small number of children who had been abducted. Runaways alone accounted for more than 90 per cent of those reported 'missing', and the same 2012 articles also explained that more than 97 per cent of the children were recovered safely within twelve months. The number of abductions of children by strangers was limited to around 115 a year.

Every child abduction, anywhere, is a tragedy, but there are not two thousand of those tragedies in America each day; in 2012, statistically, there was less than one abduction of a child by a stranger every three days. By 2020, reported *USA Today*, improvements to communication technology and policing had nearly halved the yearly missing child reports just from the 2012 numbers.[63] While trafficked-child numbers were always hard to determine, the National Center for Missing and Exploited Children identified that among children reported missing, runaways faced the greatest numerical threat of sexual exploitation: 26,500 runaways were reported to NCMEC in 2020, with one in six likely to be victims of child sex trafficking.[64]

This meant nothing to the QAnon campaign in which thousands of online accounts shared emotionally provocative images of wide-eyed small children with captions like 'A child in America today is over 66,000 times more likely to be sold to human traffickers than to die of COVID'.[65] The claims resonated beyond the online conspiracy communities and found a widespread audience in parenting groups and amid lifestyle influencers. *Rolling Stone* reported that the oft bikini-clad Instagrammer Helen Owen had posted an image of herself with her mouth bound for World Trafficking Day, using the #SaveTheChildren hashtag as she spoke up for those 'who cannot speak for themselves'.[66] Journalist Eddie Kim from men's magazine *MEL* wrote in 2020 of seeing #SaveTheChildren or #EndTrafficking hashtags posted by friends online that led back to 'accounts that espouse #Pizzagate logic elsewhere in their timelines'.[67]

After pushback from the British charity Save the Children, the dominant hashtag morphed into #SaveOurChildren, but it appeared around others with less subtlety – like #Pedowood, #PedoGate, #SymbolsWillBeTheirDownfall, #SatanicPedophiles and #PizzagateIsReal, and often alongside, of course, #GreatAwakening and #WWG1WGA.[68] Online 'child rescue' organisations sprouted that solicited PayPal donations for hazily defined activities.

In Australia, the ABC reported on how disinformation about child trafficking was being mutually amplified between QAnon agitators and a 'network of anti-human trafficking not-for-profit organisations, many emerging from the evangelical religious right'. The online article appeared in September 2020; the US elections were only a couple of months away, and ABC journalists identified that the QAnon/religious right exchange represented 'hugely influential online movements which look set to have an outsized effect on November's presidential election campaign'.[69]

Increasingly, the effects of QAnon's campaign were being registered in mainstream media, with stories both disturbing and bizarre. In August 2020, *Los Angeles Magazine* reported that stalking the social-media feeds of Hollywood stars like Chrissy Teigen, Tom Hanks, the cast of *Friends* and Oprah Winfrey had become a standard QAnon activist practice. Anons were apparently scouring for evidence that linked celebrities to the now-dead sexual predator Jeffrey Epstein.[70]

A few weeks previously, the July issue of *Elle* magazine reported that model Chrissy Teigen – wife of musician John Legend – was obliged to block a million Twitter accounts after a sustained campaign of harassment.[71] Back in 2017 she'd started to receive tweets claiming she was one of the celebrities implicated in Pizzagate. Her forceful denials attracted more abuse from the QAnon community, and the accusations metastasised. Claims were made that Teigen and Legend's names appeared on the flight logs of Jeffrey Epstein's infamous private plane.

They didn't. Neither Teigen nor Legend had ever been on the plane and, unlike Donald Trump, had never been photographed with Jeffrey Epstein either. Repetition of these facts did not quell Teigen's harassment.

Other celebrities faced similar swarms of malign QAnon nonsensing. Rumours had spread through the 'qommunity' in early 2020 that Oprah Winfrey had been arrested in Boca Raton, Florida, on charges of human trafficking. These spread to Twitter, went viral, and Oprah herself was obliged to issue a public denial that March. In July 2020, *Los Angeles Magazine* reported that the rumours had returned; a single Facebook post repeating false claims of Oprah's arrest was shared 32,000 times.[72] Then, when Oprah interviewed the Duke and Duchess of Sussex in March 2021, the old rumours found purchase once more. This time they were driven by users on a QAnon Telegram channel of 200,000 people who'd decreed – without credible evidence – that Oprah did the interview wearing an ankle monitor.[73]

Wayfair..

Trafficking company.

Justin trudeau and ellen degeneres also!!

Pedos!

Wethepeoplestruth on Telegram, 31 July 2021

Stranger still was QAnon's involvement in a controversy that involved the American e-commerce furniture brand Wayfair. In mid-2020, a QAnon 'influencer' was perusing the company's online catalogue and observed that a collection of high-priced wardrobes were labelled with girls' names. Her suspicions were shared on the 'r/conspiracy' subreddit a few weeks later. Here, believers in the QAnon myth began to insist the names of the furniture matched the names of children reported missing in the United States. The analysis was that

Wayfair were agents of the deep state. The company was accused of retailing stolen children to child-eating paedophiles and shipping them worldwide, hidden in furniture.

The problem with this theory, as the BBC pointed out at the time, was that there was no evidence to suggest that it was true.[74] Many of the 'missing children' named in the online speculation were either long found or, in the case of one girl, now an adult, had not actually been missing in the first place. This particular woman even recorded a Facebook Live to expose the rumours of her supposed abduction by Wayfair as false.

It made no difference. A frantic Wayfair felt obliged to publicly explain why larger-sized industrial furniture cost more than smaller domestic items, as well as how they used an algorithm to ascribe names to their catalogue items, before they pledged publicly to the renaming of their entire cabinet range. Despite their efforts, the story continued to travel through what was now an international pipeline of disinformation. The BBC tracked 4.4 million engagements with the story on Instagram as well as 12,000 Facebook posts about it, leading to a million engagements with it there. Outside of the United States, it had notable popularity in Turkey and Argentina. It wasn't only that online interconnectedness allowed the web centipede to have a global crawl. Readers' lack of familiarity with international 'news' sources perhaps inclined them to consider this content less critically.

Meanwhile, in the months leading up to the November 2020 election, #SaveOurChildren protests were mobilising a physical presence in towns and cities across America. NBC reported placard-bearing crowds were marching along main streets from Spokane, Washington, to New York City, chanting and regaling local media and passers-by with focused tales of child abuse and human trafficking.[75] Yet among protest signage that declared 'Stolen people = stolen dreams' and 'Children are not for sale!' and demanding an end to child trafficking, pizza symbols appeared alongside Q sayings and #WWG1WGA iconography. 'Real witches don't eat humans!' appeared on a placard with a slice of pizza and a cryptic hotdog. Organisers told NBC that they were gathering to 'raise awareness and start a conversation'.

'This is not about child protection,' Whitney Phillips, a conspiracy theory scholar and associate professor at Syracuse University, told NBC. 'This is about a conspiracy theory that's trying to couch itself in other terms to get more people involved and sympathetic.' Marc-André Argentino, a QAnon scholar from Concordia University, described 'Save the Children' Facebook groups as a 'soft front' for the conspiracy movement to draw in concerned recruits. A *New York Times* article linked an upsurge in #SaveOurChildren online activity to a period in July 2020 when Facebook and Twitter had begun a crackdown on overt QAnon accounts.[76] Argentino identified to the *Times* 114 online QAnon groups posting anti-trafficking concerns, and his discovery – at which he expressed horror – that the groups had increased their membership by '3,000 percent – yes, 3,000 percent' between July and September 2020.

NBC reported the frustration of organisations and long-term activists in anti-trafficking and safety campaigns about the effects of QAnon's disinformation – legitimate services had been 'flooded by bizarre claims and tips, as well as criticism and sometimes threats'. Reporting from the scene of a #SaveOurChildren protest held in Hollywood in October 2020, Donie O'Sullivan from CNN questioned protest organiser 'Scotty the Kid' – a singer – about whether he was actually a QAnon follower.[77] He said no, only to mysteriously fall silent when O'Sullivan presented him with a social media post he'd made only the night before in which he'd promoted QAnon explicitly. 'The truth is mind blowing and cannot be fully exposed,' Q had posted on 29 October 2017, a refrain repeated throughout the opus of the drops. Indeed, Q. Indeed.

Conspicuously, these protests made physical targets of media organisations. The #SaveOurChildren march attended by Donie O'Sullivan made CNN's bureau in Los Angeles one of their stops. 'The media writ large is a frequent target of these groups and their rallies,' O'Sullivan wrote in a subsequent article, 'because they think – falsely – that it is covering up for the people they have baselessly accused.'[78] Noting that many rally attendees were avowed Trump supporters and wearing MAGA hats, when O'Sullivan identified to them that CNN was his employer, their response was usually a variation on Trump's attack mantra of 'fake news'.

Eddie Kim made another important observation about the QAnon targeting of mainstream media in his *MEL Magazine* article.[79] It wasn't just about implying that mainstream media was a discredited source, or complicit in the exploitation of children by a supposed failure to report on it. Targeting the media boosted the egos of protest participants and those advocating Q's grand heroic narrative. There was personal value, Kim said, in the belief that the protest activism was a form of labour that other people weren't brave enough to do. Q eagerly fed this illusion of superiority and valour in the faithful. 'You are the saviours of mankind,' wrote Q on 6 November 2018. On 11 February 2019, Q said: 'You are the news now.'

Look at how China, Saudi Arabia (sword dance) India treated President Trump compared to Obama. They treated Trump like a honored hero... They hate the satanic cabal too, and all the fuckery they have pulled over the past 100 years plus.

Anonymous on 8kun, 2 April 2020

Then president Trump hardly disassociated himself from what was burbling in the online communities that praised him as a four-dimensional-chess-playing, masterfully Moloch-fighting, child-rescuing, heroic holy Christian God Emperor. As QAnon's growing online influence drew more scrutiny, Trump's relationship with the movement that lionised him did too.

On 19 August 2020, Facebook removed nearly eight hundred QAnon pages from its platform, having identified posts 'celebrating violence, showing intent to use weapons, or attracting followers with patterns of violent behaviour'.[80] This was the context of one journalist's question in a 20 August

2020 press briefing, in which she asked the president what he thought about that and what he had to say to people who were following the movement.[81]

Interviewed by NPR in the wake of this briefing, Travis View, co-host of the *QAnon Anonymous* podcast that tracked the movement's beliefs and evolutions, explained that journalist's questioning of Trump was of massive consequence to Q believers.[82] As Michael Kunzelman later said in the Associated Press, QAnon adherents had been demanding that journalists 'Ask the Q' of Trump from the conspiracy theory's beginning. 'His answer would confirm their baseless belief that he is secretly fighting deep state enemies and a cabal of Satan-worshipping cannibals operating a child sex trafficking ring,' Kunzelman said.[83] For believers, it wasn't just about getting the story into the mainstream news, Travis View told NPR: doing so would actually cue the events of 'the storm' Q had promised and lead to the mass-arrest great awakening events.[84] Will Sommer at *The Daily Beast* revealed on Twitter that he'd obtained secret service documents on a believer who'd told a Republican congressional representative's office she was willing to disguise herself as a journalist and infiltrate the White House to get the question asked.

By this stage, QAnon had been named specifically by the FBI as a source of conspiracy theory–driven extremism, but Trump did not disavow the movement.[85] Instead, he replied: 'Well, I don't know much about the movement other than I understand they like me very much, which I appreciate.' He added, 'I have heard that it is gaining in popularity,' then pivoted to lines his administration had been repeating about the racial justice protests erupting across America in the wake of the police killing of George Floyd.[86] The implication was that the Black Lives Matter movement was the real source of America's social chaos, while QAnon – according to Trump – were 'people that love our country' and 'didn't like seeing' the protests.

The journalist pressed him. 'The cause of the theory is this belief that you are secretly saving the world from this satanic cult of pedophiles and cannibals. Does that sound like something you are behind or ...? '

Trump responded that he 'hadn't heard that', but added, 'Is that supposed to be a bad thing or a good thing? I mean, if I can help save the world from problems, I'm willing to do it. I'm willing to put myself out there.'

This response did not announce the longed-for 'great awakening', but Travis View subsequently reported in *Business Insider* that the 'qommunity' greeted Trump's remarks with elation. It was a good enough response from Trump to be considered an endorsement, said View, and it cemented among believers some relief that all their time invested in baking and proofing had been worthwhile.'[87] Within the infinitely adaptable universe of Q belief, Trump's remarks were quickly interpreted as signalling the faithful to 'trust the plan' – as Q's posts had instructed so many times – that the promised storm was very much underway.

Trump's claim to not 'know much about the movement' was disingenuous. A president worshipped by a cult that the FBI had flagged as a terror threat was likely to have been briefed on the implications of engaging with them. By the time of his August 2020 remarks, however, the president had been validating QAnon for years, mostly through Twitter retweets. By the time of his spoken remarks, wrote Travis View in *Business Insider*, 'Trump [had] amplified QAnon Twitter accounts at least 216 times.'

On 27 October 2020, E.J. Dickson at *Rolling Stone* reported that Trump had begun retweeting QAnon content as early as 25 November 2017.[88] This was less than a month after the first post from Q had appeared and the president had quote-tweeted a pro-Q account called @MAGApill. By 31 July 2018, according to Dickson's article, Q supporters were appearing in the footage of Trump rallies, while on 24 August that year, a 'conspiracy analyst' from *Infowars* named Michael Lebron tweeted photos of himself visiting Trump in the White House with the hashtags #WWG1WGA and #TrustThePlan.

Over the next year, more Q signs and paraphernalia increasingly appeared at Trump rallies. Although it was later deleted, the Trump campaign shared a 'Women for Trump' ad on 9 August 2018 that featured visible QAnon signs and slogans. In November, senior Trump staffer Dan Scavino started sharing memes with imagery from popular QAnon sayings, like a ticking clock, representing the countdown to the 'mass arrests'.

Then, in December 2018, the president tweeted content from no less than @TracyBeanz, the original QAnon YouTube influencer with four thousand Russian-backed Twitter megaphones. Bear in mind, this was a full four months after the NBC article was published that identified her specific role in bringing Q to greater public attention.[89]

In July 2019, *Vanity Fair* reported that QAnon advocate Bill Mitchell had been invited to participate in a 'Social Media Summit' at the White House with Trump himself.[90] Two weeks later, *The Guardian* reported that 'Trump singled out a "beautiful baby" whose jumpsuit was adorned with the "Q" symbol' at a rally in Greenville on 17 July 2019.[91]

Online, there was more retweeting by Trump from other pro-Q accounts; in February 2020 he shared content from another popular Q influencer, @PrayingMedic.[92] At a campaign rally that same month, Trump campaign spokesperson – and White House press secretary – Kayleigh McEnany interviewed on stage a Trump fan wearing a Q t-shirt. Again in February, Q t-shirts appeared in the footage of a Las Vegas campaign rally within a Trump ad, and then in another ad shot at a rally in Arizona.

Lauren Boebert is a piece of ass. Pro-gun,
traditional, no tattoos, believes in Qanon.
She's wife material.

Anonymous on 4chan, 13 November 2020

These were not overlooked coincidences. Presidential encounters are managed carefully, and campaign material is tightly controlled, targeted propaganda. Donald Trump was not a careless Twitter user, he was president of the United States – and on 4 July 2020, that president marked America's annual Independence Day with fourteen retweets from Q-aligned Twitter accounts.[93]

The next day, Trump's disgraced former national security adviser Michael Flynn released a fifty-three-second clip to social media of his family chanting an oath that ended 'Where we go one, we go all'.[94] This was the same Michael Flynn close enough to Trump that the president had pressured then FBI director James Comey to get him out of the trouble his own lies about a meeting with a Russian ambassador had gotten him in.

Flynn denied – through his lawyer, Sidney Powell – any association to the conspiracy theory, but elsewhere, allegiances to QAnon theories were made without shame. In the run-up to the election, Trump promoted through his Twitter feed the Republican congressional candidates DeAnna Lorraine of California, Antoine Tucker of New York, and Angela Stanton-King and Marjorie Taylor Greene of Georgia, all of whom were either avowed QAnon supporters, sharers of QAnon content or otherwise publicly identified with QAnon beliefs. *Forbes* reported that Trump's endorsements drew Twitter follower accounts to the candidates in their tens of thousands, thus widening channels for amplifying QAnon content through political discourse on the internet.[95] Taylor Greene was notable for having made social media posts that disparaged George Soros and the Rothschild banking family. The *Atlanta Jewish Times*, from her own home state, has since published commentary that described her as 'a conspiracist for rent'.[96]

These were not the only QAnon advocates appearing as candidates in the lead-up to America's scheduled 3 November election. NBC reported that no less than seventy-five who'd publicly supported the QAnon theory had run in the 2020 primary elections for the US Congress, and nineteen were scheduled to appear on the ballot.[97] Jo Rae Perkins, the Republican candidate for the Senate in Oregon, stood little chance of winning in the solidly Democratic state, but NBC noted she had thundered to victory in the Republican primary. At the end of June 2020, Q-advocating Republican Lauren Boebert of Colorado had beaten a five-term, Trump-endorsed incumbent in the primaries; the next day, Trump tweeted congratulations for her primary win. 'Everything I've heard of Q, I hope that this is real,' Boebert told a podcast interview of her belief in the theory, which was reported in *The Guardian*.[98] By August 2020, both Boebert and Trump's re-election campaign director of press communications, Erin Perrine, had made appearances on the Q-themed *Patriots' Soapbox* internet show, still run by @TracyBeanz's old r/CBTS_stream offsider Coleman Rogers.

Across America's state houses, there were also dozens of QAnon-supporting candidates running. Kevin Roose, the tech columnist from *The New York Times*, observed that QAnon engagement was driving the political conversation on the online right. 'Many of the stories that end up trending on Twitter or Facebook are there because QAnon found them and pushed them,' he told *Los Angeles Magazine*. '[I]t is a lot bigger and more influential than people realize.'[99] At the 2020 Republican Party convention, Kimberly Guilfoyle, the chair of the Trump Victory Finance Committee and girlfriend of Trump's eldest son, Donald Trump Jr, gave a rousing speech in front of twelve golden-eagle-topped American flags, infamously screaming, 'The best … is yet … to come!'[100] Even if it was a coincidence that Q had posted the same words three times already in 2020, and in all caps, worth noting was that the slogan (again, in all caps) was repeated beneath a meme Q posted two weeks before the 2020 election. The image depicted Trump facing the crowds amassed for his 2016 inauguration, with the words 'WE ARE Q!' above it.

Yet Trump insisted he didn't 'know much about the movement', even as it gained followers, even as its candidates sought office and he endorsed them, even as he stood in front of its placards and t-shirts, even as his closest allies swore oaths to its slogans, even as it marched down streets across the country, even as he shared its tweets, even as his own FBI named it a potential domestic terror threat.

On 15 October 2020, less than three weeks out from the election, Trump was asked by television host Savannah Guthrie in a town hall meeting televised by NBC if he was prepared to denounce the theory and he responded: 'I don't know about QAnon.'

Guthrie reminded him that its cult-like activities had received broad press coverage, and that many of his own supporters had endorsed it.

'What I do hear about it, they are very strongly against pedophilia,' he said.

Then she reminded him that he himself had shared on Twitter a QAnon conspiracy theory claiming – without evidence – that Trump's Democratic opponent, Joe Biden, had killed a team of navy SEALs.

'That was a retweet!' Trump said. 'People can decide for themselves!'

'You're the president,' said Guthrie, 'not someone's crazy uncle.'[101]

Trump was the president, and his comments, his praise, his candidate endorsements and his failure to disavow the movement gave Q and Q's adherents what they had always craved, all the way from back when Q was on 4chan insisting fanciful, impossible claims about Hillary Clinton's impending arrest were the 'biggest drop on /pol/'. Validation.

QAnon's outrageous fantasies were finding a media audience. They drew increasing flattery from the Republican political establishment. On 21 October, Steve Bannon said in his *War Room* podcast that QAnon 'at least appears directionally to be correct' and called the conspiracy theory 'the elephant in the room'.[102] A week later on 28 October, less than a week out from the election, Trump's White House senior adviser Stephen Miller claimed candidate Joe Biden 'would incentivize child smuggling and child trafficking on an epic global scale'.[103]

When interviewed for Talia Lavin's September 2020 *New Republic* article, medieval scholar Michael Barbezat had told her that, historically, persecutions turned towards violence when the demonisation of targets as satanic got taken up by political leaders. Now, QAnon had reached such proximity to the imprimatur of the US presidency that many adherents believed they were but one Trump acknowledgement away from the violent events of 'the storm' being set in motion.

This is what made QAnon so dangerous.

The age of centralised government ruled by a
handful of people is coming to an end. It seems as
if it will come to a head first in the United States,
but once government corruption has been removed
here, it must be removed everywhere.

@PrayingMedic on Telegram, 2 August 2021

The FBI classified QAnon's potential for domestic terror in an internal memo prepared by its Phoenix field office dated 30 May 2019. The memo had been distributed as a fifteen-page document to a variety of law enforcement agencies and was published by Yahoo News on 2 August 2019. The report itself noted it was perhaps the first to identify the threat of 'conspiracy-driven domestic terrorism', but it cited numerous incidents of violence linked to conspiracy theories in support of its claim.[104]

In July 2020, researchers Amarnath Amarasingam and Marc-André Argentino published a paper in the *CTC Sentinel* at West Point's Combating Terrorism Center that examined the implications of the FBI memo of the previous year. They concluded that QAnon was contributing to the radicalisation of ideologically motivated and violent extremists, and they referred explicitly to the FBI's warning that there were conspiracy theory narratives in circulation that encouraged violence.[105] By the time their paper was published, a series of public events had supplied enough evidence to furnish the FBI's darkest predictions.

QAnon adherents, explained Adrienne LaFrance in *The Atlantic*, had 'sometimes proved willing to take matters into their own hands'.[106] By the time of the FBI memo, these matters had gone a lot further than dogpiling Chrissy Teigen on Twitter, accusing George Soros of being a secret Nazi on 8kun or even contributing to the cascading fantasies posted to Reddit that yearned for Hillary Clinton's assassination, or to see her corpse ripped to pieces by 'buzzards' or 'her blood pouring down the gutters'.

The original FBI memo noted the events of Pizzagate at Comet Ping Pong and the arrest of Maddison Welch. They also mentioned the 2018 arrest of a Californian found with bomb-making materials. Police had foiled the man's planned bombing of a holiday season display in Springfield, Illinois. The man had taken offence that free-speech campaigners the Satanic Temple had contributed a 50-centimetre 'Snaketivity' sculpture to the display alongside traditional nativity items. His stated intention for the bombing was to 'make Americans aware of Pizzagate' and the 'new world order'.[107]

The memo also cited Matthew Philip Wright, a Nevada man who on 15 June 2018 used a self-made armoured truck to block traffic on the Hoover Dam Bypass Bridge, demanding to be issued a secret 'inspector general's report' on Hillary Clinton's emails that QAnonners discussed online but which did not, in reality, exist. He fled arrest and was apprehended in Arizona, where law enforcement found body armour, two rifles, two handguns, nine hundred rounds of ammunition and a flash-bang device in his car. Wright pleaded guilty to terrorism offences. *The New York Times* reported that

Wright, an avowed QAnonner, wrote letters to Trump and other officials after his arrest, 'calling himself a "humble patriot" and making references to the QAnon slogans "Great Awakening" and "Where we go one, we go all"'.[108]

Then there was the leader of an unofficial veterans' group in Arizona, Michael Lewis Arthur Meyer, who on 29 May 2018 claimed that he'd uncovered a child sex–trafficking camp within the grounds of a privately owned cement works in Tucson. He occupied the site for nine days. When his claim was discredited, he accused law enforcement of a cover-up, and while his armed group searched out more 'camps', they doxxed and threatened their critics online. Meyer returned to the cement works site after his initial removal and was arrested for trespass.[109] What he'd insisted was a child-trafficking camp turned out to be a place where homeless people had been squatting.[110]

Not in the FBI report but of similar concern were the activities of people like Oregon man William Gregory Douglas. He was arrested in September 2018 for threatening to shoot YouTube employees for restrictions the platform had placed around his QAnon-promoting channel. A couple of months later, 22-year-old Ryan Jaselskis was caught on surveillance footage after a fire broke out at Comet Ping Pong on 23 January 2019, having shared Pizzagate material from QAnon influencers on social media the night before. Jaselskis was apprehended in a physical brawl with law enforcement outside the Washington Monument a few days later on 4 February. On 25 September 2019 came the arrest of Timothy Larson in Arizona. The QAnon supporter had swung a crowbar and smashed up the town of Sedona's Catholic Chapel of the Holy Cross while shouting that the Catholic Church engaged in human trafficking.

The accumulating incidents were of increasing seriousness. In January 2020, QAnon believer Cynthia Abcug, from Colorado, was arrested in Montana for a plot to kidnap her son with the help of other QAnon believers she'd met: she'd come to believe his foster family were 'evil Satan worshippers'.[111] On 20 March 2020, another QAnon believer, Kentucky resident Neely Blanchard, kidnapped her two daughters from their grandmother's legal custody. Then, on 11 June 2020, Boston man Alpalus Slyman led police on a thirty-kilometre car chase with his five children, aged eight months to thirteen, trapped in his vehicle. He live#streamed about QAnon while doing so, begging both Trump and QAnon for help, convinced that 'police were coming to abduct' the children or even kill them. His terrified wife had managed to get out of their van, which eventually Slyman crashed after police used stop sticks that blew one of his tyres. Slyman struck another vehicle, rammed his van into a cruiser and hit a tree before coming to a stop. He faced multiple charges for the incident, but fortunately the children were not hurt.

On 1 October 2020, it was Emily Jolley, from Utah, who was arrested in Oregon for snatching her son from his father's custody during a supervised visit. Her social media profiles contained QAnon material claiming child protective services ran adrenochrome harvesting. In the wake of Cynthia Abcug's arrest, *The Daily Beast* explained on 4 January 2020 that elements of the QAnon community had convinced themselves child-protective services were taking children into care only to sell them on to the fantasy paedophiles of the deep state cabal.[112]

Over the course of the pandemic, it seemed that paranoias grew more desperate, and the actions they provoked grew even darker. Jessica Prim of Illinois was apprehended in New York on 29 April 2020 with eighteen illegal knives in her possession. The dancer and costume-maker had pledged in a series of Facebook posts she was travelling to 'take out' Joe Biden, Hillary Clinton and John Podesta. She live streamed her arrest on a New York pier, having travelled there to seek out the US hospital ship *Comfort*, which QAnon believed was then rescuing 'mole children' from the cabal. When arrested, she was actually outside the USS *Intrepid*, a floating museum, in a state of acute distress, telling police she'd been watching the press conferences with Donald Trump on TV and she 'felt like he was talking to me'.

What stood out for researchers Amarasingam and Argentino, who examined Prim's case in detail, was the 'rapidity with which Prim apparently radicalized to violence'. Based on her Facebook posts, her first meaningful contact with QAnon propaganda was on 9 April 2020. Only twenty days passed from this date to her published threats of offline violence and doomed trip to New York City. The researchers noted that in this time she had consumed QAnon propaganda documentaries, like the notorious *Fall of the Cabal*.

The role of hospital ships used in the American response to coronavirus were the subject of much QAnon community speculation. On 1 April 2020, Eduardo Moreno, a train engineer, intentionally ran a train off a track at full speed near the hospital ship USNS *Mercy* in Los Angeles and told the FBI it was to 'wake people up' because the ship was 'suspicious'. While Moreno did not admit to QAnon influence, analysis from Amarasingam and Argentino's paper identified that his actions seemed related to the conspiracy theory. 'You only get this chance once,' Moreno told the officers who encountered him at the scene. 'The whole world is watching … People don't know what's going on here. Now they will.'

There were also incidents in Canada. *The Guardian* reported that on 3 July 2020, Corey Hurren, owner of a sausage company and a reservist in the Canadian Rangers, had rammed a truck into the grounds of Canada's prime ministerial residence in Ottawa.[113] He spent thirteen minutes in the grounds before his arrest, threatening harm to Justin Trudeau. *Vice News* had found QAnon memes on his company's Instagram account. 'Has anyone else been following "Q" and the "White Rabbit" down the rabbit hole and how this all relates to the coronavirus/Covid-19 situation? Lots of coincidences in all these "Q" posts if this turns out to be a "Nothingburger",' read a caption.[114]

In Texas, a woman named Cecilia Fulbright was driving with a blood alcohol level double the legal limit when she chased and rammed another vehicle with her car on 12 August 2020. Her own friends informed journalists she'd become immersed in QAnon theories, and the *Waco Tribune-Herald* reported that she believed the driver whose van she rammed was a paedophile, and she was rescuing a kidnapped young girl.[115] As it turned out, the van was a catering truck and the girl was the other driver's daughter. Fulbright remained convinced, even after her arrest, that Trump was 'literally taking down the cabal and the pedophile ring'.[116]

Worse was 24-year-old Anthony Comello, charged with the 13 March 2019 murder of mob boss Frank Cali. According to his own lawyer, Comello had become obsessed with the notion that Cali was a 'prominent member of the deep state'. He'd fronted to Cali's Staten Island home to make a citizen's arrest, planning to turn Cali over to 'the military', but Cali refused to comply so Comello shot him ten times and then fled, leaving Cali to die in his driveway. Again, it was Comello's lawyer who – pursuing an insanity defence – stated that Comello had become convinced 'that he was enjoying the protection of President Trump' in his actions, 'and that he had the president's full support'. Comello appeared in court with a 'Q' and other QAnon slogans scribbled on his hand. By June 2020, he was deemed mentally unfit to stand trial.[117]

This was not, alas, the first QAnon-related murder. On 6 January 2019, Buckey Wolfe, a 26-year-old QAnon believer who also identified with the male-only, Neo-Fascist Proud Boys militia group, had murdered his brother, stabbing him repeatedly in the head with a four-foot sword. *The Daily Beast* reported prosecutors had lodged court papers that referred to Wolfe's social media posts about 'the cabal' as evidence of mental illness.[118] *The Seattle Times* reported that Wolfe had called the police himself, explaining to them the murder had occurred because he'd come to believe his brother was a lizard person.[119]

On 21 January 2021 there was another murder. The Kentucky 'QAnon Mom', Neely Blanchard (now Neely Petrie-Blanchard) was arrested for the murder of amateur 'fringe legal theorist' Chris Hallett. Over the previous months, Hallett had been helping Petrie-Blanchard in legal attempts to regain custody of her children, and they'd come to nothing. He was found face down in the kitchen of his Florida home, with several gunshot wounds in his back. *The Daily Beast* reported that Petrie-Blanchard was the only named suspect in his murder and quoted a police report. 'It was speculated that the victim was shot by [Petrie-Blanchard],' it read, 'due to her belief that the victim might have been working against her, or working to assist the government, in keeping her children away from her.'[120]

And possibly the saddest crime attributed to QAnon belief yet took place in August 2021. Matthew Taylor Coleman was a forty-year-old Californian who ran a surf school and surf therapy business called Lovewater, the website of which was studded with photos of him, bearded and smiling, with his young family. On a Saturday that the family had planned to go camping together, Coleman had taken the two small children into his van and driven away, leaving his wife behind and with no explanation. They had not had an argument. He had not said where he was going. When he failed to respond to calls and text messages, his wife tracked him via a 'find my phone' function on her laptop and discovered he'd taken the children to Mexico.

Matthew Taylor Coleman had become enamoured and entranced by QAnon and Illuminati conspiracy theories. They'd enlightened him, he said, and he'd come to believe that his wife possessed 'serpent DNA'. He had taken the children he loved away because he was convinced they were contaminated with her corrupt genetic inheritance and would grow into monsters.

US law enforcement intercepted Coleman in his van a few days later when he attempted to cross the border back from Mexico. There was no sign of the children, but there was blood on his vehicle registration papers.

Matthew Taylor Coleman had taken his children to Mexico to kill them because he wanted to prevent their supposedly monstrous destiny. A Mexican farmworker found their bodies in a ditch; Coleman's three-year-old son had been stabbed twelve times, and his one-year-old daughter had been stabbed seventeen times. Their mother had never expected them to be in any danger with their dad.

When questioned by the FBI, Coleman told them that he knew what he had done was wrong. And yet he believed – he genuinely believed – it was 'the only course of action that would save the world'.[121]

These were not the full extent of crimes committed adjacent to the QAnon movement, but patterns within these were notable. Was it fair for the FBI to claim 'conspiracy theories' of themselves were a domestic terror threat? Examinations of their individual details certainly identified that at the time of their crimes, perpetrators like Buckey Wolfe, Timothy Larson, Jessica Prim, Anthony Comello and Alpalus Slyman were exhibiting signs of extreme mental distress.

Where was the dividing line between mental illness, criminal intent or a terrorist act? On 23 July 2019, in the wake of Anthony Comello's court appearances, Philip Bump pondered the question in *The Washington Post*: 'To what extent does political rhetoric, fake news and outlandish conspiracy theorizing contribute to attempted acts of violence?'

Cheryl Paradis, a professor of psychology at Marymount Manhattan College, reminded Bump that despite negative media stereotypes of the mentally ill, the 'overwhelming majority' of individual sufferers are not violent, and the likelihood of carrying out an act of violence in response to mental illness is low.[122]

Instead, the effect of conspiracy theories was felt not due to an internal pressure but when an individual's distress toward external circumstances rendered them psychologically susceptible to their influence. This was the 'flicked switch' phenomenon that researcher Cam Smith described.[123] From Jessica Prim crying on the wrong pier, to the meltdown that beset Melissa Rein Lively as she came unstuck in a Target store, or the horrific violence of Matthew Taylor Coleman, what galvanised people into these extremist acts depended on how their distress towards a world they felt they could not control was informed by the socialisation process around them. Yes, said Paradis, mentally unwell people would 'latch on to ideas that are salient to their time period', but so, of course, does everyone else. Witch hunts, fascism, pogroms and 'satanic panics' were not historical experiences conceived or managed by the organised unwell.

In their memo, the FBI openly called on social media platforms to rein in the growing 'volume and reach of conspiratorial content'. As the pandemic of 2020 wore on, it became clear that the new online communication pipelines were socialising historically unprecedented numbers of people into extreme thinking.

The West Point researchers explained that social media allowed conspiratorial thinking to be crowdsourced.[124] The combination of QAnon's enthusiastic communities and the theory's malleability enabled a constant process of refining, supplementing and localising its details. Once immersed, an individual could be instantly encouraged by their crowd of fellow believers to perceive evidence for Q's cabal in their every place, their every interaction and in every cultural product around them. In an unfamiliar hospital ship docked at a commercial port. In homeless people squatting in a cement works. In a three-year-old boy. In a one-year-old girl.

QAnon believers, the researchers pointed out, were encouraged by Q to take action into their own hands.

ok seriously, when the fuck is someone going to
lone wolf the academy awards?

Anonymous on 8kun, 6 January 2021

What each act of QAnon violence represented was a pattern of 'stochastic terror'. This was a term that had been coined in 2002 by catastrophe expert Gordon Woo. His research into computer modelling of disasters had led him to determine that there were quantifiable relationships that informed those acts of terror that otherwise appeared to be random.[125] Writing about the extremist danger of Trumpism in October 2018, White House correspondent Heather Timmons explained the immediate political context of stochastic terror in *Quartz*. Using media to incite random actors into individually unpredictable acts of terror and violence was how you could still wreak civil chaos while circumventing the modern security apparatus. Lone wolves, said Timmons, could be remote-controlled.[126]

As more was learned about the existence of Russia's 'troll farm' and its aggressive propaganda activities in the lead-up to the 2016 election, the lesson that should have been learned was that there were some political actors heavily invested in remote-controlled chaos. 'When a common sense of what is real and what is correct breaks apart, it becomes nearly impossible to reach a democratic consensus,' explained researcher Will Partin from Data & Society to *The Guardian* of the cult's disruptive power.[127] The QAnon scenario was not only the 'dark mirror' of a game, as Reed Berkowitz had described, but the dark mirror of traditional political organising. A leader did not have to be visible, tactics did not have to be clear and targets did not need to be specific. If the political aim was chaos, the only resources required were willing recruits.

In her book *Culture Warlords*, Talia Lavin identified the socialisation process that radicalised the far-right extremists she studied into committing violent acts. An online world had been created in which people could be absorbed into the rhetoric of stochastic violence twenty-four hours a day, where propaganda calling for blood to be spilled was itself in continuous flow. The thing about a constant exhortation to violence, she wrote, was that 'sooner or later, someone is going to take them up on it'.[128]

What if the veterans of the meme war decided form an actual intelligence agency outside the online forums? Like one that would be an actual cabal that would work to get some members elected into positions of power to actually make some change.

A month or two ago another anon made a post about how he was starting to lay the ground work for his own campaign right now, while he was in his 20s, and how others who are devoted to politics and law should be doing the same thing, so that we all have a better chance at getting more right leaning people into power.

Anonymous on 4chan, 6 August 2017

Meanwhile, the anxious days of the pandemic year 2020 were advancing towards the 3 November date of the US elections. Under growing scrutiny, in September 2020 Facebook and Twitter began purging accounts they identified as being linked to Russian state actors. Just as they had in 2016, fake news sites and online amplifiers had been trying to spread made-up stories in the lead-up to the election. In 2020, these had targeted the racial justice protests as well as Democratic candidates Joe Biden and Kamala Harris. As the election drew closer, Facebook had also imposed stricter rules on political advertising. A tightening of community standards regarding misinformation that might contribute to the risk of violence had been started by Facebook in 2018; by October 2020, this resulted in a determination by Facebook to outright ban QAnon content from groups, pages and Instagram accounts.

Was it too late? Two months out from the election, Talia Lavin warned in *The New Republic* that QAnon's potential to mobilise violence towards a political end remained largely untapped.[129] Anons on message boards and in baker communities insisted to the world and one another that they never used violence, and denounced posters who suggested violence as 'glowies'. This was old 4chan parlance for FBI infiltrators and referred to the 'glowing' conspicuousness of agent provocateurs. Certainly there were people coming into Q's community who probably didn't think of themselves as joining a violent political movement, and yet the Neo-Fascists, Neo-Nazis and white nationalists still saturated the spaces where QAnon was active. Meanwhile, Q's rhetoric exhorting action against shocking and unholy evil flowed without abatement.

Fredrick Brennan, the founder of 8kun, shared Lavin's view. Brennan had long fallen out with Jim and Ron Watkins and left 8kun behind. By August 2019, Brennan was on something like a forever-apology tour for the internet monster that he'd created. At 8kun, he'd seen the propaganda and the blood it left in its trail. In the wake of 2019's three 8kun-aligned mass shootings, he'd been backing calls for his creation to be permanently shut down. Pushing 8kun underground wouldn't stop its violence from happening, Brennan told *The New York*

Times, but it wouldn't be happening every few months.[130]

The Watkinses had relaunched and rebranded the imageboard at the end of 2019, in the wake of the mass shootings in Christchurch, Poway and El Paso. It had dropped the /pol/ board where the killers had publicised and celebrated their crimes. Their site was now known as 8kun, incorporating the Japanese suffix 'kun' used to address teenage boys, unlike 'chan', which addresses children. Hosting Q remained their drawcard. Brennan told Adrienne LaFrance in June 2020: 'I worry constantly that there is going to be, as early as November 2020, some kind of shooting or something related to Q if Trump loses. Or parents killing their children to save them from the hell-world that is to come because the deep state has won. These are real possibilities. I just feel like what they have done is totally irresponsible to keep Q going.'[131]

The FBI predated both with its May 2019 prediction. 'The FBI assesses these conspiracy theories very likely will emerge, spread, and evolve in the modern information marketplace, occasionally driving both groups and individual extremists to carry out criminal or violent acts.' Explicitly, *Yahoo News* reported, the FBI believed that the threat posed by the movement would increase with the progression of the 2020 presidential campaign.[132]

Q made a handful of enthusiastic posts in the fortnight before the election. Over the course of a collection of short posts on 31 October 2020, Q asked: 'Are you ready to finish what we started?' And: 'Are you ready to hold the political elites [protected] accountable?' And: 'Are you ready to take back control of this Country?' On 3 November, election day, Q posted an image with the file name 'largest_flying_flag_in_america.jpg', a snippet from Abraham Lincoln's Gettysburg Address and the words 'Together we win'.

Due to pandemic restrictions, a record number of ballots were mailed into the polls. It took days to count them. The world, and the world of the internet, sat waiting on a result that the QAnon faithful believed with the conviction of zealots the prophet Q had already foretold.

Then, at 11.24 am, 7 November 2020, news network CNN called the presidential election for Biden.

Statistically impossible to have lost the 2020 election. Big protest in D.C. on January 6. Be there, will be wild!

@realDonaldTrump on Twitter, 19 December 2020

6. BURIAL GROUND

Rosanne Boyland was a native of Kennesaw, Georgia, a city located within Cobb County, north-west of Georgia's state capital, Atlanta.

She was born in 1987. At the time, Kennesaw's economy was being stirred to new activity by the shopping malls and businesses that stretched towards it from Atlanta, connecting Kennesaw to the greater Atlanta metropolitan area. Kennesaw's name derives from the mountain that sits between its city of 30,000 and the city of Marietta nearby. The mountain is an isolated ridge with two summits. Local historians claim that the Cherokee called it Gahneesah, meaning 'burial ground' or 'place of the dead'.

The origins of the modern town sprung up with the construction of the Western and Atlantic Railroad through Cobb County in the 1830s, around which shanty towns of railway workers bloomed. The level of track in the area rose at eighteen feet per mile, and railroad workers called it 'the big grade to the shanties', later shortening it to 'big shanty grade' and eventually just 'Big Shanty'. In the 1850s, historical records show that the railroad company acquired land to build a depot and eating house for travellers within the community that had formed. This facility was known as the Lacy Hotel, after its proprietors.

After the outbreak of the American Civil War in 1861, the Georgia militia of the Confederate Army established a military training camp at Big Shanty. It was well serviced by rail and a convenient place to transport troops and supplies. A grand review of the troops was held in Big Shanty by the Confederates on 31 July 1861 and attracted a large crowd.

The role of the railroad in enabling the movement of Southern troops and supply lines hardly went unnoticed by the forces of the Union Army. On 12 April 1862, a volunteer force of Union spies and soldiers boarded a train whose steam locomotive was known as 'The General'. When the train stopped at the Lacy Hotel in Big Shanty and its crew left it to eat breakfast, the Union soldiers stole the train, in full view of the Confederate troops gathered around it.

In what was immortalised in films by both Buster Keaton and Walt Disney, a *Great Locomotive Chase* resulted as the small travelling Union force attempted to sabotage as much Confederate infrastructure as possible from the train, and to do so until the moment their enemy caught up to them. The Southerners did catch up, and though the Union soldiers fled they were all caught by their pursuers within two weeks. Eight of the men were hanged, six were kept as prisoners of war, and eight escaped and made it back to Union lines. Most of the men who participated in the raid were the first to receive the new Congressional Medal of Honor.

This was not the last of Kennesaw's significance in the Civil War. The Union Army drove the Confederates from Big Shanty on 6 June 1864, using it as a supply base and a hospital as well as a headquarters for Union soldiers. The Union march towards Atlanta, however, was obstructed by Confederate fortifications around Kennesaw Mountain. On 27 June 1864, Union Major-General William Tecumseh Sherman launched a fiery frontal assault on these positions, and the 'place of the dead' burned in a bloody battle compared by witnesses to 'a volcano as grand as Etna'.[1] The well-entrenched Southerners resisted Sherman's bombardment, imposed three thousand casualties on the Northern forces, lost only a thousand of their own, and considered the Battle of Kennesaw Mountain a Confederate victory.

Their relief was short-lived. Over the next five days, Sherman's army flanked the Confederates, who were forced to withdraw to nearby Smyrna. Now unobstructed, by August the Northerners were besieging Atlanta, which fell on 2 September 1864. As Sherman prepared for his 'March to the Sea' in late October, Confederate General John B. Hood retook Big Shanty and seized 350 Union prisoners. On 9 November 1864, Sherman issued orders for his forces to destroy the rail connections to Big Shanty and burn the Lacy Hotel to the ground. By 14 November, the Lacy Hotel was smoking rubble and Big Shanty itself lay in ruins.

It took decades for the area to recover. It became the City of Kennesaw in 1887, and a National Battlefield Park was established on Kennesaw Mountain in 1917. While there was a period of cotton-led economic revival, this was extinguished by the 1950s when the last cotton gin closed. In the 1970s, one of the abandoned cotton gin barns was repurposed to house 'The General', eventually becoming the Southern Museum of Civil War and Locomotive History.

Throughout its tribulations, Kennesaw, like the rest of Cobb County around it, like the state of Georgia itself, remained a deeply conservative place. In 1982, after the town of Morton Grove in Illinois passed a law banning guns (since repealed), the city of Kennesaw responded by passing its own law that stated 'every head of household residing in the city limits is required to maintain a firearm, together with ammunition therefore'. This law contained numerous exemptions – it was also unenforceable and largely just conservative gestural politics made for show. Yet to this day myths circulate – now, mostly, on the internet – that the law was responsible for a conspicuous drop in the local crime rate, although *Snopes* investigated the figures in 2015 and found the claim was 'mostly false'.[2] It was five years after the gun law was passed that Rosanne Boyland was born.

She came of age as local political demographics were transforming markedly; as she entered her twenties, Kennesaw, now part of Atlanta's suburban sprawl, experienced a growth in population of more than 14 per cent just in the years between 2010 and 2020. Meanwhile, by 2015, the population density in the Atlanta metro area had increased two-and-a-half times since 1970, and the non-white population had more than doubled. Simultaneously, the number of Atlantans with a college degree (or higher) increased from 12 per cent to 35.8 per cent.

Trump had won Georgia by five points in the 2016 election, but polls taken before the election of 2020 suggested that the speed of change in Georgia's metropolitan communities may have been outpacing his conservative appeal. Several tax incentives by the state over previous decades had rapidly reshaped communities around new cultural industries with inherently liberal values. By 2016, Rosanne Boyland was hitting her thirties and there were more feature films being made in Georgia than in Hollywood.

Outside of the cities there was, of course, entrenched resistance to Georgia's cultural transformation. Immediately to Cobb County's north-west lay the rural counties that made up Georgia's fourteenth congressional district, with its collection of towns through which the Western and Atlantic Railroad used to run. It was one of the safest Republican seats in the country, and in 2020 the Republicans chose far-right QAnon advocate Marjorie Taylor Greene to be their candidate, despite her history of making racist, Islamophobic and anti-Semitic videos.[3] Even as late as June 2020, *Al Jazeera* reported that 114 statues and monuments to the slave-owning, secessionist Confederacy were still standing in Georgia.[4] That same June, in Kennesaw, fierce controversy surrounded a decision by the city council to remove the Confederate battle flag that flew in downtown Kennesaw's Memorial Park on Main Street. A week earlier, there had been protests outside Wildman's, a local confederate memorabilia store. These places were only a few kilometres from where Rosanne Boyland had gone to school at North Cobb High.

The opportunities of Georgia's new industries did not flow equally to those around it. Rosanne Boyland had a brother-in-law, Justin, a landscaper who'd landed a gig as a co-host on a reality show for a couple of years. Her own life had travelled in a different direction. Friends from school remembered her as kind, and her sisters described her as a 'really happy, wonderful person', but by her early twenties, Boyland had developed a serious substance-abuse problem.[5] A collection of local court records revealed that she'd pleaded guilty to heroin and cocaine charges in 2011 and a controlled substance charge in 2013, and was charged with heroin possession or distribution at least four other times in Fulton and Cobb counties. She'd pleaded guilty to receiving stolen property, too, and faced charges for battery, obstruction of law enforcement and trespass. She was not unaware of her problems; she had the words 'beautiful disaster' tattooed on her chest.[6]

By 2020, Rosanne Boyland appeared to be emerging from addiction. She had started reaching out to old friends from school on Facebook, trying to reconnect, she said, because she wanted 'more positive people in her life'.[7] She'd joined a recovery group in Atlanta, she was enjoying sobriety and she talked to friends and family about wanting to train and work as a substance-abuse counsellor. Her sister's children called her 'Ro Ro', and she became devoted to them. She collected them from school every day. Her friends posted on Facebook that she was 'real good' to their children too.[8]

As recovery changed Rosanne Boyland's perspective on her life, her politics also appeared to change. A fan of punk whose Facebook 'likes' included avowedly progressive bands like Against Me! and System of a Down, she 'stopped blaming other people for her problems and got real conservative', a friend said.[9] She traded memes with people online, attacking liberal politics and politicians. She fervently praised and admired Donald Trump.

Her family watched a profound change take hold of Rosanne Boyland, starting midway through 2020. She'd been drawn into the baseless online rumours about home furnishings retailer Wayfair, and the accusations that they were shipping children stashed in cabinets to paedophiles. Her brother-in-law, Justin Cave, the one who'd been on the reality show, had been a spokesperson for Wayfair a few years earlier.

'She would text me some things,' said Lonna Cave, Rosanne's sister, who was married to Justin, 'and I would be like, "Let me fact-check that." And I'd sit there and I'd be like, "Well, I don't think that's actually right."'[10] The family said that Rosanne Boyland's beliefs in conspiracies 'spiralled' from the rumours about Wayfair. She shared social media posts from far-right groups like Project Veritas, and videos of Trump's rallies, and anti-vaxxer conspiracy theories. She shared QAnon material.

Her family weren't the only people concerned about her energetic engagement with the QAnon myths. One of Rosanne Boyland's old friends, Zedith Drane, had considered unfriending her on social media, put off by her right-wing comments and spreading of conspiracy theories, like QAnon material. Drane had a lot of sympathy for Boyland, understanding how serious her battle with addiction had been. He knew she was bothered by the effects of the pandemic lockdowns on addicts – she'd told him she had friends who were dying due to the isolation – but disagreed with her that masking and lockdowns were a threat to 'freedom and liberty'. Drane tried talking to her. He told her that he thought she was going down a rabbit hole. He was worried.[11]

In the lead-up to the election, Rosanne Boyland's posts in support of President Trump grew more intense, as did the hatred she expressed for Trump's presidential rival, Joe Biden, and her sharing of QAnon disinformation. Her friend Sarah Lewis described the frustration of Rosanne's friends who couldn't figure out how to intervene. '[We] all watched her decline, and go on these rabbit-trails,' Lewis said.[12]

The election began with a period of pre-election day voting. The ongoing pandemic encouraged many voters to take advantage of mail-in voting and early in-person voting, rather than just rely on in-person voting on election day. Processing eligible votes coming in from multiple sources was time-consuming, and the count was expected to take many days after election day itself. While Democrats had advised voters to exercise mail-in ballots and early in-person voting to avoid crowds on election day, Trump had campaigned loud and long against mail-in voting, insisting that an increase in such voting would somehow lead to widespread fraud. He told his voters to exercise their vote on election day. As a result, election analysts had been warning there was a likelihood of a 'red mirage' taking place on election night in areas with a larger share of mail-in voting, which would give the appearance of Trump leading the vote until all the mail-in ballots were counted.[13]

Sure enough, on election day, the red mirage appeared, and Trump insisted he would be victorious. His election surrogates echoed his positive spin. A little before midnight on election night, however, that narrative fell apart when the pro-Trump Fox News network called the state of Arizona as having 'flipped' to Joe Biden.[14] The red mirage was dispersing and there were still millions of votes to come in. Trump went on television at 2.30 am and said: 'This is a major fraud on our nation … We want all voting to stop. We don't want them to find any ballots at 4 o'clock in the morning and add them to the list … As far as I'm concerned we already have won it.'[15]

#Trump2020

Rosanne Boyland on Facebook, 4 November 2020

By 4 November, Rosanne Boyland was posting *Game of Thrones* memes on Facebook to express her anxiety at watching the count. They depicted tense pre-battle gatherings of soldiers, which she'd captioned 'Americans sitting at home like …'. While Boyland expressed her incredulity online that anyone could vote for Joe Biden, elsewhere, pro-Trump activists were frantically subscribing to 'Stop the Steal' Facebook groups, pushing outward Trump's aggressive false narrative that he was a victim of electoral fraud. *The New York Times* reported that a hundred new members were joining the largest of these pages every ten seconds, which Facebook moved neither hard or fast enough to shut down.[16] The web centipede roused its head; the *Times* noted a movement to organise pro-Trump protest rallies across the country had been seeded through a diversity of platforms and was growing.

Over the course of the next few days, the red mirage rapidly evaporated as all the votes were tallied. As the state-by-state voting totals changed, Rosanne Boyland joined the other Trump supporters online, feverishly sharing memes claiming that ballot boxes had been stuffed with fraudulent votes and the election had been stolen.[17] Trump was broadcasting this line himself; his campaign team and associated Trumpy hangers-on were preparing a monster suite of lawsuits across the country to challenge the results. Sidney Powell – Michael Flynn's lawyer, formerly one of Trump's, but now claiming to be acting independently – called the lawsuits 'The Kraken' after the giant sea monster of Norse mythology. It was an appropriate analogy because 'a dark myth was taking shape,' reported *The Guardian*, 'that the Democrats had stabbed Trump in the back'.[18]

They hadn't, as the meticulous counting and auditing of the votes revealed. The Associated Press, Fox News, Atlanta-based CNN and other major networks called the election for Joe Biden on 7 November, and a procession of state-by-state certifications confirmed the results. Biden had indeed flipped Arizona. He'd also won Michigan, Pennsylvania and Wisconsin. To many observers' electoral surprise, he won Georgia, the first time a Democratic nominee had done so in twenty-eight years. Cobb County, the home of Kennesaw and

Rosanne Boyland, had narrowly backed Hillary Clinton in 2016, but it swung heavily for Biden. He won it from Trump by fourteen points, a result that helped deliver him the state overall.

Rosanne Boyland couldn't believe it. On 8 November she posted a satirical meme on Facebook marking herself as 'safe' from 'believing that Biden won today'. She published memes insisting that Georgia's election officials – all of whom were Republicans – had conspired to change the results. Interestingly, she did not challenge the result that saw QAnon believer Marjorie Taylor Greene elected in Georgia's fourteenth congressional district on the same ballot, in the same election, in the same state and through the same processes that had acknowledged the presidential victory of Joe Biden.

If youre not questioning this ... youre stupid at this point and I can't help you dude

Rosanne Boyland on Facebook, 5 November 2020

Despite all evidence to the contrary, the Trump campaign continued to insist the election was fraudulent. There were dozens of 'Kraken' lawsuits mounted overall by a suite of different lawyers. They sourced affidavits for 'fraud' complaints from partisan poll watchers, as well as from the general public through a form on a website aligned to the Trump campaign.[19]

As the former lawyer to Michael Flynn, Sidney Powell drew the admiration and encouragement of QAnon believers.[20] Although she denied being involved with the QAnon movement herself, she went on QAnon shows like Coleman Rogers' *The Patriots' Soapbox*, engaged publicly with QAnon influencers, and repeated QAnon slogans.[21] The 2020 US election had been declared the 'most secure in American history' by Trump's own cybersecurity agency, and yet as the lawsuits progressed, QAnon supporters amplified tweets using the hashtag #ReleaseTheKraken in the hundreds of thousands.[22]

The QAnon movement latched on to Sidney Powell's lawsuit campaign with some ferocity. Donie O'Sullivan explained for CNN that there was a need within the community for Trump to be re-elected. It wasn't only that believers needed Trump to stay in office to sustain the myth that Q's predictions were true – that 'the storm' was coming, that the movement did have a purpose, that these people did have a powerful champion to believe in. It was because by late 2020 there was an industry of influencers and advocates ensconced that nurtured the faith of the 'qommunity' as a matter of income: they wrote books and made broadcasts, sold merchandise, asked for donations. O'Sullivan had attended a conference run by QAnon influencers before the election. 'Their message to the audience,' he wrote, '[b]e patient and trust Q. Everything will come true after Trump's re-election.'[23]

Now that Trump had lost, there was no small amount of desperation to maintain the myth in which so many had invested, with their finances, with their income streams, with their character and their public reputations. For people like Rosanne Boyland, who had had such passionate arguments with friends and family members about the theories she'd espoused, there was, one can imagine, no small amount of loss of face involved in admitting that none of it had been true.

This fear of losing face was perhaps the reason why adherents plastered excuses for the movement over their social media. They shifted the goalposts around Q's prognostications when the promised arrests and extraditions – of Hillary Clinton, of John Podesta – didn't come to pass. Maybe it was why QAnon believers clung to the insistence that crimes committed in the movement's name were 'false flag' operations organised by the devilish deep state. It certainly explained why, back in September 2020, there weren't QAnon walkouts or mass demands for accountability when the operator of Qmap.pub – one of QAnon's most prominent, profit-making website communities – was rumbled as a senior vice-president at Citigroup who had an interest in datamining.[24] In October 2020, writing for Australia's *Financial Review*, William Turton and Joshua Brustein reported that long-time Wall Street IT executive Jason Gelinas had started the site in 2018 as a hobby project. He was dedicated to bringing QAnon to a wider audience of white-collar workers and soccer mums who'd appreciate the site's clean lines, clear links to external references and tabs that compiled posts around areas of interests – Hillary's servers, perhaps, or nukes, or Gitmo.[25]

Gelinas dreamed of making his QAnon hobby his day job. He told a friend that he believed the movement may indeed be his calling from God. Maybe God would be willing to gamble on the project's eventual profitability; a report in the *New York Post* claimed Gelinas was earning US$3000 a month from Patreon donations on the site, while compiling valuable data on the ten million very credulous visitors to it.[26]

Welcome Patriots

Q is a movement that is changing the world. Power is being restored to the people. From dark to light, corruption is being exposed worldwide and we are winning bigly!

Qmap.pub was created to share Q's messages and organize the data in an approachable way. This website is built with modern technologies running in the cloud. If you would like to contribute to this site, please visit the links below.

Qmap.pub site info page, June 2020[27]

While those like Gelinas harvested data, Rosanne Boyland and others like her were seeing less of it. Deeply immersed in Q's theories even at the time the credible allegations against Gelinas came to light, she had become enmeshed in an alternative information universe that increasingly sealed her away from fact-based points of view. Will Partin, the research analyst with Data & Society, and Alice Marwick, from the University of North Carolina, had discovered in their research that QAnon believers were not poorly read or poorly educated but rather voracious readers and communicators who just preferred stories that were untrue. The decisions made by these people weren't technically irrational, they were just made on the basis of believing information that was empirically inaccurate, as Partin explained to *The Guardian* on 25 June 2020.[28] The amount of information they consumed on the internet was vast, but its poor quality led them towards incorrect conclusions. They had, said Partin, a fundamentally different epistemology to judge what was true from what was false.

Those who invested in QAnon's research and discussion groups often did so with an obsessive and immersive energy. The prize of being rewarded with group validation for a 'proof' of one of Q's coded messages required study of Q's words, study of established discussion around it, and lots of googling. People set alarms to notify them of new Q drops. The excitement of poring through articles posted to their groups got some believers out of bed early, while others stayed up watching YouTube videos and reading late into the night. Leila Hay, a twenty-year-old British student who'd fallen into QAnon and back out, told a journalist from *Mashable* that during her time in the movement, she often read so much QAnon material online that she'd give herself headaches and eye strain.[29]

This kind of immersion explains, in part, the phenomenon of 'QAnon orphans', loving family members and friends estranged by those whose journey down the 'rabbit hole' – like Rosanne Boyland's – was appearing to travel one way.

Ironically, it was a subreddit formed for peer support among these people that brought public attention to the intimate costs of what Will Partin and Alice Marwick had described as QAnon's 'dark participatory culture'. The sad stories of family and friends who posted on r/QAnonCasualties about the loved ones who'd abandoned them were featured in publications like *The Guardian* due to content like this:

Husband of 21 Years Turning On Me
... I took care of these people my whole adult life. But, I refuse to spend the rest of my life being treated like an enemy and like garbage. Because I'm not 100 pro gun, don't believe dems are trying to destroy America, don't believe that fricking Derek chauvin [the murderer of George Floyd] is right in what he did. I'm just tired of being attacked ...

My Best Friend... Gone.
... She started saying favorable things about Trump. She believed there were violent (Black Lives Matter) riots in the city where her parents lived, and was frantically trying to get them to flee. Even sending her video of the neighborhood and the reassurance that nothing was happening and everything was fine didn't convince her ...

First Casualty
... So my cousin started posting Q related conspiracy theories about how the left wing media stole the election away from Trump and there is a vast network silencing anyone who disagrees with Biden who is a pedo and a lizard. And my

heart broke … She is 29, attended a private liberal arts
college, publicly identifies as queer, and I have been keeping
a closer eye on my conservative retired family members and
never imagined the first to go would be her …

Sometimes the process of estrangement was gradual and cumulative. Sometimes the rupture was more sudden. Karen Stewart, the sister of the prominent Australian QAnon advocate Tim Stewart, had the latter experience. An argument between the siblings about Donald Trump blew up at an outdoor family gathering, and a drunken Tim walked away. His son Jesse remained – Jesse and Karen had always been close – and he tried to persuade her of the veracity of Q's claims. Karen told Jesse that the theories sounded like propaganda, as well as something of high risk to her mental health. Karen, as the family knew, was a survivor of childhood sexual abuse herself, and she explained that she didn't want to be drawn into Tim and Jesse's QAnon obsession with chasing imaginary paedophiles. It was a volatile discussion, and Karen's husband intervened, warning Jesse that he was acting like someone who'd been radicalised – like an extremist. Provoked, Jesse came running across the backyard, as if about to throw a punch at Karen's husband's head, and Karen had to separate them.

'That was the moment in time where I thought, okay, wherever Tim and Jesse have gone, that is the most outlandish place,' Karen says. 'I only saw them once after that. At Easter, the following year.'[30]

In Kennesaw, Rosanne Boyland was engaged in similarly powerful disagreements with her own family about her disbelieving response to the election. 'We got in fights about it, arguments,' her sister, Lonna, said about the fantasies Rosanne Boyland pushed with such enthusiasm.[31] Rosanne had been sharing material online that coronavirus was a cabal plot to steal the election.

Myths of election fraud abounded among Georgia's Trump devotees in the month after Biden's victory was declared, despite Biden's historic tally of 81,283,098 popular votes to Trump's 74,222,958. Perhaps because of it. Throughout November, Rosanne Boyland posted memes about the Biden victory that complained about fact-checks while sharing disproved conspiracy theories about Trump voters being handed Sharpie pens to vote with that would invalidate their ballots. She echoed fact-free claims made by the teams of pro-Trump lawyers, and Trump himself, about dodgy ballot practices, devious partisan poll#watchers and fraud. She was stunned by Joe Biden's huge vote total and wrote on Facebook, 'Nobody with an ounce of common sense thinks it's legit.'

She typified how deeply pro-Trump conspiracist thinking penetrated parts of the community. On 10 December, *The Washington Post* reported that Trump-supporting Georgians were chasing trucks and staking out loading docks on the hunt for suspicious boxes that might contain fraudulent absentee ballots.[32]

It didn't matter to these people that the lawsuits pursued by Sidney Powell and the others were accumulating a steady procession of losses in court. Of sixty-five reported suits, by year's end the sole victory the 'Kraken' had delivered Trump in the courts was a decision that struck down extending a deadline for Pennsylvania voters to correct mail-in ballots, something that had no meaningful impact on the election results. It didn't matter, either, that Sidney Powell's credibility was torn apart over the course of November 2020 after she claimed that voting machines used in the presidential ballot count had somehow been corrupted by either a rogue supercomputer, George Soros, the Clinton Foundation or former Venezuelan president Hugo Chavez. Perhaps conspicuously, it didn't matter that Hugo Chavez had actually been dead since 2013. It didn't even really matter that Q had made only a handful of posts after the election, a few on 12 November and one on 8 December, that barely referred to the election. The most coherent – and consoling – of these was posted on 12 November: 'Sometimes you must walk through the darkness before you see the light.'

What mattered was that the desperate need to believe Trump would remain president was being fuelled by the behaviour of Trump himself, who simply refused to concede the election. On 14 November 2020, a 'Million MAGA March' in Washington platformed Marjorie Taylor Greene and Alex Jones from *Infowars* to push Trump's own election-fraud conspiracy theories to a crowd of some thousands, and Trump circled it in his motorcade. The next day, Trump tweeted claims that the election had been 'rigged' for Biden to win, a claim he repeated in press statements.[33] Powell's lawsuits continued, and continued to fail, and the outgoing president spent the next month pressuring state officials – infamously, those in Michigan and Georgia – to overturn their states' results. They refused. Each state's electoral college met on 14 December; the votes tallied 306 to 232. Biden had beaten Trump by the same electoral college margin that Trump had beaten Clinton and claimed then was 'a landslide', but still Trump refused to concede.

With legal appeals and pressure campaigns failing, those attempting to keep Trump in power turned their attention to an upcoming joint sitting of Congress. It was the traditional session scheduled to certify the receipt of electoral votes from the states, and as a ceremonial gathering was overseen by the vice-president. In 2021 it was scheduled for 6 January.

Trump supporters organising protests mobilised behind this date, the aim being to pressure Trump's own vice-president, Mike Pence, into refusing to certify Biden's election. 'Big protest in D.C. on January 6th,' Trump himself tweeted to his followers on 19 December. 'Be there, will be wild!' He followed up on 27 December with 'See you in Washington, DC, on January 6th. Don't miss it. Information to follow'. 'JANUARY SIXTH, SEE YOU IN DC!' came on 30 December. 'The BIG Protest Rally in Washington, D.C. will take place at 11:00 A.M. on January 6th. Locational details to follow. StopTheSteal!' he tweeted on 1 January.

Trump had some familiar – and enthusiastic – megaphones also promoting the event. The outgoing president had made use of his last months in office issuing presidential pardons to close friends and allies from various legal troubles, and some of these people were overt in their support for rallies on 6 January.

Steve Bannon, for instance, was facing criminal charges for conspiracy to commit wire fraud and conspiracy to commit money laundering at the same time he sponsored a cross-country bus tour of the 'March for Trump' organisers promoting the 6 January event. In advance of the day's activities, he'd also suggested on his *War Room* podcast that the director of the FBI should be beheaded and have his head placed on a pike outside the White House, along with that of health official Dr Anthony Fauci. 'You either get with the program or you are gone,' warned Bannon, who Trump would pardon on 19 January 2021.[34]

Disgraced Lieutenant General Michael Flynn was also out promoting the 6 January events for weeks before they happened. He'd encouraged Christians – of a certain kind – to join a 'Jericho March' in Washington on that date, describing the campaign against the election results as a battle for America's heart and soul, and an occasion demanding fearlessness and sacrifice. *ABC News* in the US reported that Flynn had been personally invited by Trump to join the official 6 January rally, although Flynn skipped out during the event. Despite having pleaded guilty to lying to the FBI, Trump had pardoned Flynn on 25 November 2020.[35]

Trump's old friend and Republican operative Roger Stone had been sentenced to prison time in the wake of the Mueller investigation, found guilty of witness tampering, obstruction of justice and of lying to Congress five times. Trump pardoned him on 23 December, and by the night of 5 January, Stone was in Washington, geeing up Trump supporters at a pre-rally 'One Nation Under God' prayer event, flanked by members of the Oath Keepers militia group. His speech framed the demonstration the next day as a 'fight between dark and light'.[36]

Spruikers of the event weren't limited to political celebrities of the Trump era, of course. British newspaper the *Independent* reported on 9 January that QAnon-related accounts and pages were discussing the planned protests of the election result for weeks before they happened.[37]

Trump told his supporters to go to the capitol on January 6. He gave a speech at the Ellipse before hand. He did say do it peacefully. People went there, and a handful took it too far. They misinterpreted Trump's words. Trump accidentally caused the riot, he didn't actually mean it.

Anonymous on 4chan, 25 January 2021

Rosanne Boyland was committed to going to Washington, DC, even if it was a ten-hour drive; she had never heard Trump speak in person. Her family members 'vehemently disagreed' with her decision.[38] Her sister and brother-in-law tried to talk her out of it, but Rosanne was already sharing Facebook posts about the event. She amplified a viral post that told 'all the Patriots heading to D.C. bring EXTRA food, water, blankets, supplies, and have a plan of where to sleep. Patriots not going to D.C. please Echo this info' the week of the event. Her claim that following these instructions was necessary because authorities would be shutting hotels, restaurants and other amenities to keep protestors away was marked with a Facebook warning about misleading content, like many of her posts about the election had been.

Travis View from the *QAnon Anonymous* podcast believed that the en masse physical mobilisation of adherents was an evolution in the movement. He explained to website *FiveThirtyEight* how one of QAnon's most appealing fantasies was its premise the world could be transformed in a grand, revolutionary way by sharing memes from the comfort of your computer, so to stir QAnon believers to do something in the physical world required the heft and advertising powers of its biggest influencers. Indeed, by 9 January, *The New York Times* reported that media insights researchers at Zignal Labs had found 100,000 online exhortations among various groups to 'storm the Capitol' in the month leading up to the event.[39] For View, however, 6 January held a unique power for the QAnon community because Trump himself had promoted it.[40]

What View saw as 'advertising powers' were, to believers, holy summonses. How could Travis View – let alone Lonna and Justin Cave – have understood the spiritual significance to someone who'd 'gone full QAnon' of gathering in Washington, DC? The mythology that had been shared and repeated and shared and repeated again within its community was that 'the storm' was imminent. Q's promise was that 'Nothing can stop what's coming' – Q had said this twice in November alone. Q had described the fear of the cabal's Washington elites as 'panic in DC' around forty times. Now, Trump was calling patriots to DC. In the wake of a stolen election, it had to be one of his four-dimensional chess moves. Surely this meant Trump would seize the emergency broadcast system, announcing the launch of the promised arrests. The rounding up of evildoers was imminent. Patriots had been invited to be present for the precise moment the great awakening began. How could anyone stay home?

In an article for *The Conversation*, religion scholar Timothy Pettipiece compared the belief system of QAnon to the worldview of the gnostics of first-century Christian and Jewish sects.[41] He explained that the ancient gnostics believed that the world that people perceive is really a prison constructed by demonic powers to enslave the soul. Only a small spiritual elite, he wrote, 'are blessed with special knowledge – or *gnosis* – that enables them to unmask this deception'. Feature writer for the *Intelligencer* Kerry Howley saw the same belief in QAnonners, but with modern smugness. 'Ecstatic believers', as she called them, were going to descend on the Capitol on 6 January because there was a 'plan in place to clear the world of wicked-doing, and an all-powerful man executing that plan'. The existence of doubters functioned to make believers feel superior in their belief.[42]

Trump had invited supporters to DC on 6 January, and there was no way that Rosanne Boyland, as a believer, wasn't going. Lonna Cave did not approve of Rosanne's plans and was upset about her going. The sisters got in an argument about it. 'They have different political views,' Lonna's husband, Justin, said later. 'My wife didn't want her to go.'[43]

There were clear reasons for Lonna Cave to be concerned. Weeks of investigations, dismissed lawsuits, recounts and reports had determined that the elections were free and fair, the result certified. But maybe Lonna Cave had also seen the Trump supporters on Twitter, posting photographs under Trump's tweets of the weapons they planned to bring with them to the rally.

Rosanne Boyland assured her sister that she was not going to participate in any violence when she travelled to Washington. She promised Lonna she was just going to stand on the sidelines to show her support. Once more, the family begged her not to make the trip. Yet, as Justin Cave explained later, it was something that Rosanne felt passionate about, so she went.[44]

QAnon believers weren't the only Trump supporters who descended on Washington's Capitol on 6 January 2021, although they made themselves visible in t-shirts, banners, flags and other on-brand accoutrements, with Jacob Chansley, the self-styled 'QAnon shaman', distinguishing himself with his horned bearskin hat and face paint. But far-right militia groups like the Oath Keepers, Three Percenters and Proud Boys were there too. They'd brought with them established backgrounds of instigating violence, as well as plans about the day they'd prepared with one another on channels like Telegram.[45] Those who gathered, wrote Talia Lavin for *The New Republic* on 7 January 2021, saw the moment as one of apocalyptic confrontation between the forces of slavery and those of freedom, with the rhetoric constantly harking back to that of the American Revolution.[46] If there was a shared psychological mood to the gathering it was aspirational cosplay, located in a cultural fantasy somewhere between

Washington Crossing the Delaware and the plucky fugitives who fight the alien overlords in *V*.

Ron Watkins, son of Jim and the erstwhile administrator of Q's home, the website 8kun, had been heavily retweeted by Trump in advance of the event – Trump had shared Watkins's concern regarding 'malign foreign influence efforts in our elections'.[47] At 3.23 am on 6 January, when crowds were already gathering to get a good vantage point to see the president address the rally, Watkins had somewhat set the tone for what might take place when he denounced then vice-president Mike Pence in a tweet as a traitor, sharing a blog post that demanded Pence's 'immediate arrest' for treason.[48] Trump was maintaining his own pressure on the vice-president. 'All Mike Pence has to do is send [the votes] back to the States, AND WE WIN. Do it Mike, this is a time for extreme courage!' he tweeted at 8.17 am.[49]

At noon, Trump repeated the exhortation to Pence in a speech to the crowd that went for an hour, denouncing Pence by name six times. While Trump was still speaking, *The Washington Post* reported, Pence had released a statement that contained an explicit commitment to carry out his constitutional duty to certify the vote.[50]

Talia Lavin described Trump's performance as 'his signature peevish, Borscht-belt-inflected brand of fascist insurrectionism'.[51] Trump told the protestors, 'We're going to walk down to the Capitol.' He told them 'to fight' and to 'fight like hell'. He said they had to 'show strength'.[52] Before the speech was even finished, some of the rally attendees started moving towards the Capitol Building, where the vote to certify the election results was taking place. More people from the crowd headed that way as Trump's speech finished, and more did after that. Trump himself got in a limousine and went back to the White House.

Rosanne Boyland had made the long road trip to Washington with her friend Justin Winchell. There's a photograph of her that he took as they walked to join the crowds moving on the Capitol Building. In it she's wearing a black hoodie from a camouflage outfitter, ripped jeans, and striped socks and a pair of sneakers. She has a backpack and a placard that says 'Save America'. She's holding aloft a yellow Gadsden flag, the one that features a snake and the words 'don't tread on me'. It's a flag that was first used during the American Revolution, since appropriated by gun-rights advocates and fans of limited government.

Kerry Howley, writing for *Intelligencer*, described images of QAnon supporters taken on the day as 'images of unrestrained joy'.[53] It's in Rosanne Boyland's face in the photograph. She's walking tall and smiling. Wearing a pair of American flag–patterned sunglasses, she literally has stars in her eyes.

this is the kind of stuff they show in the articles.
the fat faceless blob in the black shirt is allegedly her.
Im more curious about the passed out black guy. no
one ever brings him up lol

Anonymous on 4chan, 12 February 2021

Rosanne Boyland's sunglasses were what *The New York Times* used to identify her in footage recording the assault of the Capitol Building by Trump's crowds.[54] At around 2.30 pm, a mob forced their way through lines of Metropolitan Police on the west side of the Capitol. This mob reached a second-level promenade and made for a security door that lay within an ornate arched tunnelway entrance to the building, trying to breach it. The crowd confronted a line of police and began pushing against it. The tunnelway was packed with rioters within thirty minutes. The police and protestors sprayed chemical irritants at one another.

Rosanne Boyland had promised her sister she would stand on the sidelines but, amped up by the president's speech, she and Justin Winchell walked up to the Capitol and joined the surge in the tunnel. A video records that at 4.19 pm, the crowd they joined made another push against police.[55] The police pushed back and rioters fell backwards, out of the arched tunnel, tumbling down some steps. Justin Winchell is visible in the video, digging through the bodies of the other rioters as more of them fall out of the doorway because he can't find Rosanne Boyland. They've been separated. Something's wrong. She's still somewhere in the crowd at 4.27 pm when two rioters attack the police again, one wielding a crutch. Irritants are being sprayed all around. Someone else attacks the police line with a hockey stick.

Suddenly, Rosanne Boyland appears in the video. She's on the ground, on her side. She's being trampled by the mob. She's not moving, and Justin Winchell can't get her out of the melee. He starts screaming that she's dying, she needs help. He has his arm underneath her, but a man falls on her, and another man steps over her. People are climbing over her to launch themselves at the police. The rioter with the crutch knocks an officer to the ground and the crowd cheers. The one with the hockey stick smashes it into the officers ten times in sixteen seconds. Rosanne Boyland is pinned to the ground. 'She's gonna die!' screams Winchell. 'I need somebody!'

The police can't help because they're still being clubbed by the men who are also pushing them, trying to breach the Capitol. Justin Winchell is begging people in the crowd to help him, but a man sprays irritant over his head into the police line. Roseanne is still being trampled. Finally, two men in the crowd manage to pull her away from the door and lay her out on the steps. Someone checks her pulse. She's unresponsive. One attempts to resuscitate her with CPR. It doesn't seem to work. A man frantically negotiates with the police to do something, to help this woman, and men carry Rosanne's body to the police line. It takes two and a half minutes. Even as this happens, there are men in the crowd still hurling poles at the police, pledging to kill them.

'By the time that they decided to pick the person up and give them to a police officer, she had blue lips and blood was coming out of her nose,' said a pro-Trump YouTuber from Portland who called himself 'Villain Report' in a video he uploaded later.[56] He was the man who had checked Rosanne Boyland's pulse. Despite everything going on around them, police managed to contact paramedics and get Rosanne Boyland inside the Capitol rotunda. Two police were performing CPR on her when paramedics eventually managed to reach her through the chaos. The paramedics took over the resuscitation attempts and raced her to hospital.

Back in Georgia, Rosanne's old friend Zedith Drane watched the reports of the events in Washington and logged on to Facebook to see what her 'hot take' may have been but found nothing – he didn't know she had gone to the protests.[57] Rosanne Boyland's family were also watching the same scenes at the Capitol, hoping Rosanne was not among the crowd.[58]

At 6.09 pm, ninety minutes after she collapsed, Rosanne Boyland, thirty-four years old, was pronounced dead at a Washington hospital.[59] Her final post on Twitter was a picture of thousands of people surrounding the Washington Monument, retweeted from the account of Trump's White House media director, Dan Scavino. *AP News* reported that the photo was taken before Trump's rally speech repeated his unfounded claims of election fraud, before he incited demonstrators to march on the Capitol while lawmakers within debated the electoral votes.[60]

If you're not out in the sun building guillotines, what are you doing with your life?

Milo Yiannopoulos (@m) on Gab, 19 August 2021

Rosanne Boyland was not QAnon's only casualty at the Capitol on 6 January 2021. Earlier, on the other side of the building, a QAnon believer named Ashli Babbitt was with a mob of Trump supporters who had managed to breach the Capitol Building.[61] They had walked through the rotunda but became agitated as they made their way towards the congressional chamber. Congressional representatives were in the process of being evacuated, and only a set of glass-paned doors and a bare defence of three police officers stood between Babbitt's group and the chamber lobby where the evacuation was taking place. As the mob approached, the officers had frantically created a furniture barricade to the lobby, locking the doors and standing in front of them. The police had no shields or riot gear.[62] Two of them didn't even have hats.

Ashli Babbitt and the protestors soon flooded the hallway that led to the glass doors, holding aloft weapons improvised from sticks and flagpoles, filming their actions on their phones, some with selfie sticks. One had a camera mounted to the helmet on his head. They were determined to get past the police barricade. They roared that they wanted the doors open. They chanted, 'Break it down! Break it down!'

The three officers held their ground, unmoving. The protestors banged on the barricaded doors, manoeuvring around the police and bashing the glass panes with their hands.[63] They were so close to the representatives being evacuated from the lobby that congressional representative Jim McGovern, Democrat of Massachusetts, could see their faces through the glass. If asked to described evil, he told *The New York Times*, that was what it looked like. The people he saw seemed crazed. "'They weren't here to make a political point," he said. They were here to destroy things.'[64]

Ashli Babbitt was at the front of the crowd. She had a Trump flag knotted around her neck like a cape and was demanding the police step aside, open the door and let them past.[65] 'They're not gonna stop,' she said of the crowd. People were thrusting flagpoles into the glass over the officers' shoulders, beside their heads. It was beginning to shatter.

The mobs across the Capitol were howling for the killing of lawmakers. In the lobby, on the other side of the doors, a lieutenant whose earpiece had told him that officers all over the building were being attacked with sticks and poles and chemical sprays could not see the police at the barricade but could see the protestors hammering at the glass. The lieutenant got into position, aiming a gun at the entry point, not knowing what weapons the protestors had.

On the other side of the rioters, a team of equipped tactical officers were approaching from behind them. The lieutenant in the lobby couldn't see that. The police at the door got word of the tactical team's imminent arrival and started moving away from the doors. A man in the crowd of rioters at the door was filming the scene and noticed the lieutenant's gun through the glass panes. He called out, 'There's a gun! There's a gun!' and filmed what he could see, but the others hadn't.[66] He kept screaming, but the protestors were still attacking the doors; no one could hear him. Wrapped in Gadsden and American flags, they were bellowing 'Fuck the blue!' and 'Fucking pussies!' at the police.[67] The man with the camera screamed again, 'There's a gun!' One or two protestors noticed, but their shouts were drowned out by the sound of the glass doors being shattered by the protestors. Ashli Babbitt was hoisted by the crowd through the smashed pane towards the lobby. She was trying to crawl through when the lieutenant stepped forward and fired.[68]

Ashli Babbitt fell to the ground, her back to the floor. The bullet had gone into her shoulder. Tactical officers were with her immediately, cradling her neck. Most of the protestors who hadn't instantly fled got out their cameras and filmed her dying. Her eyes were open. Blood was pouring out of her mouth.

Ashli Babbitt was thirty-five years old. She'd been raised in the suburbs of San Diego, California, and returned there to live in a polyamorous relationship with her husband, Aaron, and their mutual girlfriend, Kayla Joyce, after spending fourteen years in the United States Air Force. She'd spent six of these years in the Air National Guard, charged with guarding the very Washington she herself had tried to upend. Leaving the services in 2016, she relished the opportunity to speak freely about her political beliefs. She'd go on political-themed rants at barbecues. Her speeches were often tinged with conspiracy theories and sometimes the neighbours struggled to follow along.

Once proud to vote for Barack Obama, Ashli Babbitt couldn't bring herself to vote for Hillary Clinton and voted Trump.[69] Enamoured of the new president, frustrated by coronavirus and struggling to manage a pool-supplies business that was crippled by bad debt, she was feisty and political but those closest to her perhaps didn't realise the extent of her drift towards radicalisation. Although Ashli flew a QAnon flag outside their shared bungalow alongside an American one, Kayla Joyce didn't follow her on Twitter. She didn't grasp how fatally deep into QAnon thinking her girlfriend had sunk.

The Washington Post reported, 'She promoted far-right lies that Hillary Clinton has kidnapped children and described the left as modern-day enslavers.'[70] She posted QAnon material, repeated its slogans, joined the #SaveTheChildren hashtag. There were photos online of her taken at Trump 'boat parades', visual campaign events on water where supporters joined a flotilla of boats decorated with campaign material; Babbitt was featured with other people in QAnon gear.[71] On 5 January, she tweeted: 'They can try and try and try but the storm is here and it is descending upon DC in less than 24 hours ... dark to light!'[72]

On 6 January, it took three hours for police to finally clear the Capitol of protestors. Congressional representatives and senators were summoned from where they'd been evacuated, their joint sitting restored in the very chambers that the protestors had briefly overrun. Although a handful of Republicans voted with the Trump cause and against the electoral vote tallies from some states, it was a performative display. Vice President Mike Pence oversaw the certification, and Joe Biden proceeded unimpeded towards his presidential inauguration on 20 January. There was no 'storm' – there was never going to be a storm. Within a few months, all the 'Kraken' lawsuits would also be exhausted. Rosanne Boyland and Ashli Babbitt had died for beliefs that meant nothing.

Two more protestors died of medical emergencies in Washington over the course of what was, in every way, a failed, shambolic putsch. A police officer, Brian Sicknick, also died from injuries inflicted by protestors. Two more police officers committed suicide within the week. One of them was Metropolitan Police officer Jeffrey Smith, who told his wife that when he heard over his police radio that shots had been fired, he thought it was police who'd been shot. He thought he would die. Smith was still battling protestors at 5.35 pm when one of them thrust a metal pole at his helmet. He kept working to clear the building, but afterwards presented to a police medical clinic with a head injury and was put on leave. At home, his wife knew something was terribly wrong, but after a medical check-in on 14 January, he was ordered back to work. He had sandwiches and cookies his wife had packed for him as he drove his Ford Mustang to his shift the next night. On his way into work, in the car, Jeffrey Smith shot himself. His wife told *The Washington Post* she'd come to believe he just could not face returning to work after what he'd experienced on 6 January.[73] Two more officers had suicided by the start of August.[74]

There were hundreds of injuries to police, some permanent. Rocks, flagpoles, bits of metal and bottles had been wielded at them by the protestors. The experience was traumatising. 'We were battling 15,000 people,' said a detective whose experience of the day had included being grabbed by his helmet, dragged face-first down a flight of steps and being stripped of his equipment while the crowd around him chanted, 'USA!' The officer described what he saw as a medieval battle scene.[75]

Ashli Babbitt's husband and girlfriend had not come with her to Washington. They hadn't wanted her to go; they didn't like the idea of her travelling there alone.[76] Ashli negotiated that she would check in with them every thirty minutes. Then she didn't. Watching the scenes of violence unfold on TV, Aaron and Kayla frantically called her, and called again. The calls went unanswered, and Ashli's location services were off.[77] Kayla was phoning around DC hospitals trying to find her when she saw the video of Ashli being shot.[78] The family found out about her death by seeing it replayed on TV. Her mother-in-law said hearing the news left her numb with shock. 'I really don't know why she decided to do this,' she told a reporter from Fox.[79]

Initially, the reward for QAnon believer Ashli Babbitt's pro-storm sacrifice was that she was disowned by the conspiracy community. *SFGate* reported that by 11 January 2021, the QAnon Patriots account was one among many on the social-networking app Parler claiming variations of a similar story: 'Ashli Babbit was a False Flag Operation. She is alive.'[80] The insistence was she was an agent provocateur from the shadowy, oft-cited, little-found, all-purpose villains, the left-wing, anti-fascist 'antifa' militants. 'Only a small amount of her immediate family would know,' claimed the QAnon Patriots, 'the rest have to believe she's dead to keep up the illusion.' On 8 January, *Newsweek* reported that one of the lawyers from the Kraken suits, Lin Wood, tweeted the suggestion that Ashli Babbitt may have been 'conveniently photoshopped' to link her to Wood and the QAnon movement.[81]

Ashli Babbitt's very last tweet was a retweet of one of Lin Wood's. It was a list of demands for 6 January. These included, among other things, that Vice President Mike Pence be charged with treason.

#IfTrumpWereReinstated it would be especially uncomfortable for reinstated Vice-President Mike Pence, who knows that everyone who wanted Trump back considers him a traitor and would still kind of like to hang him.

@meamwayne on Twitter, 19 August 2021

Kayla Joyce laid the blame for Ashli Babbitt's death on Donald Trump.[82] So did the US Congress, who voted to impeach Trump for a historic second time on 13 January, with the Democratic Party majority receiving the votes of ten of Trump's own Republican congressional representatives to do so. On 19 January, then Senate majority leader Mitch McConnell, a Republican, joined the ranks of this opinion. He was said to be leaning towards convicting Trump in his Senate impeachment trial. That day, McConnell said from the Senate floor, 'The mob was fed lies. They were provoked by the president and other powerful people, and they tried to use fear and violence to stop a specific proceeding of the first branch of the federal government which they did not like.'[83]

By early February, as the impeachment process rolled towards a trial of Trump in the Senate, at least ten Capitol riot arrestees were also blaming Trump for their part in an insurrection, saying that he had incited their participation.[84] As president, Trump was also the commander-in-chief, they claimed, and as that commander had invited their march on the Capitol.[85]

An attempted coup to keep Trump in the presidency had failed, but those most invested in the Trump project were not yet willing to abandon all hope of its future return. Perhaps aware that conviction in the Senate trial would prevent Trump from ever being able to run for president again, more Trump allies mobilised around the narrative the QAnon accounts were fervently seeding about Ashli Babbitt as a dupe of antifa.

On 1 March 2021, *The New York Times* published an exposé of how a web centipede was roused to spread the fraudulent story that antifa activists had run the Capitol riots. They traced its media origin to the Twitter account of small-time right-wing radio host Michael D. Brown. At 1.51 pm on 6 January, Brown had posted a suspicion that antifa or even Black Lives Matter activists could have led the riot in disguise as Trump supporters. 'Come on, man,' he'd written, 'have you never heard of psyops?'[86]

Psyops – psychological operations, military tactics used to wage psychological disruption on an enemy – were an article of faith in the QAnon community. In keeping with the references to *Alice in Wonderland*, cabal manipulation and deviousness, Q had asked followers 'What is a psyop?' in two separate posts.

Whether Brown's tweet was a specific dog whistle to this community or not, the dogs came quick. The tweet was picked up by another conservative broadcaster, Todd Herman, who at the time was guest hosting the show of the nationally syndicated right-wing radio superstar Rush Limbaugh. Only minutes after Brown had mooted the false idea that antifa had something to do with what happened at the Capitol, Herman was sharing the conspiracy theory on air to Limbaugh's millions of listeners. By 2.30 pm, the right-wing *Washington Times* newspaper – founded by the rabidly pro-Trump, conservative reverend Sun Myung Moon and owned by a subsidiary of his Unification church – again shared this conjecture, with the outright untrue addition that two antifa activists had been identified in the Capitol crowds using facial recognition technology.

Singapore company XRVision were the makers of this technology, and they issued a rapid refutation. *Buzzfeed* reported that the men who *The Washington Times* had claimed were a Stalinist and a climate-activist Black Lives Matter protestor were identified by XRVision as a Neo-Nazi and a QAnon supporter. XRVision sent cease and desist communications to *The Washington Times*, demanding both a retraction of the false article and a public apology.[87] It took *The Washington Times* a tardy twenty-four hours to comply, in which time a deluge of social media comment ricocheted the accusations across the internet with the fervour of a desperate wish. Facebook calculated the fake story had received 360,000 engagements on its platform alone. In the single hour leading up to 5 pm, *The New York Times* reported, the fanciful story had gained 8700 mentions across cable media, social media and online news sources.[88]

Within hours, Fox News pundit Laura Ingraham had put the viral false story before her millions of Twitter followers, repeating it to her Fox News audience of millions later that night. Ingraham's fellow Fox pundit, once–Republican vice-presidential candidate Sarah Palin, did the same. By the time the rioters had finally been cleared from the Capitol Building and the US House and Senate were able to safely reconvene in the ransacked Capitol chambers to finish certification of the 2020 election, pro-Trump Republican representative Matt Gaetz was repeating the fake accusation from the riot-trashed congressional floor. Mere hours after the Capitol attack, congressional representative Mo Brooks was himself repeating the claims to Fox Business. Brooks doubled down on Twitter the next day, writing, 'Evidence, much public, surfacing that many Capitol assaulters were fascist ANTIFAs, not Trump supporters.' He added, 'Don't be fooled by #FakeNewsMedia whose political judgment drives their reporting.' Brooks's tweets, also, went viral.

This was the mainstream context established in which QAnon supporters could argue over the next few weeks that hapless, dead Ashli Babbitt was never one of their own. Their community's active shares and repeats of the fake antifa story empowered mainstream Trumpists with a populist momentum to make their false statements with confidence. So too did the imprimatur of that establishment allow QAnon adherents who weren't at the Capitol to convince themselves their movement remained non-violent and pure. On 6 January, Justin Winchell had been alongside his friend Rosanne Boyland, trying to breach the Capitol Building together as part of the murderous mob. By 7 January, Winchell was giving radio interviews shifting the blame to antifa for the acts of the mob that he and Boyland themselves had been in. 'She was killed by an incited event,' he told CBS46, 'and it was not incited by Trump supporters.'[89]

Winchell said Trump bore no responsibility for his friend's death. The message had been shared through committed propaganda channels, and it found its target soon enough. Despite his unambiguous statements against Trump on 19 January, by 13 February the political winds within the Republican Party had turned away from Mitch McConnell and back towards the Trumpist right. The Senate failed to reach the two-thirds majority required to convict Donald Trump in his impeachment trial and he was acquitted. Only seven Republicans had voted with the Democrats and Mitch McConnell was not one of them.

Mo Brooks of Alabama had also voted against Trump's impeachment in the House of Representatives, claiming there was 'ZERO' evidence of Trump inciting the events of the day. This was the same Mo Brooks who'd also addressed the rally that preceded the riot, telling the crowd, 'Today is the day American patriots start taking down names and kicking ass!'[90]

Six months later, when congressional Democrats had initiated a select committee to investigate the events of 6 January, Mo Brooks was dismissive of their attempt. All but two Republicans in the House boycotted the investigation, and in an interview with Jim Newell for *Slate*, Brooks repeated a popular Republican line that Democrat Nancy Pelosi, the House speaker, somehow bore the responsibility for a failure to protect the police.[91] He bragged to Newell that his own level of preparation that day had been superior – he'd slept in his office the night before and given his speech at the rally with body armour under his windcheater. 'I was warned on Monday that there might be risks associated with the next few days,' he explained.

Newell asked who had warned him. What was the risk? Brooks didn't say.

Good Morning Patriots!!!

Fuck all LIBTARDS, FUFCKTARDS, DEMORATS, Turncoats, & all who ain't fucking right!! Yes that's you too Transtesticle FUCKS!! Happy to see my Parler friends!!!! All the rest GO FUCK YOURSELVES!

@ViolentVixen on Parler, 17 February 2021

The movement around 6 January may have abandoned its victims, but Parler, at least, as well as the similarly unrestricted social media platforms Telegram and Gab, were enjoying a surge in favour.

In the wake of the failed insurrection attempt, the giant social media platforms that had pipelined the radicalisation of so many would-be insurrectionists had decided to, finally, clamp down. Twitter suspended 70,000 accounts associated with QAnon, telling the Associated Press it was acting against online behaviour 'that has the potential to lead to offline harm'.[92] Twitter was in no denial about Trump's role inciting the chaos; they even suspended his account.

There'd already been a QAnon crackdown on YouTube in October 2020, and another on Reddit a few months before in July. Facebook now made a bigger move, cracking down on Facebook groups as well as public pages that fomented hateful content. The company was already wearing the brand damage of its association with hard-right extremism and disinformation and had been under increasing global political pressure to implement stronger content moderation standards for years. It had also started restricting QAnon content the previous year as escalating incidents of real-world violence made the FBI's warning about its domestic-terror potential more difficult to ignore. Facebook's own description of QAnon as a 'militarised social movement' seemed prescient in the wake of adherents' visible involvement in the Capitol riots. Platforms as diverse as YouTube, Triller, Pinterest and even artisan marketplace Etsy also moved to restrict QAnon content.[93] After all, what viable internet business would want to be associated with a toxic product like 8kun?

Even 8kun – now known as 8kun – appeared to be taking a temperature check given external events. Two weeks after demanding Mike Pence's prosecution for treason, 8kun's scion Ron Watkins – who many suspected of being Q himself – shared an Inauguration Day message to his followers: 'We gave it our all. Now we need to keep our chins up and go back to our lives as best we are able.' He posted this on Telegram; having been kicked off Twitter and banned from Facebook, that's where his people were.[94]

In the meantime, the FBI combed through the masses of footage that so many of the Capitol rioters had captured of themselves in the fray, making identifications and beginning arrests. Their efforts were aided by many friends and family members who recognised their estranged, QAnon-believing loved ones in the images of the riots that were circulating. A woman called Leslie described to *The Guardian* the 'helpless, horrifying feeling' of seeing her QAnon mother with the rioters who scaled the Capitol scaffolding. Like others, she was hoping that calls from the FBI would serve as a 'wake up call' that QAnon belief had serious consequences.[95]

As the arrests continued, some disturbing patterns began to emerge. Researchers at the University of Maryland's National Consortium for the Study of Terrorism and Responses to Terrorism (START) identified forty QAnon adherents among four hundred or so rioters who'd been arrested by the end of May.[96] This was a significant number, and one the researchers realised was likely to increase as investigations continued. What had happened at the Capitol had borne out the concerns expressed by the FBI back in their memo of 2019.

An analysis of QAnon's Capitol offenders revealed their backgrounds were economically diverse. Michael Jensen from START told *Voice of America* that while there were certainly people who'd struggled with unemployment and drug problems among the QAnon ranks, many of QAnon's Capitol arrestees had 'affluent backgrounds' with high levels of educational attainment and no criminal history.[97] QAnon offenders also tended to skew older than arrestees from other far-right groups, and they included more women. These observations affirmed what Travis View, from the *QAnon Anonymous* podcast, told *Voice of America* on 31 March 2020: what united adherents wasn't a shared class or economic experience but a 'sense of moral righteousness that they are fighting a very noble crusade', providing them the 'moral justification to do some very dangerous and criminal things'.[98]

Trump supporters were often derided with a 'boomer-rube' stereotype that depicted them as older redneck bumpkins from struggling, working-class circumstances.[99] Political scientist Isaac Kamola, for a paper he published in May 2021, drew on the terminology of Marxist class analysis to identify QAnon adherents within the *lumpenproletariat*, a category that traditionally sweeps up the unemployed, the underemployed, the rootless and the criminal. The *lumpenproletariat* is a class ravaged by capitalism – made desperate by it – but without clear ideology or a sense of class solidarity. Without much data on the class or economic breakdown of QAnon adherents, Kamola saw the yearning of people to participate in QAnon's be-a-hero role-playing games and simple dark-into-light narrative, an understandable escapist channel away from economic dread.[100]

Kamola was right to identify that an established infrastructure of ruthless political operatives on the right saw the value in exploiting the explosive energy of a group animated by grand personal narratives of heroism and anointment. He was right, too, that QAnon attracted mercantilist and mercenary opportunists, grifting the movement for monetary gain. Yet it was the American political scientist – and conservative – Tom Nichols who seemed to nail the class colours of QAnon more precisely in a tweet on 2 July 2021. 'The more you watch the 1/6 insurrectionists,' wrote Nichols, 'the more you realize how stupid and dangerous a *lumpen-bourgeioisie* can be. They are reflexively illiberal in the name of finding kicks to relieve the dullness of their lives.'

Nichols's thinking accorded with a University of Chicago study of the Capitol rioters, which found that overall 40 per cent of those taking part were likely business owners or white-collar workers, and only 9 per cent appeared to be unemployed. Citing this study, *The Washington Post* reminded its readers of studies that had shown 'the poor and uneducated are not more likely to join extremist movements', and that ongoing research had, in fact, found the opposite.[101] What the *Post* had discovered among the initial pool of 125 insurrectionists arrested in Washington was that most of them had experienced money troubles sometime over the past two decades. These included disruptive life events like bankruptcies, evictions, foreclosures, bad debts and unpaid taxes.

Many of these people had overcome their troubles and regained their status, but Cynthia Miller-Idriss, a political science professor at American University, wrote that that these experiences could personally impress a lasting 'deep-seated feeling of precarity' – a sense of status under threat – that allowed Trump's rhetoric about undeserving victimhood to resonate. She believed 'that precarity – combined with a sense of betrayal or anger that someone is taking something away – mobilised a lot of people that day'.[102]

Political scientist Thomas McCauley clarified the ideological impetus of QAnon with some precision in a 2021 academic paper about contemporary diversities within right-wing extremism. Although QAnon embraced anti-Semitic legends within its core mythos, and while it rubbed shoulders – quite literally – at the Capitol Building on 6 January with the ranks of the white nationalist, racist right, McCauley saw QAnon's movement not as one concerned with loss of racial supremacy but fearing a loss of cultural supremacy. QAnon believers didn't police genetic identity the way Neo-Nazis or other white supremacists did, but they fiercely defended the rituals, rhetoric and iconography of a culture in which people like them inherited a privileged position. In places like the US, Australia, Britain and Canada, the attachment was to predominantly white, Christian, patriarchal, heteronormative, property-owning and xenophobic traditions that had long centred people like themselves. QAnon's fixation on government, the media and Hollywood as targets could be understood as a fight with the entities with enough power to upend an existing culture in which they perceived themselves as important. In this context, it was possible that feelings of personal precariousness might manifest in anxieties about an entire culture under desperate, existential threat.[103] McCauley's warning was that while Neo-Nazis and white nationalists were prepared to attack people of other races to relieve their feelings of grievance, QAnon and other culturalists were prepared to attack government itself.

Such expressions of cultural grievance were certainly traceable in the story of Ashli Babbitt, whose long service to her country had been undistinguished, and who had not been subsequently rewarded with success in civilian life. Only something as powerful as anger and terrible fear could motivate a woman with pro-police 'blue lives matter' stickers on her car to die amid smashed glass leading a 'medieval' attack on police.

Michael Jensen from START saw similar intensity in the QAnon-believing women whose children had experienced sexual or physical abuse, or may have been removed from their care. Amid personal chaos, resentment could easily spark radicalisation into the movement, given the QAnon story was premised on the delivery of justice to unambiguous criminals who truly deserved it.[104]

The narrative of the wronged holding the untouchable to account had powerful appeal. It was a traceable presence in the QAnon stories that Will Sommer chronicled in *The Daily Beast* in January 2020.[105] There were QAnon-believing cancer patients who were convinced the cabal was keeping a secret cancer cure to itself. There were QAnon parents who blamed the elites for their children's Down syndrome.[106]

In these last examples, academic Daniel Bessner and commentator Amber A'Lee Frost, writing for *Jacobin* in January 2021, saw the spiritual appeal of Q. It offered an experience to these people that ameliorated their feelings of disconnection from a system that they already believed to be illegitimate. It created an identity for the combination of social forces that upset them, and rebelling against it gave them an identity too.[107] Q, Bessner and Frost expanded, made people feel good, and not just in the chemical rush of likes and praise and shares and connection that the community could provide a believer on social media, or from the possession of secret knowledge Q's illusions provided, or in a refreshed sense of hope. The narrative of QAnon was one, said Bessner and Frost, in which people could be heroes, and convince themselves they were righteous and noble, virtuous, benevolent.

It was a LARP in which nobody had to admit to themselves they were LARPing. It was *The Matrix* in which every viewer also got to play Neo.

To stop believing in this image of themselves Q provided, said Bessner and Frost, would be to return to the feelings of fear and vulnerability that led them to seek Q out in the first place.

lmao omfg this qanon stuff is too funny
Anonymous on 4chan, 20 January 2021

Joe Biden was inaugurated president of the United States on 20 January 2021. Despite the riots, the storm had not come, the emergency broadcast system was not activated and Trump's election loss was not overturned. The coup had failed – and the lucky ones were those now in custody because the unlucky ones were dead. Six months after 6 January, 570 people had been arrested for their participation in the Capitol riots. The police were still seeking three hundred people in connection with arrestable offences. Trump's Twitter was not reinstated. Q remained silent.

A rash of articles appeared proclaiming the end of the movement. SBS in Australia ran with 'QAnon followers realise their baseless conspiracy was "all a lie" as President Joe Biden takes office'.[108] '"No plan, no Q, nothing": QAnon followers reel as Biden inaugurated,' said *Reuters*.[109] '"We all got played": QAnon followers implode after big moment never comes,' wrote *Forbes*.[110]

Those who'd followed the movement with, perhaps, either more sympathy or more cynicism credited the theory with more resilience, and its believers with more will. 'There's an American positivity about QAnon, a hale resistance to fatalism,' Kerry Howley explained in her piece for *Intelligencer*, published on 29 January 2021.[111] When the storm didn't come, she observed, 'Q's faithful regrouped and bounced back.' She referred to new theories being baked into bread for the community from the crumbs of the obstinate reality around them. Some suggested the Joe Biden seen on TV was an actor, deployed as a decoy to distract the cabal while Trump remained in charge, behind the scenes, writing the script. Sure, some people 'decided to abandon the movement altogether, saying they felt duped,' as Kaleigh Rogers wrote for *FiveThirtyEight*, '[b]ut others simply went back to the drawing board, hoping to find another date on which to hang their hopes'.[112] Maybe sometime in March 2021, or later in April? August? Maybe Trump's four-dimensional chess had outmanoeuvred those dastardly reptoids again!

By 26 May 2021, *Forbes* reported with some enthusiasm that a study from the Atlantic Council's Digital Forensic Research Lab had found that digital chatter related to QAnon was evaporating from mainstream social media. The interest in the conspiracy theory that had bloomed with the onset of the pandemic and peaked around the times of George Floyd's murder and then the Capitol riots had now fallen significantly. The combination of the coup's failure, Q's silence and platform crackdowns had reduced what had been a roaring online hum to a 'low murmur'.[113]

Yet, as Kerry Hawley wrote in *Intelligencer*, '[p]ositivity is endlessly plastic'. 'Trust the plan,' adherents reminded one another, as they had from the beginning when the very first promises of Hillary Clinton's impending arrest had failed to come to pass three years earlier. *Forbes* had celebrated the Atlantic Council report's suggestion that QAnon had been demobilised, unable to use alternative social media channels on anything like the scale they'd previously enjoyed on the big platforms. But only two months later, on 28 July, another report, written by digital researchers Jordan Wildon and Marc-André Argentino and published on the *GNET* website, declared QAnon very much alive as the largest extremist community on Telegram. Their research studied the thirty most influential QAnon Telegram groups, finding 135,150 accounts maintaining activity within them, and a further 639,909 accounts having engaged with them at least once.[114]

For hundreds of thousands of people who'd spent weeks, months or years fighting an online holy war, it wasn't just that a return to a pre-Q world view held little appeal. If anything, the bans had added a sense of glamour to Q's digital soldiers about the threat they posed to the status quo, about their crucial importance in the world. It entrenched a shared identity of undeserved victimhood, of persecuted righteousness. Joseph Uscinski – the conspiracy theory expert with a mother enamoured of QAnon – had expressed his scepticism to *The Guardian* in June 2020 that kicking QAnon off Facebook would do much good.

Uscinski was clear that he believed QAnon represented a set of potentially dangerous beliefs#and that the conspiracy theory was disconnected from reality, and he certainly didn't want any more people to get involved with it. 'Do the internet companies bear some responsibility?' he said of its phenomenon. 'Yes. Would it be better if they took it down? Probably. Does that take care of it? No.'[115]

The anons weren't just flocking to Telegram and Parler and Gab. They made use of WhatsApp chats and Discord servers, as well as employing coded language on Facebook and Twitter and Reddit that found a way around the suspensions and the bans. Rather than typing slogans that could get picked up by hostile algorithms, they reconnected with one another on Facebook by adding the letter q to their names or sharing memes with QAnon symbols or slogans contained within them. It was a great irony that a community that had once pored over images of celebrity shoes, jewellery, talk-show sets and hand gestures because Q had told them the cabal's 'need for symbolism will be their downfall' were now relying on replacing the 'o' in words with a 'q' or hanging their posts with pictures of storms, owls, red shoes, abused children, Pepe the Frog, Donald Trump as a holy warrior and/or the number 17 ('q' is the seventeenth letter of the alphabet) to signal one another.

An unregulated, unmoderated internet pipeline had delivered disinformation to people, and, once it had, that disinformation couldn't just be sucked back out of them. No platform, of any size, had the power to now simply delete QAnon from the minds of the community that had formed around it, just as pesky facts couldn't out-argue QAnon away from them, nor the cold fingers of the pointless dead unpeel them from the false heroic narrative into which they had enmeshed themselves. QAnon could exist without Q because the force sustaining the community was the community.

'They all sit around and share conspiracy theories, that the media is lying to them, they don't want to believe any kind of fact outside of their circle,' a woman from Texas who had reported her riot-attending family members to the FBI told *The Washington Post* in a story from 16 January 2021.[116] That could have been Karen Stewart describing how her brother and nephew engaged with QAnon. The unnamed woman from Texas compared their participation in the conspiracist community to a cult. The cult hadn't been brought into being by the manipulations or coercions of whoever Q was, or whatever Q's agenda may have been. It was a product of a desperate willingness for belief, and a community that created itself to evangelise it.

I would watch all kinds of you tube videos and
collect breadcrumbs ... one day I saw what I was
doing. Sitting in my house all day watching videos
and being alone ... If it was true that Hilliary Clinton
is a Satanic child eater cabal leader, there surely
had to have one person in the world sitting on the
news giving proof like pictures or video feed or
something. But all it was was all these Boomers
sitting in their house talking about it.

That's when it hit me, all of it is people sitting in
their homes, alone, sick, and talking about the same
bullshit. I stopped right there.

u/Uzmati66 on Reddit, 28 December 2019

In her seminal QAnon piece for *The Atlantic*, Adrienne LaFrance
had described QAnon as 'the birth of a new American
religion'.[117] By May 2020, QAnon researcher Marc-André
Argentino was discreetly attending services of the Omega
Kingdom Ministry (OKM) and writing for *The Conversation*
about how it functioned as a QAnon church.[118] OKM used
the model of 'neocharismatic' home-based evangelical
Protestantism, running Zoom services that used QAnon
conspiracy theories and the holy word of God in the Bible as
lenses to interpret one from the other. Argentino noted that
one of the pastors at OKM, Kevin Bushey, was a Republican
contesting a seat in the Maine House of Representatives.

Argentino's concern was how OKM might use Christianity to indoctrinate believers into QAnon, but QAnon evangelism already had enough energy to indoctrinate believers without institutional formality. Just like a religion, it encouraged acts of 'proclamation' in believers. Speaking the words of Q aloud could take the form of verbally haranguing a relative or neighbours with the contents of a Q post at a barbecue – like Tim Stewart did, like Ashli Babbitt did – or it could be manically sharing memes of Q-themed slogans on the internet. These were timeless religious acts, both about recruiting converts to the belief and affirming their depth of belief themselves. Like any evangelists, QAnonners were out to build the community of the faithful to bolster their own conviction, and that zeal to find connection meant that in moments of someone else's 'precarity', the ideas were pushed at them with enthusiasm. It was this energy that gave the books, the memes, the online chats and so-called documentaries, like *Fall of the Cabal,* real social power.

Like hotdogs, Crayola crayons, Nike shoes or Britney Spears, the 'American positivity' of QAnon had international appeal. German broadcaster *Deutsche Welle* reported in April 2021 that even in the wake of the Capitol riots, even amid the FBI arrests, QAnon's conspiratorial omnitheory was recruiting adherents in Japan and Germany.[119] Japanese believers were only in the hundreds, but they already had chapters like QArmy Japan Flynn, which venerated Trump's disgraced national security appointment Michael Flynn. It had an evolving, localised mythos, including a belief that Japan's devastating March 2011 'triple disaster' of an earthquake, tsunami and nuclear meltdown was an act of 'artificial tsunami terrorism' overseen by then emperor Akihito. The German reporters quoted Jun Okumura, an analyst at the Meiji Institute for Global Affairs, who identified parallels between Japanese QAnonners' self-belief in possession of secret knowledge with a similar vanity in the murderous Aum Shinrikyo doomsday cult. Back in the 1990s, Aum tried to drive Japanese society towards its prophesied End Times with sarin gas attacks in the Tokyo subways that killed thirteen people and injured as many as six thousand.

QAnonism had attracted international interest from its inception, even if you didn't count @TracyBeanz's Russian helpers. The threads containing the first Q posts had an audience on 4chan that included self-identified French, Norwegian, Canadian, Danish, Swedish, German, British and Australian users. The ideas spread internationally, and by September 2020 there were already 120,000 people engaging with the most prominent German-language Telegram channel. This was the month that German magazine *Der Spiegel* described QAnon as 'on its way to becoming the most dangerous cult in the world'.[120] In Germany, many Q recruits were coming from the 'Querdenker' scene, a German name for the movement of self-described 'unconventional thinkers' from 'natural health' and other New Age communities, which had counterparts in other countries who had similarly proved susceptible to QAnon beliefs. The Querdenkers had mobilised against lockdown restrictions and the public health restrictions to contain coronavirus. Again, as happened in other places, fronting the local movement were people such as a well-known vegan chef, a former newsreader and a musician, all of whom made recognisably pro-QAnon public statements. The last of these, Xavier Naidoo, had posted a tearful video in April 2020 about freeing 'children from the hands of pedophile networks'.[121]

QAnon had been a visible presence at a storming of the Reichstag building in August 2020 protesting coronavirus control measures. Before that, a gunman who killed ten people and then himself in the regional city of Hanau in February 2020 had made statements alluding to QAnon themes. The German journalists were unambiguous in identifying QAnon's conspicuously inherited traditions, denouncing them as centuries-old anti-Semitic fictions from a far-right fringe, and a twenty-first-century international media phenomenon that mashed the tropes of the Dreyfus affair into the pulp storytelling of Dan Brown. QAnon-believing German interviewees told *Der Spiegel* that either there would be a revolution soon or another world war.[122]

'QAnon is an American invention, but it has become a global plague,' wrote Frida Ghitis in *The Washington Post* on 10 March 2021.[123] French national broadcaster France 24 had reported in October 2020 that 'powered by fear, anger and big tech's algorithms', QAnon had established itself in a staggering seventy countries.[124] The 'web watchdog' NewsGuard, Ghitis reported, had estimated a community of up to 448,000 QAnon followers in Europe the previous year. Each of its iterations appended local variations in the detail of its unifying story of the people versus satanic elites. The theory served as a 'binding force', France 24's analysis said, for different fears agitated by the experience of coronavirus.

Alarming research confirmed that QAnon beliefs had found deep purchase in Britain. An October 2020 study by civil rights campaign group Hope Not Hate had found that 26 per cent of Britons agreed with claims that celebrities, politicians and prominent media were secretly engaging in child abuse and trafficking.[125] While specific alignment with the QAnon movement was only espoused by 6 per cent of their survey respondents, Hope Not Hate identified that the UK had become the second biggest hub for QAnon activity globally.

Cam Smith, the Australian researcher who monitors online far-right activity, had first noticed mention of QAnon in the local communities he watched as early as 2018. At the time, it looked like just a few 'tiny meetup groups on Facebook' of around twenty people. 'They were talking about, oh, we'll meet up at like some pub in [the Melbourne suburb of] Oakleigh, and we'll talk about this QAnon thing. And I didn't think it was going to be that important.'[126]

Smith's interest in the local movement was sparked again during the periods of heavy coronavirus public health restrictions in Melbourne, in 2020. To contain an outbreak of the virus within Melbourne's public housing high-rise towers, local authorities had moved quickly – and controversially – to unilaterally lock down the residential communities in the buildings. In defiance of the restrictions, a group of QAnon believers drove nearly two thousand kilometres from Queensland to protest the events, filming themselves – and espousing their theories – as they went. Smith was curious, found a way into their Facebook groups and started tracking their conversations.

What he noticed was that Facebook's algorithm was assisting the spread of disturbing content. Smith found that even engagements with Australian Facebook groups that represented softer political positions, like a small anti-vaccine community, quickly pushed him towards extremist content. 'The Facebook algorithm was like "I know some other stuff you would be interested in!"' Smith says, and it drove users within Australia's shallow Facebook pool towards political content that was much more hardcore.

As in Germany, QAnon seeded its Australian iteration through the networks of the wellness community. It was a bourgeois place in which those fearful of 'precarity' came to seek comfort. Community values here lay in promoting opportunities for personal healing through 'clean eating' and radical diets, alternative medicine, meditation, yoga and New Age beliefs. It was also a place where anti-vax conspiracy theories had lurked for some time, and, as the pandemic progressed, became a ripe channel – online and off – for QAnon influence. A friend even described to me how her first encounter with QAnon belief in Australia resulted from a 'rabbit hole' opening for her on Facebook while she searched recommendations of organic food for her dog.

Brigid Delaney, whose 2017 book, *Wellmania*, charted her adventures through the wellness industry, wrote about the emerging alliance she saw between the wellness and conspiracist communities in a 2020 piece for *The Guardian*. In the piece she revisited a concept first explained in the 1990s by Michael Kelly in *The New Yorker*. Kelly had called it 'fusion paranoia', and described it as the process of strengthening and bonding that takes place between unalike movements when they recognise they share a core belief.[127] During coronavirus lockdowns, wrote Delaney in *The Guardian*, this shared core belief was the idea that the virus was 'a cover for a plot of totalitarian proportions, designed to stifle freedom of movement, assembly, speech and – to the horror of some in the wellness industry – enforce a program of mass vaccinations'.[128]

Journalist Margaret Simons wrote a 2021 piece for *Meanjin* about QAnon's Australian iterations that considered QAnon's potential to lure the Australian mainstream.[129] Events in the wake of the Capitol riots had made the subject a local concern. Members of Australia's federally governing Liberal Party, MPs George Christensen and Craig Kelly, had been repeating QAnon talking points in a very Republican Party style; that is to say, within twenty-four hours of the Capitol riots, they'd also shared the untrue *Washington Times* article that had falsely pinned the riot on antifa. Unlike *The Washington Times*, however, the men were not moved to retract the fake claims.[130] Prime Minister Scott Morrison was one of the few Western leaders who had not condemned Donald Trump's role in inciting the riots. Now he refused to rebuke his unrepentant colleagues.[131] A third Liberal, conservative Victorian MP Bernie Finn, was also now peppering social media posts with references to the 'deep state'.

Margaret Simons interviewed political scientist Associate Professor Aaron Martin, who dismissed QAnon's capacity to influence majoritarian electoral politics in Australia. Modern Australia had been founded as a bureaucratic as much as a colonial exercise by the British. The resultant local political culture lacked the heft of revolutionary zeal, or enthusiasm of pilgrims seeking out religious freedom, and was therefore less susceptible to passionate narratives recalling the 'spirit of 1776' or dramatic images like *Washington Crossing the Delaware*. It was our national blandness, Martin argued, that was likely to save us from being stirred into the passions of a holy war.

This may have been a credible political analysis, but QAnon's evangelical project had already impacted on Australians socially, and in the very spaces of our blandness – our domestic, ordinary, material lives – where we may otherwise expect to feel most safe. The prime minister's Q-believing friend Tim Stewart became the avatar of the movement in Australia because, unlike chefs or Instagrammers who may have also engaged QAnon beliefs, Stewart presented the movement in the way that Australians found the most familiar. As he emerged as Australia's most prominent QAnon figure, a photo showing Stewart drinking beer in a polo shirt next to his friend Scott Morrison was disturbing for its screaming ordinariness.

Australia has one of the highest social media penetration rates globally, and the reach of QAnon messaging has been difficult to avoid. You can enquire about who's had QAnon encounters just among friends on Facebook and summon an overflow of responses about aggressive QAnon attempts at conversion. It is hardly surprising that in a country where the prime minister gets on the beers with local QAnon acolytes,

Australians of lesser public profile have had in-person experiences with cult advocates too.

> I live in australia and my dad is a Trump supporter
> and has been since 2016 since then he had
> been watching Alex Jones, Fox News and some
> youtube's supporting Trump. Ever since Trump
> lost the recent election he's been obsessed with Q
> conspiracies first starting with how trump is going
> to be president again and that Biden isn't the real
> president ... but now he says things about how the
> covid vax is killing people, masks are killing people,
> lockdowns are happening so people can child traffic
> and how there's all underground tunnels, hollywood
> and politicians are all clones and pediphiles. He just
> constantly glued to his phone with his headphones
> on, he is now currently not working and the family
> is running really low on money but now he wants to
> buy gold and silver like we can afford it??
>
> u/lloonabee on Reddit, 24 March 2021

On an Australian Facebook page, a woman named Victoria relates that she's lost a friend to QAnon and it 'hurts my heart seeing him spout the madness and hatred he spews'. Another woman, named Kelly, responds that 'it's the same' with her mum. 'My cousin is well and truly down the rabbit-hole,' says Lauren, as is '[o]ne of my brothers,' adds Angela. 'An ex,' says Mike. 'A friend's brother, otherwise a nice person, went bonkers' and 'came on strong with this QAnon stuff,' says Dave. 'I just unfriended someone because they believe all this conspiracy rubbish,' confesses Faye. There are hundreds more, in a single conversation. They tell of encounters in workplaces, at family gatherings, with 'the woman who runs a gift shop down the road'. A church minister was confronted by pro-Q parishioners. A woman retells being shanghaied by a QAnon believer at her garage sale. A man tells the story of being trapped in an optometrist chair having his eyes tested when the optometrist tried to entice him into a conversation about the cabal.

By 2021, those wanting to believe that QAnonism had mostly spared bland and isolated Australia had an increasing amount of evidence to ignore. Australia's experience of the coronavirus pandemic between 2020 and 2021 was dominated by a series of rolling lockdowns that trapped Australians at home with a lot of frustration and the internet for months at a time. The preponderance of anecdotal online accounts detailing encounters with QAnon could be written off as unrepresentative of what may have been going on in the broader community. Accumulating statistics, however, were a far harder boulder to shift.

A 2020 paper released by the British-based think tank the Institute for Strategic Dialogue revealed that after the US, Britain and Canada, Australia was the fourth largest producer of QAnon content worldwide. Australia created more QAnon content than Russia.[132]

Shockingly, this had been so even before the pandemic, with Australians sharing more than 105,000 QAnon tweets in the first nine months of the theory's existence between October 2017 and June 2018. QAnon researcher Marc-André Argentino was monitoring QAnon activity on 8kun and recorded the presence of six Australian QAnon research boards there in January 2020, hosting four thousand posts.[133] By the start of 2021, the number of research boards had grown to eleven. In a February 2021 feature for *The Guardian*, journalist Michael McGowan noted that QAnon's unique ability to cross-pollinate with other conspiracy theories had created fusion paranoia in Australia, not only with anti-vax communities but also anti-lockdown protestors and anti-migration and anti-Semitic believers as well as the community of anti-5G mobile phone tower activists. This was not an inconsiderable number of Australians to influence. Polling from Essential Media in McGowan's article revealed a shocking 12 per cent of Australians believed 5G towers were being used to spread coronavirus.[134]

What lay behind all of these statistics of tweets and cross-pollination and web centipedes and influence were the sad true stories of Australians mourning the loss of loved ones to 'the Qult' in places like Reddit's r/QAnonCasualties community. Statistics could measure the size of QAnon's transmission into Australia, but the unquantifiable anecdotes recorded its cost. QAnon cultism was not a phenomenon that just affected abstracted, faraway people on the internet. It was getting into families, and communities. It was hurting workplaces and friendship groups. Including mine.

My friend Meshelle – not her real name – had already had a negative encounter with another cult, many years before QAnon inserted itself in her life.[135] She'd met her partner, Dave, straight out of high school in Brisbane. Married more than twenty years, they had two teenage kids and long-term jobs when Meshelle started to suffer depression. She mentioned to her hairdresser she'd begun seeing a therapist, and the hairdresser recommended a weekend hypnotherapy course that she swore had helped her stop smoking.

Meshelle went on a weekend away with the course, and it was a transformative and positive experience. Paying for more and more courses with the same provider, she was swept into a new community that encouraged her to make changes in her life. She quit her job, left her marriage, moved into a place of her own and started her own hypnotherapy business with a guy from the course who lived interstate, with whom she'd begun a relationship while in the process of leaving Dave. Any doubts that nagged about her choices were suppressed, and her new community was eager to help her do so.

Then, one day, she received a phone call from another woman interstate who had also started a hypnotherapy business with Meshelle's new partner, with whom she was also in a relationship. The woman had stumbled upon an intimate email the man was in the process of sending to Meshelle. Between the two horrified women, they eventually discovered that the partner they shared was sharing himself with no less than twenty-one other women at the same time.

The dam of Meshelle's suppressed doubts burst. She was a smart, capable woman but she had been vulnerable to a need for positivity and encouragement, and she realised she'd been sucked into a cult. She abandoned the parallel reality she'd joined, reunited with Dave, and moved back into the family home. Her self-remonstrations were intense.

Together again, Meshelle and Dave joined a community yoga class, and it was here she had her second experience with a cult. When the couple who ran the classes split up, the yogi husband was left behind and, during the pandemic, went 'full QAnon'. Meshelle, Dave and the other students found themselves on the end of an increasing barrage of Facebook posts and other communications insisting that rejecting the conspiracy theory was rejecting yoga itself. People in the class who knew a little of Meshelle's background came to her for advice. 'They couldn't believe somebody that they respected had gone off the planet,' she says. 'They were really worried, and people were coming to me distraught; he was tearing strips off them.' Meshelle stood up to the yogi on Facebook and tried to reach out to him privately. He repeated QAnon stories to her about paedophiles, kids in tunnels under New York City, and how 'Hillary Clinton is actually in jail and that's a body double that's walking around'. She realised there was no bringing him back when he started on the 'fucking lizard people'.

The experience for Meshelle was triggering, she says, not only because of the depth and extremity of the yogi's new beliefs. It was the women from the yoga class she watched fall in behind him, agreeing about Hillary Clinton and believing in the 'lizard people'. The insecurity in these women she recognised too well. A feeling of precarity. A need to find community and to connect. She and Dave had left the class, but in their small suburban community, Meshelle realised she was being frozen out by the class members who remained behind. They dropped their eyes and went silent when she entered the cafe that they gathered at. 'I've lost friends, definitely,' Meshelle says. She had been shunned.

Noni is a Twitter friend, and someone who I got to know online – again, it's not her real name. Before her encounter with QAnon, her previous experience with cults was limited to an uncle who lived on the North Coast of New South Wales.[136] His New Age beliefs had once predisposed him more to hippie tribalism, but his more recent Facebook posts suggested that he'd gotten into QAnon and become something of a Trumpster. When coronavirus lockdowns began around Australia, Noni's home state of Western Australia didn't have the same restrictions as other states but she was still seeing distrust expressed around her social media networks – from people like her sixty-something uncle – towards a possible vaccine. She was vaguely aware of local conspiracy theories that insisted mobile phone towers were somehow evil or untrustworthy, but she wasn't really paying attention. She had other things on her mind.

Noni was pregnant, and a world in the grip of a pandemic infection was an anxious place to birth a baby. This was her fourth child, but her sixth pregnancy; she had had her first three children young, but trying to have a fourth later in life had been complicated and devastating. She'd had two previous miscarriages, and while all tests had suggested the new pregnancy was healthy and the baby likely to be brought to term, she was struggling to manage a debilitating level of anxiety. Noni needed help, but at a period of heightened psychological distress for a whole community, it was hard to access counselling, even in the relatively safe state where she lived.

It was an enormous relief when she remembered a clinical psychologist she had seen years earlier, who she'd been referred to by her doctor, and was able to get some appointments. She was given the option of having the session on Zoom, but the intimate nature of her anxiety made her feel it was best to organise face-to-face visits.

After a couple of unremarkable appointments, the psychologist began their weekly session asking Noni some questions about how she'd been coping with the virus, and the lockdowns. Noni replied that the spread of the virus was obviously concerning; she had a few friends who were immuno-compromised. 'Then,' says Noni, 'the psychologist was, like, "Yeah, I've been reading some things and watching some documentaries and videos about immunisations, and I'm just unsure about whether I'd want to get my kids immunised."'

Noni was taken aback. She politely reminded the psychologist she was a nursing student, and she'd studied the effective use of vaccines. She wondered, hasn't a trained clinical psychologist done so too? She gently tried to steer the conversation back to why she was there, the anxiety about her pregnancy, but the psychologist still wanted to talk about vaccines. She told Noni that she'd seen a video called *Plandemic*, and that she'd 'been doing lots of research', and talked about what she'd seen on YouTube, and in articles about 'alternative science'.

Noni was speechless. She was pregnant and seeking out professional mental health help for anxiety and she was trapped in a room with someone whose qualifications had required a background in research and science but who was suddenly telling her that Bill Gates, Dr Fauci and the US Center for Disease Control were involved in creating a pandemic around the world for financial gain.

Noni was an active user of social media, and familiar with the QAnon slogans that floated around online. When the psychologist mentioned that 'Hillary Clinton was in on it', Noni knew she was being QAnonned. She left that day. She did not go back.

Instead, Noni called a friend – another nurse – whose highly educated brother had also, somehow, fallen into a conspiracy cult. They talked about what had happened and, Noni says, 'had a good laugh'. Noni found some proper help at a perinatal clinic; she reported the psychologist's behaviour to them and they lodged a complaint on her behalf. 'I just thought to myself,' says Noni, 'she has a lot of kids that she sees. I hope that she's not having these conversations with vulnerable people who don't have enough experience to see through it for themselves.'

Nick is another friend of mine, and this name, once again, isn't his real one. He comes from a big, suburban Australian migrant family, where the cousins are all close, the politics are traditionally progressive and the bonds are very deep. He was at a wedding when he learned from a cousin that her own brother was 'knee-deep in QAnon'.[137]

Nick is immersed in the media; he knew about QAnon. He'd barely recovered from learning that relatives in an American branch of the family had voted for Trump in 2016. Now he sat and listened to his cousin 'aghast'. He couldn't believe it. 'Someone in my family,' he says, 'believing there were a cabal of paedophiles running a pizza shop.'

The shock weighed on him. Nick couldn't help himself and texted the cousin's QAnon-believing brother: *I heard you believe this bullshit. Is it true?*

'And then, my god,' Nick says, 'the messages I got back blew me away. He'd even adopted the language: *I'm receiving information from patriots abroad about what's going on in the US. Something big's going down on January 6.*

Nick sent back: *I bet you everything I have in my bank account on January 6 there might be trouble, but Joe Biden is going to be sworn in on January 20.* 'And,' says Nick, 'this person took the bet.'

When Nick won, he didn't cash it in. He did revisit the subject with his cousin, though, at a family dinner not long later when his cousin started to argue the coronavirus vaccines had been 'compromised'. Nick accused his cousin of believing Russian disinformation, 'because I'm guessing that's what it is, this QAnon thing'. When his cousin's eyes glazed over, Nick decided he wouldn't bring it up again. 'To be honest, I can't cope with it,' he says, 'not in someone who's so close to me.'

Yet he soon learned his cousin was still bringing it up, and in the most hurtful of ways. Nick isn't just a guy from a big family: he's a member of a parliament and has been part of a government, and he heard second-hand from relatives that his cousin had claimed Nick challenging QAnon beliefs just affirmed Nick supported 'the cabal'.

'He says I'm aware of the truth that there's a paedophile cabal and satanic cult running the country, but I choose to do nothing,' says Nick, 'and that's the part that bothers me the most: that people I love, and that I'm related to, believe that I ... I would allow that to occur. I mean, I just don't know ... I just don't know what to do. And I've ... I've tried to offer reason. Doesn't work. I've tried just arguing back, and debunking things that they've said, but none of it works. None of it works.'

The emotion grows in Nick's voice. 'But, you know, if you met this person,' he says, 'and sat down for an hour with him, and we had a conversation, you'd never know, if it didn't come up. He and his wife are both professionals, and their family's done very, very well – tertiary-educated kids, everyone's ... everyone's tertiary educated, everyone's doing well, or middle class. And they believe this, and I just ... I don't know what to do. I just stare at it, and I've just sort of ... I just ignore it. I choose not to engage in it because it just ... I don't know where it's gonna lead.'

In her article for *Meanjin*, Australian journalist Margaret Simons listed the people she knew of who'd been pulled into QAnon. There was a senior accountant, doctors, lawyers and journalists, people from all places and all ages. 'I searched for common threads,' she wrote. 'Often there was some kind of trauma – a harsh experience of life's unfairness.'[138]

Meshelle was shunned. A clinical psychologist pushed conspiracy theories on an anxiety patient. A politician was smeared with the taint of a fantasy cabal. Whose was the undeserving victimhood here?

My fiancés sister is a Qannon 'patriot' as she calls herself and is currently in Washington DC. She wholeheartedly believes that she is the daughter of Trump and that Jfk Jr is going to marry her and the three of the them are going to run the country ... Shes been clean of drugs for over a year and we don't believe shes back on them. Is Q fueling an existing mental illness we just didn't know about or has Q made her believe this?

u/Spiritual_Sweet_5806 on Reddit, 18 November, 2020

In the popular imagination, conspiratorial belief is commonly understood as intertwined with extreme psychiatric illness. However, recent studies have demonstrated that this is not so. Writing for online medical journal *Medscape* in February 2021, professor of psychiatry Ronald W. Pies and clinical professor in health sciences Joseph M. Pierre dispelled the prevailing myth. Under the heading 'Believing in conspiracy theories is not delusional', the two professors addressed recent scholarship to conclude that conspiracy theories 'are likely *not* the product of psychosis or mental illness'. To support this point, they cited a recent survey that established 50 per cent of Americans believe at least one conspiracy theory. Only one in twenty-five Americans experience extreme psychiatric illness.[139]

Dr Richard Wise is a Melbourne-based clinical psychologist who sees in the behaviour exhibited by internet conspiracy cult adherents recognisable personality phenomena widely understood by psychologists.[140]

The first phenomenon expands on the notion that feeling distress from uncertain or unstable circumstances primes people to grasp at conspiracy theories. 'We know that people are more prone to identifying with conspiracies when threatened, or sensing themselves as vulnerable or powerless,' he explains. It's an observation that contextualises the trauma that Margaret Simons identified in the QAnon people she wrote about, and the research from *The Washington Post* that revealed the large number of Capitol riot arrestees who had experienced profound economic upsets.[141] It also applies, of course, to the individual circumstances of Pizzagate believers like Maddison Welch, or the Gamergaters who so feared feminist incursion into their spaces.

What psychologists have learned, says Wise, is that conspiracy theories can be seized at by humans to inform an 'internally consistent pattern and systems of causation' that 'reduces uncertainty and bewilderment when the world is confusing and frightening'. The beliefs formed by these internal decisions are so valuable to people as a stabilising force that they are defended from challenge with psychological ferocity. Parliamentarian Nick's QAnon cousin is a good example: he's seized on a belief system that is providing him so much psychological reassurance that he is willing to bypass his critical thinking, discount evidence and destroy the reputation of someone close to him to maintain it. 'We begin to perceive and absorb only the concepts that support our beliefs, either completely miss or discount the ideas that run counter, and thereby consolidate our positions to be incredibly robust,' says Wise. The instinct to preserve beliefs is so strong, the brain will even discount sensory information – what the body can see, hear, taste, smell, feel – to maintain its decided convictions.

Those grasping at conspiracy theories might also do so to reduce the input of confusing or contradicting information into simple binaries. Wise explains this as a reduction resulting from what psychologists call the 'paranoid-schizoid' position. 'This describes a usually stress-induced psychological state in which we perceive the world to be more persecutory and tend to see things as rather black and white,' says Wise. Psychologists call it 'splitting'. He explains that dual categories are much easier for people in distress to comprehend, as well as to choose alignments within.

It is obvious to a casual observer how much within the Q posts appeals to this simplicity. There are white hats and black hats. Light and dark. Good and evil. Patriots or the cabal.

Are you a fucking moron. The pandemic in 1918 killed 100 million people you stupid fuck. There have been many pandemics since.
It is you fucking QAnon morons that spread all this bullshit ... that is what is going to fuck up the entire planet.

Anonymous on 4chan, 7 April 2021

Observe the wreckage that QAnon belief can impose on the people around the believers. There's the physical violence of its outliers and the disruption caused to political processes and community. Then there's the emotional damage adherents inflict on those who have loved them.

The digital soldiers of the movement don't see themselves as agents of violence or cruelty. In an article on QAnon believers for *Business Insider* in December 2020, journalists Jim Edwards and Jessica Davies noted the profound disconnect between how QAnon activists saw themselves and how the movement's adherents behaved in real life.[142] Claims by activists that they were peaceful, respectful truth-seekers were somewhat undermined by the journalists' direct experience of being subjected to hostility and threats when they asked believers questions or sought information from them.

QAnon on the inside, as Edwards and Davies observed, is very different from its image on the outside. In the sly community that remains on Facebook, there's a disquieting juxtaposition of radical sentiments and Hallmark-card aesthetics in many of the images. In one, an adorable photo of a smiling baby is captioned 'MAKING US CANNIBALS ONE BITE AT A TIME / SENOMYX HEK-293 ABORTED BABY FLAVOR ENHANCEMENT'. A thoughtful sepia portrait of John F. Kennedy Jr is captioned 'I WILL FIND MY FATHER'S KILLERS EVEN IF IT BRINGS DOWN THE GOVERNMENT'. In another, the caption 'Let's finish this, shall we? Please don't give up on this amazing man' appears around a painterly, patriotic image of Donald Trump standing in front of an American flag, rolling up the sleeves on a pair of unnaturally buff arms.

Amid this, individual accounts use cartoon images of themselves to compete for graphic attention between rainbows and sunshine and American flags and photos of dewy-eyed children. Although the requests in their newsfeeds that you pray for their sick children or injured pets alternate with demands to try traitors before military tribunals and some truly shocking racism, adherents online really do view their community as one of righteous comrades, brave believers brought together in the cause of purity's triumph over corruption. The darker elements of its story – lurid stories of child trafficking, the anti-vaxxing, the paedophiles, the lizard people – usually come out in memes or links, which the users tweely caption with pleas to keep fighting, to trust the plan, to remind one another of the children in underground tunnels who only meme-sharing can save.

Business Insider quoted believer Christian Suprean in December 2020 claiming QAnon was the most amazing movement with which he'd ever been involved. To him it was filled with love, and humility, and love for country and love for God.[143] Within two weeks, QAnon believers were storming the Capitol.

Suprean's comments echo Melissa Rein Lively's description of a movement of positivity that drew her in, before driving her all the way to a nervous breakdown at Target.[144] It's the 'ecstatic smile' of belief described by Kerry Howley in *Intelligencer* that accompanied Rosanne Boyland to her violent death under the feet of a Capitol Hill mob.[145] It's the heroic narrative explained by Daniel Bessner and Amber A'Lee Frost in *Jacobin* two weeks after the Capitol riots in which

Ashli Babbitt was shot while participating.[146] It's also a pure example of 'splitting', in which the monstrous, unfathomable evil of baby-eating satanic lizard people is obliged to have an equal and opposite counterpart in the beautiful, holy goodness of Q's self-recruited spiritual myrmidons.

What Christian Suprean's 'amazing movement' also speaks to is how QAnon isn't merely a phenomenon of individuals but one of socialisation. 'I have made some of the most amazing friends that will be lifelong friends throughout this journey, following Q and meeting people with Q,' he told *Business Insider.* Spend time in the online 'qommunity' on Facebook and you'll see much of the same rhetoric – users employing the slang term 'frens' to describe the specific relationship of people who may have never met in person but who share the belief that Hillary Clinton kills and eats children and who praise one another for great virtue on this basis.

The team of psychology researchers from the University of Kent who study conspiracy theories make the point in their paper 'The psychology of conspiracy theories' that 'conspiracy belief is also predicted by collective narcissism – a belief in the in-group's greatness paired with a belief that other people do not appreciate it enough'.[147] In social media spaces, it's an observable theme – particularly in advice offered by a user's unmet 'frens' encouraging them to shun their families, leave their partners and walk away from lifelong friendships with those 'sheep' – like Meshelle, like Nick – who challenge the conspiratorial world view.

The Kent researchers suggest that the 'love' that the likes of Christian Suprean claim they've experienced in movements like QAnon is actually a collective valorisation of the self and their in-group. They say this particularly appeals to people whose positive image of either has been threatened in some way.

The problem is, writes Jan-Willem van Prooijen, a psychology researcher from Vrije Universiteit Amsterdam, that participation in conspiracy communities does little to reduce the negative feelings that drove individuals there in the first place. When QAnon believers – or Pizzagaters, or Gamergaters – form groups where social activity is organised around engaging conspiracy beliefs, they mutually reinforce one another's preoccupations with what is distressing them, and 'exacerbate [their] feelings of anxiety'. Simply, people join conspiracy communities because they are frightened, and they remain frightened as long as they stay in conspiracy communities.[148]

Presenting a preferable social alternative to fear is how loved ones can recover friends and family members from the 'rabbit hole' of conspiracy cults. Richard Wise explains that this doesn't mean challenging conspiratorial beliefs with the evidence and truth, because 'the more you come across as threatening to the internal consistency' of what has been a 'quite comforting explanation', the more easily you're recruited into a binary role as the oppositional 'other' and a villain, entrenching those beliefs.[149]

It means recognising that cult participation might start with a psychological provocation but it has a sociological solution. This, fundamentally, is the argument made in American psychiatric theorist Robert Jay Lifton's landmark

1961 book, *Thought Reform and the Psychology of Totalism: A study of 'brainwashing' in China*, which has informed generations of cult-deprogramming practice across the world since publication.[150]

Lifton had studied a group of American service personnel held prisoner in Mao's China during the Korean War and subjected to coercive psychological indoctrination, which was sensationally known as 'brainwashing' but which Lifton referred to as 'thought reform'. Despite the cultural reputation that brainwashing had developed for effecting permanent change on those subjected to it, Lifton's discovery was that when the prisoners returned to America, removal from the coercive environment and resocialisation within their community returned them to normal.

Lifton's observations about how psychological coercion is achieved through desocialising people – narrowing their social contact and limiting their media exposure – are consistent with the experience of people drawn into the internet's conspiracy cults. Pandemic lockdowns even helped pre-establish these conditions. Meanwhile, Q readily offered simple binary oppositional thinking. The patriotic iconography of *Washington Crossing the Delaware* and 'one nation under God' as a continental landmass wrapped in the American flag were contrasted with photographs of the nefarious Rothschild family members attending a ball in demonic-looking masks as well as images depicting repeated patterns of mysterious, shadowy owls in the design details of public buildings or celebrity couture. Q offered an image of Trump as an ongoing mystical event and 'repetitiously all-encompassing jargon', all of which accompanied the process of 'thought reform' that Lifton had described in his seminal book.

Desocialisation defined the QAnon experience of Jitarth Jadeja. Immersion in exclusively conspiracist media – like Alex Jones's *Infowars* – was part of a radicalisation process that dangerously isolated him. The Australian had been a Bernie Sanders supporter when based in the US and became tempted into conspiracy belief – and then sucked into QAnon – when 'alternative news' fed his animosity towards Hillary Clinton. 'QAnon was all he wanted to talk about,' explained a CNN feature on him in October 2020.[151] 'That made life offline increasingly difficult for him, and he pulled away from friends.'

Conspiracy thinking does not make people happier. Eventually, an isolated and lonely Jadeja became restless with unhappiness. Just as had happened with Leila Hay, the young British student who had withdrawn from the world into QAnon and headaches, doubts accumulated and contradictions in the theory became more difficult for him to resolve.

When he reached out to an anti-QAnon subreddit with a post entitled 'Q Fooled Me' explaining his crisis of belief, he was genuinely shocked to receive support and encouragement rather than abuse. It assisted a process of resocialisation in a life where his obsession with QAnon had profoundly affected all of his existing offline relationships.

Having left the movement, he gave interviews about his experiences of QAnon. One of these, between himself and

CNN's Anderson Cooper, became an international news story when Cooper was obliged to ask Jadeja if at any point he'd truly believed high-level Democrats and celebrities were really worshipping the devil and drinking children's blood.

'I thought you did that,' Jadeja said, embarrassed, 'and I would like to apologise for that right now.' To Cooper's pale, shocked face, he repeated, 'I apologise for thinking that you ate babies.'[152]

In the wake of his own deconversion, Jadeja has appeared across a vast swathe of international media encouraging the loved ones of QAnon believers not to abandon them to the conspiracy community, but to maintain contact, and 'remind them of their life before Q'.[153] An ongoing relationship with the past, he suggests, offers a powerful means of comparison with their conspiracist life of the present, illustrating it may not be as productive, or good – and may, in fact, eventually represent to them – as it did to him – a waste of time spent trying to fill an emotional void. An account on Reddit who claimed to be a seventeen-year-old former QAnon believer spoke of how the doubts he'd suppressed about Q's failed predictions came to the front of his mind when he realised how awful his life had become. Taking a two-month break from political discussions online gave him the space to develop new hobbies and his indoctrination wore off. Another former believer, DB, participated in an 'ask me anything' discussion on Reddit about leaving QAnon, and stressed to the audience that it was unlikely for adherents to be reasoned out of beliefs they were not reasoned into. Instead, DB recommended loved ones maintained a loving connection so there was somewhere

a believer knew they could return if – when – they became
ready to leave QAnon behind.

Some American families who QAnon belief has divided
have sought help from cult deprogrammers; those who've
spoken to media agree with DB and Jadeja's advice. They
recommend long conversations that are about something
other than mocking or fighting conspiracy belief, and shared,
participatory activities that encourage resocialisation.
There are, alas, no magic words a loved one can say to get
someone out of a cult – but they offer points of social re-
entry for when the cult inevitably fails to satisfy a believer's
emotional needs.

In March and in the wake of the Capitol riots, journalist
Tovia Smith interviewed some cult deprogrammers as well
as believers for a radio feature on NPR about their work
with QAnonners.[154] One of the people interviewed was Jay
Gilley. Once a 32-year-old left-leaning pizza-delivery guy
from Alabama who'd voted for Obama, he spent three years
sucked down a rabbit hole of QAnon after getting into some
online arguments about Black Lives Matter, which drew
him towards conspiracist conversations and beliefs. Gilley
explained that'd he'd been able to come out of it thanks to a
friend who'd stuck with him and invested the time to patiently
talk him back around.

It was a crucial intervention. For a CNN piece on
4 February 2021, cult deprogrammer and mental health
counsellor Steven Hassan recommended that those who'd cut
off contact with someone radicalised by a conspiracy cult were
still powerfully capable of helping that person.[155] The first task

was to re-establish contact on neutral conversational ground. Hassan recommended asking for a 'redo', and to invest time and listen with compassion and understanding. He suggested finding activities that could provide people breaks away from obsessive media consumption, creating opportunities for input from new experiences. If questions about sensitive topics came up, Hassan recommended answering questions with quality resources, and gentleness.

For her NPR piece, Tovia Smith sat in on some of the laborious, trust-building conversations patient 'exit counsellors' had with people who were initially adamant they'd maintain their beliefs. They replicated what Jay Gilley had experienced from his friend: kind, patient conversations establishing rapport, discussing shared experiences, and always finding a way to pivot a conversation back to common ground. 'It's a tedious and time-intensive process,' Smith admitted, but it worked.

It was exactly what had worked on Steven Hassan. He himself had fallen into cult belief at the age of nineteen. He'd joined some girls for a weekend workshop and found he'd agreed to a forty-day social isolation. Two-and-a-half years later, he reunited with his family after a near-fatal van accident put him in hospital and got him away from the cult. His father had asked him just to spend five days talking to him about his new beliefs with a promise he'd personally escort him back to the cult if he hadn't changed his mind. Hassan began talking, began listening and began thinking again. His mind changed, he did stay with his family, and he's spent his life since helping people out of cults. The cult he'd been a member of was Sun Myung Moon's Unification Church, the church that still owns *The Washington Times*.

Rosanne Boyland was a passionate MAGA supporter
... Her death doesn't advance their propaganda so
they just erase her.

Christian Suprean may have tried to proclaim to the journalists from *Business Insider* and also to himself that QAnon was 'filled with love', but it wasn't love that was laborious or patient. It wasn't love that exhibited duty or responsibility. It was love entirely conditional on the maintenance of shared fear.

On 7 April 2021, three months after Rosanne Boyland's fatal participation in the Capitol riots, the medical examiner's office in Washington, DC, released the conclusions of their investigations into her death. An exhaustive post-mortem had revealed that she had not, in fact, been trampled to death. The 34-year-old aspiring drugs counsellor who'd joined a recovery group, got herself clean and sober, turned her life around, saw her family every day and had been trying to reconnect with old friends had died from accidental 'acute amphetamine intoxication' among the violent, flailing bodies in the Capitol riots. At some point during her trip to Washington, Rosanne Boyland had taken drugs again.[156]

Amphetamine overdoses are comparatively rare, but if someone overdosing can get to first aid in time, they'll most likely survive. Rosanne Boyland didn't get that assistance. As her overdose set in, she was trapped in the crowd she had joined. As she fell, no one caught her. The bodies around her were heaving against the doors of the Capitol Building, trying to stop an election that had already been won. Rosanne Boyland was considered less important than violence and fantasy in the community of strangers she'd defied her family to join.

The day she learned of Rosanne Boyland's death, Sarah Lewis, her best friend of thirty years, made an emotional video that she shared on Facebook, describing how Rosanne's world had shrunk into rabbit trails, and her decline. 'I just want to remind everybody: she is a human being,' Lewis said, tissue in hand as she wept. 'She's not a "psycho Trump supporter". She's not a "drug addict". She's a human being,' she repeated. 'And she was closer to me than a sister.

'I hope this is a wake-up call to everybody,' Lewis said. 'Check on your friends.'

Videodrome is about Marshall McLuhan's theories on media you fucking pleb

Anonymous on 4chan, 7 November 2016

... BUT THIS IS NOT THE END

Three months after she wrote her feature article 'The prophecies of Q' for *The Atlantic*, Adrienne LaFrance was interviewed on radio for NPR about her analysis of the QAnon movement.[1]

The prerecorded interview was released at an opportune time. Q no longer lurked on the internet's furthest fringes but had reached the centre of no less than the direct presidential conversation. One day earlier, on 19 August 2020, the day after Joe Biden received the official Democratic nomination for the presidency, was the day that then still US president Donald Trump was asked in a White House press briefing for his thoughts on QAnon and what he might say to its adherents. Trump's response, 'I've heard these are people that love our country' was a validation accepted with something like ecstasy among the online ranks of Q believers.

Describing her adventures with QAnon, LaFrance was conspicuously less ecstatic; she compared it to following the plot of a 'bad spy novel'. LaFrance told interviewer Dave Davies that for all the impact her article had had in bringing

Q to the broader public consciousness, she'd been frustrated in her primary objective with the piece. 'I wish I could tell you who Q is. This is something that I wanted to figure out,' she told Davies. 'I asked every single person I talked to, who do you think Q is?'

It's a journalist's question, and it also preoccupied filmmaker Cullen Hoback, who made the Q-themed HBO documentary *Q: Into the storm*, which premiered in 2021. Seeking to expose Q's identity, Hoback had amassed hours of interviews and analysed Q's photographs, images and text in attempts to work out Q's identity and location. An article about his efforts by Alyssa Rosenberg in *The Washington Post* on 5 April 2021 quoted Hoback insisting that Q's power derived from anonymity; it was Hoback's belief that exposing the human being behind the Q curtain was necessary to dilute the power of the myth that held Q's followers in such thrall.[2]

Rosenberg was not persuaded. Scrutinised, Hoback's belief was perhaps captive to the same wilfulness as any claiming that Marina Abramović uses contemporary art as a mask for diabolical witchcraft, or that feminists are secretly plotting to ruin all the sexy fun in your video games, or that Donald Trump is waging a secret war on paedophiles as a buff-armed, child-rescuing warrior-Christ.

The reality was that Q had maintained a faithful following despite repeated prophetic failures, platform bans, relentless public fact-checking and the invincible-chess-grandmaster Trump's conclusive, humiliating and verified electoral defeat.

It was the power of Q's narrative to overwhelm facts that had always been the essence of the movement's appeal. For adherents, the loathed 'mainstream media' of investigators and researchers dedicated to truth are ever just servants of the wicked cabal. If Hoback, LaFrance or anyone else successfully unmasks Q, the discovery will be irrelevant to believers.

It says much about the disconnect in realities between the conspiracy community and those trying to understand it that LaFrance found herself 'really perplexed' by her discovery that true believers did not seem to care about Q's identity. They seemed, she said, to have almost no interest in it as a question.

Of course QAnonners were uninterested. Given Q's origin among 4chan LARPers, one could argue Q's only real identity was an impassioned desire to participate in a shared fantasy of personal specialness. Cult deprogrammer Diane Benscoter explained to NPR that cult participation often fills a psychological void with righteousness.[3] The sense of purpose provided is invigorating and addictive, she said; it was like you found yourself fighting a battle for goodness, and in it, you were a hero. Benscoter had experienced this feeling for herself. She was another person who'd got herself into and out of Sun Myung Moon's Unification Church.

For a *lumpenbourgeoisie* who were not struggling materially but who guessed a changing culture had no reasons to flatter their specialness, Q's role-playing game of hero had a powerful appeal. Perhaps that was why it took only four days for @TracyBeanz and people like her to decide that anonymous, unverifiable public messages on an emotionally adolescent imageboard simply had to be credible insights from a well-placed government insider who'd decided the best people to share their national security secrets with were whoever happened to be on 4chan at the time. In equivalent circumstances, it's why Edgar Maddison Welch never actually did the 'recon' on Comet Ping Pong before striding into the restaurant with an assault rifle, or why an entire community of online gamers elected themselves the morality police of Zoë Quinn, a stranger whose life had never touched their own. In a fantasy, playing hero doesn't oblige ethics or precision; it just requires some villains. In the past, this wilful fabulism was what led ancient mobs to punish Jews for invented, improbable sins. In the present, tales of imaginary child-eaters squatting in positions of cultural power propelled Ashli Babbitt and Rosanne Boyland towards the Capitol Building, and ultimately to their deaths.

Whoever is behind the nonsensical Q posts, it's the audience of willing conspiracists who are the real authors of Q, as much as it is any congregation whose will to believe is what moulds and shapes a god. Yes, if Q didn't exist, it would be necessary to invent Q, if only because taking lease of people's 'eyes and ears and nerves' to manipulate them – as Marshall McLuhan predicted of new media – is always so much easier when those body parts are volunteered. If Q's author is its audience, the more important search is for who it is that most stands to profit from their fealty.

For what it's worth, Hoback, LaFrance and even 8kun's founder, Fredrick Brennan, have advanced, with credible evidence, that the most recent incarnation of Q behind the tripcode on 8kun is likely to be the 8kun imageboard owner operators, Ron Watkins and/or his father, Jim Watkins – maybe individually, maybe together, maybe as the organisers of a posse of posters summoned to share the task. Jim Watkins certainly has a talent for compartmentalisation. After the El Paso shooting in 2019, Jim Watkins was subpoenaed to appear before a US congressional homeland security committee. There had been three fatal mass shootings that year linked to what was then 8kun, dozens of innocent people were dead, and he was asked how he planned to address the proliferation of extremist content on his site. He read from prepared remarks to the congressional committee and said, '8kun has no intent of deleting constitutionally protected hate speech' – and he did so while wearing a QAnon pin.[4]

The younger Watkins, Ron, had been made famous by his association with QAnon. The proximity had delivered him a prominent social media platform and great visibility – especially when retweeted by the not uninfluential then president of the United States, Donald Trump – yet when asked he outright denied that he is the secret author of Q.[5] Apparently, Ron Watkins tried to convince Cullen Hoback that Q had to be Steve Bannon.[6]

It's not an unreasonable suggestion, although Bannon is a busy man. Given how well Q has served Bannon's interests, the posts could arguably be the work of one of his talented minions from Breitbart, or Cambridge Analytica, or the Government Accountability Institute, or even a new Bannon project with a name the public is yet to learn, one more scheme among his many to ensure the politics that flow downstream from culture are of the hard-right, nationalist flavour he prefers. Right-wing blogs have also pondered if Q could even be disgraced Lieutenant General Michael Flynn. Given how well Q has also served Flynn's interests and reputation, a connection to him is, again, not improbable. The QAnon discourse helped revive his destroyed brand as a patriot. That's quite a triumph for a man forced out of the White House, twenty-four days into his term, having been caught out misleading the vice-president as well as lying to the FBI about his surreptitious meetings with the Russians.

Whoever is behind Q may have something to do with Sidney Powell or her fellow 'Kraken' lawyer Lin Wood, or Rudy Giuliani. Q's fanbase was of use to all of them in their staging of courtroom distraction theatre in the wake of Trump's election loss, theatre since denounced as a historic and profound abuse of the legal process by a US federal judge.[7] Alternatively, Q might be employed by Erik Prince, Betsy DeVos's brother, given as CEO of Blackwater he's in the private business of black ops, and his family – like the Mercers, and others of the fascism-friendly rich – certainly have the money to throw around on the right talent for something like this. Or Q could be a project of any number of Trump's friends, employees or offsiders tasked with the responsibility for its coordination.

QAnon's online faithful might sometimes speculate that no less than omnipotent God Emperor Trump himself contributes to the Q account – although it doesn't actually matter if Q is Trump, Watkins, Bannon, Tracy Diaz and her old Reddit collaborators, a handful of anonymous channers, or a smarmy left-wing prank against the right that got completely out of hand. What matters is that someone, somewhere, understood the web centipede well enough to know where to poke a thing like Q with a stick to make the creature move where they wanted it to.

It was interesting to learn, on 25 August 2021, that the US Congress Select Committee investigating the events of 6 January demanded the communication records of many names of prominence within the conspiracy cult community. These not only included Steve Bannon, Michael Flynn, Sidney Powell, Rudy Giuliani and Roger Stone but also George Papadopoulos, the infamous former drinking companion of Alexander Downer, who'd been charged with making false statements to the Mueller investigation and was pardoned by Trump on 22 December 2020. Conspicuously, records were also demanded from Pizzagate's Alex Jones and Jack Posobiec, as well as from Tracy Diaz. Among others, the committee investigators specifically requested 'All documents and communications referring or relating to QAnon'.[8]

In the wake of the Capitol riots, Ashli Babbitt was initially denounced as an antifa plant, a dupe and a fraud, a crisis actor who'd faked her own death, maybe to frighten Trump's supporters, maybe to make them look bad. Yet within six months of 6 January, dead Ashli Babbitt's reputation was suddenly rehabilitated. With an adjustment of messaging – if not actually of the facts – she was transformed from conniving provocateur into a peaceful patriot, a wrongly murdered hero and a martyr to the Trumpist cause. Her name was lionised in speeches given by Trump himself.

There was a disinformation campaign here. It was to historically rewrite the events of a failed putsch in which Ashli Babbitt had died trying to smash her way into the congressional chamber, part of a mob bellowing to hang Vice President Mike Pence. To twist that much remembered history requires an army to disseminate disinformation. Fortunately, the campaign had one: the digital soldiers of the conspiracy communities.

On 11 February 2021, posters in a 'great awakening' channel on Telegram were sharing fake news stories claiming no ambulance was ever sent to retrieve Ashli Babbitt's body from the Capitol. One poster declared, 'If Ashli Babbit comes out as a witness for a good guys. I will literally pee my pants. Lol.' On 26 February, the same channel shared fake news links claiming Babbitt's real name was Ashley Nylen and that she was from a family of Democrats, one of whom was supposedly a doctor in DC.

But by 13 July, new posts being shared on Telegram had links to a video of Trump ally Rudy Giuliani claiming there was a 'whole plot' behind Babbitt's death. By 8 August, posts were appearing with headlines like 'Ashli Babbitt's family claim she was "recklessly ambushed" by police in Capitol'. These last two were on the same great awakening channel as the earlier two stories. They were posted by the channel admin.

There's great political value in a volunteer army of online warriors one need only flick a switch to deploy. Isaac Kamola made the sharp point in his essay 'QAnon and the digital lumpenproletariat' that 6 January may indeed have been bankrolled by the corporations and Republican megadonors who provided the infrastructure, but it was QAnon that helped rouse the mob.[9]

In a post on 8 September 2020, Q had called out for these digital soldiers. What Q was actually recruiting were digital brownshirts and had been for some time. Their exposure to the imageboards, subreddits, Facebook groups, Twitter campaigns, fake news sites and data voids, their social isolation – especially from family – and the mistrust encouraged in them towards all other media had sealed some of these people into a closed propaganda bubble for years. The result was a cadre of oath-taking ideologues, pumped up with apocalyptic rhetoric and offered an irresistible image of themselves as righteous heroes in a holy war. Amid tales they'd already swallowed of white hats, black hats, tunnels, clones, warlocks and lizard people, they could be convinced the real was unreal, the impossible possible, and make themselves forget what they had furiously argued only weeks earlier. They could be turned out for street protests or provoked to stochastic terror. With targeted messaging – as the Capitol showed – they could be convinced to storm a seat of government. Yes, they were definitely brownshirts – just ones who hadn't realised that their shirts were brown.

The old hard-right movements certainly saw their value. The alt-right, old right, white supremacists, Neo-Nazis and Neo-Fascists had been marginalised from mainstream political conversation for so long, only through building numbers and enough of a critical presence could they shoulder their way back in. Colin P. Clarke from global security think tank the Soufan Group told *Voice of America* in March 2021 that in the wake of Trump's defeat and the Capitol riots, online chatter in far-right channels discussed how the 'useful fools' of the qommunity could be recruited to their own operations.[10] The gateway for this recruitment by Neo-Nazis, according to Clarke, were the anti-Semitic tropes QAnon adherents were primed in, so many unconsciously.

Bannon knew their value, too, especially to the web of scheming ideological influence networks that he'd created. As a disposable army they could be deployed variously as fundraisers, or voters in a primary process, or in turnouts to events. They were aggressively public fans and fundraisers for the politicians – like Trump, Marjorie Taylor Greene and others – who are willing to nod at their codewords. There'd be few Republican Party operatives in the United States unaware of a *Daily Kos*/Civiqs poll of September 2020 that discovered a solid 55 per cent of Republican voters believe at least some of the QAnon conspiracy theory is true.

Beyond domestic manipulators there are nefarious foreign actors jostling for control in the influence space. There are no longer merely Russian-backed influence operations boosting conspiracy material in the West. A report released in April 2021 – again by the Soufan Group – revealed that in the past year, China, Iran and Saudi Arabia had engaged disinformation operations 'to sow societal discord and even compromise legitimate political processes' by encouraging the conspiracists.[11] In 2020 and the first two months of 2021, almost 20 per cent of all QAnon posts on Facebook originated from administrators overseas, with China emerging as the primary foreign actor sourcing QAnon narratives online.

The internet pipeline into these communities that allows disinformation to be internationally weaponised is also what allows it to be profit-making. Brandy Zadrozny is one of the journalists from NBC News who broke the story early about the spread of QAnon, examining the role of @TracyBeanz and *The Patriots' Soapbox* as 'conspiracy entrepreneurs'. For an interview with *The Washington Post* in August 2020, Zadrozny spoke with palpable cynicism about lower-rent manipulators of the QAnon community.[12] QAnon, said Zadrozny, is the 'product of some small-time grifters who took an old anon trope and expertly fed it through a pipeline of social media (4chan -> Reddit -> YouTube -> Twitter and Facebook) for profit'. Then, she added, 'the pandemic lit it all on fire'.

The flames remind us while agitators and influencers can act as a conspiracy theory's accelerant, the spark comes from people's willingness to believe. Marshall McLuhan warned the danger of interactive media was about the 'lease' it may allow 'on our eyes and ears and nerves'. The terrible realisation in the self-confessed examples of mask-stand-destroying Melissa Rein Lively and Anderson Cooper's interlocutor Jitarth Jadeja is that within this fraught conspiratorial epoch, we – the ordinary people – are more than capable of burning our houses down ourselves.

Writing in *The Washington Post* on 5 April 2021, Alyssa Rosenberg lamented Cullen Hoback's *Q: Into the storm* for what she believed was its misplaced focus on unmasking Q.

Rather, Rosenberg said, '[f]or society at large, the task ahead is to find a way to restore a shared sense of reality and agreed-upon tools for determining what's true and what's fake'.[13]

Regulating the technology platforms that allow disinformation to proliferate is only partially useful to this project. Blocks, bans and other limitations imposed by Twitter, Facebook, Instagram and YouTube on disinformation posters are somewhat akin to shutting the stable door after the horse has joined the riots at the Capitol. Similarly, political commitments to transparency, accountability and committed truth-telling – such as the one in which US President Joe Biden has joined European leaders, a 'Pledge for Election Integrity' document that commits its signatories to act against 'falsified, fabricated, doxxed or stolen' data – are only helpful to a point.

On 19 November 2020, disinformation scholar Nina Jankowicz advocated in an essay for *Foreign Affairs* that governments had to start taking the theatre of disinformation seriously and assign meaningful resources towards fighting it.[14] She suggests the installation of 'counter-disinformation czars' and a whole-of-government take on the problem. Given the growing activism of foreign governments in the disinformation space, doing so is inarguably a matter of national security. Working across departments from defence to education, and cooperatively with private sector and civil society groups, according to Jankowicz, would enable governments to 'monitor the information system' and identify threats before they metastasise into movements. She recommends targeted outreach projects, too, to improve the media literacy of communities, and to bolster those institutions – like public libraries and national broadcasters – that already enjoy recognition by citizens as arbiters of trustworthy and reliable information.

Jankowicz's recommendations are a collective solution to a general problem, but, on the level of 'rabbit-holed' individuals, the solution is also collective. The oft-repeated plea for advice on how to recover someone from the cult has its answer in a process of resocialisation.

When interviewed on this subject by Australia's ABC on 23 May 2021, social psychologist Jolanda Jetten from the University of Queensland explained that conspiracy belief is an 'all-absorbing identity'.[15] It's an identity that's bestowed through participating in a community that represents itself as attentive and supportive and can be incredibly difficult to leave behind. Steven Hassan, himself a cult survivor, was also interviewed and concurred. It was an incredible help for those trying to climb out of the rabbit hole to find themselves surrounded by those 'who do not share their past beliefs'.

The intervention of friends and family talking through the conspiracist's relationship with QAnon sounds emotionally involving and exhausting because it is. The nuanced, orthodox practicality of personal contact is antithetical to the simplistic, seductive heresies of the online conspiracy cults. Again and again, though, it's this kindness, patience and respect from friends and loved ones that those who leave the cults describe as their 'pathway back to society', away from the shallow, tribal relationships of an online community that exists to stoke and nurture their fear.

Former QAnonner Ashley Vanderbilt spoke on US television chat show *The View* about leaving the community. She described a transformative moment of reconnection with her mother. Before the day of Joe Biden's inauguration, she prepped for Q's 'blackout' by 'stocking up on groceries and filling up her car's gas tank'. When Q's promises did not come true, Vanderbilt found herself in psychological freefall, believing her 'worst nightmare' may be coming true. She called her mother in terror. Her mother spoke calmly and reminded her she need not be afraid. The quiet, reasoned reassurance provoked a moment of sudden self-awareness in Vanderbilt that snapped her back to reality. As she rejoined her life outside QAnon, Vanderbilt told *The View*, she left 'disappointment and anger and lies' behind.[16]

Reddit has become the place where support groups of ex–QAnon believers form and gain followers. The subreddit r/ReQovery attracted ten thousand members in its first year. In these communities, redditors share stories of their 'wake-up' moments, like Vanderbilt's. Someone called u/Being_Certain describes simply feeling 'betrayed'. u/Realistic_Hornet_536 took 'great offence' to being told by qommunity members that 'Hitler was a good guy'. Another called u/StickNutzMan – a former Republican – cites the Capitol riots as the catalyst for his reconversion. 'I now find myself center-left politically,' the poster confesses, 'but I live in deep red Trump territory. I got the first round of the vaccine, but I literally can't tell anyone but my left leaning friends without getting a condescending look.'

While the subreddit's content is heartening, and the community of ex-QAnonners continues to grow, it would be a dangerous mistake to believe that the forces that created QAnon are a problem with a definitive solution, or that they are part of a transitory phenomenon that will inevitably reach an end point.

Conspiracy theories fall in and out of popularity. They're just as subject to changing tastes as any form of cultural expression. What the journey from Gamergate to Pizzagate to QAnon demonstrates, though, isn't that conspiratorial thinking itself comes and goes like an item of fashion. It's that conspiracist ideas adapt to evolving contexts like a dynamic organism. They repurpose hateful old tropes to attack new targets: the nocturnal ritual fantasies of the Romans become the blood libel of the Middle Ages. A 'satanic panic' of the 1980s that insists the devilish Luciferians are everywhere becomes Pizzagate, becomes QAnon. The organism feeds on the desperate will that ever exists for us-and-them binary thinking.

Those who feel powerless seize at these evidence-free stories of conspiracy and deviousness because they want to feel in control. They join internet conspiracy cults to have these ideas affirmed. But whoever gains control of a fantasy narrative – whether it's the prophecies of Q, a slut-shaming campaign dreamed up by 4chan or a war-on-Christmas monologue on Fox News – also gains control over every single person who allows themselves to believe it.

Even if we could blow up the internet and every computer it connects tomorrow, we can't erase conspiracy thinking. But we can monitor these ideas and intervene with the people who hold them. We can build up our institutions and improve critical literacy and keep exerting pressure on internet platforms to adapt their services against influence operations and extremism. We can also resist the *Videodrome*-like pull of seductive fantasies about our world and ourselves that internet technology passively puts before us, and fight to retain possession of our eyes and ears against the dangerous temptation of believing things merely because we'd prefer they were true.

Finally, we can – and must and should – keep contact alive with those we love who might be lured towards conspiracy communities and ensure that no matter how far someone travels down a rabbit hole, they can always find their way home again.

For the Rosanne Boylands. For the Edgar Maddison Welches. For the Tim and Jesse Stewarts. For everyone who loved these people and was devastated to lose them to their fantasies, we must stay visible. Even if we can't bring back the lost. Even if we can only help those we love to unfollow the white rabbits, one rabbit at a time.

ENDNOTES

Internet posts have been reproduced verbatim, errors and all.

References to posts attributed to 'Q' have been sourced from the online archive qagg.news. Some references attributed to 8kun were originally published on 8chan but were archived as 8kun. Conflicting time stamps from imageboard posts may result from automatic time-zone adjustments. For researchers, a newer, comprehensive database of online posts and commentary associated with the QAnon movement is available at dchan.qorigins.org.

This is the beginning ...

1   Bryan Anderson, 'Tech pioneer Vint Cerf offers optimistic view
     of future of the internet, artificial intelligence', *Elon News Network*,
     elonnewsnetwork.com/article/2016/10/vint-cerf, 30 September 2016.
2   Steven Levy, 'Indecent proposal: Censor the net', *Newsweek*, newsweek.
     com/indecent-proposal-censor-net-181706, 2 April 1995.
3   Vinton Cerf, Yogen Dalal and Carl Sunshine, 'Specification of
     internet transmission control program', ietf.org/rfc/rfc0675.txt,
     December 1974.
4   David Weinberger, 'The internet that was (and still could be)', *The
     Atlantic*, theatlantic.com/technology/archive/2015/06/medium-is-the-
     message-paradise-paved-internet-architecture/396227/, 22 June 2015.
5   CBS News, '45 years ago: First message sent over the internet', *CBS
     News*, cbsnews.com/news/first-message-sent-over-the-internet-45-
     years-ago/, 29 October 2014.
6   Marshall McLuhan, *Understanding Media: The extensions of man*, New
     York: McGraw-Hill, 1964.

7   Nick Carr, 'McLuhan would blow hot and cool about today's internet', *The Guardian*, theguardian.com/technology/2007/nov/01/comment.internet, 2 November 2007.

8   McLuhan, *Understanding Media*, p. 15.

9   Hamish Patton, 'Oz: Commie bushpig Van Badham condemns Reclaim Australia', *Jew World Order*, jewworldorder.org/oz-commie-bushpig-van-badham-condemns-reclaim-australia/, 8 April 2015.

10   Van Badham, 'If your friends or family have fallen for an internet conspiracy cult, here's what you should do', *The Guardian* (via Facebook), facebook.com/theguardianaustralia/posts/3492827204085674, 28 September 2020.

11   Weinberger, 'The internet that was (and still could be)'.

12   Tovia Smith, 'Experts in cult deprogramming step in to help believers in conspiracy theories', transcript from *All Things Considered*, NPR, npr.org/2021/03/02/972970805/experts-in-cult-deprogramming-step-in-to-help-believers-in-conspiracy-theories, 2 March 2021.

13   Karen Douglas, 'The internet fuels conspiracy theories – but not in the way you might imagine', *The Conversation*, theconversation.com/the-internet-fuels-conspiracy-theories-but-not-in-the-way-you-might-imagine-98037, 28 June 2018.

14   Smith, 'Experts in cult deprogramming step in'.

15   David Cronenberg, *Videodrome* [film], Toronto: Universal Pictures, 1983.

1. A small role in a reality TV show

1   Christopher Knaus and Josh Taylor, 'Revealed: The QAnon conspiracy theorist who is friends with Australian PM Scott Morrison', *The Guardian*, theguardian.com/australia-news/2019/oct/05/qanon-conspiracy-theorist-friends-australian-prime-minister-scott-morrison, 5 October 2019.

2   Sam Shead, 'YouTube radicalized the Christchurch shooter, New Zealand report concludes', *CNBC*, cnbc.com/2020/12/08/youtube-radicalized-christchurch-shooter-new-zealand-report-finds.html, 8 December 2020.

3   Elias Groll, 'How the Christchurch shooter played the world's media', *Foreign Policy*, foreignpolicy.com/2019/03/15/how-the-christchurch-shooter-played-the-worlds-media, 15 March 2019.

4   David Hardaker, 'Scott Morrison's conspiracy-theorist friend claims he has the PM's ear — and can influence what he says', *Crikey*, crikey.com.au/2019/10/31/scott-morrison-qanon/, 31 October 2019.

5   Karen Stewart, interview with the author, 9 July 2021.

6   Will Sommer, 'QAnon's newest hero is D-List "Vanderpump Rules" star Isaac Kappy', *The Daily Beast*, thedailybeast.com/qanons-newest-hero-is-a-d-list-vanderpump-rules-star, 7 August 2018.

7   Fiona Barnett, 'Luciferian cult & MK ultra survivor Australia — Fiona Barnett Part 1' [video], BitChute, bitchute.com/video/ST6sPIQbjS5p/, 18 July 2018.

8   Karen Stewart, interview with the author, 9 July 2021.

9   Hardaker, 'Scott Morrison's conspiracy-theorist friend claims he has the PM's ear'.

10 Gayland W. Hurst and Robert L. Marsh, 'Satanic cult awareness', *US Department of Justice*, ojp.gov/pdffiles1/Photocopy/140554NCJRS.pdf, date stamped 27 January 1993.

11 Matthew Bevan and Ruby Jones, 'The drink that started the Mueller investigation: George Papadopoulos and Alexander Downer tell us everything', *ABC News*, abc.net.au/news/2019-05-24/mueller-investigation-george-papadopoulos-alexander-downer-speak/11107712?nw=0, 24 May 2019.

12 Knaus and Taylor, 'Revealed'.

13 ABC Television, 'The great awakening: A family divided by QAnon' [television program], *Four Corners*, ABC Television, abc.net.au/4corners/the-great-awakening/13387338, 14 June 2021.

14 Australian Senate, *Finance and Public Administration Legislation Committee — Estimates*, aph.gov.au/Parliamentary_Business/Hansard/Hansard_Display?bid=committees/estimate/578b189d-5bd2-4879-8af7-df3a39a133f7/&sid=0006, 21 October 2019.

15 Knaus and Taylor, 'Revealed'.

16 Katharine Murphy, 'Vector of influence: Labor grills officials about QAnon family friend of Scott Morrison', *The Guardian*, theguardian.

com/australia-news/2020/oct/21/vector-of-influence-labor-grills-officials-about-qanon-family-friend-of-scott-morrison, 21 October 2020.

17   Knaus and Taylor, 'Revealed'.

18   ABC Television, 'The great awakening'.

19   Prime Minister Scott Morrison, 'National apology address: Transcript', *Prime Minister of Australia*, pm.gov.au/media/national-apology-address, 22 October 2018.

20   Richard Bartholomew, 'Australian Prime Minister Scott Morrison and "ritual sexual abuse"', *Bartholomew's Notes*, barthsnotes. com/2018/10/26/australian-prime-minister-scott-morrison-and-ritual-sexual-abuse/, 26 October 2018.

21   Richard Bartholomew, interview with the author, 20 July 2021.

22   BBC News, 'Carl Beech: Liar, fraudster and paedophile', *BBC News*, bbc.com/news/uk-49048972, 26 July 2019.

23   Richard Bartholomew, 'Lurid VIP paedophile and murder claims hit Australia's MSM', *Bartholomew's Notes*, barthsnotes.com/2015/10/25/lurid-vip-paedophile-and-murder-claims-hit-australias-msm/, 25 October 2015.

24   Stephen Rice, 'Key ABC witness Peter Alexander Priest is a serial conspiracy theorist', *The Australian*, theaustralian.com.au/nation/key-abc-witness-peter-alexander-priest-is-a-serial-conspiracy-theorist/news-story/73c60d96619a76e6300836e163140f6b, 20 June 2021.

25   ABC Television, 'The great awakening'.

26   Sandi Keane, interview with the author, 19 July 2021.

27   Negan [@NeganHQ], 'Treason +++ Violation of basic human rights and Nuremberg Code ...' [online forum post], Gab, gab.com/NeganHQ/posts/106549866269651061, 9 July 2021.

28   Karen Stewart, interview with the author, 9 July 2021.

29   Australian Senate, *Finance and Public Administration Legislation Committee – Estimates*, aph.gov.au/Parliamentary_Business/Hansard/Hansard_Display?bid=committees/estimate/2a895067-c4f7-4f6b-991a-784a4a8ff0ba/&sid=0002, 25 May 2021.

30   Olivia Rubin, Lucien Bruggeman and Will Steakin, 'QAnon emerges as recurring theme of criminal cases tied to US Capitol siege', *ABC*

News, abcnews.go.com/US/qanon-emerges-recurring-theme-criminal-cases-tied-us/story?id=75347445, 20 January 2021.

31   Miles Taylor, interview with the author, 23 July 2021.

32   ABC Television, 'The great awakening'.

33   David Hardaker, 'PM defies his own expert panel during apology speech to child sex abuse survivors', *Crikey*, crikey.com.au/2019/11/18/scott-morrison-qanon-apology-advice/, 18 November 2019.

34   Bartholomew, 'Australian Prime Minister Scott Morrison and "ritual sexual abuse"'.

2. Gateway drugs

1   Jesselyn Cook and Sebastian Murdock, 'Dahvie Vanity raped a child. Police gave him a warning. Now 21 women accuse him of sexual assault', *Huffpost*, huffpost.com/entry/dahvie-vanity-botdf-sexual-assault_n_5c82afb8e4b0d9361627ca1f, 5 April 2019.

2   Peter Farquhar, 'Jessi Slaughter and the 4Chan trolls – the case for censoring the internet', *News.com.au*, accessed on *Internet Archive*, web.archive.org/web/20100721182813/news.com.au/technology/jessi-slaughter-and-the-4chan-trolls-the-case-for-censoring-the-internet/story-e6frfro0-1225894369199, 20 July 2010.

3   James Cook, 'The Emma Watson naked photo countdown was more than just the work of serial internet hoaxers', *Business Insider*, businessinsider.com.au/emma-watson-naked-photo-countdown-hoax-2014-9, 25 September 2014.

4   Michael Bernstein, Andrés Monroy-Hernández, Drew Harry, Paul André, Katrina Panovich and Gregory Vargas, '4chan and /b/: An analysis of anonymity and ephemerality in a large online community' [conference paper], *Proceedings of the Fifth International Conference on Weblogs and Social Media*, Barcelona, Spain, 17–21 July 2011.

5   Jamie Bartlett, '4Chan: The role of anonymity in the meme-generating cesspool of the web', *Wired*, wired.co.uk/article/4chan-happy-birthday, 1 October 2010.

6   'Message to Scientology' [video], *ChurchOfScientology*, YouTube, youtube.com/watch?v=JCbKv9yiLiQ, 22 January 2008.

7   Chad Perrin, 'The so-called group called Anonymous', *Tech Republic*, techrepublic.com/blog/it-security/the-so-called-group-called-anonymous/, 23 September 2008.

8   Jacob Siegel, 'Dylann Roof, 4chan, and the new online racism', *The Daily Beast*, thedailybeast.com/dylann-roof-4chan-and-the-new-online-racism?ref=author, 14 April 2017.

9   Keegan Hankes, 'How Reddit became a worse black hole of violent racism than Stormfront', *Gawker*, gawker.com/how-reddit-became-a-worse-black-hole-of-violent-racism-1690505395, 3 October 2015.

10   Siegel, 'Dylann Roof, 4chan, and the new online racism'.

11   Simon Parkin, 'Zoe Quinn's Depression Quest', *The New Yorker*, newyorker.com/tech/annals-of-technology/zoe-quinns-depression-quest, 9 September 2014.

12   Michael Salter, 'Gamergate and the subpolitics of abuse in online publics' in *Crime, Justice and Social Media*, New York: Routledge, 2017, p. 43.

13   Keith Stuart, 'UK gamers: More women play games than men, report finds', *The Guardian*, theguardian.com/technology/2014/sep/17/women-video-games-iab, 17 September 2014; Monica Anderson, 'Views on gaming differ by race, ethnicity', *Pew Research Center*, pewresearch.org/fact-tank/2015/12/17/views-on-gaming-differ-by-race-ethnicity/, 17 December 2015.

14   Alice Clarke, 'The state of Australian gamers in 2019', *The Sydney Morning Herald*, smh.com.au/technology/video-games/the-state-of-australian-gamers-in-2019-20190801-p52cuk.html#:~:text=Though%20the%20average%20age%20of,been%20for%20around%20a%20decade, 4 August 2019.

15   Feminist Frequency, 'Support my Kickstarter project – tropes vs women in video games' [video], *Feminist Frequency*, YouTube, youtube.com/watch?v=l8I0Wy58adM, 5 June 2019.

16   Anita Sarkeesian, 'Harassment via Wikipedia vandalism' [blog post], *Feminist Frequency*, Tumblr, feministfrequency.com/2012/06/10/harassment-and-misogyny-via-wikipedia/, 10 June 2012.

17   Sophie Riche, 'Anita Sarkeesian VS 4chan: The fight against a background of sexism' *Madmoizelle*, madmoizelle.com/anita-sarkeesian-vs-4chan-108249, 7 June 2012.

18   Jordan Owen, *The Sarkeesian Effect: Inside the world of social justice warriors* [film], 2015.

19   David Futrelle, 'JordanOwen42 on the couch: Two wannabe Sarkeesian muckrakers react to the horrible news that she's been telling the truth', *We Hunted the Mammoth*, wehuntedthemammoth. com/2014/09/19/jordanowen42-on-the-couch-two-would-be-sarkeesian-documentaries-react-to-the-horrible-news-that-shes-been-telling-the-truth/, 19 September 2014.

20   P.E. Tetlock, 'Social-functionalist frameworks for judgment and choice: The intuitive politician, theologian, and prosecutor', *Psychological Review*, no. 109, 2002, pp. 451–72.

21   Karen M. Douglas, Robbie M. Sutton and Aleksandra Cichocka, 'The psychology of conspiracy theories', *Current Directions in Psychological Science*, vol. 26, no. 6, 2017, pp. 538–42, journals.sagepub. com/doi/pdf/10.1177/0963721417718261.

22   J.W. van Prooijen and N.B. Jostmann, 'Belief in conspiracy theories: The influence of uncertainty and perceived morality', *European Journal of Social Psychology*, no. 43, 2013, pp. 109–15.

23   Meg Jayanth, '52% of gamers are women – but the industry doesn't know it yet', *The Guardian*, theguardian.com/commentisfree/2014/ sep/18/52-percent-people-playing-games-women-industry-doesnt-know, 19 September 2014.

24   Zoë Quinn, *Crash Override*, Cambridge, MA: Perseus Books, 2017 p. 2.

25   Zachary Jason, 'Game of fear', *Boston*, bostonmagazine.com/ news/2015/04/28/gamergate/2/, 28 April 2015.

26   John Bain [@Totalbiscuit], 'What the hell just happened?' [online post], *Twit Longer*, twitlonger.com/show/n_1s4nmr1, 19 August 2014.

27   Stephen Totilo, 'In recent days I've been …', *Kotaku*, kotaku.com/ in-recent-days-ive-been-asked-several-times-about-a-pos-1624707346, 20 August 2014.

28   Jason, 'Game of fear'.

29   Jason, 'Game of fear'.

30   Quinn, *Crash Override*, p. 3.

31   Salter, 'Gamergate and the subpolitics of abuse in online publics'.

32 Leigh Alexander, '"Gamers" don't have to be your audience. "Gamers" are over', *Gamasutra*, gamasutra.com/view/news/224400/ Gamers_dont_have_to_be_your_audience_, 28 August 2014.

33 Ben Cotton, 'Troll repellent: Fighting online harassment with open source', *Opensource.com*, opensource.com/life/15/7/interview-randi-harper-online-abuse-prevention-initiative, 2 July 2015.

34 Torill Elvira Mortensen, 'Anger, fear, and games: The long event of #GamerGate', *Games and Culture*, vol. 13, no. 8, April 2016.

35 Taylor Wofford, 'Is GamerGate about media ethics or harassing women? Harassment, the data shows', *Newsweek*, newsweek.com/ gamergate-about-media-ethics-or-harassing-women-harassment-data-show-279736, 25 October 2014.

36 Bob Garfield, 'Condemning #GamerGate' [radio broadcast], *On the Media*, WNYC, wnyc.org/story/codemning-gamergate/, 24 October 2014.

37 Quinn, *Crash Override*, p. 3.

38 David Futrelle, 'Zoe Quinn's screenshots of 4chan's dirty tricks were just the appetizer. Here's the first course of the dinner, directly from the IRC log', *We Hunted the Mammoth*, wehuntedthemammoth. com/2014/09/08/zoe-quinns-screenshots-of-4chans-dirty-tricks-were-just-the-appetizer-heres-the-first-course-of-the-dinner-directly-from-the-irc-log/, 8 September 2014.

39 Michael Heron, 'Sexism in the circuitry: Female participation in male-dominated popular computer culture', *ACM SIGCAS Computers and Society*, vol. 33, no. 4, 2014, pp. 18–29.

40 Montreal Gazette, 'Alt-right in Montreal: Shining a light on the local neo-Nazi network', *Montreal Gazette*, montrealgazette.com/news/local-news/alt-right-in-montreal-shining-a-light-on-local-neo-nazi-network, 20 May 2018.

41 Shannon Carranco, Jon Milton and Christopher Curtis, 'Alt-right in Montreal: The war against women', *Montreal Gazette*, montrealgazette. com/news/local-news/alt-right-in-montreal-the-war-against-women, 18 May 2018.

42 Shannon Carranco, Jon Milton and Christopher Curtis, 'An online culture of harassment and hate', *Montreal Gazette*,

accessed via *Pressreader*, pressreader.com/canada/montreal-gazet
te/20180519/281732680141436, 20 May 2018.

43   Jason Wilson, 'Cultural Marxism: A uniting theory for rightwingers
who love to play the victim', *The Guardian*, theguardian.com/
commentisfree/2015/jan/19/cultural-marxism-a-uniting-theory-for-
rightwingers-who-love-to-play-the-victim, 19 January 2015.

44   Mortensen, 'Anger, fear, and games'.

45   Scott Kaufman, 'Actor Adam Baldwin: #GamerGate defeated the
left, but there will be no parade', *Raw Story*, rawstory.com/2014/11/
actor-adam-baldwin-gamergate-defeated-the-left-but-there-will-be-
no-parade/, 20 November 2014. (Tweets are deleted but referred to
in Salter, 'Gamergate and the subpolitics of abuse in online publics'.)

46   Stephen Richter, 'Steve Bannon the destroyer: Trump's top aide is
the anti Jimmy Carter', *Salon*, salon.com/2017/03/17/steve-bannon-
the-destroyer-trumps-top-aide-is-the-anti-jimmy-carter_partner/,
17 March 2017.

47   Gabrielle Levy, 'Steve Bannon: "I'm not a white nationalist … I'm
an economic nationalist"', *US News*, usnews.com/news/politics/
articles/2016-11-18/steve-bannon-im-not-a-white-nationalist-im-an-
economic-nationalist, 18 November 2016.

48   Mike Snider, 'Steve Bannon learned to harness troll army from
"World of Warcraft"', *USA Today*, usatoday.com/story/tech/
talkingtech/2017/07/18/steve-bannon-learned-harness-troll-army-
world-warcraft/489713001/, 18 July 2017.

49   Joshua Green, 'This man is the most dangerous political operative in
America', *Bloomberg*, bloomberg.com/politics/graphics/2015-steve-
bannon/, 8 October 2015.

50   Emily Tillett, 'Christopher Wylie: Bannon wanted "weapons" to fight
a "culture war" at Cambridge Analytica', *CBS News*, cbsnews.com/
live-news/senate-cambridge-analytica-whistleblower-christopher-
wylie-live-stream-updates-today-2018-05-16/, 16 May 2018.

51   Carole Cadwalladr, '"I made Steve Bannon's psychological warfare
tool": Meet the data whistleblower', The Guardian theguardian.
com/news/2018/mar/17/data-war-whistleblower-christopher-wylie-
faceook-nix-bannon-trump, 18 March 2018.

52   Keach Hagey, 'Breitbart to announce new management', *Politico*,
      politico.com/blogs/media/2012/03/breitbart-to-announce-new-
      management-117836, 19 March 2012.

53   James Oliphant and Steve Holland, 'After firing, Bannon returns to his
      "killing machine"', *Reuters*, reuters.com/article/us-usa-trump-bannon-
      right-idUSKCN1AY2JQ, 19 August 2017.

54   Noah Friedman, Josh Barro and Lamar Salter, 'Here's how Steve
      Bannon used angry white gamers to build himself up to Trump's
      chief strategist', *Business Insider*, businessinsider.com.au/steve-bannon-
      white-gamers-seinfeld-joshua-green-donald-trump-devils-bargain-
      sarah-palin-world-warcraft-gamergate-2017-7, 22 July 2017.

55   Sarah Posner, 'How Donald Trump's new campaign chief created an
      online haven for white nationalists', *Mother Jones*, motherjones.com/
      politics/2016/08/stephen-bannon-donald-trump-alt-right-breitbart-
      news/, 22 August 2016.

56   Sean Illing, '"Flood the zone with shit": How misinformation
      overwhelmed our democracy', *Vox*, vox.com/policy-and-
      politics/2020/1/16/20991816/impeachment-trial-trump-bannon-
      misinformation, 6 February 2020.

57   Dorian Lynskey, 'The rise and fall of Milo Yiannopoulos: How
      a shallow actor played the bad guy for money', *The Guardian*,
      theguardian.com/world/2017/feb/21/milo-yiannopoulos-rise-and-
      fall-shallow-actor-bad-guy-hate-speech, 22 February 2017.

58   Aja Romano, 'Milo Yiannopoulos still has alt-right fans', *Vox*, vox.
      com/culture/2017/2/23/14681712/milo-yiannopoulos-alt-right-fan-
      base-support, 23 February 2017.

59   Milo Yiannopoulos, 'Zoe Quinn is the perfect person to address the
      UN on Cyber Bullying', *Breitbart*, breitbart.com/politics/2015/09/21/
      zoe-quinn-is-the-perfect-person-to-address-the-un-on-cyberbullying/,
      21 September 2015; Milo Yiannopoulos, 'Harping on: The hypocrisy
      and lies of Twitter's most notorious "anti-abuse" activist, Randi
      Harper, part 1' *Breitbart*, breitbart.com/the-media/2015/06/29/
      harping-on-the-hypocrisy-and-lies-of-twitters-most-notorious-anti-
      abuse-activist-randi-harper-part-1/, 29 June 2015; Mytheos Holt,
      'Let's stop pretending Anita Sarkeesian is an art critic', *Breitbart*,

breitbart.com/tech/2015/11/02/lets-stop-pretending-anita-sarkeesian-art-critic/, 2 November 2015; Milo Yiannopoulos, 'The wacky world of Wu: The tortured history of Gamergate's self-styled feminist martyr', *Breitbart*, breitbart.com/europe/2015/02/13/the-wacky-world-of-wu-the-tortured-history-of-gamergates-self-styled-feminist-martyr, 13 February 2015.

60   Yiannopoulos, 'Zoe Quinn is the perfect person to address the UN'.

61   Joseph Bernstein, 'Top conservative writer is a group effort, sources say', *Buzzfeed News*, buzzfeednews.com/article/josephbernstein/top-conservative-writer-is-a-group-effort-sources-say#.ldyQmnYbp, 31 March 2016.

62   Lynskey, 'The rise and fall of Milo Yiannopoulos'.

63   Joseph Bernstein, 'Here's how Breitbart and Milo smuggled white nationalism into the mainstream', *Buzzfeed News*, buzzfeednews.com/article/josephbernstein/heres-how-breitbart-and-milo-smuggled-white-nationalism, 5 October 2017.

64   Milo Yiannopoulos, 'Donald Trump, king of trolling his critics, should be the internet's choice for president', *Breitbart*, breitbart.com/politics/2015/06/19/donald-trump-king-of-trolling-his-critics-should-be-the-internets-choice-for-president/, 19 June 2015.

65   Milo Yiannopoulos, 'How disgraced blogger Leigh Alexander torpedoed a games studio', *Breitbart*, breitbart.com/the-media/2015/06/23/how-disgraced-blogger-leigh-alexander-torpedoed-a-games-studio/, 23 June 2015.

66   Milo Yiannopoulos, 'Why I'm winning', *Breitbart*, breitbart.com/the-media/2015/11/23/why-im-winning/, 23 November 2015.

67   Joseph Bernstein, 'In 2015, the dark forces of the internet became a countercult', *Buzzfeed News*, buzzfeednews.com/article/josephbernstein/in-2015-the-dark-forces-of-the-internet-became-a-countercult, 23 December 2015.

68   Friedman, Barro and Salter, 'Here's how Steve Bannon used angry white gamers'.

69   Betsy Swan, 'Inside Virginia's creepy white-power wolf cult', *The Daily Beast*, thedailybeast.com/inside-virginias-creepy-white-power-wolf-cult, 13 April 2017.

70   Milo Yiannopoulos, 'Meme magic: Donald Trump is the
internet's revenge on lazy elites', *Breitbart*, breitbart.com/social-
justice/2016/05/04/meme-magic-donald-trump-internets-revenge-
lazy-entitled-elites/, 4 May 2016.

71   Tara Golshan, '2 big takeaways from a scandalous report on internal
Breitbart documents', *Vox*, vox.com/2017/10/5/16433172/buzzfeed-
report-breitbart-documents-milo, 5 October, 2017.

72   Jo Livingstone, 'Our algorithms, ourselves', *The New Republic*,
newrepublic.com/article/150562/algorithms, 10 August 2018.

73   Tom Sear and Michael Jensen, 'Russian trolls targeted Australian
voters on Twitter', *UNSW Canberra*, unsw.adfa.edu.au/newsroom/
news/russian-trolls-targeted-australian-voters-twitter, 23 August
2018.

74   David Kushner, '4chan's overlord Christopher Poole reveals why
he walked away', *Rolling Stone*, rollingstone.com/culture/culture-
features/4chans-overlord-christopher-poole-reveals-why-he-walked-
away-93894/, 13 March 2015.

75   Steven Levy, 'Indecent proposal: Censor the net', *Newsweek*, newsweek.
com/indecent-proposal-censor-net-181706, 2 April 1995.

76   Jamie Bartlett, '4chan: The role of anonymity in the meme-generating
cesspool of the web', *Wired*, wired.co.uk/article/4chan-happy-
birthday, 1 October 2013.

77   Drew Harwell, 'Three mass shootings this year began with hateful
screed on 8kun, its founder calls it a terrorist refuge in plain sight', *The
Washington Post*, washingtonpost.com/technology/2019/08/04/three-
mass-shootings-this-year-began-with-hateful-screed-chan-its-founder-
calls-it-terrorist-refuge-plain-sight/, 4 August 2019.

78   Robert Evans, 'Ignore the Poway Synagogue shooter's manifesto:
Pay attention to 8kuns /pol/ board', *Bellingcat*, bellingcat.com/
news/americas/2019/04/28/ignore-the-poway-synagogue-shooters-
manifesto-pay-attention-to-8kuns-pol-board/, 28 April 2019.

3. Cheese pizza

1   Keith L. Alexander and Susan Svrluga, '"I am sure he is sorry
for any heartaches he has caused," mother of alleged "Pizzagate"

gunman says', *The Washington* Post, washingtonpost.com/local/
public-safety/i-am-sure-he-is-sorry-for-any-heartaches-he-has-
caused-mother-of-alleged-pizzagate-gunman-says/2016/12/12/
ac6f9068-c083-11e6-afd9-f038f753dc29_story.html, 12 December
2016.

2   Jonathan Drew and Jessica Gresko, 'The man fake news sent to
Washington', *Maclean's*, macleans.ca/news/edgar-maddison-welch-
fake-news-pizza/, 7 December 2016.

3   Gideon Resnick, 'Pizzagate gunman said he would sacrifice the "lives
of a few for the lives of many"', *The Daily Beast*, thedailybeast.com/
pizzagate-gunman-said-he-would-sacrifice-the-lives-of-a-few-for-the-
lives-of-many, 13 April 2017.

4   Spencer S. Hsu, '"Pizzagate" gunman says he was foolish,
reckless, mistaken – and sorry', *The Washington Post*,
washingtonpost.com/local/public-safety/pizzagate-shooter-
apologizes-in-handwritten-letter-for-his-mistakes-ahead-of-
sentencing/2017/06/13/f35126b6-5086-11e7-be25-3a519335381c_
story.html, 14 June 2017.

5   Associated Press, 'NC shooter drover to DC for a "closer look"',
WFMYNews2, wfmynews2.com/article/news/crime/nc-shooter-drove-
to-dc-for-a-closer-look/83-366033371, 12 August 2016.

6   Adam Goldman, 'The Comet Ping Pong gunman answers our
reporter's questions', *The New York Times*, nytimes.com/2016/12/07/
us/edgar-welch-comet-pizza-fake-news.html, 7 December 2016.

7   Marc Fisher, John Woodrow Cox and Peter Hermann, 'Pizzagate:
From rumor, to hashtag to gunfire in D.C.', *The Washington Post*,
washingtonpost.com/local/pizzagate-from-rumor-to-hashtag-
to-gunfire-in-dc/2016/12/06/4c7def50-bbd4-11e6-94ac-
3d324840106c_story.html, 6 December 2016.

8   Goldman, 'The Comet Ping Pong gunman answers our reporter's
questions'.

9   Spencer Hsu, 'Pizzagate gunman sentenced to four years in prison,
as prosecutors urged judge to deter vigilante justice', *The Washington
Post*, washingtonpost.com/local/public-safety/pizzagate-gunman-
sentenced-to-four-years-in-prison-as-prosecutors-urged-judge-to-

deter-vigilante-justice/2017/06/22/a10db598-550b-11e7-ba90-f5875b7d1876_story.html, 22 June 2017.

10   Hsu, '"Pizzagate" gunman says he was foolish'.

11   Geneva Sands, '"Pizzagate" gunman recorded "goodbye" video message to his family', *ABC News*, abcnews.go.com/US/pizzagate-gunman-recorded-goodbye-video-message-family/story?id=48235100, 24 June 2017.

12   Goldman, 'The Comet Ping Pong gunman answers our reporter's questions'.

13   Shawn Musgrave, 'I get called a Russian bot 50 times a day', *Politico*, politico.com/magazine/story/2017/08/09/twitter-trump-train-maga-echo-chamber-215470/ , 9 August 2017. (Note: Eagle Wings/@NIVIsa4031 has changed their online name to Connie's Corner/@CRRJA5, but it's the same account.)

14   Caroline Hallemann, 'What we do and don't know about Jeffrey Epstein', *Town and Country*, townandcountrymag.com/society/money-and-power/a28352055/jeffrey-epstein-criminal-case-facts/, 2 July 2020.

15   Warthog76, 'I have inside sources and can confirm privately to a mod my credentials ...' [online forum post], *Godlike Productions*, godlikeproductions.com/forum1/message3341662/pg1?disclaimer=1, 30 October 2016.

16   C. Eugene Emery Jr, 'Evidence ridiculously thin for sensational claim of huge underground Clinton sex network', *Politifact*, politifact.com/factchecks/2016/nov/04/conservative-daily-posxt/evidence-ridiculously-thin-sensational-claim-huge-/, 4 November 2016.

17   Amanda Robb, 'Anatomy of a fake news scandal', *Rolling Stone*, rollingstone.com/feature/anatomy-of-a-fake-news-scandal-125877/, 16 November 2017.

18   Kate Bennett, 'The Podesta brothers are ready to cook for Hillary', *Politico*, politico.com/story/2015/10/kgb-podestas-cook-214286, 10 January 2015.

19   Gregor Aisch, Jon Huang and Cecilia Kang, 'Dissecting the #Pizzagate conspiracy theories', *The New York Times*, nytimes.com/interactive/2016/12/10/business/media/pizzagate.html, 16 December 2016.

20   Anne Applebaum, 'Opinion: What "cheese pizza" means to the internet's conspiracy-mongers', washingtonpost.com/blogs/post-partisan/wp/2016/12/09/what-cheese-pizza-means-to-the-internets-conspiracy-mongers/, 9 December 2016.

21   Aisch, Huang and Kang, 'Dissecting the #Pizzagate conspiracy theories'.

22   Cecilia Kang, 'Fake news onslaught targets pizzeria as nest of child-trafficking', *The New York Times*, nytimes.com/2016/11/21/technology/fact-check-this-pizzeria-is-not-a-child-trafficking-site.html, 21 November 2016.

23   Christina Cauterucci and Jonathon L. Fischer, 'Comet is D.C.'s weirdo pizza place. Maybe that's why it's a target', *Slate*, slate.com/human-interest/2016/12/comet-ping-pong-is-a-haven-for-weirdos-and-now-a-target.html, 6 December 2016.

24   Fisher, Woodrow Cox and Hermann, 'Pizzagate'.

25   Robb, 'Anatomy of a fake news scandal'.

26   John Hayward, 'Erik Prince: NYPD ready to make arrests in Anthony Weiner case', *Breitbart*, breitbart.com/radio/2016/11/04/erik-prince-nypd-ready-make-arrests-weiner-case/, 4 November 2016.

27   Benjamin Lee, 'Marina Abramović mention in Podesta emails sparks accusations of satanism', *The Guardian*, theguardian.com/artanddesign/2016/nov/04/marina-abramovic-podesta-clinton-emails-satanism-accusations, 5 November 2016.

28   Eric Levitz, 'Report: Clinton linked to satanic rituals involving kidnapped children and Marina Abramović', *Intelligencer*, nymag.com/intelligencer/2016/11/spirit-cooking-explained-satanic-ritual-or-fun-dinner.html, 4 November 2016.

29   teresafae, 'The faerie ring' [blog post], Tumblr, tereseafae.tumblr.com/post/153580179242/pizzagate-podesta-washingtons-occult-elite/amp.

30   Andrew Russeth, 'Marina Abramović on right-wing attacks: It's absolutely outrageous and ridiculous', *ARTnews*, artnews.com/art-news/news/marina-abramovic-on-right-wing-attacks-its-absolutely-outrageous-and-ridiculous-7255/, 4 November 2016.

31   Robb, 'Anatomy of a fake news scandal'.

32   Tim Mak and Ben Collins, 'Hannity and Drudge cite WikiLeaks
      to claim Clinton campaign worships Satan', *The Daily Beast*,
      thedailybeast.com/hannity-and-drudge-cite-wikileaks-to-claim-
      clinton-campaign-worships-satan, 13 April 2017.

33   Burt Helm, 'Pizzagate nearly destroyed my restaurant. Then my
      customers helped me fight back', *Inc*, inc.com/magazine/201707/
      burt-helm/how-i-did-it-james-alefantis-comet-ping-pong.html, July/
      August 2017.

34   Will Sommer, 'Alt right conspiracy theorists obsess over Comet
      Ping Pong', *Washington City Paper*, washingtoncitypaper.com/
      article/327515/alt-right-conspiracy-theorists-obsess-over-comet-ping-
      pong/, 6 November 2016.

35   Sommer, 'Alt right conspiracy theorists obsess'.

36   Robb, 'Anatomy of a fake news scandal'.

37   Emery Jr, 'Evidence ridiculously thin'.

38   Before It's News, '"Pizzagate": How 4Chan uncovered the sick world
      of Washington's occult elite', *Before It's News*, beforeitsnews.com/
      eu/2016/11/pizzagate-how-4chan-uncovered-the-sick-world-of-
      washingtons-occult-elite-2615694.html, 21 November 2016.

39   EU Times, 'Wikileaks exposes Clinton satanic ritual, FBI calls Hillary
      the Antichrist', *The European Union Times*, eutimes.net/2016/11/
      wikileaks-exposes-clinton-satanic-ritual-fbi-calls-hillary-the-antichrist/,
      5 November 2016.

40   Kang, 'Fake news onslaught targets pizzeria'.

41   Efe Kerem Sozeri, 'How the alt-right's PizzaGate conspiracy hid real
      scandal in Turkey', *Daily Dot*, dailydot.com/debug/pizzagate-alt-right-
      turkey-trolls-child-abuse/, 23 November 2016.

42   Laura Hayes, 'The consequences of "Pizza Gate" are real at
      Comet Ping Pong', *Washington City Paper*, washingtoncitypaper.com/
      article/193701/the-consequences-of-pizza-gate-are-real-at-comet-
      ping-pong/, 15 November 2016.

43   Kang, 'Fake news onslaught targets pizzeria'.

44   Kim LaCapria, 'Is Comet Ping Pong pizzeria home to a child abuse
      ring led by Hillary Clinton', *Snopes*, snopes.com/fact-check/pizzagate-
      conspiracy/, 21 November 2016.

45   Abby Ohlheiser, 'Fearing yet another witch hunt, Reddit bans Pizzagate', *The Washington Post*, washingtonpost.com/news/the-intersect/wp/2016/11/23/fearing-yet-another-witch-hunt-reddit-bans-pizzagate/, 23 November 2016.

46   Hayes, 'The consequences of "Pizza Gate" are real'.

47   Eric Hananoki, 'Alex Jones deletes video in which he had told his audience to personally "investigate" "Pizzagate" restaurant', *Media Matters*, mediamatters.org/alex-jones/alex-jones-deletes-video-which-he-had-told-his-audience-personally-investigate-pizzagate, 16 December 2016.

48   Hananoki, 'Alex Jones deletes video'.

49   WikiLeaks, 'Re Farmers L update and welcome Mat', *WikiLeaks*, wikileaks.org/podesta-emails/emailid/42356, 8 October 2015.

50   Hananoki, 'Alex Jones deletes video'.

51   Tom O'Connor, 'Alex Jones apologizes for "Pizzagate" fake news' *Newsweek*, newsweek.com/alex-jones-apologize-pizzagate-fake-news-574025, 24 March 2017.

52   Christine Grimaldi, interview with the author, 17 January 2021.

53   Mike Cernovich, 'Podesta Spirit Cooking emails reveal Clinton's inner circle as sex cult with connections to human trafficking' [blog post], *Dangerous Reading*, accessed via *Internet Archive*, web.archive.org/web/20161117024439/https://dangerandplay.com/2016/11/03/podesta-emails-reveal-clintons-inner-circle-as-sex-cult-with-connections-to-human-trafficking/, 3 November 2016.

54   Brian Stelter, 'Fake news, real violence: "Pizzagate" and the consequences of an internet echo chamber', *CNN*, money.cnn.com/2016/12/05/media/fake-news-real-violence-pizzagate/index.html, 6 December 2016.

55   Fisher, Woodrow Cox and Hermann, 'Pizzagate'.

4. 'Are you all larping as larpers?'

1   Steve Almond, 'The disturbing evolution of "lock her up"', *Wbur*, wbur.org/cognoscenti/2018/07/25/lock-her-up-jeff-sessions-steve-almond, 25 July 2018; Chris Cillizza, 'How "lock her up!" just blew

up', *CNN*, edition.cnn.com/2020/01/10/politics/hillary-clinton-donald-trump-justice-department/index.html, 10 January 2020.

2 A. Tychsen, M. Hitchens, T. Brolund and M. Kavakli, 'Live action role-playing games: Control, communication, storytelling, and MMO RPG similarities', *Games and Culture*, 2006, vol.1, no. 3, pp. 252–75.

3 F. Stenseng, J. Rise and P. Kraft, 'Activity engagement as escape from self: The role of self-suppression and self-expansion', *Leisure Sciences*, 2012, no. 34, pp. 19–38.

4 The Q Origins Project, interview with the author, 3 February 2021.

5 The Q Origins Project, interview with the author, 3 February 2021.

6 Abby Ohlheiser, '"We actually elected a meme as president": How 4chan celebrated Trump's victory', *The Washington Post*, washingtonpost.com/news/the-intersect/wp/2016/11/09/we-actually-elected-a-meme-as-president-how-4chan-celebrated-trumps-victory/, 9 November 2016.

7 Ohlheiser, '"We actually elected a meme as president"'.

8 Paul Waldman, 'Opinion: Steve Bannon is the most powerful person in the Trump White House. That should terrify us', *The Washington Post*, washingtonpost.com/blogs/plum-line/wp/2017/02/01/steve-bannon-is-the-most-powerful-person-in-the-trump-white-house-that-should-terrify-us/, 1 February 2017.

9 John Wagner and Callum Borchers, 'New Trump book: Bannon's "treasonous" claim, Ivanka's presidential ambitions and Melania's first-lady concerns', *The Washington Post*, washingtonpost.com/news/the-fix/wp/2018/01/03/new-trump-book-bannons-treasonous-claim-ivankas-presidential-ambitions-and-melanias-first-lady-concerns/, 3 January 2018.

10 Jessica Taylor, 'Comey: Trump asked for "loyalty", wanted him to "let" Flynn investigation "go"', *NPR*, npr.org/2017/06/07/531927032/comey-trump-asked-for-loyalty-wanted-him-to-let-flynn-investigation-go, 7 June 2017.

11 Taylor, 'Comey: Trump asked for "loyalty"'.

12 Maggie Haberman, Matthew Rosenberg, Matt Apuzzo and Glenn Thrush, 'Michael Flynn resigns as national security advisor', *The New York Times*, nytimes.com/2017/02/13/us/politics/donald-

trump-national-security-adviser-michael-flynn.html, 13 February 2017.

13   Yair Rosenberg, '"Jews will not replace us": Why white supremacists go after Jews', *The Washington Post*, washingtonpost.com/news/acts-of-faith/wp/2017/08/14/jews-will-not-replace-us-why-white-supremacists-go-after-jews/, 14 August 2017.

14   Maggie Haberman and Glenn Thrush, 'Bannon in limbo as Trump faces growing calls for the strategist's ouster', *The New York Times*, nytimes.com/2017/08/14/us/politics/steve-bannon-trump-white-house.html, 14 August 2017.

15   Chuck Todd, Mark Murray and Carrie Dann, 'August proves to be a cruel month for Trump', *NBC News*, nbcnews.com/politics/first-read/august-proves-be-cruel-month-trump-n797691, 31 August 2017.

16   Andrew Prokop, 'Steve Bannon's exit from the Trump White House, explained', *Vox*, vox.com/policy-and-politics/2017/8/18/16145188/steve-bannon-fired-resigns, 18 August 2017.

17   Eliza Relman, 'Steve Bannon says Ivanka Trump is dumb as a brick', *Business Insider*, businessinsider.com/steve-bannon-says-ivanka-trump-is-dumb-as-a-brick-2018-1?r=AU&IR=T, 4 January 2018.

18   Anthony Zurcher, 'Trump's "brain" Steve Bannon emerges from the shadows', *BBC*, bbc.com/news/world-us-canada-38996534, 24 February 2017.

19   Prokop, 'Steve Bannon's exit from the Trump White House, explained'.

20   Dan Duray, 'Milo Yiannopoulos threw a party after Twitter banned him', *Vanity Fair*, vanityfair.com/news/2016/07/milo-yiannopoulos-twitter-rnc, 20 July 2016.

21   Phoebe Luckhurst, 'Who is Milo Yiannopoulos? Everything you need to know about Donald Trump's alt-right poster boy', *Evening Standard*, standard.co.uk/lifestyle/london-life/who-is-milo-yiannopoulos-everything-you-need-to-know-about-donald-trump-s-altright-poster-boy-a3404921.html, 26 November 2016.

22   German Lopez, 'Meet the 16-year-old Canadian girl who took down Milo Yiannopoulos', *Vox*, vox.com/policy-and-

politics/2017/2/24/14715774/milo-yiannopoulos-cpac-pedophile-video-canada, 24 February 2017.

23   Lopez, 'Meet the 16-year-old Canadian girl'.

24   Tina Nguyen, 'Steve Bannon half-heartedly disowns Milo Yiannopoulos', *Vanity Fair*, vanityfair.com/news/2017/10/steve-bannon-disowns-milo-yiannopoulos, 23 October 2017.

25   Tina Nguyen, '"Holy sh—t": Allies shocked as Bob Mercer renounces Milo, dumps his stake in Breitbart', *Vanity Fair*, vanityfair.com/news/2017/11/bob-mercer-defunds-milo-yiannopoulos-sells-stake-in-breitbart, 2 November 2017.

26   Anonymous [ID: BQ7V3bcW], 'Mockingbird ...' [online forum post], 4chan [archive of Politically Incorrect board], archive.4plebs.org/pol/thread/146981635/#q147023341, 29 October 2017.

27   Carl Bernstein, 'The CIA and the media', *Carl Bernstein*, carlbernstein.com/magazine_cia_and_media.php, 20 October 1977.

28   Jennifer Wang, 'The new Forbes philanthropy score: How we ranked each Forbes 400 billionaire based on their giving', *Forbes*, forbes.com/sites/jenniferwang/2020/09/08/the-new-forbes-philanthropy-score-how-we-ranked-each-forbes-400-billionaire-based-on-their-giving/?sh=18171e129eba, 8 September 2020.

29   Matthew Yglesias, 'The (((echo))), explained', *Vox*, vox.com/2016/6/6/11860796/echo-explained-parentheses-twitter, 6 June 2016.

30   Narjas Zatat, 'Donald Trump warns of "calm before the storm" as he poses for photo with US military chiefs', *Independent*, independent.co.uk/news/world/americas/donald-trump-calm-storm-military-staff-photo-white-house-iran-isis-north-korea-a7985871.html, 6 October 2017.

31   Stephen M. Walt, 'The worst mistake of Trump's first 100 days', *Foreign Policy*, foreignpolicy.com/2017/04/26/the-worst-mistake-of-trumps-first-100-days/, 26 April 2017.

32   Scott Adams, '2-D chess players take on a 3-D chess master (part of my Trump persuasion series)' [blog post], *Scott Adams Says*, scottadamssays.com/2015/09/15/2-d-chess-players-take-on-a-3-d-chess-master-part/, 15 September 2015.

33   Scott Adams, 'Trump VS Bush: Persuasion wars' [blog post], *Scott Adams Says*, scottadamssays.com/2015/08/24/trump-vs-bush-persuasion-wars/, 24 August 2015.

34   Alexandra Topping, 'Sweden, who would believe this? Trump cites non-existent terror attack', *The Guardian*, theguardian.com/us-news/2017/feb/19/sweden-trump-cites-non-existent-terror-attack, 20 February 2017.

35   John Herrman, 'The enduring appeal of seeing Trump as chess master in chief', *The New York Times Magazine*, nytimes.com/2017/05/31/magazine/the-enduring-appeal-of-seeing-trump-as-chess-master-in-chief.html, 31 May 2017.

36   Reed Berkowitz, 'A game designer's analysis of QAnon', *Medium*, medium.com/curiouserinstitute/a-game-designers-analysis-of-qanon-580972548be5, 1 October 2020.

37   The Q Origins Project, interview with the author, 3 February 2021.

38   Amber Athey, 'Trey Gowdy stops just short of calling collusion on the Clintons and the DOJ', *Daily Caller*, dailycaller.com/2017/05/16/gowdy-clinton-doj-connections-run-deep-video/, 16 May 2017.

39   Karoun Demirjian and Devlin Barrett, 'How a dubious Russian document influenced the FBI's handling of the Clinton probe', *The Washington Post*, washingtonpost.com/world/national-security/how-a-dubious-russian-document-influenced-the-fbis-handling-of-the-clinton-probe/2017/05/24/f375c07c-3a95-11e7-9e48-c4f199710b69_story.html, 24 May 2017.

40   The Q Origins Project, interview with the author, 3 February 2021.

41   'Casey Drexler', interview with the author, 14 June 2021.

42   Mike Nunn, 'A captivating comedy ...' [review], *Goodreads*, goodreads.com/review/show/615953071?book_show_action=true&from_review_page=1, 15 May 2013.

43   David Leonhardt and Stuart A. Thompson, 'Trump's lies', *The New York Times*, nytimes.com/interactive/2017/06/23/opinion/trumps-lies.html, 14 December 2017.

44   Angela Wang and Sawyer Click, 'We analysed every message ever posted by "Q", the enigmatic person that started the QAnon

conspiracy theory', *Business Insider*, businessinsider.com/every-qanon-message-q-drop-analyzed-2020-10?r=AU&IR=T, 4 November 2020.

45 The Q Origins Project, interview with the author, 3 February 2021.

46 The Q Origins Project, interview with the author, 3 February 2021.

47 Charlie Spiering, 'Donna Brazile: Team Clinton controlled DNC in 2015 before winning primary', *Breitbart*, breitbart.com/politics/2017/11/02/brazile-clinton-controlled-dnc-2015-winning-primary/, 2 November 2017.

48 Tom Fitton, '2,800 Huma Abedin government documents on husband Weiner's laptop', *Breitbart*, breitbart.com/politics/2017/10/27/2800-abedin-government-documents-husband-weiners-laptop/, 27 October 2017.

49 Jordyn Phelps, 'Trump "disappointed" in Justice Department for not focusing on Hillary Clinton and Democratic National Committee', *ABC News*, abcnews.go.com/Politics/trump-disappointed-justice-department-focusing-hillary-clinton-democratic/story?id=50907101, 4 November 2017.

50 ABC News, 'How Russia-linked hackers stole the Democrats' emails and destabilised Hillary Clinton's campaign', *ABC News*, abc.net.au/news/2017-11-04/how-russians-hacked-democrats-and-clinton-campaign-emails/9118834, 5 November 2017.

51 Donie O'Sullivan, 'How a conspiracy theory closed part of a major US seaport', *CNN Business*, money.cnn.com/2017/06/16/media/port-of-charleston-dirty-bomb-conspiracy-theory-shutdown/index.html, 16 June 2017.

52 tracybeanz, 'She stood in the storm' [blog post], Steemit, steemit.com/drama/@tracybeanz/she-stood-in-the-storm, 17 May 2018.

53 'Team', *UncoverDC*, uncoverdc.com/team/.

54 Brandy Zadrozny and Ben Collins, 'How three conspiracy theorists took "Q" and sparked Qanon', *NBC News*, nbcnews.com/tech/tech-news/how-three-conspiracy-theorists-took-q-sparked-qanon-n900531, 15 August 2018.

55 tracybeanz, 'She stood in the storm'.

56 S. Zannettou, T. Caulfield, E. De Cristofaro, N. Kourtellis, I. Leontiadis, M. Sirivianos, G. Stringini and J. Blackburn, 'The web centipede:

Understanding how web communities influence each other through the mainstream and alternative news sources', *The 2017 Internet Measurement Conference*, 2017, doi: 10.1145/3131365.3131390.

57   Tiffany Westry, 'Study says fringe communities on Reddit, 4chan influence flow of alternative news to Twitter', *The University of Alabama at Birmingham*, uab.edu/news/research/item/8840-study-says-fringe-communities-on-reddit-4chan-influence-flow-of-alternative-news-to-twitter, 1 November 2017.

58   Jeremy Blackburn [@jhblackb], 'Is this how the Web *really* works? ...' [tweet], Twitter, twitter.com/jhblackb/status/866702758132559876?s=20, 23 May 2017.

59   Adam Taylor, 'Before "fake news," there was Soviet "disinformation"', *The Washington Post*, washingtonpost.com/news/worldviews/wp/2016/11/26/before-fake-news-there-was-soviet-disinformation/, 26 November 2016.

60   Ellen Nakashima, 'Russian government hackers penetrated DNC, stole opposition research on Trump', *The Washington Post*, washingtonpost.com/world/national-security/russian-government-hackers-penetrated-dnc-stole-opposition-research-on-trump/2016/06/14/cf006cb4-316e-11e6-8ff7-7b6c1998b7a0_story.html?hpid=hp_rhp-banner-main_dnc-hackers-1145a-banner%3Ahomepage%2Fstory&utm_term=.e8bf3382d30a, 14 June 2016.

61   DHS Press Office, 'Joint statement from the Department of Homeland Security and Office of the Director of National Intelligence on election security', *Department of Homeland Security*, dhs.gov/news/2016/10/07/joint-statement-department-homeland-security-and-office-director-national, 7 October 2016.

62   Adam Entous, Ellen Nakashima and Greg Miller, 'Secret CIA assessment says Russia was trying to help Trump win White House', *The Washington Post*, washingtonpost.com/world/national-security/obama-orders-review-of-russian-hacking-during-presidential-campaign/2016/12/09/31d6b300-be2a-11e6-94ac-3d324840106c_story.html?utm_term=.2afc5b50552a, 9 December 2016.

63 Shane Harris, Ellen Nakashima and Craig Timberg, 'Through email leaks and propaganda, Russians sought to elect Trump, Mueller finds', *The Washington Post*, washingtonpost.com/politics/through-email-leaks-and-propaganda-russians-sought-to-elect-trump-mueller-finds/2019/04/18/109ddf74-571b-11e9-814f-e2f46684196e_story.html, 18 April 2019.

64 Harris, Nakashima and Timberg, 'Through email leaks and propaganda'.

65 Eric Geller, 'Collusion aside, Mueller found abundant evidence of Russian election plot', *Politico*, politico.com/story/2019/04/18/mueller-report-russian-election-plot-1365568, 18 April 2019.

66 Joseph Menn, 'QAnon received earlier boost from Russian accounts on Twitter, archives show', *Reuters*, reuters.com/article/us-usa-election-qanon-cyber-idUSKBN27I18I, 2 November 2020.

67 Nina Jankowicz, interview with the author, 10 April 2021.

68 Tracy Beanz, 'The quickening: A guide' [blog post], *Beanz Bungalow*, medium.com/@tracybeanz/the-quickening-a-guide-bf3585b40d4b, 23 October 2017.

69 Mark Sweney, 'Is Facebook for old people? Over 55s flock in as the young leave', *The Guardian*, theguardian.com/technology/2018/feb/12/is-facebook-for-old-people-over-55s-flock-in-as-the-young-leave, 12 February 2018.

70 K. Quinn, 'Cognitive effects of social media use: A case of older adults', *Social Media + Society*, 2018, vol. 4, no. 3, pp. 1–9, doi: 10.1177/2056305118787203.

71 Limelight Networks, *The State of the User Experience*, second annual edition, img03.en25.com/Web/LLNW/%7Be52345e6-02a4-4332-9514-937c853c61cb%7D_2015StateofUser.pdf, 2015.

72 A. Guess, J. Nagler and J. Tucker, (2019), 'Less than you think: Prevalence and predictors of fake news dissemination on Facebook', *Science Advances*, 2019, vol. 5, no. 1, p. 108, doi: 10.1126/sciadv.aau4586.

73 Michael Golebiewski and danah boyd, 'Data voids: Where missing data can be easily exploited', *Data & Society*, datasociety.net/wp-content/uploads/2018/05/Data_Society_Data_Voids_Final_3.pdf, May 2018.

74 Matt Binder, 'Why some baby boomers are eating up the QAnon conspiracy', *Mashable*, mashable.com/article/qanon-conspiracy-baby-boomers-4chan#et9YVgLnbiqH, 7 August 2018.

75 Brian Friedberg, 'The dark virality of a Hollywood blood-harvesting conspiracy', *Wired*, wired.com/story/opinion-the-dark-virality-of-a-hollywood-blood-harvesting-conspiracy/, 31 July 2020.

76 Julia Carrie Wong, 'Down the rabbit hole: how QAnon conspiracies thrive on Facebook', *The Guardian*, theguardian.com/technology/2020/jun/25/qanon-facebook-conspiracy-theories-algorithm, 25 June 2020.

77 Zadrozny and Collins, 'How three conspiracy theorists'.

78 Reed Berkowitz, 'A game designer's analysis of QAnon', *Medium*, medium.com/curiouserinstitute/a-game-designers-analysis-of-qanon-580972548be5, 1 October 2020.

79 Christopher Knaus and Josh Taylor, 'Revealed: The QAnon conspiracy theorist who is friends with Australian PM Scott Morrison', *The Guardian*, theguardian.com/australia-news/2019/oct/05/qanon-conspiracy-theorist-friends-australian-prime-minister-scott-morrison, 5 October 2019.

80 Jason McGahan, 'Inside QAnon, the conspiracy cult that's devouring America', *Los Angeles Magazine*, lamag.com/citythinkblog/qanon-gop/, 17 August 2020.

81 Clive Thompson, 'QAnon is like a game – a most dangerous game', *Wired*, wired.com/story/qanon-most-dangerous-multiplatform-game/, 22 September 2020.

82 Berkowitz, 'A game designer's analysis of QAnon'.

83 Zadrozny and Collins, 'How three conspiracy theorists'.

84 Adrienne LaFrance, 'The prophecies of Q', *The Atlantic*, theatlantic.com/technology/archive/2020/09/reddit-qanon-ban-evasion-policy-moderation-facebook/616442/, June 2020.

85 Gene Park, 'Conspiracy theorists misidentify Minnesota Reddit user as Madden shooter', *The Bemidji Pioneer*, bemidjipioneer.com/news/4491765-conspiracy-theorists-misidentify-minnesota-reddit-user-madden-shooter, 28 August 2018.

86 McGahan, 'Inside QAnon, the conspiracy cult that's devouring America'.

87 Dave Davies, 'Journalist enters the world of QAnon: "It's almost like a bad spy novel"', *NPR*, npr.org/2020/08/20/904237192/journalist-enters-the-world-of-qanon-it-s-almost-like-a-bad-spy-novel, 20 August 2020.

88 Kelly Weill, 'Pinterest moms share parfait recipes next to QAnon memes', *The Daily Beast*, thedailybeast.com/pinterest-moms-share-parfait-recipes-next-to-qanon-memes, 15 August 2018.

89 Timothy McLaughlin, 'The weird, dark history of 8kun', *Wired*, wired.com/story/the-weird-dark-history-8kun/, 8 June 2019.

90 McLaughlin, 'The weird, dark history of 8kun'.

91 Zadrozny and Collins, 'How three conspiracy theorists'.

92 Zadrozny and Collins, 'How three conspiracy theorists'.

5. The great awakening

1 Will Rahn and Dan Patterson, 'What is the QAnon conspiracy theory?', *CBS News*, cbsnews.com/news/what-is-the-qanon-conspiracy-theory/, 29 March 2021.

2 Reed Berkowitz, 'A game designer's analysis of QAnon', *Medium*, medium.com/curiouserinstitute/a-game-designers-analysis-of-qanon-580972548be5, 1 October 2020.

3 'Casey Drexler', interview with the author, 14 June 2021.

4 Tarpley Hitt, 'How QAnon became obsessed with "adrenochrome", an imaginary drug Hollywood is "harvesting" from kids', *The Daily Beast*, thedailybeast.com/how-qanon-became-obsessed-with-adrenochrome-an-imaginary-drug-hollywood-is-harvesting-from-kids, 14 August 2020.

5 Jason McGahan, 'Inside QAnon, the conspiracy cult that's devouring America', *Los Angeles Magazine*, lamag.com/citythinkblog/qanon-gop/, 17 August 2020.

6 Hitt, 'How QAnon became obsessed with "adrenochrome"'.

7 Jennifer Walker-Journey, 'Untangling the medical misinformation around adrenochrome', *How Stuff Works*, science.howstuffworks.com/adrenochrome.htm, 14 April 2021.

8   Josie Adams, 'The truth about adrenochrome', *The Spinoff*, thespinoff.
     co.nz/society/07-04-2020/explainer-adrenochrome-the-drug-that-
     doesnt-exist/, 7 April 2020.

9   Brian Friedberg, 'The dark virality of a Hollywood blood-harvesting
     conspiracy', *Wired*, wired.com/story/opinion-the-dark-virality-of-a-
     hollywood-blood-harvesting-conspiracy/, 31 July 2020.

10   David Emery, 'Is a Hillary Clinton "snuff film" circulating on the
     dark web?', *Snopes*, snopes.com/fact-check/hillary-clinton-snuff-film/,
     16 April 2018.

11   Rahn and Patterson, 'What is the QAnon conspiracy theory?'.

12   Tangentman123, 'Bell from the Honey Fitz? Not so much' [online
     forum post], Reddit, reddit.com/r/Qult_Headquarters/comments/
     g662f8/bell_from_the_honey_fitz_not_so_much/, 23 April 2020.

13   Michael E. Miller, 'JFK assassination conspiracy theories: The grassy
     knoll, Umbrella Man, LBJ and Ted Cruz's dad', *The Washington
     Post*, washingtonpost.com/news/retropolis/wp/2017/10/24/jfk-
     assassination-conspiracy-theories-the-grassy-knoll-umbrella-man-lbj-
     and-ted-cruzs-dad/, 27 October 2017.

14   Hatewatch staff, 'What you need to know about QAnon', *Southern
     Poverty Law Center*, splcenter.org/hatewatch/2020/10/27/what-you-
     need-know-about-qanon, 27 October 2020.

15   E.J. Dickson, 'QAnon followers think JFK Jr. is coming back on the
     4th of July', *Rolling Stone*, rollingstone.com/culture/culture-features/
     qanon-jfk-jr-conspiracy-theory-854938/, 3 July 2019.

16   Olga Oksman, 'Conspiracy craze: Why 12 million Americans
     believe alien lizards rule us', *The Guardian*, theguardian.com/
     lifeandstyle/2016/apr/07/conspiracy-theory-paranoia-aliens-
     illuminati-beyonce-vaccines-cliven-bundy-jfk, 8 April 2016.

17   Rachel E. Greenspan, 'QAnon builds on centuries of anti-Semitic
     conspiracy theories that put Jewish people at risk', *Insider*, insider.com/
     qanon-conspiracy-theory-anti-semitism-jewish-racist-believe-save-
     children-2020-10, 25 October 2020.

18   Australian Associated Press, 'Psychiatrist struck off for posting
     "bizarre" QAnon conspiracy theories', *The Guardian*, theguardian.

QAnon and On

com/australia-news/2020/feb/07/psychiatrist-struck-off-for-posting-bizarre-qanon-conspiracy-theories, 7 February 2020.

19 Milo Yiannopoulos, 'Why I'm winning', *Breitbart*, breitbart.com/the-media/2015/11/23/why-im-winning/, 23 November 2015.

20 Adrienne LaFrance, 'The prophecies of Q', *The Atlantic*, theatlantic.com/magazine/archive/2020/06/qanon-nothing-can-stop-what-is-coming/610567/, June 2020.

21 Richard J. Evans, 'Anti-Semitism lurks behind modern conspiracy theories', *The Irish Times*, irishtimes.com/opinion/anti-semitism-lurks-behind-modern-conspiracy-theories-1.4485495, 16 February 2021.

22 Peter Baker, 'Bush tells group he sees a "third awakening"', *The Washington Post*, washingtonpost.com/wp-dyn/content/article/2006/09/12/AR2006091201594.html, 13 September 2006.

23 LaFrance, 'The prophecies of Q'.

24 Alex Nichols, '"Q" the end credits for the internet's lamest conspiracy theory', *The Outline*, theoutline.com/post/6883/qanon-conspiracy-theory-end-times, 13 December 2018.

25 Paul A. Djupe and Jacob Dennen, 'Christian nationalists and QAnon followers tend to be anti-Semitic. That was seen in the Capitol attack', *The Washington Post*, washingtonpost.com/politics/2021/01/26/christian-nationalists-qanon-followers-tend-be-anti-semitic-that-was-visible-capitol-attack/, 26 January 2021.

26 PRRI staff, 'Trumpism after Trump? How Fox News structures Republican attitudes', *Public Religion Research Institute*, prri.org/research/trumpism-after-trump-how-fox-news-structures-republican-attitudes/, 18 November 2020.

27 Tucker Carlson, 'Tucker Carlson: The real reason so many Christians are willing to support Trump', *Fox News*, foxnews.com/opinion/tucker-carlson-christians-support-trump, 24 December 2019.

28 David Emery, 'A history of the "war on Christmas"', *Snopes*, snopes.com/news/2017/11/29/the-war-on-christmas/, 29 November 2017.

29 Fox News, 'Christians victims of rising "hostility" from gov't and secular groups, report says', *Fox News*, foxnews.com/us/christians-

victims-of-rising-hostility-from-govt-and-secular-groups-report-says,
30 November 2015.

30   Perry Chiaramonte, 'Christians most persecuted group in the world as
      vicious attacks grow', *Fox News*, foxnews.com/world/christians-most-
      persecuted-group-in-the-world-as-vicious-attacks-grow, 14 April 2017.

31   Aila Slisco, '"Fox & Friends" host claims Christians are "most
      persecuted religion on the planet" after New York Hanukkah
      stabbing', *Newsweek*, newsweek.com/fox-friends-host-claims-christians-
      are-most-persecuted-religion-planet-after-new-york-1479766,
      30 December 2019.

32   PRRI staff, 'Trumpism after Trump?'.

33   Thomas J. Froehlich, 'A disinformation-misinformation ecology:
      The case of Trump', *IntechOpen*, intechopen.com/online-first/74337,
      7 December 2020.

34   Djupe and Dennen, 'Christian nationalists and QAnon followers tend
      to be anti-Semitic'.

35   The Q Origins Project, interview with the author, 3 February 2021.

36   Anita Chabria, 'QAnon now pushes alarming conspiracy myths
      targeting China and Jewish people', *Los Angeles Times*, latimes.com/
      california/story/2021-03-23/qanon-conspiracy-evolves-new-world-
      order-china-jewish-people, 23 March 2021.

37   Evans, 'Anti-Semitism lurks behind modern conspiracy theories'.

38   Yair Rosenberg, '"Jews will not replace us": Why white supremacists
      go after Jews', *The Washington Post*, washingtonpost.com/news/
      acts-of-faith/wp/2017/08/14/jews-will-not-replace-us-why-white-
      supremacists-go-after-jews/, 14 August 2017.

39   Henry Ford and the editors of *The Dearborn Independent*, 'The
      International Jew: The world's foremost problem', *Internet Archive*,
      archive.org/details/TheInternationalJew_655/page/n271/
      mode/2up?view=theatre, 1921.

40   Ben Kamisar, 'Trump: We're saying Merry Christmas again', *The Hill*,
      thehill.com/homenews/administration/355303-trump-were-saying-
      merry-christmas-again, 13 October 2017.

41   Peter Wade, 'Trump: People are saying "Merry Christmas again"
      thanks to him', *Rolling Stone*, rollingstone.com/politics/politics-news/

people-are-saying-merry-christmas-again-thanks-to-trump-930898/, 23 December 2019.

42 Thomas Colson, 'Trump suggests Joe Biden will try to take the word Christmas "out of vocabulary"', *Business Insider*, businessinsider.com. au/trump-suggests-biden-will-take-christmas-out-of-the-vocabulary-2020-12?r=US&IR=T, 7 December 2020.

43 Mike Rothschild, 'QAnon isn't newly anti-Semitic – it's always been that way', *Daily Dot*, dailydot.com/debug/qanon-anti-semitism-russia/, 7 August 2020.

44 Rothschild, 'QAnon isn't newly anti-Semitic'.

45 United States Holocaust Memorial Museum, 'Protocols of the elders of Zion' (c. 1903), *Holocaust Encyclopedia*, encyclopedia.ushmm.org/content/en/article/protocols-of-the-elders-of-zion.

46 Evans, 'Anti-Semitism lurks behind modern conspiracy theories'.

47 Talia Lavin, *Culture Warlords: My journey into the dark web of white supremacy*, London: Hachette Books, 2020.

48 Talia Lavin, 'QAnon, blood libel, and the satanic panic', *The New Republic*, newrepublic.com/article/159529/qanon-blood-libel-satanic-panic, 30 September 2020.

49 Djupe and Dennen, 'Christian nationalists and QAnon followers tend to be anti-Semitic'.

50 Greenspan, 'QAnon builds on centuries of anti-Semitic conspiracy theories'.

51 Patrick Beuth, Marie Groß, Roman Höfner, Max Hoppenstedt, Judith Horchert, Katrin Kuntz, Alexandra Rojkov, Alexander Sarovic, Christoph Scheuermann and Daniel C. Schmidt, 'QAnon's inexorable spread beyond the U.S.', *Spiegel International*, spiegel.de/international/world/the-most-dangerous-cult-of-our-times-qanon-s-inexorable-spread-beyond-the-u-s-a-e2b13c80-246a-43e5-945b-80ad7767a170, 24 September 2020.

52 Rothschild, 'QAnon isn't newly anti-Semitic'.

53 Jeremy Fuster, 'Steve Bannon called Jared Kushner a "cuck" behind his back', *The Wrap*, thewrap.com/bannon-jared-kushner-cuck/, 6 April 2017.

54   Greenspan, 'QAnon builds on centuries of anti-Semitic conspiracy theories'.

55   Timothy Pettipiece, 'History repeats itself: From the New Testament to QAnon', *The Conversation*, theconversation.com/history-repeats-itself-from-the-new-testament-to-qanon-156915, 22 March 2021.

56   Joanna Slater, 'India's devastating outbreak is driving the global coronavirus surge', *The Washington Post*, washingtonpost.com/world/interactive/2021/india-covid-cases-surge/, 19 April 2021.

57   Karen M. Douglas, Robbie M. Sutton and Aleksandra Cichocka, 'The psychology of conspiracy theories', *National Center for Biotechnology Information*, ncbi.nlm.nih.gov/pmc/articles/PMC5724570/pdf/10.1177_0963721417718261.pdf, 2017.

58   Cam Smith, interview with the author, 9 April 2021.

59   Cam Smith, interview with the author, 9 April 2021.

60   Pettipiece, 'History repeats itself'.

61   The Forward and Molly Boigon, 'She was a Jewish QAnon supporter. And she warns it could happen to you', *Haaretz*, haaretz.com/us-news/she-was-a-jewish-qanon-supporter-and-she-warns-it-could-happen-to-you-1.9531287, 11 February 2021.

62   Barbara Goldberg, 'Missing children in the U.S. nearly always make it home alive', *Reuters*, reuters.com/article/us-usa-missing-children/missing-children-in-u-s-nearly-always-make-it-home-alive-idUSBRE83P14020120426, 27 April 2012.

63   Matthew Brown, 'Fact check: Mask-wearing not connected to child trafficking', *USA Today*, usatoday.com/story/news/factcheck/2020/08/11/fact-check-mask-wearing-not-connected-child-trafficking/3318642001/, 11 August 2020.

64   National Center for Missing and Exploited Children, 'Our impact', *National Center for Missing and Exploited Children*, missingkids.org/footer/media/keyfacts.

65   Kim LaCapria, 'How COVID-19 triggered a #SaveTheChildren child trafficking panic', *Truth or Fiction?*, truthorfiction.com/how-covid-19-triggered-a-savethechildren-child-trafficking-panic/, 10 August 2020.

66 E.J. Dickson, 'What is #SaveTheChildren and why did Facebook block it?', *Rolling Stone*, rollingstone.com/culture/culture-features/savethechildren-qanon-pizzagate-facebook-block-hashtag-1041812/, 12 August 2020.

67 Eddie Kim, 'How "Save the Children" became a conspiracy grift', *MEL Magazine*, melmagazine.com/en-us/story/save-the-children-qanon-child-trafficking, 6 August 2020.

68 CNN, 'QAnon has hijacked the name of a real organization trying to save children' [video], *CNN*, edition.cnn.com/videos/tech/2020/10/19/save-the-children-qanon-conspiracy-gr-orig.cnn, 19 October 2020.

69 Elle Hardy, 'Inside the Save The Children conspiracy theory targeting suburban mums in the US', *ABC News*, abc.net.au/news/2020-09-20/how-growing-conspiracy-movement-critical-to-us-election/12661592, 20 September 2020.

70 McGahan, 'Inside QAnon, the conspiracy cult that's devouring America'.

71 Katie O'Malley, 'A helpful summary of the Chrissy Teigen conspiracy theorist drama', *Elle*, elle.com/uk/life-and-culture/culture/a33333809/chrissy-teigen-conspiracy-theorist-drama-jeffrey-epstein/, 16 July 2020.

72 McGahan, 'Inside QAnon, the conspiracy cult that's devouring America'.

73 Rachel E. Greenspan, 'QAnon recycles a false claim that Oprah is part of the "deep state" after Harry and Meghan interview', *Insider*, insider.com/qanon-oprah-conspiracy-theory-meghan-and-harry-interview-2021-3, 10 March 2021.

74 Marianna Spring, 'Wayfair: The false conspiracy about a furniture firm and child trafficking', *BBC News*, bbc.com/news/world-53416247, 15 July 2020.

75 Stephanie Keith, 'QAnon looks behind nationwide rallies and viral #SavetheChildren hashtags', *NBC News*, nbcnews.com/tech/tech-news/qanon-looms-behind-nationwide-rallies-viral-hashtags-n1237722, 22 August 2020.

76 Kevin Roose, 'How "Save the Children" is keeping QAnon alive', *The New York Times*, nytimes.com/2020/09/28/technology/save-the-children-qanon.html, 28 September 2020.

77 CNN, 'QAnon has hijacked the name of a real organization'.

78 Donie O'Sullivan, 'Analysis: A CNN reporter went to two different QAnon events. Here's what he found', *CNN Business*, edition.cnn.com/2020/10/19/tech/qanon-events-cnn-reporter/index.html, 19 October 2020.

79 Kim, 'How "Save the Children" became a conspiracy grift'.

80 Reuters staff, 'Trump says he doesn't know much about QAnon but has heard it likes him', *Reuters*, reuters.com/article/us-usa-trump-qanon-idUSKCN25F2SI, 20 August 2020.

81 The White House, 'Remarks by President Trump in press briefing', *Internet Archive*, web.archive.org/web/20210104143032/https://whitehouse.gov/briefings-statements/remarks-president-trump-press-briefing-august-19-2020/, 19 August 2020.

82 Michel Martin, '"QAnon Anonymous" host on the conspiracy movement's growing influence' transcript from *All Things Considered*, NPR, npr.org/2020/08/23/905266582/qanon-anonymous-host-on-the-conspiracy-movements-growing-influence, 23 August 2020.

83 Michael Kunzelman, 'AP explains: What's behind Trump's town hall answer on QAnon', *AP News*, apnews.com/article/trump-town-hall-qanon-explained-b4614edad1aae27a0cbcb9dfe0c0c44c, 17 October 2020.

84 Martin, '"QAnon Anonymous" host'.

85 Zeke Miller, Jill Colvin and Amanda Seitz, 'Trump praised the supporters of QAnon, a conspiracy theory the FBI says is a domestic terrorism threat', *Chicago Tribune*, chicagotribune.com/nation-world/ct-nw-trump-qanon-conspiracy-theory-20200820-m6oeff7wojf77dyeupvl7u6xbu-story.html, 19 August 2020.

86 Philip Bump, '"They like me very much": Why Trump's QAnon comments are dangerous', *The Washington Post*, washingtonpost.com/politics/2020/08/19/trump-gives-more-oxygen-dangerous-qanon-movement-they-like-me-very-much/, 20 August 2020.

87 Travis View, 'Trump's public embrace of QAnon was the culmination of years of waiting, and will likely drive the conspiracy movement to new extremes', *Business Insider*, businessinsider.com.au/opinion-trump-

qanon-praise-inevitable-likely-further-encoyrage-extreme-2020-8,
21 August 2020.

88   E.J. Dickson, 'A timeline of Trump's QAnon presidency', *Rolling Stone*,
      rollingstone.com/culture/culture-features/qanon-trump-timeline-
      conspiracy-theorists-1076279/, 27 October 2020.

89   Brandy Zadrozny and Ben Collins, 'How three conspiracy theorists
      took "Q" and sparked QAnon', *NBC News*, nbcnews.com/tech/tech-
      news/how-three-conspiracy-theorists-took-q-sparked-qanon-n900531,
      15 August 2018.

90   Alison Durkee, 'Trump's "Social Media Summit" is a far-right troll
      convention', *Vanity Fair*, vanityfair.com/news/2019/07/trump-social-
      media-summit-far-right, 8 July 2019.

91   Jason Wilson, 'Conspiracy theories like QAnon could fuel
      "extremist" violence, FBI says', *The Guardian*, theguardian.com/
      us-news/2019/aug/01/conspiracy-theories-fbi-qanon-extremism,
      2 August 2019.

92   Dickson, 'A timeline of Trump's QAnon presidency'.

93   Tina Nguyen, 'Trump isn't secretly winking at QAnon. He's
      retweeting its followers', *Politico*, politico.com/news/2020/07/12/
      trump-tweeting-qanon-followers-357238, 7 December 2020.

94   Marshall Cohen, 'Michael Flynn posts video featuring QAnon
      slogans', *CNN Politics*, edition.cnn.com/2020/07/07/politics/michael-
      flynn-qanon-video/index.html, 8 July 2020.

95   Jack Brewster, 'Trump RTs help QAnon candidates rack
      up huge followings on Twitter', *Forbes*, forbes.com/sites/
      jackbrewster/2020/08/19/trump-rts-help-qanon-candidates-rack-up-
      huge-following-on-twitter/?sh=7e26b6e77837, 19 August 2020.

96   Jan Jaben-Eilon, 'QAnon attracts Jewish believers despite anti-Semitic
      leanings', *Atlanta Jewish Times*, atlantajewishtimes.timesofisrael.
      com/qanon-attracts-jewish-believers-despite-anti-semitic-leanings/,
      3 February 2021.

97   NBC News, 'Inside the rise of Qanon-affiliated candidates for
      Congress – NBC News NOW' [video], YouTube, youtube.com/
      watch?v=_uBZetRxygY, 11 August 2020.

98   Joanna Walters, 'Who is Lauren Boebert, the QAnon sympathizer
      who won a Republican primary?', *The Guardian*, theguardian.com/us-
      news/2020/jul/01/who-is-lauren-boebert-republican-primary-qanon-
      trump, 2 July 2020.

99   McGahan, 'Inside QAnon, the conspiracy cult that's devouring
      America'.

100   USA Today, 'Enthusiastic Kimberly Guilfoyle says "the best is yet to
      come" with Pres. Trump' [video], *USA Today*, usatoday.com/videos/
      news/politics/2020/08/25/rnc-enthusiastic-kimberly-guilfoyle-says-
      best-yet-come-pres-trump/5629473002/, 24 August 2020.

101   Jason Abbruzzese, 'Trump and Biden town halls: Highlights and
      analysis' [blog post], *NBC News*, nbcnews.com/politics/2020-election/
      live-blog/trump-biden-town-halls-start-time-how-watch-live-
      updates-n1243511/ncrd1243628#blogHeader, 16 October 2020.

102   Madeline Peltz, 'After being indicted and then having his Biden smear
      flop, Steve Bannon turns to QAnon', *Media Matters*, mediamatters.org/
      qanon-conspiracy-theory/after-being-indicted-and-then-having-his-
      biden-smear-flop-steve-bannon?fbclid=IwAR1Un8N9EsjLUNidsq-ya
      b8MupEtJV14hcsWJE6nPL175z6SykeLeMjem0U, 21 October 2019.

103   Arno Rosenfeld, 'Stephen Miller claims Biden would "incentivize"
      child trafficking', *Forward*, forward.com/fast-forward/457414/stephen-
      miller-biden-child-trafficking/, 29 October 2020.

104   Jana Winter, 'Exclusive: FBI document warns conspiracy theories are
      a new domestic terrorism threat', *Yahoo News*, news.yahoo.com/fbi-
      documents-conspiracy-theories-terrorism-160000507.html, 2 August
      2019.

105   Amarnath Amarasingam and Marc-André Argentino, 'The QAnon
      conspiracy theory: A security threat in the making?', *CTC Sentinel*,
      July 2020, vol. 13, no. 7, pp. 37–44, ctc.usma.edu/wp-content/
      uploads/2020/07/CTC-SENTINEL-072020.pdf.

106   LaFrance, 'The prophecies of Q'.

107   Lois Beckett, 'QAnon: A timeline of violence linked to the conspiracy
      theory', *The Guardian*, theguardian.com/us-news/2020/oct/15/
      qanon-violence-crimes-timeline, 16 October 2020.

108 Mike McIntire and Kevin Roose, 'What happens when QAnon seeps from the web to the offline world', *The New York Times*, nytimes.com/2020/02/09/us/politics/qanon-trump-conspiracy-theory.html, 9 February 2020.

109 Tim Steller, 'Steller column: Sex-trafficking conspiracy catches fire despite lack of evidence', *Tucson*, tucson.com/news/local/steller-column-sex-trafficking-conspiracy-catches-fire-despite-lack-of-evidence/article_b6b6c798-22a3-5ccb-9fb2-99cdccfc73d9.html, 7 June 2018.

110 KOLD News 13 staff, 'Founder of homeless veterans camp Michael Lewis Arthur Meyer arrested', *KOLD News 13*, kold.com/2019/08/06/founder-homeless-veterans-camp-michael-lewis-arthur-meyer-arrested/, 7 August 2019.

111 Elisha Fieldstadt, 'Colorado woman, inspired by QAnon conspiracy, sought to kidnap her own child, police say', *NBC News*, nbcnews.com/news/crime-courts/colorado-mom-inspired-qanon-conspiracy-sought-kidnap-her-own-child-n1111711, 8 January 2020.

112 Will Sommer, 'QAnon believer teamed up with conspiracy theorists to plot kidnapping, police say', *The Daily Beast*, thedailybeast.com/cynthia-abcug-qanon-conspiracy-theorist-charged-in-kidnapping-plot, 4 January 2020.

113 Leyland Cecco, 'Armed man roamed Justin Trudeau's grounds for 13 minutes after ramming gates', *The Guardian*, theguardian.com/world/2020/jul/03/armed-man-roamed-justin-trudeaus-grounds-for-13-minutes-after-ramming-gates, 4 July 2020.

114 Mack Lamoureux, 'Armed man who allegedly stormed Trudeau's residence appears to have posted QAnon content', *Vice*, vice.com/en/article/z3ez39/armed-man-corey-hurren-who-allegedly-stormed-justin-trudeaus-residence-rideau-hall-appears-to-have-posted-qanon-content, 7 April 2020.

115 Kristin Hoppa, 'Affidavit: Drunk driver who rammed car claimed to be chasing pedophile', *Waco Tribune-Herald*, wacotrib.com/news/local/crime-and-courts/affidavit-drunk-driver-who-rammed-car-claimed-to-be-chasing-pedophile/article_5989fa98-49fb-5db1-a5f2-2cef7a42e009.html, 13 August 2020.

116 Julian Feeld, 'Texas QAnon supporter used car to attack strangers she believed were "pedophiles"', *Right Wing Watch*, rightwingwatch.org/post/texas-qanon-car-attack-cecilia-fulbright/, 20 August 2020.

117 E.J. Dickson, 'Killer says he murdered reputed mafia boss to protect Trump', *Rolling Stone*, rollingstone.com/culture/culture-news/frank-cali-murder-mafia-boss-qanon-motive-anthony-comello-861777/, 22 July 2019.

118 Will Sommer, 'Qanon-believing Proud Boy accused of murdering "lizard" brother with sword', *The Daily Beast*, thedailybeast.com/proud-boy-member-accused-of-murdering-his-brother-with-a-sword-4, 9 January 2019.

119 Sara Jean Green, '"God told me he was a lizard": Seattle man accused of killing his brother with a sword', *The Seattle Times*, seattletimes.com/seattle-news/crime/god-told-me-he-was-a-lizard-seattle-man-accused-of-killing-his-brother-with-a-sword/, 8 January 2019.

120 Will Sommer, 'Qanon mom arrested for murder of fringe legal theorist', *The Daily Beast*, thedailybeast.com/qanon-mom-arrested-for-murder-of-fringe-legal-theorist-in-florida, 27 January 2021.

121 Jamie Ross and Justin Rohrlich, 'Surf school owner killed kids after being "enlightened" by QAnon: Feds', *The Daily Beast*, thedailybeast.com/matthew-taylor-coleman-surf-school-owner-arrested-after-his-kids-1-and-3-found-stabbed-to-death, 12 August 2019.

122 Philip Bump, 'How fake news, online conspiracy theories and Trump's rhetoric may fit into two acts of violence', *The Washington Post*, washingtonpost.com/politics/2019/07/23/how-fake-news-online-conspiracy-theories-trumps-rhetoric-fit-into-two-acts-alleged-violence/, 23 July 2019.

123 Cam Smith, interview with the author, 10 April 2021.

124 Amarasingam and Argentino, 'The QAnon conspiracy theory'.

125 Mihai Andrei, 'What stochastic terrorism is and why the US may see more of it', *ZME Science*, zmescience.com/other/feature-post/stochastic-terrorism-matters/, 6 April 2021.

126 Heather Timmons, 'Stochastic terror and the cycle of hate that pushes unstable Americans to violence', *Quartz*, qz.com/1436267/trump-stochastic-terror-and-the-hate-that-ends-in-violence/, 27 October 2018.

127 Julia Carrie Wong, 'Down the rabbit hole: How QAnon conspiracies thrive on Facebook', *The Guardian*, theguardian.com/technology/2020/jun/25/qanon-facebook-conspiracy-theories-algorithm, 25 June 2020.

128 Lavin, *Culture Warlords*.

129 Lavin, 'QAnon, blood libel, and the satanic panic'.

130 Kevin Roose, '"Shut the site down," says the creator of 8kun, a megaphone for gunmen', *The New York Times*, nytimes.com/2019/08/04/technology/8kun-shooting-manifesto.html, 4 August 2019.

131 LaFrance, 'The prophecies of Q'.

132 Jana Winter, 'FBI warns of increasing extremist threats to the 2020 elections', *Yahoo News*, news.yahoo.com/fbi-warns-of-increasing-extremist-threats-to-the-2020-elections-155602354.html, 11 September 2020.

6. Burial ground

1 F. Cleaves, *Rock of Chickamauga: The life of General George H. Thomas*, Norman, US: University of Oklahoma Press, 1986.

2 Kim LaCapria, 'Mandatory gun ownership in Kennesaw, Georgia', *Snopes*, snopes.com/fact-check/kennesaw-gun-law/, 9 October 2015.

3 Ally Mutnick and Melanie Zanona, 'House Republican leaders condemn GOP candidate who made racist videos', *Politico*, politico.com/news/2020/06/17/house-republicans-condemn-gop-candidate-racist-videos-325579, 18 June 2020.

4 Mohammed Haddad and Usaid Siddiqui, 'Mapping the hundreds of Confederate statues across the US', *Al Jazeera*, aljazeera.com/news/2020/6/11/mapping-the-hundreds-of-confederate-statues-across-the-us, 11 June 2020.

5 Kristen Reed and Jon Shirek, 'Kennesaw woman among deaths at U.S. Capitol insurrection', *11 Alive*, 11alive.com/article/news/local/kennesaw/kennesaw-woman-among-deaths-at-us-capitol/85-23f73eda-c2ef-426c-9b0c-5fd3414c5765, 16 January 2021.

6 Pilar Melendez, Ana Lucia Murillo, Will Lennon and Matt Taylor, 'Police officer Brian Sicknick, Iraq War veteran defending Congress

from Trump rioters', *Daily Beast*, thedailybeast.com/benjamin-philips-kevin-greeson-rosanne-boyland-were-the-three-others-who-died-during-the-capitol-riot?source=articles&via=rss, 8 January 2021.

7   Wayne Drash and Sarah Rose, 'Kennesaw woman who died amid D.C. chaos was among Trump's "biggest fans"', *GPB*, gpb.org/news/2021/01/08/kennesaw-woman-who-died-amid-dc-chaos-was-among-trumps-biggest-fans, 8 January 2021.

8   Reed and Shirek, 'Kennesaw woman among deaths at U.S. Capitol insurrection'.

9   Sudhin Thanawala, Stefanie Dazio and Jeff Martin, 'Family: Trump supporter who died followed QAnon conspiracy', *Associated Press*, apnews.com/article/election-2020-joe-biden-donald-trump-police-elections-7051411972c58cfbbf079876ce527ab4, 9 January 2021.

10   Sudhin Thanawala, Stefanie Dazio and Jeff Martin, 'Rosanne Boyland, Trump supporter who died, followed QAnon conspiracy, family says', *USA Today*, usatoday.com/story/news/nation/2021/01/09/rosanne-boyland-trump-supporter-who-died-followed-qanon-family/6608289002/, 9 January 2021.

11   Drash and Rose, 'Kennesaw woman who died amid D.C. chaos'.

12   Reed and Shirek, 'Kennesaw woman among deaths at U.S. Capitol insurrection'.

13   Luke Harding, 'The vanishing "red mirage": How Trump's election week soured', *The Guardian*, theguardian.com/us-news/2020/nov/07/red-mirage-donald-trump-election-week-soured, 7 November 2020.

14   Annie Karni and Maggie Haberman, 'Fox's Arizona call for Biden flipped the mood at Trump headquarters', *The New York Times*, nytimes.com/2020/11/04/us/politics/trump-fox-news-arizona.html, 4 November 2020.

15   The Jakarta Post, 'As far as I'm concerned we already have won it: Trump falsely claims' [video], *The Jakarta Post*, YouTube, youtube.com/watch?v=XQvzO7dNoKM, 5 November 2020.

16   Sheera Frenkel, 'The rise and fall of the "Stop the Steal" Facebook group', *The New York Times*, nytimes.com/2020/11/05/technology/

stop-the-steal-facebook-group.html, 5 November 2020; Brian Fung
and Donie O'Sullivan, '"Stop the steal" groups hide in plain sight on
Facebook', *CNN*, cnn.com/2021/01/15/tech/facebook-stop-the-steal-
evasion/index.html, 15 January 2021.

17 Thanawala, Dazio and Martin, 'Rosanne Boyland, Trump supporter
who died'.

18 Harding, 'The vanishing "red mirage"'.

19 Andrew Feinberg, 'Judge suggests "Kraken" lawsuits were meant to
"make the public believe" Trump's false election claims', *Independent*,
independent.co.uk/news/world/americas/us-politics/trump-kraken-
powell-wood-giuliani-b1882871.html, 12 July 2021.

20 Keith Kloor, 'The #MAGA lawyer behind Michael Flynn's
scorched-earth legal strategy', *Politico*, politico.com/news/
magazine/2020/01/17/maga-lawyer-behind-michael-flynn-legal-
strategy-098712, 17 January 2020.

21 Reality Check team and BBC Monitoring, 'The Kraken: What is it
and why has Trump's ex-lawyer released it?', *BBC*, bbc.com/news/
election-us-2020-55090145, 28 November 2020.

22 Cybersecurity and Infrastructure Security Agency, 'Joint statement
from Elections Infrastructure Government Coordinating Council
& the Election Infrastructure Sector Coordinating Executive
Committees', *Cybersecurity and Infrastructure Security Agency*, cisa.
gov/news/2020/11/12/joint-statement-elections-infrastructure-
government-coordinating-council-election, 12 November 2020.

23 Donie O'Sullivan, 'Sidney Powell is a beacon of hope to sad QAnon
supporters', *CNN Business*, edition.cnn.com/2020/11/24/business/
sidney-powell-qanon/index.html, 24 November 2020.

24 William Turton and Jenny Surane, 'Citigroup employee who operated
QAnon website on paid leave', *Financial Review*, afr.com/world/north-
america/citigroup-employee-who-operated-qanon-website-on-paid-
leave-20200917-p55wew, 17 September 2020.

25 William Turton and Joshua Brustein, 'QAnon was on the fringe until
this Citigroup executive came along', *Financial Review*, afr.com/world/
north-america/qanon-was-on-the-fringe-until-this-citigroup-executive-
came-along-20201013-p564j7, 14 October 2020.

26   Thornton McEnery, 'Citigroup employee who ran popular QAnon
      website put on paid leave', *New York Post*, nypost.com/2020/09/17/
      citigroup-employee-who-ran-popular-qanon-site-put-on-leave/,
      17 September 2020; William Turton, 'QAnon website shuts down
      after N.J. Man identified as operator', *Bloomberg*, bloomberg.com/
      news/articles/2020-09-11/qanon-website-shuts-down-after-n-j-man-
      identified-as-operator, 12 September 2020.

27   'Site info', *Qmap.pub*, *Internet Archive*, web.archive.org/
      web/20200621195743/https://qmap.pub/info, archived 21 June
      2020.

28   Julia Carrie Wong, 'Down the rabbit hole: How QAnon
      conspiracies thrive on Facebook', *The Guardian*, theguardian.com/
      technology/2020/jun/25/qanon-facebook-conspiracy-theories-
      algorithm, 25 June 2020.

29   Rebecca Ruiz, 'Conspiracy theories are a mental health crisis',
      Mashable, mashable.com/article/mental-health-disinformation-
      conspiracy-theories-depression, 27 June 2021.

30   Karen Stewart, interview with the author, 9 July 2021.

31   Thanawala, Dazio and Martin, 'Family: Trump supporter who died
      followed QAnon conspiracy'.

32   Dan Zak, 'A Kraken is loose in America', *The Washington Post*,
      washingtonpost.com/lifestyle/style/kraken-trump-election-powell-
      giuliani/2020/12/09/6f6944ea-381e-11eb-bc68-96af0daae728_story.
      html, 10 December 2020.

33   Zack Budryk, 'Trump walks back tweet saying Biden "won"
      election', *The Hill*, thehill.com/homenews/campaign/526027-
      trump-says-biden-won-while-promoting-election-conspiracy-theories,
      20 November 2020.

34   Will Steakin, Matthew Mosk, James Gordon Meek and Ali Dukakis,
      'Longtime Trump advisers connected to groups behind rally that led
      to Capitol attack', *ABC News*, abcnews.go.com/US/longtime-trump-
      advisers-connected-groups-rally-led-capitol/story?id=75261028,
      16 January 2021.

35   Steakin, Mosk, Meek and Dukakis, 'Longtime Trump advisers
      connected to groups behind rally'.

36　Ryan Goodman and Justin Hendrix, 'Exclusive: New video of Roger Stone with Proud Boys leaders who may have planned for Capitol attack', *Just Security*, justsecurity.org/74579/exclusive-new-video-of-roger-stone-with-proud-boys-leaders-who-may-have-planned-for-capitol-attack/, 6 February 2021.

37　Danielle Zoellner, 'Extremists planning more violent events for Inauguration Day after US Capitol riots, experts warn', *Independent*, independent.co.uk/news/world/americas/us-election/inauguration-day-rioters-us-capitol-b1784935.html, 9 January 2021.

38　Jack Healy, 'These are the 5 people who died in the Capitol riot', *The New York Times*, nytimes.com/2021/01/11/us/who-died-in-capitol-building-attack.html, 22 February 2021.

39　Dan Barry, Mike McIntire and Matthew Rosenberg, '"Our president wants us here": The mob that stormed the Capitol', *The New York Times*, nytimes.com/2021/01/09/us/capitol-rioters.html, 9 January 2021.

40　Kaleigh Rogers, 'QAnon has become the cult that cries wolf', *FiveThirtyEight*, fivethirtyeight.com/features/qanon-has-become-the-cult-that-cries-wolf/, 26 March 2021.

41　Timothy Pettipiece, 'History repeats itself: From the New Testament to QAnon', *The Conversation*, theconversation.com/history-repeats-itself-from-the-new-testament-to-qanon-156915, 22 March, 2021.

42　Kerry Howley, 'QAnon and the bright rise of belief', *Intelligencer*, nymag.com/intelligencer/article/qanon-capitol-riot-bright-rise-belief.html, 29 January 2021.

43　La Porsche Thomas, 'NYT: Kennesaw woman "trampled" at U.S. Capitol insurrection, later dies', *11 Alive*, 11alive.com/article/news/local/protests/nyt-kennesaw-woman-trampled-at-us-capitol-insurrection-later-died/85-51e1337a-8953-43bc-8583-f06fd5a3a161, 17 January 2021.

44　Thanawala, Dazio and Martin, 'Rosanne Boyland, Trump supporter who died'.

45　Joseph Choi, 'Feds charge members of Three Percenters militia group over Jan. 6 attack', *The Hill*, thehill.com/regulation/court-battles/557901-feds-charge-members-of-three-percenters-militia-group-over-jan-6, 6 October 2021.

46   Talia Lavin, 'The violent crescendo of the MAGA conspiracies', *The New Republic*, newrepublic.com/article/160814/trump-protesters-attack-us-capital, 7 January 2021.

47   Darragh Roche, 'Donald Trump retweets leading figure in QAnon conspiracy theory', *Newsweek*, newsweek.com/donald-trump-retweets-leading-figure-qanon-conspiracy-theory-1554744, 15 December 2020.

48   David Gilbert, 'QAnon supporters are calling for violence at pro-Trump protests', *Vice*, vice.com/en/article/pkdqq7/qanon-supporters-are-calling-for-violence-at-pro-trump-protests, 7 January 2021.

49   Shayna Greene, 'Fact check: Can Pence send votes back to states for "correction" as Trump says?', *Newsweek*, newsweek.com/fact-check-can-pence-send-votes-back-states-correction-trump-says-1559398, 1 June 2021.

50   Anne Gearan and Josh Dawsey, 'Trump issued a call to arms. Then he urged his followers "to remember this day forever!"', *The Washington Post*, washingtonpost.com/politics/trump-election-capitol-building/2021/01/06/3e9af194-5031-11eb-bda4-615aaefd0555_story.html, 6 January 2021.

51   Lavin, 'The violent crescendo of the MAGA conspiracies'.

52   Brian Naylor, 'Read Trump's Jan. 6 speech, a key part of impeachment trial', *NPR*, npr.org/2021/02/10/966396848/read-trumps-jan-6-speech-a-key-part-of-impeachment-trial, 10 February 2021.

53   Howley, 'QAnon and the bright rise of belief'.

54   Evan Hill and Arielle Ray, 'Body camera footage shows Capitol rioters trampling over woman', *The New York Times*, nytimes.com/2021/01/28/us/capitol-riot-woman-trampled.html, 28 January 2021.

55   Evan Hill, Arielle Ray and Dahlia Kozlowsky, 'Videos show how rioter was trampled in stampede at Capitol', *The New York Times*, nytimes.com/2021/01/15/us/rosanne-boyland-capitol-riot-death.html, 15 January 2021.

56   Hill, Ray and Kozlowsky, 'Videos show how rioter was trampled in stampede at Capitol'.

57   Drash and Rose, 'Kennesaw woman who died amid D.C. chaos'.

58   Steve Fennessy and Sean Powers, 'Georgia today: Insurrection shines a light on militant groups', *Georgia Public Broadcasting*, gpb. org/news/2021/01/13/georgia-today-insurrection-shines-light-on-militant-groups, 13 January 2021.

59   Hill, Ray and Kozlowsky, 'Videos show how rioter was trampled in stampede at Capitol'.

60   Thanawala, Dazio and Martin, 'Family: Trump supporter who died followed QAnon conspiracy'.

61   Healy, 'These are the 5 people who died in the Capitol riot'.

62   Laurel Wamsley, 'What we know so far: A timeline of security response at the Capitol on Jan. 6', *NPR*, npr. org/2021/01/15/956842958/what-we-know-so-far-a-timeline-of-security-at-the-capitol-on-january-6, 15 January 2021.

63   Wamsley, 'What we know so far'.

64   Adam Goldman and Shaila Dewan, 'Inside the deadly Capitol shooting', *The New York Times*, nytimes.com/2021/01/23/us/capitol-police-shooting-ashli-babbitt.html, 23 January 2021.

65   Healy, 'These are the 5 people who died in the Capitol riot'.

66   Goldman and Dewan, 'Inside the deadly Capitol shooting'.

67   Luke Mogelson, 'Among the insurrectionists', *The New Yorker*, newyorker.com/magazine/2021/01/25/among-the-insurrectionists, 15 January 2021.

68   Goldman and Dewan, 'Inside the deadly Capitol shooting'.

69   Bellingcat Investigations Team, 'The journey of Ashli Babbitt', *Bellingcat*, bellingcat.com/news/2021/01/08/the-journey-of-ashli-babbitt/, 8 January 2021.

70   Peter Jamison, Hannah Natanson, John Woodrow Cox and Alex Horton, '"The storm is here"', *The Washington Post*, washingtonpost. com/dc-md-va/2021/01/09/ashli-babbitt-capitol-shooting-trump-qanon/, 10 January 2021.

71   BBC News, 'Ashli Babbitt: The US veteran shot dead breaking into the Capitol', *BBC News*, bbc.com/news/world-us-canada-55581206, 8 January 2021.

72   Jamison, Natanson, Woodrow Cox and Horton, '"The storm is here"'.

73   Peter Hermann, 'Two officers who helped fight the Capitol mob died by suicide. Many more are hurting', *The Washington Post*, washingtonpost.com/local/public-safety/police-officer-suicides-capitol-riot/2021/02/11/94804ee2-665c-11eb-886d-5264d4ceb46d_story.html, 12 February 2021.

74   Kevin Breuninger and Dan Mangan, 'Two more police officers die by suicide after defending Capitol during riot by pro-Trump mob, tally now 4', *CNBC*, cnbc.com/2021/08/02/3rd-police-officer-gunther-hashida-kills-himself-after-capitol-riot-by-trump-mob.html, 3 August 2021.

75   Peter Hermann, 'We got to hold this door', *The Washington Post*, washingtonpost.com/dc-md-va/2021/01/14/dc-police-capitol-riot/, 14 January 2021.

76   Miranda Green, 'Who dies for Donald Trump? The case of the Capitol riot's Ashli Babbitt', *Intelligencer*, nymag.com/intelligencer/2021/01/who-dies-for-trump-the-case-of-capitol-riots-ashli-babbitt.html, 11 January 2021.

77   Green, 'Who dies for Donald Trump?'.

78   Tamar Lapin, 'Ashli Babbitt, Air force vet killed at Capitol, was in a "throuple": Reports', *News.com.au*, nypost.com/2021/01/14/ashli-babbitt-husband-were-reportedly-in-a-throuple/, 14 January 2021.

79   BBC News, 'Ashli Babbitt: The US veteran shot dead breaking into the Capitol', *BBC News*, bbc.com/news/world-us-canada-55581206, 8 January 2021.

80   Katie Dowd, 'The far-right propaganda machine doesn't know what to do with Ashli Babbitt', *SFGate*, sfgate.com/politics/article/capitol-trump-riots-storming-coverage-deaths-15861812.php, 11 January 2021.

81   Ewan Palmer, 'QAnon supporters think Capitol shooting victim Ashli Babbitt is still alive', *Newsweek*, newsweek.com/qanon-ashli-babbitt-alive-conspiracy-lin-wood-1559989, 8 January 2021.

82   Green, 'Who dies for Donald Trump?'.

83   Aaron Rupar, 'McConnell commemorates President Trump's last day by blaming him for a riot', *Vox*, vox.com/2021/1/19/22239007/mcconnell-blames-trump-capitol-riot, 19 January 2021.

84　Erin Snodgrass, 'At least 10 people charged in the Capitol siege are blaming Trump for their involvement in the attack', *Insider*, businessinsider.com/10-charged-in-capitol-siege-blame-trump-for-their-involvement?r=AU&IR=T, 10 February 2021.

85　Jan Wolfe, '"He invited us": Accused Capitol rioters blame Trump in novel legal defense', *Reuters*, reuters.com/article/us-usa-trump-capitol-defense-idUSKBN2A219E, 2 February 2021.

86　Michael M. Grynbaum, Davey Alba and Reid J. Epstein, 'How pro-Trump forces pushed a lie about antifa at the Capitol riot', *The New York Times*, nytimes.com/2021/03/01/us/politics/antifa-conspiracy-capitol-riot.html, 1 March 2021.

87　Craig Silverman, 'A facial recognition company says that viral Washington Times "antifa" story is false', *Buzzfeed News*, buzzfeednews.com/article/craigsilverman/facial-recognition-antifa-washington-times-false, 7 January 2021.

88　Grynbaum, Alba and Epstein, 'How pro-Trump forces pushed a lie about antifa at the Capitol riot'.

89　Zac Summers, 'Friend of Kennesaw woman killed in Capitol riot recounts her final moments', *CBS46*, cbs46.com/news/friend-of-kennesaw-woman-killed-in-capitol-riot-recounts-her-final-moments/article_c36b3146-515c-11eb-adfd-a32b248f9815.html, 7 January 2021.

90　Jim Newell, 'Turns out Mo Brooks was wearing body armour to Trump's very peaceful Jan. 6 rally', *Slate*, slate.com/news-and-politics/2021/07/mo-brooks-body-armor-jan-6-rally.html, 28 July 2021.

91　Newell, 'Turns out Mo Brooks was wearing body armour'.

92　AP, 'Twitter blocks 70,000 QAnon accounts after US Capitol riot', *AP News*, apnews.com/article/twitter-blocks-70k-qanon-accounts-171a5c9062be1c293169d764d3d0d9c8, 12 January 2021.

93　Kevin Rose, 'YouTube cracks down on QAnon conspiracy theory, citing offline violence', *The New York Times*, nytimes.com/2020/10/15/technology/youtube-bans-qanon-violence.html, 15 October 2020.

94　Shayan Sardarizadeh and Olga Robinson, 'Biden inauguration leaves QAnon believers in disarray', *BBC News*, bbc.com/news/blogs-trending-55746304, 21 January 2021.

95   Kari Paul, '"I had no qualms": The people turning in loved ones for the
      Capitol attack', *The Guardian*, theguardian.com/us-news/2021/jan/17/
      capitol-attack-reporting-family-internet-sleuths-qanon, 17 January 2021.

96   Michael Jensen and Sheehan Kane, 'QAnon offenders in the United
      States', START Research Brief, University of Maryland, start.umd.
      edu/sites/default/files/publications/local_attachments/START%20
      QAnon%20Research%20Brief_5_26.pdf, May 2021.

97   Masood Farivar, 'FBI director concerned about QAnon's potential for
      violence', *VOA News*, voanews.com/usa/fbi-director-concerned-about-
      qanons-potential-violence, 14 April 2021.

98   Masood Farivar, 'Capitol riot exposed QAnon's violent potential',
      VOA News, voanews.com/usa/capitol-riot-exposed-qanons-violent-
      potential, 31 March 2021.

99   Jason Lemon, 'Ivanka Trump blasts viral CNN Don Lemon segment
      "mocking accents" of "boomer-rube" Trump supporters: "Smug
      ridicule is disgusting"', *Newsweek*, newsweek.com/ivanka-trump-blasts-
      viral-cnn-don-lemon-segment-mocking-accents-boomer-rube-trump-
      supporters-1484390, 28 January 2020.

100   Isaac Kamola, 'QAnon and the digital lumpenproleteriat', *New
      Political Science*, 2021, vol. 43, no. 2, pp. 231–34, tandfonline.com/doi/
      abs/10.1080/07393148.2021.1925835?journalCode=cnps20.

101   Todd C. Frankel, 'A majority of the people arrested for Capitol
      riot had a history of financial trouble', *The Washington Post*,
      washingtonpost.com/business/2021/02/10/capitol-insurrectionists-
      jenna-ryan-financial-problems, 10 February 2021.

102   Dr Cynthia Miller-Idriss [@milleridress], 'Really enjoyed helping
      interpret these findings …' [tweet], Twitter, twitter.com/milleridriss/
      status/1359573633564368898, 11 February 2021.

103   Thomas McCauley, 'Race war or culture war: The diversity in right-
      wing extremism', *Dynamics of Asymmetric Conflict*, April 2021, vol. 14,
      no. 2, pp. 192–208, tandfonline.com/doi/full/10.1080/17467586.202
      1.1917771.

104   Farivar, 'Capitol riot exposed QAnon's violent potential'.

105   Will Sommer, 'QAnon-ers' magic cure for coronavirus: Just drink
      bleach!', *The Daily Beast*, thedailybeast.com/qanon-conspiracy-

theorists-magic-cure-for-coronavirus-is-drinking-lethal-bleach, 28 January 2020.

106 Daniel Bessner and Amber A'Lee Frost, 'How the QAnon cult stormed the Capitol', *Jacobin*, jacobinmag.com/2021/01/q-anon-cult-capitol-hill-riot-trump, 19 January 2021.

107 Bessner and Frost, 'How the QAnon cult stormed the Capitol'.

108 Rashida Yosufzai, 'QAnon followers realise their baseless conspiracy was "all a lie" as President Joe Biden takes office', *SBS News*, sbs.com.au/news/qanon-followers-realise-their-baseless-conspiracy-was-all-a-lie-as-president-joe-biden-takes-office, 21 January 2021.

109 Joseph Menn, Elizabeth Culliford, Katie Paul and Carrie Monahan, '"No plan, no Q, nothing": QAnon followers reel as Biden inaugurated', *Reuters*, reuters.com/article/us-usa-biden-qanon-idUSKBN29P2VO, 21 January 2021.

110 Jack Brewster, '"We all got played": QAnon followers implode after big moment never comes', *Forbes*, forbes.com/sites/jackbrewster/2021/01/20/we-all-got-played-qanon-followers-implode-after-big-moment-never-comes/?sh=ad013633a06b, 20 January 2021.

111 Howley, 'QAnon and the bright rise of belief'.

112 Rogers, 'QAnon has become the cult that cries wolf'.

113 Jack Brewster, 'QAnon content is "evaporating" from the internet, new report finds', *Forbes*, forbes.com/sites/jackbrewster/2021/05/26/qanon-content-is-evaporating-from-the-internet-new-report-finds/?sh=2d981b0812b7, 26 May 2021.

114 Jordan Wildon and Marc-André Argentino, 'QAnon is not dead: New research into Telegram shows the movement is alive and well', *GNET*, gnet-research.org/2021/07/28/qanon-is-not-dead-new-research-into-telegram-shows-the-movement-is-alive-and-well/, 28 July 2021.

115 Wong, 'Down the rabbit hole: How QAnon conspiracies thrive on Facebook'.

116 Hannah Knowles and Paulina Villegas, 'Pushed to the edge by the Capitol riot, people are reporting their family and friends to the FBI', *The Washington Post*, washingtonpost.com/nation/2021/01/16/capitol-riot-family-fbi/, 16 January 2021.

117 Adrienne LaFrance, 'The prophecies of Q', *The Atlantic*, theatlantic. com/magazine/archive/2020/06/qanon-nothing-can-stop-what-is-coming/610567/, June 2020.

118 Marc-André Argentino, 'The church of QAnon: Will conspiracy theories form the basis of a new religious movement?', *The Conversation*, theconversation.com/the-church-of-qanon-will-conspiracy-theories-form-the-basis-of-a-new-religious-movement-137859, 18 May 2020.

119 Deutsche Welle, 'US: QAnon followers tied to Capitol riot arrested, FBI says', *Deutsche Welle*, dw.com/en/us-qanon-followers-tied-to-capitol-riot-arrested-fbi-says/a-57205833, 14 April 2021.

120 Patrick Beuth, Marie Groß, Roman Höfner, Max Hoppenstedt, Judith Horchert, Katrin Kuntz, Alexandra Rojkov, Alexander Sarovic, Christoph Scheuermann and Daniel C. Schmidt, 'QAnon's inexorable spread beyond the U.S.', *Der Spiegel*, spiegel.de/international/world/the-most-dangerous-cult-of-our-times-qanon-s-inexorable-spread-beyond-the-u-s-a-e2b13c80-246a-43e5-945b-80ad7767a170, 24 September 2020.

121 Katrin Bennhold, 'QAnon is thriving in Germany. The extreme right is delighted', *The New York Times*, nytimes.com/2020/10/11/world/europe/qanon-is-thriving-in-germany-the-extreme-right-is-delighted. html, 11 October 2020.

122 Beuth et al., 'QAnon's inexorable spread beyond the U.S.'.

123 Frida Ghitis, 'Opinion: QAnon is an American invention, but it has become a global plague', *The Washington Post*, washingtonpost.com/opinions/2021/03/10/qanon-japan-germany-colombia-conspiracy-theories-disinformation/, 10 March 2021.

124 Hong Kong AFP, 'QAnon conspiracies go global in pandemic "perfect storm"', *France 24*, france24.com/en/20201006-qanon-conspiracies-go-global-in-pandemic-perfect-storm, 6 October 2020.

125 Chris Baynes, 'QAnon: One in four Britons believe conspiracy theories linked to movement', *Independent*, independent.co.uk/news/uk/home-news/qanon-uk-conspiracy-theories-hope-not-hate-trump-survey-b1222574.html, 22 October 2020.

126 Cam Smith, interview with the author, 9 April 2021.

127 Michael Kelly, 'The road to paranoia', *The New Yorker*, newyorker.com/magazine/1995/06/19/the-road-to-paranoia, 19 June 1995.

128 Brigid Delaney, '"Evil forces": How Covid-19 paranoia united the wellness industry and rightwing conspiracy theorists', *The Guardian*, theguardian.com/commentisfree/2020/jun/05/wellness-advocates-used-to-talk-about-bali-trips-and-coconut-oilnow-its-bill-gates-and-5g, 8 June 2020.

129 Margaret Simons, 'Q for conspiracy', *Meanjin*, meanjin.com.au/essays/q-for-conspiracy/, Autumn 2021.

130 Paul Karp, 'Australian liberal MP Craig Kelly stands by US Capitol "antifa" claim, despite discredited evidence', *The Guardian*, theguardian.com/australia-news/2021/jan/08/australian-liberal-mp-craig-kelly-us-capitol-antifa-claim, 8 January 2021.

131 Daniel Hurst, 'Scott Morrison refuses to condemn Trump for inciting "distressing" violence in US Capitol', *The Guardian*, theguardian.com/australia-news/2021/jan/07/scott-morrison-refuses-to-condemn-trump-for-inciting-distressing-violence-in-us-capitol, 7 January 2021.

132 Aoife Gallagher, Jacob Davey and Mackenzie Hart, *The Genesis of a Conspiracy Theory: Key trends in QAnon activity since 2017*, Institute for Strategic Dialogue, isdglobal.org/wp-content/uploads/2020/07/The-Genesis-of-a-Conspiracy-Theory.pdf, 2020.

133 Marc-André Argentino, '6/ next up is the Australia Q board …' [tweet], Twitter, twitter.com/_MAArgentino/status/1219011805785284610, 20 January 2020.

134 Michael McGowan, 'How Australia became fertile ground for misinformation and QAnon', *The Guardian*, theguardian.com/australia-news/2021/feb/16/how-australia-became-fertile-ground-for-misinformation-and-qanon, 16 February 2021.

135 'Meshelle', interview with the author, 12 April 2021.

136 'Noni', interview with the author, 1 April 2021.

137 'Nick', interview with the author, 2 May 2021.

138 Margaret Simons, 'Q for conspiracy'.

139 Ronald W. Pies and Joseph M. Pierre, 'Believing in conspiracy theories is not delusional', *Medscape*, medscape.com/viewarticle/945290, 4 February 2021.

140 Dr Richard Wise, interview with the author, 12 April 2021.

141 Frankel, 'A majority of the people arrested for Capitol riot'.

142 Jim Edwards and Jessica Davies, 'What QAnon's own activists said when we told them we were publishing a list of the movement's 200 most important people', *Business Insider*, businessinsider.com.au/qanon-activists-respond-database-of-activists-2020-12, 24 December 2020.

143 Edwards and Davies, 'What QAnon's own activists said'.

144 The Forward and Molly Boigon, 'She was a Jewish QAnon supporter. And she warns it could happen to you', *Haaretz*, haaretz.com/us-news/she-was-a-jewish-qanon-supporter-and-she-warns-it-could-happen-to-you-1.9531287, 11 February 2021.

145 Howley, 'QAnon and the bright rise of belief'.

146 Bessner and Frost, 'How the QAnon cult stormed the Capitol'.

147 Karen M. Douglas, Robbie M. Sutton and Aleksandra Cichocka, 'The psychology of conspiracy theories', *Current Directions in Psychological Science*, 2017, vol. 26, no. 6, pp. 538–42, doi: 10.1177/0963721417718261.

148 Jan-Willem van Prooijen, 'The psychology of Qanon: Why do seemingly sane people believe bizarre conspiracy theories?', *NBC News*, nbcnews.com/think/opinion/psychology-qanon-why-do-seemingly-sane-people-believe-bizarre-conspiracy-ncna900171, 14 August 2018.

149 Richard Wise, interview with the author, 12 April 2021.

150 Robert Jay Lifton, *Thought Reform and the Psychology of Totalism: A study of 'brainwashing' in China*, New York: W.W. Norton & Company, 1961.

151 Bronte Lord and Richa Naik, 'He went down the QAnon rabbit hole for almost two years. Here's how he got out', *CNN*, edition.cnn.com/2020/10/16/tech/qanon-believer-how-he-got-out/index.html, 18 October 2020.

152 Anderson Cooper, 'Former QAnon supporter to Cooper: I apologize for thinking you ate babies' [video], *CNN*, edition.cnn.com/videos/us/2021/01/30/anderson-cooper-former-qanon-supporter-special-report-sot-ac360-vpx.cnn, 30 January 2021.

153 Bronte Lord and Richa Naik, 'How Jitarth Jadeja escaped the Qanon social media rabbit hole', *7 News*, 7news.com.au/technology/how-

jitarth-jadeja-escaped-the-qanon-social-media-rabbit-hole-c-1403038, 17 October 2020.

154 Tovia Smith, 'Experts in cult deprogramming step in to help believers in conspiracy theories', *NPR*, npr.org/2021/03/02/972970805/experts-in-cult-deprogramming-step-in-to-help-believers-in-conspiracy-theories, 2 March 2021.

155 Steven Hassan, 'I was a member of a cult. Here's how to bring QAnon believers back to reality', *CNN*, edition.cnn.com/2021/02/04/perspectives/qanon-cult-truth/index.html, 4 February 2021.

156 Pilar Melendez, 'Capitol rioter Rosanne Boyland died from drug overdose, not trampling: M.E.', *The Daily Beast*, thedailybeast.com/capitol-rioter-rosanne-boyland-died-from-acute-amphetamine-intoxication, 7 April 2021.

... But this is not the end

1 Dave Davies, 'Journalist enters the world of QAnon: "It's almost like a bad spy novel"', *NPR*, npr.org/2020/08/20/904237192/journalist-enters-the-world-of-qanon-it-s-almost-like-a-bad-spy-novel, 20 August 2020.

2 Alyssa Rosenberg, 'The only question about QAnon that really matters', *The Washington Post*, washingtonpost.com/opinions/2021/04/05/only-question-about-qanon-that-really-matters, 5 April 2021.

3 Tovia Smith, 'Experts in cult deprogramming step in to help believers in conspiracy theories', *NPR*, npr.org/2021/03/02/972970805/experts-in-cult-deprogramming-step-in-to-help-believers-in-conspiracy-theories, 2 March 2021.

4 Makena Kelly, '8kun "has no intent of deleting constitutionally protected hate speech," owner tells Congress', *The Verge*, theverge.com/2019/9/5/20850791/8kun-hate-speech-delete-jim-watkins-infinitechan-el-paso-shooting-racist-white-supremacist, 5 September 2019; Rachel E. Greenspan, 'Who is Q? Why QAnon's ringleader may have been hiding in plain sight all along', *Insider*, insider.com/who-is-q-why-people-think-jim-watkins-qanon-8kun-2020-10, 9 April 2021.

5   Drew Harwell and Craig Timberg, 'A QAnon revelation suggests the truth of Q's identity was right there all along', *The Washington Post*, washingtonpost.com/technology/2021/04/05/ron-watkins-qanon-hbo/, 5 April 2021.

6   The Daily Beast, 'How Q tried to pin the whole thing on Steve Bannon', *The Daily Beast*, thedailybeast.com/how-q-tried-to-pin-the-whole-thing-on-steve-bannon, 7 April 2021.

7   Alison Durkee, 'Sidney Powell, "Kraken" attorneys sanctioned for bringing Michigan election fraud lawsuit', *Forbes*, forbes.com/sites/alisondurkee/2021/08/25/sidney-powell-kraken-attorneys-sanctioned-for-bringing-michigan-election-fraud-lawsuit/?sh=582c55921124, 25 August 2021.

8   Select Committee to Investigate the January 6th Attack on the United States Capitol, request to David S. Ferriero, archivist of the United States, january6th.house.gov/sites/democrats.january6th.house.gov/files/NARA.8.25.pdf, 25 August 2021.

9   Isaac Kamola, 'QAnon and the digital lumpenproleteriat', *New Political Science*, 2021, vol. 43, no. 2, pp. 231–34, tandfonline.com/doi/abs/10.1080/07393148.2021.1925835?journalCode=cnps20.

10   Masood Farivar, 'Capitol riot exposed QAnon's violent potential', *Voice of America*, voanews.com/usa/capitol-riot-exposed-qanons-violent-potential, 31 March 2021.

11   CNN, 'China and Russia "weaponised" QAnon conspiracy around time of US Capitol attack, report says', *9 News*, 9news.com.au/world/qanon-conspiracy-weaponised-by-russia-and-china-capitol-violence/d005e2ba-5c9b-4152-96da-7b13aad0577f, 20 April 2021.

12   Philip Bump, 'How to talk – and ask – about QAnon', *The Washington Post*, washingtonpost.com/politics/2020/08/20/how-talk-ask-about-qanon/, 20 August 2020.

13   Rosenberg, 'The only question about QAnon that really matters'.

14   Nina Jankowicz, 'How to defeat disinformation', *Foreign Affairs*, foreignaffairs.com/articles/united-states/2020-11-19/how-defeat-disinformation, 19 November 2020.

15   Gemma Conroy, 'Believers in QAnon and other conspiracy theories reveal how they climbed out of the rabbit hole', *ABC News*, abc.net.

au/news/science/2021-05-23/ex-conspiracy-theorists-reveal-how-they-got-out-qanon/100153732, 23 May 2021.

16   Joanne Rosa, 'How QAnon conspiracies took over one mom's life: "It made me emotionally unavailable"', *ABC News*, abcnews.go.com/Politics/qanon-conspiracies-moms-life-made-emotionally-unavailable/story?id=75840525, 16 February 2021.

ACKNOWLEDGEMENTS

All books represent a collective effort, but the complexity of research around this one has been extraordinarily demanding and only made possible through extraordinary help.

My particular thanks to the courageous Karen Stewart, as well as to Dr Richard Wise, Richard Bartholomew, Cam Smith, the Q Origins Project, Nina Jankowicz, Miles Taylor and the small army of anonymous contributors who told me their stories of cult participation and survival. Thank you to Laura Lippman, Talia Lavin, Jo Parker, Andy Fleming and my beloved old friend, Phil Roberts who provided the invaluable service of connecting me to other people, and to Lisa France and Christine Grimaldi, who helped me map out the mental territory of neighbourhoods I couldn't visit with an invisible killer virus suddenly in the way. Thank you to Monica Attard and Tim Laurie at UTS for pointing me towards connections I would never have made on my own.

Thank you to my mentor, Jenna Price, who got me through the early drafts, and to Jay Luxembourg and Johann Hari, whose personal support and timely encouragement to persist with this project are the reason it came to fruition. Thank you to Jamila Rizvi and Liberty Sanger, who took some very nutty phone calls, Jen Hudaverdi, who refused to let me live in squalor and Bec Carey-Grieve, Heather Marsh and Donna Hughes, who got me out of the house and away from the internet – lifesaving time after time. Thank you to Jo Porter at the Queen Victoria Women's Centre, Dom Sweeney at CSU, my musical partner Jonny Berliner, my stage muse Amber McMahon and Svetlana Stankovic at *The Guardian*, who were endlessly patient with the complex juggling of my other work commitments around this project. And a second thank you to Svetlana – as well as to Bridie Jabour – at *The Guardian*, whose commissioning of my piece 'If your friends or family have fallen for an internet conspiracy cult, here's what you should do' began this whole wild conspiracy-cult ride.

It has been both great fun and an honour to realise this project with Hardie Grant, and my gratitude goes to Julie Pinkham, Roxy Ryan, Loran McDougall, Arwen Summers – the patient, unflappable Arwen Summers – Jo Butler and Simone Ford for their literally tireless work on the manuscript. Special acknowledgement goes to Alex Grennhalgh at Shanahans who – with Jessamy Gleeson – made a Herculean effort cleaning up the footnotes, and I apologise that it had to be in an Augean Stables kind of way.

My gratitude goes also to my family: to my mother, Barbara Badham, and cousin Preston Wall, and my two mothers-in-law, Fiona Davison and Kim Delahey, and of course to my amazing, wonderful partner, Ben Davison, who cooked, cleaned, gardened and kept the household functional while I raved into the night about lizard people and disinformation pipelines. I am fortunate to also have found a family in my work colleagues: my agent, Sally McLennan, and management team of Emma J. Hawkins and Jessamy Gleeson. Ever my indomitable major-domo, this project has relied on Jessamy from footnotes to fact-checks to screaming GET OFF TWITTER at every moment that mattered. The book would not have made it without her.

Thank you, most of all, to the thousands of journalists, academics and extremism monitors who, when faced with seemingly impassable mountains of lies and fantasy, chip and chip and chip away at rock until the truth finds its way through.

QAnon and On was written with the generous support of a residency provided by Booranga Writers' Centre, Wagga Wagga. It was made possible by The Grotto.

About the author

Van Badham is an internationally award-winning writer and theatremaker. As a journalist, she's written for *The New York Times*, *Bloomberg*, *The Telegraph* (UK) and *The Age*, and she maintains a regular column for *The Guardian*. Widely published as an essayist and poet, she's appeared in anthologies for Hardie Grant, Black Inc, MUP and QUP, and wrote the novel *Burnt Snow* for Pan Macmillan. Her plays include *Banging Denmark* for STC, *The Bloody Chamber* for Malthouse and *The Bull, the Moon and the Coronet of Stars* for Griffin Theatre. Van appears regularly on television and radio as a commentator, critic and activist.